INDEFENSIBLE

INDEFENSIBLE

DEMOCRACY, COUNTERREVOLUTION, AND THE RHETORIC OF ANTI-IMPERIALISM

Rohini Hensman

Haymarket Books
Chicago, Illinois

Published in 2018 by
Haymarket Books
P.O. Box 180165
Chicago, IL 60618
773-583-7884
www.haymarketbooks.org
info@haymarketbooks.org

ISBN: 978-1-60846-911-6

Trade distribution:
In the US, Consortium Book Sales and Distribution, www.cbsd.com
In Canada, Publishers Group Canada, www.pgcbooks.ca
In the UK, Turnaround Publisher Services,
www.turnaround-uk.com
All other countries, Ingram Publisher Services International,
IPS_Intlsales@ingramcontent.com

Cover design by Rachel Cohen. Cover photograph by Teun Voeten of life
amid the rubble in Aleppo, 2015.

This book was published with the generous support of Lannan Foundation
and Wallace Action Fund.

Printed in Canada by union labor.

Library of Congress Cataloging-in-Publication data is available.

10 9 8 7 6 5 4 3 2 1

To my beloved grandchildren, Amlan, Zinedine, Anisa and Rafael

Contents

Abbreviations   ix

Introduction   1

Part 1: Understanding Imperialism

1 The Politics of Anti-imperialism   21

Part 2: Case Studies

2 Russia and Ukraine   53
3 Bosnia and Kosovo   95
4 Iran   119
5 Iraq   151
6 Syria: The Assad Regime   195
7 The Syrian Uprising   209

Part 3: Looking for Alternatives

8 What Can We Do?   279

Acknowledgments   303
Notes   305
References   311
Index   367

Abbreviations

AQI	Al Qaeda in Iraq
ASP	Arab Socialist Party
BOALs	Basic Organizations of Associated Labour (Yugoslavia)
CDF	Committee for the Defense of Democratic Freedoms and Human Rights in Syria
CND	Campaign for Nuclear Disarmament
DiEM25	Democracy in Europe Movement
EFPs	Explosively Formed Projectiles
EU	European Union
FPÖ	Freedom Party of Austria
FSA	Free Syrian Army
FSB	Federal Security Service of the Russian Federation
GFIW	General Federation of Iraqi Women
GRU	Main Intelligence Directorate (Russia)
HDZ	Croatian Democratic Union
HNC	High Negotiations Commission (Syria)
HRAS	Human Rights Association in Syria
HVO	Croatian Defence Council
ICC	International Criminal Court
ICP	Iraqi Communist Party
ICTY	International Criminal Tribunal for Former Yugoslavia
IDPs	Internally Displaced Peoples
IFTU	Iraqi Federation of Trade Unions
IGC	Interim Governing Council (Iraq)
ILO	International Labour Organization

IMF	International Monetary Fund
IRGC	Islamic Revolutionary Guard Corps
IRI	Islamic Republic of Iran
IRIB	Islamic Republic of Iran Broadcasting
IRP	Islamic Republican Party
ISCI	Islamic Supreme Council of Iraq
JAMA	Revolutionary Movement of the Iranian People
JCPOA	Joint Comprehensive Plan of Action
KDP	Kurdish Democratic Party
KLA	Kosovo Liberation Army
KRG	Kurdish Regional Government
LCCs	Local Coordination Committees of Syria
LTTE	Liberation Tigers of Tamil Eelam
MKO	People's Mujahedin of Iran
MPRP	Muslim People's Republican Party (Iran)
NATO	North Atlantic Treaty Organization
NDF	National Defence Forces
NOC	National Oil Corporation (Libya)
OCHA	UN Office for the Coordination of Humanitarian Affairs
OPCW	Organisation for the Prohibition of Chemical Weapons
OPEC	Organisation of the Petroleum Exporting Countries
OUN	Organization of Ukrainian Nationalists
OWFI	Organization of Women's Freedom in Iraq
PDPA	People's Democratic Party of Afghanistan
PJAC	Free Life Party of Kurdistan
PKK	Kurdistan Workers' Party
PLFP-GC	Popular Front for the Liberation of Palestine – General Command
PLO	Palestine Liberation Organization
PUK	Patriotic Union of Kurdistan
PYD	(Kurdish) Democratic Union Party
RCC	Revolutionary Command Council (Iraq)
RG	Rossyiskaya Gazeta
RPR	Reanimation Package of Reforms (Ukraine)

SAVAK	Iranian secret police under the shah
SCIRI	Supreme Council for the Islamic Revolution in Iraq
SDF	Syrian Democratic Forces
SSO	Special Security Organization (Iraq)
StWC	Stop the War Coalition
SWP	Socialist Workers Party (UK)
UCM	Unity of Communist Militants (Iran)
UDHR	Universal Declaration of Human Rights
UNHRC	United Nations Human Rights Council
UNMIK	UN Mission in Kosovo
UNPROFOR	UN Protection Force
VEVAK	Secret police of the Islamic Republic of Iran
WDTUM	Workers' Democratic Trade Union Movement (Iraq)
WMD	Weapons of Mass Destruction
WPC	World Peace Council
WPI	Worker-Communist Party of Iran
WSWS	World Socialist Web Site
WTO	World Trade Organization

Introduction

In September 2015, the image of little Aylan Kurdi, whose dead body washed up on a beach in Turkey, temporarily jolted the conscience of European politicians who had been preoccupied up until then with turning back the tide of refugees from Syria. The compassion and kindness of those who welcome refugees to their countries is certainly admirable, especially in contrast with the cruelty of the far right, which seeks to exclude them. We must ask, however: Is this enough? As a member of the advocacy group The Syria Campaign pointed out soon afterwards,

> Since the picture of Aylan hit headlines across the world, 6 children have been killed in Syria every day – the majority from barrel bombs and missiles from Syrian government aircraft. But their bloodied and blown apart corpses don't make the front page of any newspaper. None of the other 10,000 children killed in the fighting have. What broke my heart this week was a cartoon by Neda Kadri, a Syrian artist, that pictured Aylan in heaven being welcomed by children: *'you are so lucky Aylan! We're victims of the same war but no one cared about our death.'* (Nolan 2015)

Despite the tendency of the mainstream media to conflate 'migrants' and 'refugees', it is important to remember that they are different. Refugees are fleeing violence. Therefore, the only viable solution to the refugee crisis would be to end the violence that has killed hundreds of thousands and displaced millions.

That is, however, easier said than done. Ending the Syria crisis would entail, first and foremost, identifying its causes. For some of those who call themselves anti-imperialists, there is only one cause: Western (that is, North American and Western European) imperialism, which is responsible for all the bloodshed – including the rise of the Islamic State in Iraq and al-Sham (ISIS),[1] which, according to them, is responsible for most of the violence in Syria. An example of this argument is an article in the *Guardian* by Seamus Milne (2015) titled 'Now the truth emerges: how the US fuelled the rise of Isis in Syria and Iraq'.

Milne supports his allegation by referring to a recently declassified US intelligence file, in order to claim that the US 'effectively welcomed' a Salafi principality in Iraq and Syria. Yet the document actually says the following:

> If *the situation unravels* there is the possibility of establishing a declared or undeclared Salafist principality in Eastern Syria ... The *deterioration* of the situation *has dire consequences on the Iraqi situation* and are as follows: This creates the ideal atmosphere for AQI to return to its old pockets in Mosul and Ramadi, and will provide a renewed momentum under the presumption of unifying the jihad among Sunni Iraq and Syria ... ISI could also declare an Islamic State through its union with other terrorist organizations in Iraq and Syria, *which will create grave danger in regards to unifying Iraq and protecting its territory.* (Judicial Watch 2015, emphasis added)

It is surely a perverse reading of such phrases as 'the situation unravels', 'deterioration', 'dire consequences on the Iraqi situation' and 'grave danger in regards to unifying Iraq and protecting its territory' to say that it consti-tutes an effective welcome of this outcome. Attributing this to Obama is also strange, given that the usual criticism of him by human rights defenders is that the drone strikes in his relentless war on Al Qaeda and ISIS killed hundreds of civilians (Serie 2016).

After describing ISIS and Nusra Front gains, Milne observes, 'Some Iraqis complain that the US sat on its hands while all this was going on.' He doesn't make it clear where he stands on this issue, but the general tenor of his article suggests that he sympathises with the complaint. Who was complaining? A year earlier, then–prime minister Nouri al-Maliki had pub-licly called on the US to bomb ISIS (Freeman 2014), and subsequently the Iraqi government had complained that the US was not providing air support to Iranian troops and Shia militias attempting to retake Tikrit from ISIS (Barnard 2015a). The Obama administration reportedly feared that there would be large-scale civilian casualties and revenge attacks on Sunni civilians by the Iranian troops and Shia militias, who were already abducting, tor-turing and killing Sunni civilians with impunity (Cockburn 2014). In fact, the Iraqi government's complaint contradicts Milne's claim that the US was mounting 'joint military operations with Iran against Isis in Iraq': what the Iran-backed militias were complaining of was precisely that the US was *not* coordinating with them.

By this stage, one is totally confused about what Milne is advocating. Does he want the US to ignore pleas from the Iraqi government and stop bombing ISIS? Or to bomb more indiscriminately and kill more civilians as demanded by Maliki and the sectarian Shia militias? He castigates the US for bombing some rebels while supporting others in Syria, which apparently makes no sense to him except as a divide-and-rule tactic. But does he really think that ISIS and the Kurdish PYD/YPG would be together if not for the US bombing one and supporting the other? He does not distinguish between them, but to any informed observer it would be evident that their interests are very different. Throughout this discussion, he scrupulously avoids mentioning the pro-democracy uprising in Syria which is being attacked brutally by the state, thereby helping to cover up the mass murder unleashed by Bashar al-Assad (see Chapter 7).

Milne ends by saying that it is the people of the region who can solve its problems, but it is precisely these people who are conspicuous by their absence from his article. Not a single Iraqi or Syrian civilian is quoted. Perhaps he did not have the resources to meet them, but could he not at least quote from reports of those who did? If he had bothered to look for or listen to the voices of these civilians, he would, for example, have come across a blog post slamming the Obama administration, not for providing weapons to the Syrian opposition, but for its *arms blockade* against it – along with a long list of 'Friday slogans,' including many condemning Assad's atrocities and Hezbollah, Iran and Russia for their complicity in them (NotGeorgeSabra 2013). He would have come across a photograph of Syrians holding up a banner responding to Obama's patronising and ignorant *refusal* to arm the Syrian opposition that says, 'Yes, Mr President Obama! Dentists, farmers and students are the ones who lead dignity revolutions; criminals kill while idiots talk' (Karadjis 2014). And surely these Syrians are right: Che Guevara was a doctor, Camilo Torres was a priest, and many of the Vietnamese who battled against US imperialism were farmers and students, yet they all took up arms against intolerable oppression. Moreover, since all Syrian adult males have been through compulsory military service, and many of those fighting against the regime are defectors from the regime's army, a large number have received training to handle weapons.[2]

Jacob Siegel, in an article analysing responses to the intelligence report cited by Milne, debunked the way in which 'Hawks and anti-imperialists alike are flogging a recently declassified U.S. intelligence report. Depending on who's spinning it, the report either proves that Washington ignored dire warnings about the rise of ISIS or that the U.S. was in a secret alliance that fueled the jihadi army's rise' (Siegel 2015). In fact, careful analyses of this intelligence file by Michael Karadjis and Gilbert Achcar suggest that it probably reports inputs from an Iraqi regime informant, explaining its understandable anxiety about the effects on Iraq (Karadjis 2015). But even after Siegel's critique, Seema Mustafa (2015) published a cruder version of Milne's allegations. What is most striking is the convergence of these self-professed socialists with the far right, including Donald Trump, who made exactly the same allegation of 'Barack Hussein Obama'. As Trump put it, 'He's the founder of ISIS' (Corasaniti 2016).

Another example of this type of argument is Brad Hoff's article, 'ISIS leader Omar al-Shishani fought under US umbrella as late as 2013' (Hoff 2015). Anyone reading this article would conclude that al-Shishani, trained by the US, continued to be supported by the US when he entered Syria and fought under the banner of ISIS in the battle for Menagh Airbase under US-supported Free Syrian Army (FSA) colonel Abdul Jabbar al-Okaidi, who, according to Hoff, 'had been in a position of operational command over ISIS terrorists'.

If one takes the trouble to check just one of the references in his article, it becomes clear that to say that Hoff's account is economical with the truth would be an understatement. The reference describes how al-Shishani – a Georgian named Tarkhan Batirashvili with a Chechen mother – had started off a follower of the moderate Sufi Islam prevalent in Chechnya and Georgia, and as a teenager had fought alongside Chechen separatists, before being trained by the US to fight against Putin's invasion of Georgia in 2008. After being sent to prison by the Georgian authorities because they feared he had been radicalised, he was released and travelled to Turkey, and from there to Syria, where he formed the Jaish al-Muhajireen to fight against Assad. In August 2013, al-Shishani led the assault on the Menagh Airbase in collaboration with the FSA. *Only in November 2013* did he join ISIS and start targeting FSA units, much to the dismay of some of the Syrians who had formerly fought under him, who at this point broke with him (Prothero 2015). So the allegation that al-Okaidi was 'in operational command over ISIS terrorists' is a lie on two counts: firstly, he was not in command over al-Shishani or the latter's fighters; secondly, at the time they fought alongside each other, al-Shishani (later killed by US bombs) was not in ISIS.

Milne, Mustafa and Hoff are not the only 'so-called anti-imperialists' who align themselves with the Assad regime and 'relentlessly slander the uprising every step of the way in every conceivable way' (NotGeorgeSabra 2013). An article by Shamus Cooke, which alleges that 'for well over two years ISIS and other al-Qaeda-style groups have been the main driving force in the Syrian war' (Cooke 2014), is effectively demolished by Michael Karadjis (2014), who provides ample evidence that 'the only force in the region, apart from the Syrian Kurds, who have been fighting ISIS are the FSA and its allies,' and that 'they have been the "driving force" in the revolt against the regime, not ISIS'. Like Milne and Mustafa, Cooke covers up the fact that over 90 per cent of the killings are by Assad's forces (The Syria Campaign 2015), thereby becoming another accomplice to his crimes against humanity.

The overall message communicated by the omissions, distortions and outright lies in such accounts is that, firstly, there is no democratic opposition to Assad; and secondly, that it is the West, due to its support for extremist Islamists, that is responsible for most of the current bloodshed in Iraq and Syria, rather than the Assad regime, Hezbollah, the Iraqi Shia militias, and the Iranian and Russian forces. These writers cover up the real causes of the massive refugee exodus, enabling the war crimes and crimes against humanity to continue, leading to more deaths, continuing Islamist radicalisation, and the continuing outflow of refugees. By implying that the Sunnis (including children) being slaughtered by Assad and his allies are all Islamist extremists, they endorse collective punishment of all Sunnis for the crimes of ISIS.[3] In the eyes of blogger NotGeorgeSabra, this is part of an 'imperialist-anti-imperialist alliance [which] … speaks with one voice, endlessly repeating a narrative on Syria that is so at odds with the truth: that extremists are the only/main actors in the Syrian opposition; that brutality, torture, sectarianism, and atrocities are the only/main activities of the opposition; that Saudi Arabia, Qatar, Turkey, and Israel are the only/main sponsors or beneficiaries of opposition activism' (NotGeorgeSabra 2013). It is worth noting that their critics are just as critical of Western powers, *but for exactly the opposite reasons*.

I have taken the example of Syria in this introduction because, on the one hand, anyone with an iota of humanity would agree that the massive humanitarian catastrophe there should be ended, while on the other, most accounts conceal its real causes, and, by doing so, provide support for the main perpetrators to continue their mass murder. The Syria Campaign highlights that it is scarcely registered on the internet that well over 90 per cent of the killings in Syria have been perpetrated by the Assad regime, asking, 'Why has the world chosen to ignore Assad's crimes? Is it because he claims to be a secular leader? Is it because he is clean shaven and wears a suit? Is it because we don't realise that by ignoring these crimes by the regime, we are becoming recruiting cheerleaders for Isis?' (The Syria Campaign 2015). The reference to 'becoming recruiting cheerleaders for Isis' links to a report of the Syrian regime's bombing of a market in Douma on August 16, 2015, which killed at least one hundred civilians and wounded many more; the report comments, 'While much is made of the vaunted propaganda of the Islamic State, there is nothing the group could produce that will draw as many supporters or recruits as Assad's atrocities' (The Soufan Group 2015). In fact, as we shall see in Chapters 6 and 7, the Assad regime has been responsible for supporting ISIS in more direct ways too.

How has this happened? How have some anti-imperialists, who in 2003 exposed the lies about Iraqi weapons of mass destruction and stood in solidarity with the oppressed people of Iraq, ended up repeating the lies of the oppressors in Syria and vilifying the oppressed? The Syrian case is only the biggest of the humanitarian disasters that have been facilitated in this way by people who call themselves anti-imperialists. There are others – including the Russian annexation of Crimea and invasion of eastern Ukraine – where they actually support imperialism.

'Having masterminded the coup in February against the democratically elected government in Kiev, Washington's planned seizure of Russia's historic, legitimate warm-water naval base in Crimea failed,' John Pilger (2014) tells us. According to him, the 'Russians defended themselves' against 'threat and invasion from the west' as well as 'fascist forces' launching 'attacks on ethnic Russians in Ukraine' – a curiously uncritical regurgitation of Russian propaganda justifying their invasion of Ukraine from the east. As Nina Potarskaya, a socialist-feminist participant in the Maidan movement, explained, anger at social and economic deterioration

> exploded after the non-ratification of the Ukraine-EU Association Agreement, which led to the first Maidan demonstrations, towards the end of November 2013. And every two or three weeks that followed, the evolution of the political

situation provoked an escalation, as a growing number of people were taking over the streets, especially after special police forces began to beat and even kill demonstrators. The situation was different in the East, because Russian-speaking people, who are predominantly listening to Russian media, populate the Eastern part of Ukraine, and their information about Maidan had nothing to say about the actual reasons for these protests. They heard about an uprising led by neo-Nazis, which had to be stopped by all means. Of course, the far right played an important role at Maidan, but it was wrong to say that it was a right-wingers movement. (Potarskaya and Batou 2014)

Indeed, the results of the Ukrainian parliamentary elections of October 2014, in which the right-wing parties fared very poorly (Pifer 2014), confirm Potarskaya's claim.

Pilger fails to mention that the overwhelming majority in the Ukrainian parliament, and even former president Viktor Yanukovych himself, had supported the association agreement between Ukraine and the EU (Euronews 2013) until the Russian government twisted their arms by suspending imports from Ukraine in August 2013, leading to the cancellation of the agreement (EU observer 2013) and the subsequent Maidan protests. He seems unable to comprehend that popular protests against elected representatives who fail to carry out their mandate, or who become agents of a foreign power, are not a 'coup' but, on the contrary, evidence of a thriving democratic current in civil society. And if he thinks that 'Washington' could have 'masterminded' (as opposed to having supported) those massive demonstrations, he must believe that 'Washington' is all-powerful and that most Ukrainians would passively accept being ruled from Moscow. He seems to be ignorant of the 1994 Budapest Memorandum on Security Assurances, in which Russia, in return for Ukraine giving up the world's third-largest nuclear arsenal, undertook to 'respect the independence, sovereignty and existing borders of Ukraine,' and to 'refrain from the threat or use of force against the territorial integrity or political independence of Ukraine' (StopFake 2016) – undertakings which Putin violated when he annexed Crimea and invaded eastern Ukraine. According to the same logic, the 1979 overthrow by the Sandinistas of Anastasio Somoza, the 'democratically elected' president of Nicaragua, would also have to be classified as a 'coup,' 'masterminded' by Moscow and Havana. At the time, Pilger, along with other anti-imperialists, supported the Sandinistas – so why the double standard?

In fact, it was the movement in the East that could more accurately be described as 'fascist'. In his preface to *Imperialism, the Highest Stage of*

Capitalism (1917), Lenin made it clear that he considered Ukraine to have been colonised by Russian imperialism (see Chapter 1). It became an independent Soviet Socialist Republic after the revolution, only to be subordinated to Russia once again within a few years. In the 1930s, Stalin's policies of mass murder of Ukrainian intellectuals and priests, and forcible extraction of grain from Ukrainian peasants even as millions of them starved to death between 1932 and 1933 alone, were described by Raphael Lemkin, who invented the term 'genocide', as 'the classic case of Soviet genocide' (Lemkin 1953, Coates 2014).[4]

Given this history, it is not surprising that in 1991 over 90 per cent of Ukrainians voted for independence from the Soviet Union, with majorities in every region – including Donetsk, Luhansk and Crimea, where Russian speakers are the majority (Lalpychak 1991). Over the long years of Russian and Soviet rule, Russians had settled in Ukraine, especially in the East, and in some cases intermarried with Ukrainians; these people and their descendants became Ukrainian citizens. They surely had a right to continue to use their own language, but the idea that the areas in eastern Ukraine where they were concentrated should be part of Russia is akin to Hitler's claim to the Sudetenland in Czechoslovakia on the grounds that it was inhabited mainly by German-speaking people.

This is exactly the idea that inspired a key player in the Ukraine war, Russian citizen Igor Girkin, better known as Igor Strelkov. Strelkov said in in an interview published by Russia's *Zavtra* newspaper, 'I was the one who pulled the trigger of this war,' claiming, 'If our unit hadn't crossed the border, everything would have fizzled out' (Dolgov 2014). In Lucian Kim's words (2014), '*Zavtra* is the ideological home for ultranationalists who miss Russia as a great power, whether it was called the Russian Empire or Soviet Union.' As Kim notes, another contributor to the publication was Alexander Borodai, a Russian citizen who served as the prime minister of the self-proclaimed Donetsk People's Republic, which declared its independence from Ukraine in 2014. Strelkov, who was later removed from his post (possibly because he revealed facts about the heavy involvement of Russian military forces in Ukraine, which the Kremlin wanted to keep under wraps), was openly admired by his *Zavtra* interviewer, editor Alexander Prokhanov (Kim 2014). Extreme right-wing elements like Strelkov and Prokhanov have flourished in Vladimir Putin's Russia; as Jean Batou said of the Russian state (2015), 'Embracing an ultra-nationalist ideology that gives a good deal of space to racism, anti-Semitism, and homophobia, its authoritarian neoconservatism has become a veritable standard for the European extreme right.'

As for Russia's 'legitimate' claim to the Crimean naval base, this is founded on a 1997 treaty between Ukraine and Russia in which Ukraine agreed to lease major parts of its facilities in Crimea to the Russian Black Sea Fleet until 2017. In 2010, under pressure from Russia, pro-Russian president Yanukovych extended the lease to 2042, with an option for an additional five years. In other words, the base is on Ukrainian territory leased to Russia, just as Guantanamo Bay is on Cuban territory leased to the US by the Cuban-American Treaty of 1903. If Pilger thinks that Crimea is part of Russia because it has a Russian naval base on its territory, does he also think Guantanamo is part of the US because it has a US naval base on its territory? In fact, the naval bases at Sevastopol were *not* solely Russian; there was also a Ukrainian naval base, and far from the US seizing the Russian base, it was the Russians who seized two Ukrainian naval bases, including the one at Sevastopol (Vasovic and Kiselyova 2014).

Pilger implies that Crimea has always been part of Russia when he says that in Crimea 'the Russians defended themselves'. This is simply not true. Crimean Tatars were the most numerous indigenous ethnic group in Crimea when it was annexed by the Russian empire in 1783 during the reign of Catherine the Great, who proceeded to settle it with Russian colonisers. Under Lenin, the Crimean Tatars gained special status, but they were deported en masse by Stalin in 1944, a crime against humanity in which almost half of the population perished. Some returned when Crimea was transferred to Ukraine in 1954 by Krushchev, and others returned in large numbers from the late 1980s onward under Gorbachev (International Committee for Crimea n.d.; Uehling n.d.). They enjoyed considerable autonomy after Ukraine became independent, and were understandably upset to find their homeland forcibly re-annexed by Russia in 2014. Tatar leader Refat Chubarov condemned the 'so-called referendum' conducted to justify Russian annexation of Crimea as 'illegal', pointing out that 'it is being carried out even as foreign troops have occupied the whole of Crimea' (DW 2014). The executive arm of the Congress of the Crimean Tatar People, the Mejlis, called for a boycott of the referendum, and legendary leader of the Crimean Tatars Mustafa Dzemilev confirmed that 99 per cent of his people heeded the call, while only 30 to 50 per cent of Crimean inhabitants turned out to vote at all (Ryzhkov 2014).

In a passionate condemnation of Russian policy, Russian historian and opposition politician Vladimir Ryzhkov (2014) protested against the banning of the Tatar remembrance of the seventieth anniversary of their deportation – which 'remains the most terrible tragedy in their history' – as well as the searching of mosques, schools, firms and private homes by the security forces, the barring of Dzemilev and Chubarov from entering their homeland, and the grim accounts of abductions, torture, killings and enforced disappearances of Crimean Tatar activists. Given that Pilger has stood up for the rights of the aboriginal people of Australia, he might have been expected to share Ryzhkov's sympathy for the Crimean Tatars, but in this case his sympathies are all with the colonial settlers.

There are many others who, like Pilger, support Russian imperialism in Ukraine, including Michel Chossudovsky (2014), editor of *Global Research*, and 'investigative historian' Eric Zuesse (2015). I shall refer to these supporters of Assad and Putin as 'pseudo-anti-imperialists'. The spurious character of their anti-imperialism is demonstrated not just by their support for Russian imperialism, but also by their kid-glove treatment of Donald Trump, despite his repeated threats to 'take' Iraqi oil (Borger 2016).

◆

At this point, a disclosure is in order: I have been an anti-imperialist for as long as I can remember. Although born in Ceylon (now Sri Lanka) a short while after it gained independence, and therefore never living directly under colonial rule, I grew up with parents who consistently opposed imperialism in every part of the world. However, for my parents, anti-imperialism was only part of a more general support for democracy and human rights. Although it was many years before my mother would call herself a feminist, she was a fierce advocate of equality between women and men, and inculcated this belief in the numerous generations of girls whom she taught, as well as her own children. My father, whose own mother had left her husband because he tried to stop her working as a nurse, supported her fully. Both of them were socialists, supporting workers' rights and a welfare state, but were never Stalinists.[5] Their brand of anti-imperialism led them to oppose decolonisation measures that were combined with the oppression of minorities, such as the replacement of English with 'Sinhala Only' rather than Sinhala and Tamil, or the nationalisation of foreign-owned plantations accompanied by physical assaults, eviction and starvation of Tamil plantation workers. They condemned the anti-Tamil pogroms and authoritarian transformation of the state under President J. R. Jayawardene; later, when the Tamil nationalism of the Liberation Tigers of Tamil Eelam (LTTE) resulted in terrorist attacks and the ethnic cleansing of Sinhalese and Muslims from the areas it controlled, they opposed it too.

After leaving home, I became more clearly self-identified as a Marxist and later a feminist. Although I disagreed with some of my parents' positions – for example, I became more critical of Maoist China – I saw no reason to reject their anti-imperialism. And so I was a regular participant in demonstrations and meetings supporting the Vietnamese struggle against US imperialism, the Palestinian struggle against Israel, the anti-Apartheid struggle in South Africa, the Prague Spring, and so on. After moving to India, I was active on issues of women's rights, labour rights and minority rights in both India and Sri Lanka, while continuing to write and demonstrate against the US wars on Afghanistan and Iraq, and against Israeli oppression and massacres in Palestine. In the early 1980s, our group also organised a meeting for Polish activists from Solidarnosc to address left and trade union activists.

It is because of this background that I am so appalled at what is happening. How has the rhetoric of anti-imperialism come to be used in support of anti-democratic counterrevolutions around the world? And what can we do about it?

◆

Pseudo-anti-imperialists can be divided into roughly three categories. The first category includes people like Milne, Mustafa and Cooke, who have taken progressive positions on domestic politics in Britain, India and the United States respectively, as well as Brad Hoff, who, after serving in the US Marines during the invasion of Iraq, subsequently made a commendable effort to understand the people of the region by spending time in Syria. Such commentators, however, seem unable to deal with complexity, including the possibility that there may be more than one oppressor in a particular situation; for them, 'the West' has to be the only oppressor in *all* situations. Unfortunately for them, ISIS has made no secret of its fascistic and genocidal policies, making it impossible for them to characterise it as a progressive force opposed to the West. How do they deal with this dilemma? They swallow propaganda alleging that Obama sponsored ISIS, despite the absence of any evidence to support it. The possibility that there may be many oppressors of the Syrian people, including Assad, Hezbollah, the Islamic Republic of Iran (IRI) and Russia, is beyond their comprehension – as is the idea that it is not the West that wants the removal of Assad but the Syrian people themselves (see Chapter 7). So, again, they swallow Russian and Syrian state propaganda alleging that all those opposing Assad are terrorists. Having decided a priori that all oppression in the world is the result of Western imperialism, these commentators 'spin' carefully selected information to bolster this view and leave out the reams of information contradicting it – not unlike the way mainstream Western media converted non-existent Iraqi weapons of mass destruction (WMD) into a 'fact', leading to a catastrophic war.

Some members of this category are not so ignorant or naïve as to believe that Assad is innocent of atrocities, but when confronted about their scandalous lack of solidarity with besieged Syrians, concede (as did John Rees of the British Socialist Workers Party [SWP] and Stop the War Coalition [StWC]) they feel that their only task is to oppose the West (NotGeorgeSabra 2015). The World Socialist Web Site (WSWS) of the International Committee of the Fourth International goes further in its support of Assad. When on May 1, 2013 over two hundred intellectuals, academics, artists and activists from more than thirty countries issued a statement beginning, 'We, the undersigned, stand in solidarity with the millions of Syrians who have been struggling for dignity and freedom since March 2011. We call on the people of the world to pressure the Syrian regime to end its oppression of and war on the Syrian people' (Socialist Worker 2013), the WSWS responded by alleging that 'the thoroughly reactionary and politically sinister character of this document is virtually self-evident' – since, in their view, there are no Syrians struggling against Assad for freedom and dignity, only Islamist extremists and imperialists (North and Lantier 2013). The WSWS covers up Assad's slaughter of the democratic opposition and their families and communities by repeating his propaganda that these people – including their fellow Trotskyists in the León Sedov Brigade who fought against Gaddafi in Libya and Assad in Syria (Roche 2017) – never existed, and, thereby, collude in the massacres.

This category of commentators suffers from a West-centrism which makes them oblivious to the fact that people in other parts of the world have agency too, and that they can exercise it both to oppress others and to fight against oppression; an Orientalism which refuses to acknowledge that Third World peoples can desire and fight for democratic rights and freedoms taken for granted in the West; and a complete lack of solidarity with people who do undertake such struggles. A good illustration of this is Brad Hoff's article, 'A Marine in Syria'. Towards the end of a long, idyllic description of life in Syria prior to the uprising, he casually mentions that 'political dissent was not tolerated', that there were 'limitations on personal political freedoms', and that government policy was 'backed by an authoritarian police state'; but, he felt, this seemed 'a sensibly practical, even if unjust, solution' (Hoff 2015). Clearly 'they' (Syrians) are different from 'us' (Americans): 'they' can make do with an authoritarian police state which denies them freedom of expression, association and peaceful assembly, while 'we', of course, would never accept such a condition of unfreedom – and perish the thought that 'they' might ever rise up against that police state!

The second category consists of neo-Stalinists. (I call them 'neo-Stalinists' because although they are apologists for Russian imperialism, most of them no longer pretend to be Marxists.) As Syrian Marxist Jalal al-'Azm (2013) explains, after the Cold War the left split into a large bloc that pursued human rights, equality before the law, and democratic rights and freedoms in general, while a smaller bloc hardened its dogmatic, sectarian positions. The latter refuse to recognise the numerous instances where tsarist Russia, the Soviet Union, and, since the demise of the latter, Russia, has invaded, looted, dominated, exploited and annexed weaker countries while propping up allies who are every bit as brutal as the dictators propped up by the US. Many Maoists think along the same lines, and the Chinese political leadership upholds a notion of sovereignty according to which the state has the right to slaughter its own people without being held accountable by anyone in other parts of the world. These pseudo-anti-imperialists will support any regime that is supported by Russia, no matter how right wing it may be – just like WikiLeaks founder Julian Assange, whose affinity to Putin led him to help Trump win the US presidency and continue to support him thereafter (Beauchamp 2017; Boot 2017; Ioffe 2017). The neo-Stalinists influence many people in category one who may not be Stalinists and may even call themselves Trotskyists, like the International Committee of the Fourth International.

Finally, the third category consists of tyrants and imperialists, perpetrators of war crimes, crimes against humanity, genocide and aggression, who, as soon as they face a hint of criticism from the West, immediately claim that they are being criticised because they are anti-imperialists. While the most cursory examination of their history would prove this claim to be unfounded, members of categories one and two often accept these claims because they conform with their own preconceptions. This is especially dangerous in cases where the despots have well-funded and fairly sophisticated state media through which they disseminate a mixture of genuine news and propaganda (like the Russian *RT* and the Iranian *Press TV*), as well as paid and unpaid ideologues who do the same.

I have seen how this worked in the case of Sri Lanka. After the bloody finale of the civil war in 2009, the ruling Rajapaksa regime claimed to be anti-imperialist when EU nations, Canada and several others in the United Nations Human Rights Council (UNHRC) asked for an independent investigation into and accountability for the huge civilian death toll, as well as unhindered access of humanitarian agencies to hundreds of thousands of internally displaced people (IDPs) detained in military camps (Human Rights Council 2009a). Instead, with strong support from Cuba, Nicaragua, Bolivia and other countries including Russia and China, a resolution was passed *commending the government for addressing the needs of the IDPs* and welcoming 'the continued commitment of Sri Lanka to the promotion and protection of all human rights' (Human Rights Council 2009b). Hugo Chávez was reported to be similarly congratulatory. In 2014, by which time the regime's continued military occupation of Tamil-majority areas in the north and east, attacks on the independence of the judiciary, murderous assaults on critics, and scandalous corruption should have been abundantly clear, Evo Morales of Bolivia conferred a Peace and Democracy award on Mahinda Rajapaksa (Dalima 2014).

There seem to be two articles of faith underlying pseudo-anti-imperialism: (1) the 'West' is always my enemy and I will always oppose it, no matter what it happens to be doing at the time; and (2) the enemies of my enemy are always my friends, and I will always support them, regardless of what they are doing at the time.

It is legitimate to question the motives of Western governments or their double standards when they support human rights and democracy in certain instances and not in others; but what justification is there for *opposing* them when they ask for accountability for war crimes and crimes against humanity, and for *supporting* regimes that have been looting, torturing, raping and killing their own citizens? That is exactly what these 'anti-imperialist' icons of twenty-first-century socialism were doing in the case of Sri Lanka. There was no question of sanctions against Sri Lanka, much less military action; all that was being debated were the UNHRC resolutions that might have embarrassed the regime in power *and helped opponents* to replace it with one which had more respect for human rights and democracy. While that did not materialise in 2009, it did in subsequent years. When Sri Lankans did eventually manage to bring about regime change in 2015, it was no thanks to the pseudo-anti-imperialists.

I have concentrated on the way in which the claim of being 'anti-imperialist' has been used to provide implicit or explicit support to far-right regimes. But this blinkered view of the world also infects antiwar movements, leading them to take positions that prolong wars and that enable despots to carry out massacres. This book is thus an appeal to anti-imperialists to oppose *all* oppression by one country of another; to antiwar activists to understand that by opposing the right to self-defence and defence of one's community one becomes complicit in bloodbaths; to socialists to understand that socialist internationalism demands solidarity with democratic revolutions, not with the counterrevolutions trying to crush them; and to humanitarians to support the right of people in *all* countries to demand democratic rights and freedoms without being subjected to arbitrary arrest and incarceration, torture, rape and extrajudicial killings. The book will have eight chapters, divided into three parts:

Part I: Understanding Imperialism

Chapter 1: The Politics of Anti-imperialism. The first chapter will lay out the theoretical argument underpinning my case studies of situations in which self-professed liberals and socialists have taken right-wing positions. Marxist and left-liberal theories of imperialism (including those of Marx, Hobson, Hilferding, Lenin, Trotsky, Luxemburg, and Bauer) saw the division of the world by imperialist powers as a way in which capitalism was forcibly spread to all parts of the globe. Lenin's analysis, in particular, has gained wide acceptance. Today it is clear that it conflates two distinct phases of capitalism, but at least it embodies a clear progressive politics of support for the oppressed classes and for democracy in all countries. This position was debased beyond recognition when Stalin came to power and, in the name of building 'socialism in one country', reconstituted Russian imperialism, leading to inter-imperialist rivalry with the US in the Cold War. Once a global capitalist world economy had materialised, US imperialism degenerated into neoconservatism, a doctrine supporting global military dominance. In tandem, pseudo-anti-imperialism developed: a mindless opposition to 'the

West', and, in some cases, an equally mindless support for Russian neo-conservatism. By opposing democratic revolutions, neo-Stalinists sabotage struggles against neoliberalism and capitalism.

The purpose of Part I will be to outline an alternative narrative on imperialism and global capitalism to that of the pseudo-anti-imperialists.

Part II: Case Studies

Chapter 2: Russia and Ukraine. This chapter traces how Stalin replaced Lenin's anti-imperialism with Russian imperialism. This policy was abandoned under Gorbachev but revived by Putin, who also pushed the state far to the right. Pseudo-anti-imperialists justified the annexation of Crimea and the intervention of Russian troops in eastern Ukraine by repeating Russian propaganda that the Euromaidan movement was a fascist one, that Crimea was always part of Russia, and that there were no Russian soldiers in eastern Ukraine. All these claims, however, have been disproved. While right-wing Ukrainian nationalists have certainly been involved in the fighting in eastern Ukraine, so have right-wing Great Russian nationalists; and unlike the defence forces of Ukraine, which are politically diverse, the separatist fighters in Ukraine are uniformly right wing. The position of the pseudo-anti-imperialists in fact supports Russian imperialism, while denying solidarity to both Russians and Ukrainians attempting to carry out democratic revolutions in their countries and to end the war.

Chapter 3: Bosnia and Kosovo. Josip Broz Tito's authoritarian response to a nascent democratic revolution in the early 1970s facilitated the growth of ethnic nationalism in the former Yugoslavia. The disintegration of Yugoslavia was triggered by Slobodan Milošević's drive to build a Greater Serbia, starting in Kosovo. When Bosnia-Herzegovina declared independence in 1992, it was surrounded and invaded by the Serb army and militias as well as by Croatian militias. What followed was the systematic destruction of the Muslim heritage of Bosnia, ethnic cleansing and genocide in which the UN and NATO were shamefully complicit. NATO intervened with airstrikes only after images emerged of death camps in which Bosnians were starved and tortured, and the Srebrenica massacre took place under the noses of the UN forces that were supposed to protect the victims. Pseudo-anti-imperialists like Michel Chossudovsky, James Petras and Edward S. Herman covered up the mass rape, torture and murder carried out by the Serb nationalists; they attacked the US and NATO not for failing to protect Bosnian Muslims, but for halting the genocide.

Chapter 4: Iran. Saudi Arabia is rightly denounced by anti-imperialists for the reactionary policies of its regime and the consequences this has both at home and abroad, yet the theocratic Islamic Republic of Iran (IRI) is supported by pseudo-anti-imperialists. This support goes well beyond objections to threats of military attacks on Iran, or to sanctions which hurt ordinary citizens, which should certainly be condemned. In many cases it extends to support for everything the regime does, including its sectarian, expansionist interventions in Iraq and Syria. The rationale for these double standards is simple: the Saudis are seen as allies of the US, while Iran is opposed to the US; therefore, supporting the Iranian regime constitutes 'anti-imperialism'. But is this an adequate argument for ditching the struggles of Iranians against Iranian imperialism and for their own democratic revolution, including women's liberation, trade union rights, the rights of ethnic and sexual minorities, and freedom of expression? Should we ignore the contribution of the Islamic Republic's leadership to the carnage in Syria and Iraq simply because they organise demonstrations chanting 'Death to America! Death to Israel!'?

Chapter 5: Iraq. It is undeniable that the 2003 US/UK invasion of Iraq is responsible for much of the chaos and slaughter that followed, but events that preceded it (a brutal dictatorship, the Iran-Iraq war, the 1991 invasion of Kuwait followed by the US bombing of Iraq, sanctions) are also implicated. So are subsequent events, such as the destruction of Saddam's Baath regime, which allowed a Shia Islamist regime controlled by Iran to entrench itself and at the same time allowed Al Qaeda into Iraq. The lethal combination of Iraqi ex-Baathists and Al Qaeda Islamists (which later mutated into ISIS) began during this period. The IRI and Iraqi government sponsored Shia militias that carried out atrocities against Sunni civilians, making ISIS appear to some, at least temporarily, as the lesser evil. Pseudo-anti-imperialists who blame everything on Western intervention fail to recognise local and regional factors contributing to the crisis in Iraq, including Iranian imperialism. Iraq also raises the question: Should 'humanitarian' Western military interventions always be opposed? An examination of this question in relation to the 2003 invasion of Iraq and the 2014 intervention against the ISIS genocide of Yazidis leads to the conclusion that support or opposition must depend not on subjective motives but on the objective circumstances and outcome of the intervention.

Chapter 6: Syria – The Assad Regime. This chapter looks at the background to the Syrian conflict, including early democracy movements, Hafez al-Assad's authoritarian regime, his sabotage of the Palestinian struggle, and the transition to his son Bashar. It also examines Bashar al-Assad's role in sponsoring Islamists during the Iraq war, thus fostering the rise of ISIS. The Assad regime was supported by pseudo-anti-imperialists because of its links with Russia.

Chapter 7: The Syrian Uprising. This chapter looks at the 2011 uprising and the militarisation of the democratic opposition in response to the brutal repression carried out by the state. Assad, like Gaddafi, is credited with being a secular ruler and therefore a bulwark against the rise of extremist Islamist forces like ISIS; but in reality, he has fostered sectarianism and has had a symbiotic relationship with ISIS. The vicious intervention of the Iranian state, Lebanese Hezbollah, Iraqi Shia militias and the Russian military to crush the democratic uprising and slaughter civilians is examined. Syria typifies the moral and political degeneration of pseudo-anti-imperialists who support, or fail to oppose, the brutal crushing of a democratic revolution by a totalitarian state and foreign powers.

In each of these cases, there will be a brief overview of the background to the conflict and of the conflict itself, followed by an examination of contemporary sources showing how pseudo-anti-imperialists systematically take right-wing, counterrevolutionary positions.

The aim in Part II is to challenge both factually and morally the accounts of pseudo-anti-imperialists who support authoritarianism and imperialism, and to suggest alternative narratives in each case, providing enough detail to enable genuine anti-imperialists, antiwar activists, socialists and humanitarians from other countries to identify the people with whom they should be expressing solidarity. Given that I have not lived in these countries, nor do I know their languages, this section has relied on the accounts of others that are either written in or translated into English. My experience of struggles for democracy in Sri Lanka and India nevertheless provides important insights. For example, the civil war in Sri Lanka demonstrates clearly that so far as democracy activists are concerned, the enemy of my enemy can be equally my enemy, and that totalitarian forces engaged in a fight to the death against each other can be united in their hostility to human rights defenders. India demonstrates the terrifying speed with which religious bigotry can be transformed into gruesome violence, as well as the right-wing obsession with rewriting history. Both countries illustrate how the 'war against terror' has been used to target entire communities, and both exemplify the complex ways in which struggles for women's rights, workers' rights, minority rights, and other democratic rights and freedoms intersect and interact with one another. Furthermore, these case studies fit together like pieces of a jigsaw puzzle – a fact that confirms the validity of each.

Part III: Looking for Alternatives

Chapter 8: What Can We Do? With anti-imperialists and the left divided and confused about the struggle against non-Western imperialisms and the brutal authoritarian regimes they support, Chapter 8 identifies some of the ways in which we can fight back: by pursuing and propagating the truth; by reaffirming the moral value of opposing oppression and proclaiming solidarity with the victims of violence; by making a critique of ideologies, especially on the left, that devalue democracy and thereby promote authoritarianism; by reasserting the importance of internationalism; and, finally, by examining the concept of national sovereignty – as well as international humanitarian, human rights and criminal laws and the institutions created to implement these – and proposing reforms that would better promote democracy and help to end mass slaughter.

The purpose of this book is to examine some examples of the betrayal of all that anti-imperialism should stand for, and to identify the people in each country with whom we should be expressing solidarity. The very least we can do is to listen to their voices of courage, wisdom and humanity, and amplify them in whatever way we can.

1. The Politics
of Anti-imperialism

Lenin's analysis of imperialism, written during World War I, has the merit of opposing all imperialisms, including Russian imperialism, and of supporting the oppressed classes and democracy in all countries. However, it conflates two distinct phases of capitalism – imperialism and finance capital – and this has created immense confusion on the left. The idea that finance capital and foreign investments constitute imperialism would lead to absurd conclusions; for example, that China is an imperialist power in the US, or India in the UK. Instead, imperialism should be defined as political, and sometimes military, intervention in another country in order to install or keep in power a regime that acts more in the interests of the imperialist power than in the interests of any class – even capitalists – in its own country. Its driving force is nationalism in the imperialist country. Imperialism is opposed by struggles for national liberation,[1] which constitutes one element in a democratic revolution – the people cannot rule themselves so long as they are ruled by another nation-state – but not the only one. Genuine anti-imperialists oppose all imperialisms, while pseudo-anti-imperialists oppose some while supporting others.

Theories of Imperialism

The main argument in pacifist-liberal economist J. A. Hobson's *Imperialism: A Study*, first published in 1902, is that imperialism is directed by the search of investors, backed by the great financial houses, for profitable investment opportunities. For Marxist Rudolf Hilferding, too, in *Finance Capital: A Study of the Latest Phase of Capitalist Development*, written in 1910, the 'export of capital' is what marks imperialism (1981). Drawing on both of these works, V. I. Lenin's *Imperialism, the Highest Stage of Capitalism* (1917) defined imperialism as (a) the dominance of international capitalist monopolies, (b) the merging of bank capital with industrial capital to create 'finance capital', (c) the export of capital rather than the export of commodities, and (d) the territorial division of the world among the biggest capitalist powers. Taking off from Marx's analysis of the tendency of the rate of profit to fall,[2] he identified the driving force of imperialism as the fact that

> an enormous 'surplus of capital' has arisen in the advanced countries. ... As long as capitalism remains what it is, surplus capital will be utilised not for the purpose of raising the standard of living of the masses in a given country, for this would mean a decline in profits for the capitalists, but for the purpose of increasing profits by exporting capital abroad to the backward countries. In these backward countries profits are usually high, because capital is scarce, the price of land is relatively low, wages are low and raw materials are cheap. (Lenin 1917)

According to Otto Bauer, 'Imperialism increases the number of workers who are forced to sell their labour power to capital. It accomplishes this by destroying the old modes of production in colonial areas and thereby forcing millions either to emigrate to capitalist areas or to serve European or American capital in their native land' (Bauer 1913, 873–74; cit. Luxemburg 1972 [1921], 141). As in Lenin's account, imperialism involves the destruction of the old modes of production in the colonies and their replacement with capitalist relations through the export of capital.

Rosa Luxemburg's theory of imperialism in *The Accumulation of Capital*, first published in 1913, locates the drive for imperialist expansion in capital's need for constantly expanding markets (Luxemburg 2003). Similarly, Leon Trotsky thought that capitalist states were being driven into compulsory competition with one another for markets; hence, 'The future development of the world economy on capitalist foundations will mean an uninterrupted struggle for newer and newer divisions of the same world surface as an object of capitalist exploitation' (Trotsky 1923, 76).

Although Marx refers to 'the colonial system' rather than imperialism, he too wrote about the struggle for markets as well as the draining of wealth from the colonies to the 'mother country': 'The colonies provided a market for the budding manufactures, and a vast increase in accumulation which was guaranteed by the mother country's monopoly of the market. The treasures captured outside Europe by undisguised looting, enslavement and murder flowed back to the mother country and were turned into capital there' (Marx 1976 [1867], 918). He also pointed out that 'by ruining handicraft production of finished articles in other countries, machinery forcibly converts them into fields for the production of its raw material', making India, for example, a producer of cotton and market for textiles, whereas it had formerly been a major producer of textiles (Marx 1976, 579).

We have here two very different conceptions of the relationship between the imperial power and its colonies. In the latter conception, the colonies are treated as captive markets and sources of raw materials, their wealth drained and their production of finished articles ruined; the flow of wealth is unambiguously from the colonies to the imperial power, leading to the impoverishment of the colonies. In the former, imperialism is identified as monopoly or finance capital exporting capital to the colonies by way of foreign investments. What was actually happening at the time Lenin was writing, in 1916?

In fact, income from overseas investment by Britain, then the dominant imperialist power, exceeded the outflow of capital throughout most of the nineteenth century and up to 1914; furthermore, the emergence of monopolistic firms was slow before the 1920s (Barratt Brown 1972, 54). While praising the 'vision and incisiveness' of Marx's analysis of British imperialism in India and accepting that the concerns of industrialists did play a role, Cain and Hopkins (2002, 277) felt that 'it overstates the role of the forces associated with industrialisation'. According to them, the main beneficiaries of British imperialism were a 'gentlemanly capitalist class': 'As the world economy expanded and opportunities for foreign investment grew, the numbers of socially acceptable investment outlets multiplied and the vast flows of returning income which resulted helped first to reproduce this gentlemanly elite and then, slowly, to recreate it in a new form' (Cain and Hopkins 2002, 182–83).

Classic imperialism of the British type seems to conform more closely to the analyses of Luxemburg, Trotsky and Marx, where the colonies constitute markets, and sources of wealth and raw materials for the 'mother country'. Indeed, this also helps to explain what Lenin was mainly preoccupied with in *Imperialism* – the support of supposedly working-class social-democratic parties for their respective bourgeoisies in World War I – if we conclude that the inflow of wealth from their empires allowed these bourgeoisies to make concessions to sections of the working class ('the labour aristocracy') in their countries.

However, export of capital was indeed beginning to take place. Hilferding (1981, 426n) cites a typical example: the combination, in 1906, of the four largest British sewing thread firms into J. & P. Coats Ltd., which absorbed many smaller British companies and roughly fifteen American ones, and set up factories in the United States to bypass US tariffs. This pattern of capital exports had started in the mid-1860s, with the German Friedrich Bayer taking a share in an aniline plant in New York State in 1865, the Swedish Alfred Nobel setting up an explosives plant in Hamburg in 1866, and the US Singer sewing machine company building its first overseas factory in Glasgow in 1867 (Tugendhat 1973, 33). There were various reasons why these companies chose to invest abroad, but the main one was to overcome tariff barriers created by the spread of protectionism. The rationale for this strategy was outlined by William Lever, founder of the Lever Brothers soap empire: 'When the duty exceeds the cost of separate managers and separate plants, then it will be an economy to erect works in the country that our customers can more cheaply be supplied by them' (Tugendhat 1973, 35). By 1914, the two principal Dutch margarine companies each had seven factories in Germany, and Bayer had dyestuff factories in Moscow, Flers (France) and Schoonaarde (Belgium); the American emphasis on research and innovation, along with the high cost of American labour, put them at the forefront of this movement, with the American-owned Westinghouse factory becoming the largest single industrial plant in Britain, Standard Oil becoming the largest oil company in Europe, and Ford producing a quarter of its cars in Britain (Tugendhat 1973, 35–36).

This was certainly export of capital, but to advanced capitalist countries rather than the colonies; and it was a struggle for markets waged not between imperialist powers but between capitalist firms on the basis of their competitiveness. If 'the territorial division of the world among the biggest capitalist powers' is seen as a defining feature of imperialism, as it was by Lenin, then there is no reason to label this 'imperialism' at all. Lenin's mistake was to conflate two different phases of capitalism: an older phase, where imperialist powers were striving to bring as much territory as possible under their own control, and a newer phase of foreign investments by firms, which did not depend on the state to exercise territorial control over the countries in which they invested. Lenin can hardly be blamed, given that he was writing in conditions of exile and war, and had very limited access to research materials; it is his doctrinal followers who are to blame for perpetuating the notion that foreign investments constitute imperialism. This was already questionable at the time Lenin was writing, when most export of capital was to other advanced capitalist countries; in the twenty-first century, with Chinese investments in the US and Indian investments in Britain, it becomes downright absurd.

One obvious challenge faced by imperialism was the set of national liberation struggles of colonised peoples. Less obviously, once the capitalist economy encompassed more or less the entire globe, imperialism itself became a problem for capital. Geared as it was to accumulation in the 'mother' countries, its treatment of Third World countries predominantly as markets and sources of cheap raw materials and consumption goods led it to distort many of their economies into primary-product ones (Fuentes 1963). Even where this fate was avoided, as in India, imperialism blocked the development of heavy industry (Bagchi 1972, 44). Such policies contradicted the most potent means of counteracting the tendency of the rate of profit to fall, namely the full-scale development of capitalism in these countries where the rate of profit was high. Even the aim of using them as markets was stymied by the impoverishment of their populations: starving peasants are not a promising market for manufactured goods. Furthermore, the division of the world into empires, insulated from each other by protective barriers, became an obstacle to the global reach of multinational corporations and finance capital.

The interests of nascent capitalists in Third World countries and those of capitalists in imperialist countries overlapped in one respect: both would benefit from industrialisation in the Third World. Where they differed was on the question of protectionism, with capitalists in imperialist countries wanting access to markets and investment opportunities in former colonies, while local capitalists wished to protect their domestic markets and infant industries. However, as the examples cited by Tugendhat show, that was no reason why they could not reach a modus vivendi. Logically, as national liberation struggles and independence movements succeeded in decolonising the Third World, imperialism should have shrunk and disappeared. So why did it persist?

Imperialism During the Cold War

An indispensable requirement for the spread of multinationals and finance capital was that countries should be open to foreign investment, and this was to become the driving force of US imperialism. US firms could prevail against other firms by virtue of their competitiveness, but this was possible only if they were able to invest in countries throughout the world. Given the existence of the Soviet Union and later China as alternative models and sources of support for Third World countries at a time of rapid decolonisation, 'communism' became the foremost enemy. Any government, no matter how willing to be friendly with the US, was suspected of the dreaded disease if it tried to escape the control of US corporations backed by the US government. It had to be overthrown and replaced with one more subservient to the US.

There are numerous examples, but a few will suffice to illustrate the way this operated. In Iran, nationalist feeling since the end of World War I had been directed against foreign ownership of the country's oil; there was opposition not just to British ownership of the Anglo-Iranian Oil Company, but also to a proposed oil concession demanded by the Soviet Union in the north. The leader of the oil protest movement, Mohammad Mossadegh, was elected prime minister in 1951, leading a coalition called the National Front, which enjoyed wide support in Tehran and other cities. 'The oil industry was nationalized soon after Mossadeq became premier and within a few months his government was in direct conflict with the Shah and through the Shah with the USA, despite Mossadeq's initial attempts to win the latter over … There is now no doubt that the US government, and specifically the CIA, played an active part in organizing the coup on 19 August 1953 that ousted Mossadeq' (Halliday 1979, 25). Thus 'a nationalist and secular democratic movement led by Prime Minister Muhammad Mossadegh had established constitutionalism, until it was crushed by a coup engineered by the CIA and the British secret service in 1953' and replaced with a brutal dictatorship (Bayat 2010, 6).

In Guatemala, Juan José Arévalo was elected president in 1944, and a democratic constitution, which made many references to the US Declaration of Independence, Constitution and Four Freedoms, was passed. However, the United Fruit Company (which owned millions of acres of land, the only port on Guatemala's Atlantic coast, and all the railways) had outlawed workers' and peasants' unions and strikes and made extensive use of forced labour, and it was not happy. There were several coup attempts during Arévalo's six years in office. Jacobo Árbenz, who succeeded him in 1950, went a step further, attempting to carry out land reform by redistributing fallow land to the rural poor. Most of United Fruit's land was fallow, and even though they were compensated for it at the rate they had declared for tax purposes, the company, the CIA and the Eisenhower administration decided that Árbenz had to go. He was overthrown by a CIA-backed coup in 1954, leading to a succession of far-right military dictatorships and a civil war in which hundreds of thousands died (Schlesinger and Kinzer 2005 [1982]).

Mossadegh could be described as a secular nationalist, Árbenz as a social democrat. Salvador Allende was more explicitly a socialist, and an admirer of Fidel Castro and the Cuban revolution, but rather than coming to power through armed struggle, he was elected president of Chile in 1970, proceeding with a programme that included the nationalisation of banking and copper mines, public health care, education and housing, employment creation, and workers' rights. He was willing to negotiate the terms of nationalising the telephone companies owned by the US company ITT, but instead the corporation became part of a plot to overthrow him. Indeed, declassified documents show that his peaceful road to socialism was a prime reason why the Nixon administration made every effort, first, to prevent him from being elected, and then to overthrow him with a coup. Among other things, the coup involved assassinating the commander-in-chief of the Chilean armed forces, who opposed military interference in government; economic sabotage to stir up dissatisfaction with the Allende presidency; and a barrage of propaganda against him. Finally, Allende was overthrown and killed by a US-backed military coup in 1973; thousands were murdered and tens of thousands imprisoned and tortured during the subsequent dictatorship of Augusto Pinochet (Zipper 1989; Kornbluh 2003).

Spanning the entire period of the Eisenhower, Kennedy, Johnson and Nixon administrations is the case that can be seen as paradigmatic of US imperialism: Vietnam. Beginning with US assistance to French colonialism and escalating steeply after the French were defeated at Dien Bien Phu, the US war on Vietnam left tens of thousands of Americans and millions of Vietnamese dead (BMJ 2008), in addition to poisoning the land with its weapons of mass destruction for decades afterwards. All this was driven by the 'domino theory', which held that if Vietnam 'fell to communism', the contagion would spread to the rest of Southeast Asia and beyond. In June 1956, Kennedy outlined the fundamental thesis as follows:

> Vietnam represents the cornerstone of the Free World in Southeast Asia, the Keystone to the arch, the finger in the dike. Burma, Thailand, India, Japan, the Philippines and, obviously, Laos and Cambodia are among those whose security would be threatened if the red tide of Communism overflowed into Vietnam. (Chomsky 1972/1973)

It is true that in each of these cases, existing or potential investments by US corporations were part of the picture, but the nature of those investments was very different from the export of capital to advanced capitalist countries, where local accumulation was the goal. Instead, as Baran and Sweezy (1966, 112) noted, in 1963 'the return flow of interest and dividends (not to mention remittances disguised in the form of payment for services and the like) soon repays the original investment many times over – and still continues to pour capital into the coffers of the parent corporation in the United States.' So although globally the average rate of profit was boosted by these foreign investments, the profits constituted an outflow of wealth from the Third World to the US. In this respect they resembled classical imperialism, as also in the patently racist attitudes to Third World peoples, who were treated as inferior beings whose lives were of little or no importance.

Meanwhile, on the other side of the Iron Curtain, the situation was no better. Tsarist imperialism – which, like other Eastern European empires and the Ottoman Empire, had grown by annexing adjacent territories rather than overseas ones – was no less brutal than Western European and US imperialism. When Lenin's *Imperialism* was published in 1917, he explained in the Preface that

> In order to show the reader, in a guise acceptable to the censors, how shamelessly untruthful the capitalists and the social-chauvinists who have deserted to their side … are on the question of annexations; in order to show how shamelessly they *screen* the annexations of *their* capitalists, I was forced to quote as an example – Japan! The careful reader will easily substitute Russia for Japan, and Finland, Poland, Courland, the Ukraine, Khiva, Bokhara, Estonia or other regions peopled by non-Great Russians, for Korea. (Lenin 1917)

As a genuine anti-imperialist, Lenin was as opposed to Great Russian imperialist annexation of the territories of non–Great Russian peoples as he was to Western imperialism.

At the time he wrote this, he and most of the other Russian and European revolutionaries were hoping that revolutions in Western Europe would come to the rescue of the beleaguered Russian revolution and establish socialism throughout Europe. When those revolutions failed to materialise, the Russian revolutionaries were forced to adapt to an unforeseen situation. During the civil war that followed the revolution, emergency measures such as a highly centralised administration of industry and the compulsory requisition of grain from peasants came to be known as 'war communism'. The peasants reluctantly put up with these, so long as the defeat of the revolution threatened a feudal restoration and loss of their lands, but once the war was over at the end of 1920, they became increasingly restive. With a severely devalued currency and a dearth of goods, peasants were reluctant to deliver grain to the towns. Moreover, the death of many workers and the destruction of industry in the civil war threatened to bring down the economy.

> The antidote, familiarly known to history as NEP [the new economic policy] ...
> began by striking at the point of greatest danger, as an agricultural policy to
> increase the supply of food by offering fresh inducements to the peasant; it devel-
> oped into a commercial policy for the promotion of trade and exchange, involv-
> ing a financial policy for a stable currency; and finally, reaching the profoundest
> evil of all, it became an industrial policy to bring about that increase in industrial
> productivity which was a condition of the building up of a socialist order. (Carr
> 1966, 271–72)

The Bolsheviks had succeeded because the promise of land distribution – a key measure in a bourgeois revolution – had bought them the support of the peasantry, who constituted around 80 per cent of the population. Once the emergency of the civil war was over, they found it prudent to keep their promise to the peasants, while also reintroducing capitalist management in industry. Thus at the beginning of the 1920s the Bolsheviks, who were revolutionary socialists, were in the anomalous position of having taken power in circumstances that made a socialist revolution impossible.

But the illusion that it was a socialist revolution persisted, and was used by many (possibly the majority) of Lenin's colleagues to oppose his policies favouring national liberation for Russia's colonies. After Finland's independence was recognised in 1917, no other nation received the same treatment. However, the larger nations of Ukraine, Belorussia, Georgia, Armenia and Azerbaijan became independent Soviet republics, while smaller nations within the boundaries of the Russian Soviet Federative Socialist Republic (including the Central Asian nations) became autonomous republics and autonomous regions responsible for matters of local government, education, culture and agriculture. The Soviets promoted the national, economic and

cultural development of non-Russian peoples through a set of policies including giving 'priority to the local language, a massive increase in native language
schools, development of national cultures, and staffing the Soviet administration as far as possible with local nationals. Collectively, these policies were
known as *korenizatsiya*, or "rooting"' (Smith 2004).

The priority of Lenin's *Imperialism* had been to explain how the supposedly working-class Social-Democratic parties of the Second International
came to support their own bourgeoisies in World War I, and to insist that
the working class in imperialist countries must always oppose the bourgeoisies of their own countries, who were struggling to divide up the world among
themselves. However, subsequently, the Communist International (the
Third International or Comintern) had to be far more specific and detailed.
In Lenin's draft theses on this question for the Second Congress of the Comintern in 1920, he emphasised that making 'a clear distinction between the
interests of the oppressed classes, of working and exploited people, and the
general concept of national interests as a whole, which implies the interests
of the ruling class' was as important as making 'an equally clear distinction
between the oppressed, dependent and subject nations and the oppressing,
exploiting and sovereign nations'. He went on to argue that the Comintern's
policy on the national and the colonial questions 'should rest primarily on a
closer union of the proletarians and the working masses of all nations and
countries for a joint revolutionary struggle to overthrow the landowners and
the bourgeoisie'. His specific recommendations were as follows:

> With regard to the more backward states and nations, in which feudal or pa-
> triarchal and patriarchal-peasant relations predominate, it is particularly im-
> portant to bear in mind:
>
> first, that all Communist parties must assist the bourgeois-democratic
> liberation movement in these countries [...];
>
> second, the need for a struggle against the clergy and other influential
> reactionary and medieval elements in backward countries [...];
>
> fourth, the need, in backward countries, to give special support to the
> peasant movement against the landowners, against landed proprietorship, and
> against all manifestations or survivals of feudalism [...];
>
> fifth, the need for a determined struggle against attempts to give a com-
> munist colouring to bourgeois-democratic liberation trends in the backward
> countries. (Lenin 1920)

One could summarise these recommendations as proposing that communists should assist bourgeois-democratic liberation movements and peasant

movements against landowners in what would later be known as the Third World, while at the same time maintaining a distinction between themselves, as embodying the interests of the working and exploited people, and the bourgeoisie or 'national interest'. They should certainly *not* support 'reactionary and medieval elements', or 'Pan-Islamism and similar trends' in these countries, but instead struggle against them. For Lenin, national liberation is part of a process of democratisation, replacing an imperial government over which subject peoples have no control with national governments over which they have a limited yet significant amount of control; moving from imperial to local backward-looking or theocratic rule constitutes no progress at all. Lenin implicitly abandons the vision he had shared not only with contemporaries like Luxemburg and Trotsky, but also with Marx and Engels, of a socialist or communist revolution confined to Europe, instead envisaging a joint revolutionary struggle of 'the proletarians and the working masses of all nations and countries'.

Lenin did not arrive at these positions on his own. Indeed, in the early twentieth century, his position and that of the *Iskra* current to which he belonged was extremely unsympathetic to national liberation struggles in the colonies of the Tsarist Empire. It was non-Russian Marxist parties in the empire's periphery – especially in Poland, Latvia, Lithuania, Ukraine and the Caucasus – who were arguing the positions subsequently articulated by Lenin (Blanc 2016). These parties, despite their commitment in theory and practice to opposing ethnic nationalism and to building proletarian unity across national divisions, emphasised the need for national independence as well as the autonomy of their own parties in relation to the Russian Social Democratic Workers' Party. Luxemburg was even more hostile to national independence struggles, although she, like *Iskra*, opposed the oppression of one nation by another.

This issue was complicated by the fact that the Eastern European and Ottoman empires, unlike Western European empires, had expanded by annexing adjacent territories, so that it was much easier to slip into the error of confusing empire with nation-state. Thus, as Blanc puts it, *Iskra*'s perspective of a centralised empire-wide party 'tended to conflate the dynamics in Central Russia with that of the empire as a whole' (2016). On the contrary, however, even by 1903–4, Polish, Jewish, Lithuanian, Ukrainian, Latvian, and Finnish socialists had built regional parties of their own. This was one factor in the opposition to *Iskra*'s approach, which favoured centralisation into a Russian party despite the fact that many of the peripheral parties were 'far bigger than their Russian comrades in this period' (Blanc 2016). Another was the concern that centralisation in Russia would mean that the interests of non-Russian workers – including national liberation – would become sidelined.

Lenin became supportive of national liberation struggles as a result of the debate with borderland Marxists, the capitulation of Second International leaders to their ruling classes' war drives in World War I, and his own analysis of imperialism. The central leadership in the party largely stood with him.

Another complication was migration within the empire, which resulted in people of one ethnicity settling in countries where another ethnicity was predominant. In the case of the Russian empire, the largest number of such migrants tended to be Russians. Among them, as also among Russified militants of local origin, 'Russian chauvinism and nationalism tended to be the strongest. ... Particularly after 1914, this gap between Lenin's approach and those of his comrades on the ground became a major source of internal conflict within Bolshevism. Historian Jeremy Smith notes that the history of Bolshevik national policy between 1917 and 1923 is "largely the story of a struggle between the center and the periphery in which it was, perhaps surprisingly, the center which supported local autonomy"' (Smith 1999, cit. Blanc 2016). Subject peoples too had migrated to other countries within the empire and settled in scattered clusters. The debate between Lenin and Luxemburg on the right to self-determination suffered from the failure, on both sides, to distinguish between colonies of an imperial power and enclaves of minority ethnic communities. In the former case, Lenin's argument for the right to independence was correct; in the latter case, language and cultural rights as advocated by Luxemburg made more sense.

Lenin died in January 1924 and, after a short interregnum, was succeeded by Josef Stalin, whose position was diametrically opposed to Lenin's on Great Russian chauvinism and the right to national liberation of Russia's colonies. Despite being of Georgian origin, 'he was the most "Russian" of the early leaders not only in his rejection of the west, but in his low rating of the local nationalisms of the former Russian Empire. He became the protagonist not only of "socialism in one country", but of a socialism built on a predominantly Russian foundation' (Carr 1970, 195–96). In fact, 'socialism in one country' was a euphemism for state capitalist primitive accumulation involving the dispossession and proletarianisation of the peasantry and industrialisation through extreme exploitation of the working class. Raya Dunayevskaya (1941) was an early exponent of this theory, and Tony Cliff (born Ygael Gluckstein), a Palestinian Trotskyist of Polish Jewish origin, developed it in the first edition of his *State Capitalism in Russia* in 1947.

Trotsky contended that although the Soviet Union had undergone a political counterrevolution under Stalin, it remained a 'degenerate workers' state', but Cliff pointed out that unions had been stripped of their right to negotiate over wages, which were instead fixed unilaterally by the state; piecework and competition between workers were used to atomise the working class; workers were denied the freedom to change their place of work, and there were severe punishments for arriving late, idling at work, and so forth; strikes were prohibited and punished with twenty years of a penal sentence. While the conditions of all workers were grim, with long hours and unhealthy working conditions, the condition of women workers was 'appalling', with women sometimes working twenty-four-hour shifts in freezing temperatures. These descriptions echo those of the misery of workers during the industrial revolution in Britain, but conditions in Russia's slave labour camps – to which people could be condemned for petty offences like the theft of bread, not to mention political dissidence – were even worse. In 1942, it was estimated that the population of these camps consisted of eight to fifteen million men, women and children (Cliff 1974, Chapter 1, Part 1).

From 1928 onwards, consumption was subordinated to accumulation, with massive investments in heavy industry while investments in light industry were insufficient to maintain the standard of living of the workers. Industrial products were subsidised heavily, and armaments production received the greatest subsidies and investment (Cliff 1974, Chapter 1, Part 2). During the harvest, *kolkhoz* (collective farm) workers had to work from 5:30 a.m. to 9:00 p.m. without breaks, while dairymaids were required to work from 4:30 a.m. to 8:00 p.m., 365 days a year, with a break of only 1.5 hours a day. Taxes on consumption goods (the 'turnover tax') fell most heavily on staples consumed by the poorest: 73 to 74 per cent on wheat, and 70 to 80 per cent on salt (Cliff 1974, Chapter 1, Part 3).

Egalitarianism, which had been promoted after the revolution, became a crime under Stalin. This is a graphic description of the class differentiation in place:

> A maid with two children, one of ten and another of three, told Alexander Werth in 1942: 'The children live chiefly on bread and tea; the little one receives substitute milk – what can you do? – stuff made of soya beans, without taste and of little nutritive value. With my meat coupons this month I only got

a little fish. Sometimes I get a little soup left over at the restaurant – and that's about all.' At the same time, Alexander Werth could write in his diary: 'That lunch at the National today was a very sumptuous affair, for, in spite of the food shortage in Moscow, there always seems to be enough of the best possible food whenever there is reason for any kind of big feed, with official persons as guests. For *zakuski* there was the best fresh caviare, and plenty of butter, and smoked salmon; then sturgeon and, after the sturgeon, chicken cutlets *à la Maréchal*, then ice and coffee with brandy and liqueurs; and all down the table there was the usual array of bottles.' (Cliff 1974, Chapter 1, Part 4)

Thus, as Don Filtzer writes, 'the working class became the object of exploitation of a new elite which itself took shape during industrialization', and the fact that a significant proportion of the pampered elite was drawn from the working class 'does not alter the basic relationship between the elite and the workforce: the latter creates a surplus product which the former expropriates' (Filtzer 1987, 8–9).

Charles Bettelheim had a very different starting point. He started visiting the Soviet Union in the 1930s and admired its economic successes, believing that 'the economic and social development of the Soviet Union provided a sort of "model" for the building of socialism' (Bettelheim 1976, 10). Only after the Soviet invasion and occupation of Czechoslovakia in 1968 did he come to a similar conclusion to that of Cliff: that the USSR had a militaristic imperialist-style foreign policy driven by competition with the USA for world domination, and its social relations of production constituted 'a specific form of capitalism just as oppressive and aggressive as the "classical" forms', with accumulation propelled by competition with Western capitalism (Bettelheim 1976, 18). Like Cliff, he saw the development of the monstrous authoritarian state apparatus of the Soviet Union as evidence of a furious class struggle waged against the proletariat. Paul Mattick (1978) characterised the Russian and Chinese revolutions as 'state-capitalist revolutions … which were no longer determined by market competition but controlled by way of the authoritarian state'.

In fact, referring to the internal repression as 'class struggle' understates its ferocity massively, as two examples will show. The first is the 'radical – one could maintain genocidal – attack on the so-called kulaks, the supposed rich farmers … a group that in practice was often defined by owning a few head of cattle and oxen or having a tin roof over their huts' (Naimark 2010, 55–56). Peasants labelled as kulaks were deported or shot as families, abused as swine, dogs, cockroaches, scum, vermin, filth and garbage, and depicted as apes, 'dehumanized and racialized into beings inherently inferior to others'. Some thirty thousand were killed outright, while the rest were sent to 'special settlements' where large numbers died of 'hunger, disease, filth, privation, fierce cold, and inadequate shelter and food'. As Naimark argues, 'Stalin surely knew and understood that these conditions were ubiquitous and that the kulak population of the special settlements was being decimated month after month by the horrid conditions in which they lived ... Indeed, a good argument can be made that Stalin intended to wipe out the kulaks physically as a group of people – not just metaphorically as a class' (2010, 59; 60–61; 63).

The other example is Stalin's extermination of opponents, rivals (including the entire Bolshevik leadership) and dissidents, both real and imagined. The Bolshevik leaders, unless they committed suicide like Tomsky or escaped abroad like Trotsky, were tortured and blackmailed into confessing in show trials that they had committed grotesque and impossible crimes, before they were executed; Trotsky was tracked to Mexico by one of Stalin's agents who killed him by sticking an icepick in his head in 1940. 'We know a lot about the fearsome browbeating, torture, and threats to family members that lay behind many of the confessions. That Stalin directed the trials behind the scenes is not a matter of historical dispute. He systematically eliminated his political rivals through this process of trials, confession, and execution' (Naimark 2010, 102). In 1937 and 1938, at least 1,575,000 people and probably many more were arrested and brought to 'trial' in this way; at least 681,692 were executed and the rest sent to exile and potential death in the Gulag. An estimated 800,000 more victims were shot in secret and buried in unmarked graves without their families being informed of what had happened to them (Naimark 2010, 109; 111). Thus unspeakable cruelty was used to ensure Stalin's absolute and total power.

Many admirers of the Soviet Union, like Bettelheim, were disillusioned when it invaded Hungary in 1956 or Czechoslovakia in 1968. However, evidence of the imperialist character of Stalinist Russia long preceded these events. In the Introduction I already referred to the Ukrainian genocide, in which not only were millions of people exterminated in a single year, but the culture, language, religion and intelligentsia (teachers, writers, artists, thinkers, political leaders) were also sought to be wiped out. It was the most extreme example, but not the only one:

> It has had its matches within the Soviet Union in the annihilation of the Ingerian nation, the Don and Kuban Cossacks, the Crimean Tatar Republics, the

Baltic Nations of Lithuania, Estonia and Latvia. Each is a case in the long-term policy of liquidation of non-Russian peoples by the removal of select parts. ... What we have seen here is not confined to Ukraine. The plan that the Soviets used there has been and is being repeated. It is an essential part of the Soviet programme for expansion, for it offers the quick way of bringing unity out of the diversity of cultures and nations that constitute the Soviet Empire. That this method brings with it indescribable suffering for millions of people has not turned them from their path. If for no other reason than this human suffering, we would have to condemn this road to unity as criminal. But there is more to it than that. This is not simply a case of mass murder. It is a case of genocide, of destruction, not of individuals only, but of a culture and a nation. (Lemkin 1953)

Historians who had portrayed the Tsarist Empire as the oppressor of non-Russians were discredited, and the official version of history shifted to one in which the Tsarist Empire had brought progress and civilisation to backward peoples. The relationship between Soviet imperialism and its colonies was similar to classical imperialism, with the colonies plundered for raw materials and food to serve the industrialisation of Russia. There was an increasing dominance of Russians in non-Russian regions, and the Russian language was made compulsory in non-Russian schools. Deportations of indigenous people were combined with settlement of Russians in non-Russian nations, shifting the demographic makeup of these regions (Smith 2004). The Muslim nations of the Caucasus and Crimea were especially targeted; between 1943 and 1944 the entire Karachai population, Kalmyks, Chechen and Ingush peoples, Balkars, Crimean Tatars and Meshketian Turks were rounded up and expelled; those who could not be moved were shot, their villages burned to the ground (Snyder 2010, 330–31).[3] Kazakh villagers were used as guinea pigs to test the results of 456 nuclear tests between 1949 and 1989 (BBC World Service 2016).

The Hitler-Stalin pact signed by Ribbentrop and Molotov on August 23, 1939 also had a strong imperialist dimension. Stalin was well aware of Hitler's politics by then, but that did not deter him from forming an alliance with him, and even going so far as to adorn Moscow airport with swastikas when Ribbentrop arrived there. The pact did not merely guarantee mutual non-aggression; its secret protocols committed the Soviet Union to providing food products and raw materials to the Nazis in return for finished products like machinery from Germany, effectively making Stalin a Nazi collaborator for most of the first two years of the war. Such a pact would have been unthinkable had the two men not been so similar: 'Both were dictators who killed vast numbers of people on the European continent. ... Both destroyed their countries and societies, as well as vast numbers of people inside and outside their own states. Both – in the end – were genocidairs' (Naimark 2010, 137). Hannah Arendt (1968) has drawn extensive parallels between their regimes in her monumental work *The Origins of Totalitarianism*. In the secret protocols, Hitler agreed to give Finland, Estonia, Latvia, Lithuania and part of Poland to the Soviet Union. Within days of signing the non-aggression pact, Hitler invaded Poland, setting off a declaration of war by Britain and France, while Stalin moved in to occupy the territory offered to him by Germany; both slaughtered tens of thousands of Poles (Snyder 2010, 116; 119–141). It was not Stalin but Hitler who abrogated the pact, attacking Russian positions on June 22, 1941 and forcing Stalin to fight back.

After the Yalta Conference in February 1945, Moscow-dominated regimes were set up in Poland, Hungary, Czechoslovakia, Romania, Bulgaria, Albania, and later East Germany. The only exception was Yugoslavia, where Josip Broz Tito, leader of the Yugoslav communists and partisans, had taken power without the help of Stalin, and remained independent of him (Arendt 1968, 308; Snyder 2010, 353). This pattern resembles US imperialism, with friendly dictators being installed and supported by the imperial power, and military incursions only when the regime is threatened with being overthrown. The Russian equivalent of the US intervention in Vietnam was Afghanistan. The Moscow-affiliated People's Democratic Party of Afghanistan (PDPA), established in 1965, was opposed from the beginning by the *Jam'iyyat-i Islami* party, founded by theology professors who had studied in Cairo's Al-Azhar University. The Jam'iyyat 'protested the official founding of the PDPA in 1965 by publishing a leaflet entitled 'Tract of the Holy War' and 'conducted zealous protests against Israel, the U.S., the Afghan monarchy, and most of all, communism' (Kohlmann 1999, 6). A PDPA coup in 1978 faced tribal revolts that developed into a full-scale uprising by December 1979, when the Russians invaded and occupied Afghanistan.[4]

The military campaign that followed resembled the US campaign in Vietnam in its brutality to civilians, and like the Americans in Vietnam, the Russians in Afghanistan left a cruel legacy that went on maiming Afghan children long after they had left: 'millions of plastic mines disguised as pens, watches, and even toys' (Kohlmann 1999, 19). The war had reached a stalemate in the mid-1980s when Reagan, who was already supporting the mujahideen, agreed to supply them with Stinger anti-aircraft missiles. These weapons turned the tide against the Russians, who finally withdrew in 1989, leaving power in the hands of Najibullah of the PDPA. He managed to survive until the mid-1990s due to infighting among the mujahideen, but was finally hanged when the Taliban, who had been fostered in Pakistan by the ISI, took over.

With Stalin's adoption of the 'theory of socialism in one country', which held that socialism could be built in the Soviet Union even in the absence of revolutions elsewhere, theoretical justification was created for subordinating revolutionary movements throughout the world to his conception of the national interests of Russia. One way this was done in the Third World was to argue that the struggle of the masses in these countries at this stage was anti-imperialist, and therefore that the Chinese Communist Party, for example, should remain in the Kuomintang, which represented a bloc of four classes, namely the workers, peasantry, urban petty bourgeoisie and national bourgeoisie (Stalin 1927, 675): a very different proposition from having alliances with parties like the Kuomintang while maintaining independence from them, as Lenin had advocated. Stalin's insistence that the Communists remain in the Kuomintang despite growing evidence of Chiang Kai-shek's hostility to them ended in the catastrophe of 1927, when the armed workers, having gained control of Shanghai, were ordered to bury their arms and open the gates to Chiang's army (Brandt 1966 [1958], 110–14).

The results of this utterly disastrous policy were described graphically by Victor Serge: 'There is a savage repression in the countryside; there are arrests, executions and assassinations in the towns. The Communists are outlawed, the trade unions dissolved; fascist formations are masters of the streets. The government of a great national party that still pretended to represent the anti-imperialist revolution in mid-July represents no more than bourgeois counter-revolution, the natural ally of the imperialists' (Serge 1927a). Serge opined that the 'young unknown militant Mao Zedong' was right when he asserted that the revolution against feudalism and imperialism could not succeed without a peasant uprising (Serge 1927b), and after the 1927 bloodbath, Mao was canny enough to chart his own course even while paying lip service to Stalin's leadership.

Lenin did not always practice what he preached, but unlike his more Eurocentric predecessors (Marx, Engels) and contemporaries (Trotsky, Luxemburg), he had a vision of anti-imperialist socialist internationalism that remains relevant even today. It is all the more tragic that his legacy was sidelined in favour of that of his authoritarian, sadistic, racist, genocidal successor, for whom 'anti-imperialism' meant Russian imperialism, 'anti-fascism' included collaboration with Hitler, and 'socialism' meant super-exploitation of working people and extermination of all political opposition. We can trace the origins of pseudo-anti-imperialism to support for Stalin's Russian imperialism.

After the Cold War:
The Rise of Neoconservative Imperialism

Russia's war in Afghanistan contributed to the collapse of the Soviet Union in 1991. However, it was Mikhail Gorbachev – who became general secretary of the Politburo in 1985 and president of the USSR in 1990, and whose policies of *perestroika* (restructuring) and *glasnost* (openness) allowed for greater freedom of expression of anti-Soviet sentiments in the non-Russian republics and, indeed, even in Russia itself – who was seen, by conservative hardliners, as responsible for the impending catastrophe. The result was the coup carried out against him in August 1991. Paradoxically, the coup hastened the collapse of the USSR by weakening Gorbachev, who wanted to replace it with a looser union rather than dissolve it altogether, and empowering Boris Yeltsin. Yeltsin wanted full sovereignty for the Russian Federation, which entailed the end of the Soviet Union.

The dissolution of the Eastern Bloc and the Soviet Union can be seen from an anti-imperialist perspective as a process of decolonisation and democratisation.[5] Even twenty-five years later, East Germans were grateful to Gorbachev for ruling out a Russian invasion of East Germany in November 1989 and thereby allowing the Berlin Wall to be brought down peacefully (Croucher 2014). His policy of perestroika involved not only internal reform, but a novel approach to foreign affairs, including policies for nuclear disarmament and the rejection of military intervention abroad. As *Guardian* columnist Jonathan Steele described it in a 2011 interview with Gorbachev, under perestroika,

> no country was an island or should act unilaterally. The new Soviet policy of non-intervention allowed the eastern European states to produce internal regime change by peaceful means. [As Gorbachev states:] 'What we were able to achieve within the country and in the international arena was of enormous importance. It predetermined the course of events in ending the cold war, moving toward a new world order and, in spite of everything, producing gradual movement away

from a totalitarian state to a democracy'. (Steele and Gorbachev 2011)

In subsequent years, Yeltsin, who became the first president of the Russian Federation, signed a far-reaching Partnership and Cooperation Agreement between Russia and the EU in 1994, and pledged to support European integration; there was a real prospect that Russia would join the EU (2015). Even more significantly, Russia joined the North Atlantic Cooperation Council in 1991; received a visit from then–NATO secretary general Manfred Warner in 1992; joined Partnership for Peace (PfP) in 1994; and entered the Euro-Atlantic Partnership Council in 1997. As Yuriy Davydov, a NATO research fellow, wrote in a report titled 'Should Russia Join Nato?' (2000): 'Russia's participation since early 1996 in the Implementation Force (IFOR) and then in the Stabilisation Force (SFOR) alongside NATO Allies are seen by many Western and Russian experts as a model for their military co-operation, especially in the peacekeeping field. Indeed, NATO and Russian troops have worked together effectively.' It looked as if the world was heading for a post-imperialist period of peace. Unfortunately, that did not materialise.

In retrospect, it is evident that the Cold War was a prolonged period of intense rivalry between US imperialism and Russian imperialism. The US appeared to have won when the Soviet Union disintegrated, but it was a pyrrhic victory because, by then, imperialism had lost its usefulness to global capital.

So long as military conquest resulted in the expansion of the capitalist world economy into new parts of the world, military expenditure contributed to capitalist accumulation on a world scale. But with decolonisation resulting in the development of capitalism in former colonies, and the disintegration of the Eastern Bloc and the USSR creating a truly global capitalist economy, military spending not only became unnecessary for capital, but actually held back productivity and competitiveness. Seymour Melman shows how the huge percentage of US research and development funding going into military production, compared with a much smaller proportion in Japan and Germany (55.3 per cent, as against 6 per cent and 8.5 per cent respectively), resulted in productivity in the US lagging far behind productivity in Japan and Germany (2001, 110–14, 124–26). The belief that 'military Keynesianism' could compensate for this loss in competitiveness and the loss of jobs to other countries was based on a faulty premise. As Chalmers Johnson explains, 'By military Keynesianism, I mean the mistaken belief that public policies focused on frequent wars, huge expenditures on weapons and munitions, and large standing armies can indefinitely sustain a wealthy capitalist economy. The opposite is actually true.' The mistake lies, Chalmers argues, in 'treat[ing] military output as an ordinary economic product, even though it makes no contribution to either production or consumption' (2008).

Militarism constituted not just an *indirect* deduction from capitalist accumulation by competing with state investments in infrastructure, the social sector, and civilian research and development, but was also a *direct* deduction, because it was financed by taxes on profits and wages (Mattick 1981, 215). In that sense, it was 'economically parasitic activity, that yields no return to society' (Melman 2008, 6). In a globalised world economy, where productivity was the key to success, militarism became an impediment to economic power.

By the mid-1990s, imperialism, which relies on militarism, had outlived its usefulness for capital. One reason why this is not immediately apparent is that Lenin's definition of imperialism included finance capital, which was of course thriving at this time. However, David Harvey emphasises the importance of seeing 'the territorial and capitalist logics of power as distinct from each other' (2003, 29). Once this is done, it becomes evident that by the early twenty-first century 'there appears to be a deep inconsistency if not outright contradiction between the two logics' (Harvey 2003, 204). When finance capital and foreign investment are delinked from territorial domination, and seen as separate phenomena with dynamics of their own, the contradiction between imperialism and a strong capitalist economy becomes more evident.

'Neoliberalism' was the term used to describe the measures taken to counteract the crisis of profitability that took place in the 1970s, and it was promoted assiduously by the International Monetary Fund (IMF) and the International Bank for Reconstruction and Development (World Bank). The short-term stabilisation measures they imposed in return for loans included cutbacks in government expenditure, high interest rates and currency devaluation, while the longer-term adjustment measures centred on deregulating the economy, privatising state enterprises, and liberalising trade and investment. This last measure came to be known as 'globalisation', because it liberalised trade and capital flows around the globe, and it led to the formation of the World Trade Organization (WTO) in 1995. The IMF/World Bank regime, sometimes called the 'Washington Consensus', at first reinforced US dominance over the world economy at the cost of wrecking the economies of Third World countries and Russia (Stiglitz 2000). However, in the longer term it had the opposite effect. By the early 2000s, manufactured products and IT services from China, India and other Third World countries were increasingly dominating the world market; much of this was by way of outsourcing or offshoring, as companies in North America and Western Europe gave up the struggle to compete, instead using the more competitive production in Third World countries to their own advantage (Hensman 2011, 42, 47).

How did this happen? As Harvey writes (2003, 187), globalisation created 'an increasingly transnational capitalist class', which 'paid very little heed to place-bound or national loyalties or traditions. It could be multi-racial, multi-ethnic, multicultural, and cosmopolitan. If financial exigencies and the quest for profit required plant closures and the diminution of manufacturing capacity in their own backyard, then so be it. US financial interests were perfectly content to undermine US hegemony in production.' To call this 'imperialism' is surely absurd. Who are the imperialists here? China, which is the main beneficiary of this new global order? Or the US, which appears to be committing economic hara-kiri? Neither fits the bill. Is it, then, the multiracial, multiethnic, multicultural and cosmopolitan capitalist class? But they represent no state; they are representatives of global capital. The crucial link between state and capital which defines imperialism is missing here; this is global capitalism, pure and simple.

However, the 1970s also saw the emergence in the US of a different political ideology – neoconservatism – which had very distinct imperialist overtones. As John Mearsheimer and Stephen Walt (2007, 129) explain, 'Viewing U.S. leadership as "good both for America and for the world," to quote the website of the neoconservative Project for [the] New American Century, neoconservatives generally favor the unilateral exercise of American power'; the way to exercise this power is, of course, through military force. Neoconservatism found its electoral base among socially conservative fundamentalist Christians opposed to women's equality and LGBT rights: 'In the wake of 9/11, for example, Jerry Falwell and Pat Robertson ... expressed the view that the event was a sign of God's anger at the permissiveness of a society that tolerated abortion and homosexuality' (Harvey 2003, 190–91).

The neoconservative charter for foreign policy, as laid out in the Project for the New American Century in 1997, was to put the US 'in a military and geostrategic position to control the whole globe militarily and, through oil, economically' (Harvey 2003, 199). Israel, to which they uniformly show unapologetic support, appears to be the linchpin of their strategy from both a military and ideological point of view, and within Israel they support the most right-wing elements: 'It was a group of eight neoconservatives ... that drafted the 1996 "Clean Break" study for incoming Likud Prime Minister Benjamin Netanyahu. That study advocated that Israel abandon the Oslo peace process and use bold measures – including military force – to topple unfriendly Middle Eastern regimes' (Mearsheimer and Walt 2007, 130). A peculiarity of neoconservatism is that its vision is stuck in an earlier stage of capitalism, where militarism was an asset and not a liability; thus its protagonists fail to understand that their programme for world domination undermines the economic viability of the very state whose interests they believe they are supporting.

When George W. Bush came to power in 2000, his administration enabled a large number of neoconservatives like Dick Cheney, Paul Wolfowitz, Scooter Libby, Richard Perle, John Bolton and Elliot Abrams, who 'had advocated toppling Saddam Hussein since the mid-1990s and believed this step would benefit the United States and Israel alike', to move in and shape foreign policy (Mearsheimer and Walt 2007, 238–39). It was sustained pressure from these figures that resulted in the US invasion of Iraq in 2002. Mearsheimer and Walt (2007, 231) argue that 'the war was motivated at least in good part by a desire to make Israel more secure', and indeed this was made clear in a letter from Project for the New American Century to President Bush in September 2001 in the wake of the 9/11 attacks (History Commons, n.d.). In July 2016, the Chilcot Report confirmed officially – in more polite language – what those of us who opposed the war on Iraq had been arguing all along, namely that evidence for Saddam Hussein's weapons of mass destruction had been fabricated (Brinded 2016); but the pretext for attacking Afghanistan – that the alleged mastermind of the 9/11 terrorist attacks, Osama bin Laden, was hiding there – is hardly more convincing, whether you accept the allegation that the war was at least partly about oil (Monbiot 2001) or reject it (Stevenson 2001).

The wars did nothing to improve America's security, and the massive expenses involved helped to drive up the national debt to over $9 trillion, a huge sum which could be largely explained by defence expenditures. Simultaneously, there was a severe erosion of democratic rights. In *Nemesis: The Last Days of the American Republic*, Chalmers Johnson had warned: 'We are on the cusp of losing our democracy for the sake of keeping our empire. Once a nation is started down that path, the dynamics that apply to all empires come into play – isolation, overstretch, the uniting of forces opposed to imperialism, and bankruptcy. Nemesis stalks our life as a free nation' (Johnson 2006). Two years later, his prediction came true, and he concluded that 'our short tenure as the world's "lone superpower" has come to an end' (Johnson 2008).

Obama, who inherited two wars and an economy in crisis, got the message. While his administration did little to rein in the neoliberal forces that had stoked the crash, commentators who are politically poles apart acknowledged that it managed to restore the US economy to comparative health (Egan 2015; Drum 2015). A careful evaluation of its policies also shows that it broke with the neoconservatism of the previous administration. Obama's support for abortion rights and LGBT rights clashed with the social conservatism of the Bush administration. He had opposed the invasion of Iraq in 2003 and criticised US imperialism before becoming president; once in power he pledged to end the practice of torture and close down the Guantanamo Bay prison facility, and before leaving office commuted the 35-year prison sentence of Chelsea Manning, the whistleblower who had revealed US war crimes in Iraq (McFadden et al. 2017). Normalising relations with Cuba was a step towards putting the lingering legacy of the Cold War to rest.

Most significantly, by contrast with the neoconservative threat to wage war on Iran, Obama made it a priority to push through a nuclear deal with Iran despite stubborn opposition from many members of Congress, acknowledging that 'we had some involvement with overthrowing a democratically elected regime in Iran' (Friedman 2015). In the process, his relationship with Israeli prime minister Benjamin Netanyahu deteriorated to the point where it was described as 'the worst relationship between a US president and an Israeli prime minister ever,' with Obama openly referring to the taboo subject of Israel's nuclear weapons, and Netanyahu's opponents recirculating a video of him using exactly the same discredited arguments in support of the Iraq war as he was currently using to oppose the Iran nuclear deal (Tibon and Shalev 2015). In December 2016, through its abstention in a vote on a resolution describing Israeli settlements in Palestinian territories occupied in 1967 as a 'flagrant violation' of international law, the Obama administration allowed it to be passed in the UN Security Council (Beaumont 2016).

It is true that drone strikes continued to kill civilians, the surveillance apparatus crossed all boundaries, US troops remained in Afghanistan, and Congress put obstacles in the way of closing Guantanamo Bay. But it would be naïve to think that a country which has been a superpower for decades could become a normal member of the international community in the span of a few years. As Lao Tzu said, a journey of one thousand miles begins with a single step, and the first few steps were taken by the Obama administration (although promptly retraced by Obama's successor). Its military interventions in Afghanistan and Iraq were undertaken at the request of their governments in order to combat enemies who are acknowledged to be malignant even by pseudo-anti-imperialists (the Taliban in Afghanistan and ISIS in Iraq). The interventions in Libya and Syria will be taken up in Chapter 7, but it is worth mentioning here that they took place in the context of popular uprisings and were *not* aimed at crushing them. Persistent attacks from the right on the decline in military strength and global dominance of the US during Obama's presidency are testimony to his administration's withdrawal from the role of superpower (Adams and Sokolsky 2015).

Meanwhile, in Russia, Yeltsin's ill health and incompetence combined with the IMF's 'shock therapy' had ensured that Russia's valuable public sector assets were privatised and grabbed by a small number of oligarchs who were subsequently linked to the state. Its state capitalism was thus transformed into state-supported oligarchic capitalism, while the bulk of the population suffered cruel austerity measures and plummeting living standards. The devastation of the economy was exacerbated by low oil prices. Yeltsin was forced to resign in 1999, and Vladimir Putin took over as acting president, becoming president in 2000. A decade later, Gorbachev, who had done the most to democratise Russia, was appalled at what was happening to his country under Putin, calling it a 'sham' democracy and condemning its leaders for reversing the democratic gains of the 1990s (cit. Elder 2011). Gorbachev described United Russia, Putin's ruling party, as a 'throwback' to the Communist Party, with a destructive effect on the political life of the country: 'The monopoly ends in rotting and hampers the development of democratic processes.' Bemoaning the loss of independence of the judiciary, he highlighted the case of the court clerk, Natalya Vasilieva, who had revealed that the judge in the Khodorkovsky trial had been subject to influence.

The Russian economy did well under Putin as oil prices rose, but neither diversified to reduce dependence on hydrocarbons – indeed, oil and gas increased from less than half of Russia's exports in 2002 to two-thirds a decade later – nor tackled rampant corruption, which 'is without exaggeration the biggest threat to our development', as Putin himself acknowledged in 2012, by which time falling oil prices were already putting pressure on the budget (Schuman 2012). Instead of diversifying the economy and eliminating corruption, however, Putin set out to rebuild Russia as a superpower, drawing on both its Soviet and pre-Soviet imperial history. In 2005, expressing nostalgia for an epoch when Russians who had settled in non-Russian colonies were the bosses there, he said, 'The collapse of the Soviet Union was a major geopolitical disaster of the century. As for the Russian nation, it became a genuine drama. Tens of millions of our co-citizens and compatriots found themselves outside Russian territory' (Putin 2005). Ten years later, he justified the Nazi-Soviet Pact, which he had more diplomatically condemned during a visit to Poland in 2009 (Dolgov 2015). And in the debate over the right to self-determination, he made it clear where his sympathies lay. In a speech in which he accused Lenin of placing a 'time-bomb' under Russia, Putin criticised Lenin's notion of a federative state from which regions could secede; on this point, he suggested, Stalin's unitary state model had been preferable. It was the federative model favoured by Lenin, on the contrary, that had hastened the breakup of the Soviet Union (Associated Press 2016a).[6]

In her (2014) article, Mary Elise Sarotte speculates that Putin, who was a KGB agent in East Germany when protesters pulled down the Berlin Wall and toppled the regime in 1989, was traumatised by the events: 'For someone who believed deeply in the cold war order, it was most likely an excruciating experience. It is clear that he returned home soon afterwards in disgust, full of bitterness that lingers to this day', and which shapes his responses to peaceful mass protests in Russia and Ukraine. Since then, he has become more and more of a neo-Stalinist, celebrating Stalin's role in defeating the Nazis in World War II (Thoburn 2016), whereas it should be obvious that the death toll, especially of Russians, would have been considerably lower had he fought against Hitler from the start instead of forming an alliance with him, and had he refrained from sabotaging the war effort by executing competent officials and generals who were contributing to it.

We will return to an examination of Putin's politics in Chapter 2; the point to note here is that he is a neo-Stalinist neoconservative. Peter Beinart (2014) lists the ways in which Putin resembles American neocons: (1) Like them, he is obsessed with the threat of 'appeasement' of enemies, and vows to fight back, thus gaining the admiration of US neoconservatives; (2) like them, he insists on principles of foreign policy – like non-intervention in other countries – so long as they apply to others, but not if they constrain his own country's imperialism; (3) like them, he wishes to expand his country's global military footprint without regard to the negative impact on Russia's economy; and (4) just for good measure, his government opposes abortion and LGBT rights. His shock-and-awe air campaign in Syria, and his position that anyone opposing his protégé Assad is a 'terrorist', are strongly reminiscent of George W. Bush.

Pseudo-anti-imperialists like Putin, his allies, and their supporters are neo-Stalinists engaged in rehabilitating Stalin, who in his time had rehabilitated tsarist imperialism; this accounts for their single-minded opposition to liberal democracy. They are proponents of neoconservative imperialism, living in a time warp where economic power depends on military dominance and where the US seeks to control global oil production – ignoring the facts that the US is now that a major oil producer thanks to fracking (Harlan 2015), and that a global oil glut and mounting stockpiles have led to a steep fall in oil prices (Durdan 2015). In one sense, history has left them behind; in another sense they are very modern in their ability to flood the electronic media, social media and internet with their propaganda, often influencing even sincere anti-imperialists who do not take the trouble to check their 'facts' (Weiss 2015b). This is what explains how pseudo-anti-imperialism has succeeded in colonising left-wing discourse in a way it had not been able to do since Stalin's lifetime.

Fighting Imperialism and Authoritarianism

Over the twentieth century, Western imperialism changed from being a key component of the capitalist drive for global expansion to being a major contributor to capitalist crisis. Russian imperialism, which had once helped Soviet state capitalism to develop at breakneck speed, became a major contributor to the demise of the Soviet Union. In both cases, the colossal military expenditures required to maintain an empire were instrumental in leading to economic collapse. But if imperialism is no longer of any use to global capitalism, what explains its persistence? Part of the answer is that one section of capitalists – those involved in the military-industrial complex – has a vested interest in the continuation of imperialism because of its dependence on militarism, and Mearsheimer and Walt (2007) do indeed show that this section was deeply involved in the neoconservative imperialist project in the United States. However, this by itself cannot explain the persistence of imperialism in the twenty-first century.

The desire to wield power over others, through structures ranging from patriarchy to absolute monarchy to empire, predates capitalism by millennia. Capitalism neither eliminates these power structures automatically, nor invariably fosters them as a 'divide and rule' strategy. Rather, capital employs an opportunistic policy of using or dumping them according to its own needs, and different sections or types of capital may even have different needs at the same historical juncture. It is also important to note that what Marxists misleadingly call 'bourgeois-democratic revolutions' – misleading because this term suggests there is an organic connection between capitalism and democracy, which is certainly not the case – are actually the confluence of two revolutions, one bourgeois and the other democratic. A bourgeois revolution may involve the popular masses and give them a chance to put forward their democratic agenda, but crush them subsequently. Capitalism can survive for decades without democracy; only the unremitting struggle of the popular masses can succeed in carrying out a democratic revolution, which is a necessary condition for the socialist transformation of society.

I would argue, therefore, that we need to redefine what we mean by 'right-wing' (reactionary or backward-looking) and 'left-wing' (progressive or socialist). If we keep in mind that today the whole world is dominated by capitalism and that the differences between private capitalism, state capitalism, and state-supported oligarchic capitalism are merely superficial – they all exploit wage labour (and in the worst cases slave labour) in order to accumulate capital – then the notion that being 'right-wing' entails support for private capitalism while being 'left-wing' entails support for state capitalism, or for state-supported oligarchic capitalism, is seriously flawed. It is true that neoliberal policies in the West – favouring the rule of the market in all spheres, promoting privatisation of just about everything, opposing state expenditure on social security and welfare, and being hostile to trade unions – are inimical to the working class. However, it is equally true that state capitalist or former state capitalist regimes have drastically cut back state expenditure on social security and welfare, clamp down ferociously on workers' unions that attempt to be independent of the state, and are characterised by enormous and increasing inequality between a small rich minority and a vast impoverished majority.

The key difference, therefore, is between democratic states that allow working people to *fight back* against the forces exploiting and oppressing them, and authoritarian states that *block such struggles* in multiple ways: by opposing freedom of association, expression and peaceful assembly; jailing and killing critics and dissidents; eliminating free and fair elections; and promoting authoritarianism and inequality in society through means such as patriarchy, racism, nationalism and religious bigotry. It is far more useful to characterise as 'left-wing' those who prioritise the struggle to establish the conditions in which oppressed and exploited people can fight back, and as 'right-wing' those who crush such struggles and/or promote authoritarian ideologies and inequality in society.

Much of the left has ignored or downplayed the importance of fighting against authoritarian relationships and inequality in civil society, and this has stymied its fight against fascism. Take, for example, Clara Zetkin's (1923) report on fascism: she is remarkably prescient in writing about its dangers, yet she lambasts the 'reformists' and trade unions not for failing to fight against anti-Semitism but for letting down the workers' struggle against capitalism; she does not even mention her own work for women's liberation as contributing to the struggle against fascism, although, as Wilhelm Reich later shows in *The Mass Psychology of Fascism* (1946, 34–44), patriarchal, authoritarian families are the breeding ground of fascists. It is true that the rapid growth of unemployment and poverty *can* feed into the development of fascist movements, but poverty and unemployment do not automatically result in pogroms; the dissemination of fascist beliefs and ideologies and the organisation of violence are necessary to encourage the anger generated by capitalism and the ruling class to be redirected against helpless victims.

In fact, at least some of the barbarism unleashed by right-wing movements is of no use whatsoever to capital. One of the examples used by Israel Shahak (1994, 111n.) to illustrate 'the irrational, demonic character which racism can sometimes acquire' is that 'during the eight months between June 1942 and February 1943 the Nazis probably used more railway wagons to haul Jews to the gas chambers than to carry much needed supplies to the army. Before being taken to their death, most of these Jews, at least in Poland, had been very effectively employed in production of equipment for the German army.' Thus *even* for those sections of German capital who profited from the war, it would have been logical to use these Jews for production; but the logic of genocidal racism dictated that they be exterminated. The two logics are at odds here.

Conversely, there are cases where the needs of capital may have emancipatory potential for oppressed sections. For example, a report by the McKinsey Global Institute (2016) found that promoting women's participation in the economy identically to men could add trillions to global growth. We can conclude from this that global capital, for its own reasons, needs more women to join the wage-labour force. While feminists might challenge the way in which current calculations of GDP leave out the value contributed by unwaged labour (mostly performed by women), or the argument that gender equality should be promoted only because it adds to GDP, it would be self-defeating to *oppose* gender equality just because capital seems to need it at this juncture (Nandy and Hensman 2015). Similarly, if 'gender and LGBT equality are increasingly upheld as a paradigmatic "European" value by some states and supranational institutions such as the EU' (Stella and Nartova 2016, 18), we may contest the specifically 'European' character of these values, but it would be foolish to oppose them in the name of anti-imperialism.

These examples show that we need to disentangle capitalism from forms of oppression like racism and sexism. It is undeniable that capitalism is responsible for unspeakable atrocities and must be fought,[7] but this should not detract from the fight against other forms of oppression. If anything, the struggle against racism and religious bigotry, patriarchy, misogyny and homophobia, xenophobia, nationalism and all forms of authoritarianism should be a priority, because a working class dominated and divided by these ideologies and politics can never defeat neoliberalism, much less capitalism. Nor can the struggle against capitalism be won without the freedom to express oneself freely, to debate, discuss and organise. Therefore, the establishment of these facets of constitutional democracy is *essential to the struggle against capitalism*. It is true that because liberal democracy can coexist with capitalism, it is restricted in its scope. However, what neo-Stalinists refuse to recognise is that state capitalism and state-supported oligarchic capitalism are *also* forms of capitalism, and that capitalism *without* liberal democracy is much worse than capitalism with it. Those who have the luxury of living without constant dread of arbitrary arrest, detention, torture and execution for themselves or their loved ones may lack the imagination or empathy to understand what it feels like to be in that position. As filmmaker Nanfu Wang (2016) put it, 'I'm not a paranoid person, but my experience making a film about human rights in China gave me a sense of fear that I think Westerners don't comprehend.' To support authoritarian states by word or deed in the name of opposing capitalism or imperialism is a betrayal of struggles against both.

Yet opposing everything said or done in the advanced capitalist countries of North America and Western Europe ('the West') entails doing precisely that. Pseudo-anti-imperialists for whom opposing the West is always the priority do not seem to care that opposing US and EU calls for accountability for war crimes in Sri Lanka makes them proponents of impunity for war crimes; that disagreeing with Laurent Fabius, François Hollande and Barack Obama when they say 'Assad must go' (France 24 2012, The Economic Times 2015) makes them accomplices to Assad's war crimes and crimes against humanity; that opposing US air strikes supporting the Kurdish offensive to enable encircled Yazidis to escape makes them accomplices in the ISIS genocide of Yazidis; that supporting the Russian invasion of Ukraine makes them supporters of imperialism. In every one of these cases, they take positions that are diametrically opposed to those taken by genuine anti-imperialists, because they support oppressors against the oppressed, authoritarianism against democracy.

Genuine anti-imperialists do, of course, oppose Western states when they invade and occupy countries, impose authoritarian regimes on Third World peoples, or kill civilians in airstrikes. But pseudo-anti-imperialists, by opposing 'the West' as such, are also rejecting the democratic revolutions carried out by labour activists, feminists, LGBT activists and anti-racists in the West. This is evident in some of the reactions to the ISIS attacks of November 2015 in Paris, many of which attributed them either to 'blowback' from Western intervention in Muslim countries, or to a reaction to racist discrimination against people of African origin in France and Belgium. Yet, as more perceptive observers pointed out, 'The terrorists did not target symbols of the French state or of French militarism ... They targeted, rather, the areas and the places where mainly young, anti-racist, multi-ethnic Parisians hang out. ... The other venue attacked was the Stade de France, the national football stadium ... But the Stade de France, like France's national football team, also has great cultural resonance. "Les Bleus" – as the team is known – are seen by many as an embodiment of multicultural France, a team consisting of "noir, blanc, beur" (black, white, Arab) players' (Malik 2015). 'The attackers targeted sites of inclusiveness and conversation' (Kinstler 2015), and 'explaining' this right-wing assault in any other way than recognising it for what it is entails participating in targeting the most progressive features of 'the West'.

There has been much talk of a 'new Cold War', but what has been happening, on the contrary, is a consolidation of the far right that cuts across the erstwhile Iron Curtain. The alliance between Putin and extreme right parties in Europe is long-standing, and it is strong enough for him to have invited them as observers of the Crimean referendum held directly after Russia's military intervention in 2014, prior to Crimea's annexation, for they could be trusted to endorse it (Shekhovtsov 2014b). The French Front Nationale (FN), whose leader Marine Le Pen is frank about her admiration for Putin, 'has confirmed taking Russian money. The First Czech Russian bank in Moscow has lent the party a whopping 9.4m Euros' (Harding 2014). Most strikingly, Putin supported Donald Trump's bid for the US presidency (Walker 2015): the same climate change denier who wanted to build a wall to keep out 'rapist' Mexicans and ban Muslims from entering the US, who promised to resume waterboarding and other forms of torture because 'if it doesn't work they deserve it anyway', who called for surveillance of mosques, who repeated a disproved rumour that thousands of Muslims cheered as the Twin Towers came down, and who used a 'dog-whistle' anti-Semitic advertisement (Johnson 2015; Marshall 2016b).[8] Trump, on his side, expressed open admiration for Putin and supported his role in Syria (Hanchett 2015). This alliance between neo-Stalinists (who may not even pretend to be Marxists, although some do) and neo-fascists (who may not all be anti-Semites, although some are) is a twenty-first century version of the Hitler-Stalin pact, epitomised by the endorsement of neo-fascist Le Pen in the French presidential election by neo-Stalinist James Petras (2017). Trump, like Putin, emphasises military power without counting the cost to the economy (Shear and Steinhauer 2017) and identifies with his neo-fascist supporters to such an extent that he refused to condemn them outright after their rampage in Charlottesville (Shear and Haberman 2017). Both are authoritarian neo-conservatives who rely on neo-fascist support.

2. Russia and Ukraine

The belief that Stalinist Russia was an example of socialism has led its proponents to condone and cover up horrific crimes committed by the regime in both Russia and the former tsarist colonies. A closer look at what was happening in Russia after the 1917 revolutions makes it clear that the authoritarian degeneration of the revolution began even before Stalin took over the party, and intensified massively during his rule; to believe that this was 'socialism' or 'communism' is to believe that a socialist or communist society is compatible with brutal exploitation and oppression of workers, peasants, ethnic minorities and colonised peoples. However, pseudo-anti-imperialists go even further when they support Putin, who does not even pretend to be a socialist or communist, and openly associates with the far right; their advocacy extends to support for Putin's efforts to annexe or establish subservient regimes in parts of the former Russian empire, like Ukraine.

Lenin's Last Struggle

In the last two years of his life, Lenin was tormented not only by three debilitating strokes but also by a terrible feeling that the revolution he had led was going down the drain. Part of the problem had to do with circumstances over which he had no control. The revolution took place in a country where the proletariat was a small minority which was further decimated by the civil war that followed. This necessitated the recruitment of managers to run industry, while the old tsarist bureaucracy retained a major role in administration. Winning the war brought its own problems. Victorious commanders of the Red Army assumed leading posts in the Soviets and

53

in the administration, bringing with them the authoritarian culture of the
military, which rendered them incapable of pushing back against the authoritarian culture of the bureaucracy. As Lenin commented ruefully, 'Let
us take the case of Moscow: 4,700 Communist leaders and an enormous
mass of bureaucrats. Who is leading whom? I very much doubt if it can be
said that the Communists are leading. I think it can be said that they are
being led' (Lewin 1968, 10).

However, policies that Lenin played a role in formulating and implementing were also to blame. The prohibition of factions in the party, enacted
after the civil war, helped to stifle debate within the party on crucial issues,
while empowering the secret police[1] and the most authoritarian elements
within the party: 'In 1919 Stalin "jokingly" threatened dissenting Ukrainian
Communists, Mazlakh and Shakhrai, with the Cheka for protesting against
centralization there' (Blank 1990, 156). The negation of democratic government was illustrated most starkly by the crushing of the rebellion in the
naval town of Kronstadt by the Bolsheviks in March 1921. On March 1, a
mass meeting of fifteen to sixteen thousand people in Anchor Square, Kronstadt, passed a resolution raising fifteen demands, including free elections
to the Soviets and freedom of speech, press, assembly and organisation for
workers, peasants, anarchists and left socialists. The next day, a conference
of 303 delegates from the ships' crews, army units, the docks, workshops,
trade unions and Soviet institutions endorsed the resolution and formed a
Provisional Revolutionary Committee which raised the original slogan of
the 1917 revolution – 'All Power to the Soviets!' – to which they added: 'and
not to parties'. The government issued an ultimatum, alleging falsely that the
uprising had been organised by ex-tsarist officers, and it was crushed by the
Red Army in a bloody battle, after which thousands of prisoners were shot
or sent to forced labour camps (Anarchist Writers 2008).

At this point, it did not seem to have occurred to Lenin, Trotsky and
many of their associates that the assault on democracy within the party and
in society as a whole was putting enormous power in the hands of a nascent
state capitalist class; even the Left Communists did not protest against the
repression, despite believing that 'Kronstadt was the beginning of a fresh,
liberating revolution for popular democracy' (Serge 2012, 150), and it was
left to anarchist Emma Goldman (1923) to voice an impassioned denuncia-
tion of the slaughter. It was a different issue altogether that alerted Lenin to
the looming danger: the future of tsarist Russia's colonies.

Lenin fell seriously ill towards the end of 1921, and he suffered a stroke that left his right hand and leg paralysed and his speech impaired in May 1922, the year in which Stalin was appointed general secretary; thus Lenin's power declined as Stalin's increased. During 1920 and 1921, the relations between the Russian Federation and Ukraine, Byelorussia, Georgia, Azerbaijan and Armenia were governed by a series of bilateral treaties that treated them as independent republics. When Lenin proposed the economic unification of the latter three republics into a Transcaucasian Federation, Sergo Ordzhonikidze, himself a Georgian and a close associate of Stalin, was sent to initiate the change, but he faced opposition from Georgian communists, who were particularly incensed 'by the proconsular way in which he dismissed the opinion of local leaders'; at that point, Lenin conceded that the project was premature (Lewin 1968, 44–45).

This did not deter Stalin, however. In August 1922, he set up a commission headed by himself and drew up a resolution that provided for the inclusion of all these currently independent republics in the Russian Federation as 'autonomous republics'. The representatives of Azerbaijan and Armenia agreed, but the Communist Party central committees of the other republics objected, the Georgian communists stating explicitly that they wanted to retain their independence. Subsequently the Ukrainian Central Committee too voted to remain independent (Lewin 1968, 46–49). When Lenin, who was convalescing, asked for and received the dossier about the matter, he wrote a letter rejecting Stalin's plan and suggesting instead a federation of republics enjoying equal rights; but Stalin opposed him in a covering letter to the Politburo, accusing him of both 'national liberalism' and, conversely, of overhasty centralism. Subsequently, in a brief note to Kamenev, Lenin wrote, 'I declare war to the death on dominant-nation chauvinism' (Lewin 1968, 51–53). Stalin and Ordzhonikidze continued with their plan for a Transcaucasian Federation regardless, and in one confrontation the latter struck a Georgian communist who opposed him.

Alarmed by a letter from an old Georgian communist accusing Ordzhonikidze of threatening them, Lenin sent Alexei Rykov to Georgia to investigate. Rykov returned and reported back to Lenin in early December 1922, and Lenin was deeply upset by the 'image of a Communist governor behaving like a satrap in a conquered country'. He suffered more attacks, and this time, being in the Kremlin, was subject to Stalin's orders that only his wife Nadezhda Krupskaya, his sister, three or four secretaries and the medical staff should have access to him, and they were forbidden to inform him of current state affairs; when Krupskaya broke these orders – with the doctor's permission – to write a note dictated by Lenin, Stalin phoned her and, in her own words, 'piled unworthy abuse and threats' on her (Lewin 1968, 69; 71). The degree of Stalin's surveillance over Lenin gives credence to the claim by German communist trade unionist Heinrich Brandler that in 1921, Lenin's phone was already being tapped (Blank 1990, 163). Despite his illness, Lenin insisted on dictating what he called his 'journal' for five minutes a day, which increased to forty-five minutes a day by the end of December; with a supplement dated January 4, 1923, this is what came to be called his 'Testament', although five articles he wrote in January and February 1923 could also be considered part of this (Lewin 1968, 73–74).

The first three entries of the 'Testament', written on December 23, 24 and 25, 1922, are a letter to the next Party Congress. In it he suggests a considerable expansion of the Central Committee, and expresses a prescient fear that the 'qualities of the two outstanding leaders of the present C.C. [Stalin and Trotsky] can inadvertently lead to a split, and if our Party does not take steps to avert this, the split may come unexpectedly'. In a postscript to this letter on January 4, 1923, he adds, 'Stalin is too rude and this defect, although quite tolerable in our midst and in dealing among us Communists, becomes intolerable in a Secretary-General. That is why I suggest that the comrades think about a way of removing Stalin from that post and appointing another man in his stead who in all other respects differs from Comrade Stalin ... being more tolerant, more loyal, more polite and more considerate to the comrades, less capricious, etc' (Lenin 1922–1923).

On 30–31 December came his reflections on the national and colonial question:

> I suppose I have been very remiss with respect to the workers of Russia for not having intervened energetically and decisively enough in the notorious question of autonomisation, which, it appears, is officially called the question of the Soviet socialist republics. When this question arose last summer, I was ill; and then in autumn I relied too much on my recovery and on the October and December plenary meetings giving me an opportunity of intervening in this question. However, I did not manage to attend the October Plenary Meeting (when this question came up) or the one in December, and so the question passed me by almost completely.
>
> [...] From what I was told by Comrade Dzerzhinsky, who was at the head of the commission sent by the C.C. to 'investigate' the Georgian incident, I could

only draw the greatest apprehensions. If matters had come to such a pass that Orjonikidze could go to the extreme of applying physical violence, as Comrade Dzerzhinsky informed me, we can imagine what a mess we have got ourselves into. Obviously the whole business of 'autonomisation' was radically wrong and badly timed.

[...] It is quite natural that in such circumstances the 'freedom to secede from the union' by which we justify ourselves will be a mere scrap of paper, unable to defend the non-Russians from the onslaught of that really Russian man, the Great-Russian chauvinist, in substance a rascal and a tyrant, such as the typical Russian bureaucrat is. There is no doubt that the infinitesimal percentage of Soviet and sovietised workers will drown in that tide of chauvinistic Great-Russian riffraff like a fly in milk.

[...] I think that Stalin's haste and his infatuation with pure administration, together with his spite against the notorious 'nationalist-socialism' [Stalin criticised the minority nations for not being 'internationalist' because they did not want to unite with Russia], played a fatal role here. In politics spite generally plays the basest of roles.

I also fear that Comrade Dzerzhinsky, who went to the Caucasus to investigate the 'crime' of those 'nationalist-socialists', distinguished himself there by his truly Russian frame of mind (it is common knowledge that people of other nationalities who have become Russified over-do this Russian frame of mind) and that the impartiality of his whole commission was typified well enough by Orjonikidze's 'manhandling'. I think that no provocation or even insult can justify such Russian manhandling and that Comrade Dzerzhinsky was inexcusably guilty in adopting a light-hearted attitude towards it.

[...] Here we have an important question of principle: how is internationalism to be understood?

In my writings on the national question I have already said that an abstract presentation of the question of nationalism in general is of no use at all. A distinction must necessarily be made between the nationalism of an oppressor nation and that of an oppressed nation, the nationalism of a big nation and that of a small nation.

In respect of the second kind of nationalism we, nationals of a big nation, have nearly always been guilty, in historic practice, of an infinite number of cases of violence; furthermore, we commit violence and insult an infinite number of times without noticing it. It is sufficient to recall my Volga reminiscences of how non-Russians are treated; how the Poles are not called by any other name than Polyachiska, how the Tatar is nicknamed Prince, how the Ukrainians are always Khokhols and the Georgians and other Caucasian nationals always Kapkasians.

That is why internationalism on the part of oppressors or 'great' nations, as they are called (though they are great only in their violence, only great as bullies), must consist not only in the observance of the formal equality of nations but even in an inequality of the oppressor nation, the great nation, that must make up for the inequality which obtains in actual practice. Anybody who does not understand this has not grasped the real proletarian attitude to the national question, he is still essentially petty bourgeois in his point of view and is, therefore, sure to descend to the bourgeois point of view.

What is important for the proletarian? For the proletarian it is not only important, it is absolutely essential that he should be assured that the non-Russians place the greatest possible trust in the proletarian class struggle. What is needed to ensure this? Not merely formal equality. In one way or another, by one's attitude or by concessions, it is necessary to compensate the non-Russian for the lack of trust, for the suspicion and the insults to which the government of the 'dominant' nation subjected them in the past.

I think it is unnecessary to explain this to Bolsheviks, to Communists, in greater detail. And I think that in the present instance, as far as the Georgian nation is concerned, we have a typical case in which a genuinely proletarian attitude makes profound caution, thoughtfulness and a readiness to compromise a matter of necessity for us. The Georgian [Stalin] who is neglectful of this aspect of the question, or who carelessly flings about accusations of 'nationalist-socialism' (whereas he himself is a real and true 'nationalist-socialist', and even a vulgar Great-Russian bully), violates, in substance, the interests of proletarian class solidarity, for nothing holds up the development and strengthening of proletarian class solidarity so much as national injustice ...

[...] It must be borne in mind that ... the harm that can result to our state from a lack of unification between the national apparatuses and the Russian apparatus is infinitely less than that which will be done not only to us, but to the whole International, and to the hundreds of millions of the peoples of Asia, which is destined to follow us on to the stage of history in the near future. It would be unpardonable opportunism if, on the eve of debut of the East, just as it is awakening, we undermined our prestige with its peoples, even if only by the slightest crudity or injustice towards our own non-Russian nationalities. The need to rally against the imperialists of the West, who are defending the capitalist world, is one thing. There can be no doubt about that and it would be superfluous for me to speak about my unconditional approval of it. It is another thing when we ourselves lapse, even if only in trifles, into imperialist attitudes towards oppressed nationalities, thus undermining all our principled sincerity, all our principled defence of the struggle against imperialism. But the morrow of world history will be a day when the awakening peoples oppressed by imperialism are finally aroused and the decisive long and hard struggle for their liberation begins. (Lenin 1922)

These notes were suppressed by Stalin, and they were not published until 1956. I have quoted them at length because they are among the most incisive statements of anti-imperialist principles made by any Marxist, yet have been largely ignored by Marxists, apart from C. L. R. James (1986) and a few others; Lenin notes, for example, the racial abuse used by Russians towards the peoples their empire has colonised, a common phenomenon even today, but one not pointed out by many of his contemporaries. It is also significant that by this stage, he sees revolutionary upheavals coming from 'the hundreds of millions of the peoples of Asia'. Where did this insight come from?

Mirsaid Sultan-Galiev, the son of a Tatar schoolteacher, joined the Bolshevik Party as a young man. As Maxime Rodinson (2004) writes,

> The Tartars were a Muslim minority within the Tsarist Empire, with a character all of their own. There were about three and a half million of them scattered throughout the Empire, but they were concentrated to some extent in the 'Government' of Kazan, their political and cultural centre. They were mainly peasants, and the few Tartar industrial workers still kept close ties to rural life. But there was also a bourgeoisie: a few industrialists and many shopkeepers, from which a Muslim 'clergy' and an intelligentsia had emerged. This bourgeoisie and these intellectuals were active, dynamic and ambitious. Many had long been 'modernists' in their attitude towards Muslim dogma, and 'advanced' in their attitudes to the traditional Muslim way of life. Their teaching activities often led them to penetrate and even establish themselves in areas inhabited by their less evolved co-religionists, such as Central Asia, Siberia and the Caucasus. In so doing, they introduced new ideas and modern ways, and generally stirred things up. ... All this was naturally viewed with great suspicion by the reactionary Khans.
>
> Then came the October Revolution. An important part of the Tartar intelligentsia supported it, thinking that the socialism established by the new regime would realise and deepen the reformist movement's programme. Naturally enough they particularly appreciated Bolshevism's internationalist orientation. They hoped that this would lead to equality between ethnic groups and put an end to Great-Russian domination, a domination the 'Whites' would re-impose should they be victorious.
>
> Sultan Galiev joined the Bolshevik Party in November 1917, and, thanks to his talents as an orator and organiser, soon became an important figure as the representative of this 'colonial' intelligentsia. He became a member and then president of the 'Central Muslim Commissariat', a new body affiliated to the Narkomnats (The People's Commissariat for Nationalities), a Commissariat presided over by a Bolshevik leader still relatively unknown at the time, Joseph Stalin.

Sultan-Galiev expounded his ideas in two articles published in *Zhizn' Natsional'nostei* (Life of the nationalities) in 1919. In the first of these articles, he affirms his belief that the socialist revolution must be international because otherwise the Russian revolution would soon be overwhelmed by worldwide imperialism, but he criticises the leaders of the October Revolution for looking to the West for a continuation of their revolution, rather than to the East:

> It is true that the West European states, including their ally America, appear to be the countries where all the material and 'moral' forces of international imperialism are concentrated, and it would seem that their territories are destined to become the chief battlefield in the war against imperialism. But in no way can we confidently say that there is enough strength in the Western proletariat to overthrow the Western bourgeoisie. This bourgeoisie is international and worldwide, and its overthrow demands a concentration of all the revolutionary will and all the revolutionary energy of the entire international proletariat, including the proletariat of the East.
>
> In attacking international imperialism only with the West European proletariat, we leave it full freedom of action and maneuver in the East. As long as international imperialism, represented by the Entente, dominates the East, where it is the absolute master of all natural wealth, then so long is it guaranteed of a successful outcome in all its clashes in the economic field with the working masses of the home countries, for it can always 'shut their mouths' by satisfying their economic demands. (cit. Alexander 2016)

In the second article, Sultan-Galiev outlines the way in which the extermination of indigenous peoples, slavery and colonialism have contributed to the development of Western capitalism (there are echoes of both Marx and Lenin here), but then goes on to say,

> We must never forget that, if on the one hand the East as a whole is completely enslaved by the West, on the other hand its own national bourgeoisie applies a no less heavy 'internal' pressure on the laboring masses of the east.
>
> We ought not for a minute forget the fact that the development of the international socialist revolution in the east must in no case limit itself only to the overthrow of the power of Western imperialism, but must go further. After this first stage, a second stage must be reached. This second stage is the complex question of overthrowing the Oriental clerical-feudal bourgeoisie, which pretends to be liberal, but which in reality is brutally despotic and which is capable, for the sake of its own selfish interests, to instantly change its stance toward its former foreign adversaries. (cit. Alexander 2016)

Here we have a genuine theoretical advance on previous Marxists, including Marx, because Sultan-Galiev is saying that the socialist revolution in the imperialist heartlands cannot succeed unless it is linked to the socialist revolution in their former colonies. He develops a strategy for winning over the Muslim masses while combating Muslim fundamentalism and theocracy, lessons that are still valid today. We can see the influence of his ideas on Lenin's draft theses on the national and colonial question for the second Congress of the Comintern in 1920 (see Chapter 1), and on his reflections on the national and colonial question in 1922. At this point, Sultan-Galiev retains a socialist internationalist outlook. But within a few years, baffled by the conundrum of carrying out socialist revolutions in countries where the proletariat barely existed, and embittered by the imperialist attitudes of some of the Bolsheviks, he moved towards a more Third Worldist outlook, seeing the colonial and semi-colonial countries as pitted against the imperialist countries, including their working classes.

Sultan-Galiev's story ends in betrayal and tragedy. From June 9 to 12, 1923, he was subjected to a show trial – the first show trial of a Bolshevik – accusing him of (a) treason for conspiring with an insurgent group, the Basmachi, and (b) unlawful factional activity and the formation of a deviant line – Sultangalievism or 'national communism' – opposed to the party line (Blank 1990, 155). There is overwhelming evidence that the arrest and trial took place on Stalin's initiative, and that the first of the two charges was trumped up, based on fabricated evidence (Blank 1990, 162–63). As for the second, the very fact that it was a 'charge' testifies to the lack of intra-party democracy under Stalin's leadership. Other Muslim delegates, who also came under attack, averred that the situation in Central Asia was no better than it had been under tsarism and confirmed that the 'fear of being arrested or shot' prevented them from speaking freely. Grigory Zinoviev, Lev Kamenev and Trotsky – who were subsequently to suffer the same treatment as Sultan-Galiev – failed abysmally to defend him or oppose Stalin's Great Russian chauvinism (Blank 1990, 170–72). In order to stay alive, Sultan-Galiev was left with no option but to recant and promise good behaviour in the future. 'Apart from the profound consequences for nationality policy; the outcome and proceedings of this conference strongly suggested that Stalin was abandoning debate with his rivals in favor of destroying them politically, psychologically, and personally. Tragically, this was only realized when it was too late' (Blank 1990, 175). Sultan-Galiev was expelled from the party, rearrested in the late 1930s, and shot in 1940 (Alexander 2016).

Lenin would not have known about Sultan-Galiev's trial. He had suffered another stroke on March 10, 1923, paralysing the right side of his body and rendering him unable to speak. On May 15, he was moved from his apartment in the Kremlin to his country house at Gorki. However, in July his health began to improve; he began to take walks, and he practised writing with his left hand. On October 18 Lenin visited Moscow, went to the Kremlin, wandered the streets, went back to his office, took out some books and returned to Gorki. Several visitors came to see him, brought him news, and talked to him about current affairs. At the beginning of 1924, he attended a Christmas party, and 'between January 17 and 20 his time was mainly taken up with reading the report of the Thirteenth Party Congress ... On January 21, 1924, Lenin's health suddenly deteriorated. He died at 6:50 p.m.' (Lewin 1968, 176). He was 53.

At a clinicopathological conference in 2012, doctors gathered to try and ascertain the cause of his death. They thought that the strokes he suffered could be the result of high cholesterol and arteriosclerosis, from which his father too had apparently suffered. But prior to his death he had experienced severe seizures, suggesting to the doctors not a stroke but poisoning. Russian historian Dr Lev Lurie concurred: poison was indeed the most likely cause of Lenin's death, and it was probably Stalin who had poisoned him. He was planning a political attack on Stalin, Dr. Lurie said.

> And Stalin, well aware of Lenin's intentions, sent a top-secret note to the Politburo in 1923 claiming that Lenin himself asked to be put out of his misery. The note said: 'On Saturday, March 17th in the strictest secrecy Comrade Krupskaya told me of 'Vladimir Ilyich's request to Stalin,' namely that I, Stalin, should take the responsibility for finding and administering to Lenin a dose of potassium cyanide' ... [T]here is one other puzzling aspect of the story. Although toxicology studies were done on others in Russia, there was an order that no toxicology be done on Lenin's tissues. (Kolata 2012)

Stalin's note to the Politburo, in his own handwriting, has been found (Gregory 2009), but it seems unlikely that Lenin would request Stalin to poison him at a time when he was in the midst of a battle against Stalin. On the contrary, his repeated recoveries suggest a strong attachment to life and commitment to his last struggle.

Lenin has rightly been criticised for the part he played in the inauguration of a post-revolution authoritarian state (Serge 2012, 155–58), but he has not been given sufficient credit for fighting to the death against Russian imperialism. Had he lived, the Union of Soviet Socialist Republics may not have become merely a euphemism for the Russian State Capitalist Empire.

Stalin's War on the Truth

Stalin's totalitarian state ruling Russia and its colonies was distinguished not only by its extreme brutality but also by a systematic war on the truth, analogous to the Nazi use of the big lie repeated over and over again. His propaganda machine was responsible for literally rewriting history to propagate falsehoods, and for cropping and airbrushing photographs to eliminate his victims from them as they themselves were liquidated. These fabricated stories and images were then internationalised by means of the vast propaganda apparatus of the Comintern. Vicious censorship made it impossible to find alternative accounts or challenge the falsification without risking death (Bailey 1955; King 1997).

Stalin's alliance with Hitler for the first years of World War II also had to be covered up. This was done by propagating the myth of the 'Great Patriotic War' that began not in 1939 but 1941; and it, too, required murder. In January 1948, Solomon Mikhoels, chairman of the Jewish Anti-Fascist Committee and director of the Moscow Yiddish Theater, was invited to the country house of the head of the Soviet Belarusian state police, who had him murdered (Snyder 2010, 339). Why was he killed? 'After the war, Mikhoels found himself unable to let the mass murder of the Jews pass into historical oblivion,' and wanted to publish documentation of the killing of around 1.6 million Soviet Jews (Snyder 2010, 340). But this was not something that Stalin could allow, because it would reveal that 'the Soviet citizens who suffered most in the war had been brought by force under Soviet rule right before the Germans came – as a result of a Soviet alliance with Nazi Germany. This was awkward. The history of the war had to begin in 1941, and these people had to be "peaceful Soviet citizens" ... If the Stalinist notion of the war was to prevail, the fact that the Jews were its main victims had to be forgotten' (Snyder 2010, 345). Thus the myth of the Great Patriotic War includes an element of Holocaust denial.

The February and October revolutions in Russia were followed by a counterrevolution that wiped out every gain except the transition to state capitalism. 'The Stalinist elite carried out this struggle under the name of socialism and communism, but it could do this only by totally debasing the classical concepts of socialism and communism, which shared nothing in common with Soviet reality' (Filtzer 1987, 270). Stalin exterminated communists as ruthlessly as Hitler, and converted the Communist International into an arm of the Russian state capitalist empire. The fact that the Cold War was a case of inter-imperialist rivalry was recognised by Marxists who coined the slogan 'Neither Washington nor Moscow but international socialism,' and initially also by the Non-Aligned Movement, which made use of both sides but refused to pledge allegiance to either. This situation prevailed for sixty years.

Another Revolution ... and Counterrevolution

When Mikhail Gorbachev became general secretary of the Communist Party in 1985, there were economic problems in the USSR, but they did not suggest impending doom. As Leon Aron (2011) describes, 'From the regime's point of view, the political circumstances were even less troublesome. After 20 years of relentless suppression of political opposition, virtually all the prominent dissidents had been imprisoned, exiled, ... forced to emigrate, or had died in camps and jails.' Nor was there mounting external pressure. 'The Soviet Union seemed to have adjusted to undertaking bloody "pacifications" in Eastern Europe every 12 years – Hungary in 1956, Czechoslovakia in 1968, Poland in 1980 – without much regard for the world's opinion. This, in other words, was a Soviet Union at the height of its global power and influence, both in its own view and in the view of the rest of the world' (Aron 2011).

The impetus for the revolution came, first and foremost, from ideas and ideals:

> The core of Gorbachev's enterprise was undeniably idealistic: He wanted to build a more moral Soviet Union. For though economic betterment was their banner, there is little doubt that Gorbachev and his supporters first set out to right moral, rather than economic, wrongs.
>
> [...] 'A new moral atmosphere is taking shape in the country,' Gorbachev told the Central Committee at the January 1987 meeting where he declared glasnost – openness – and democratization to be the foundation of his perestroika, or restructuring, of Soviet society. ... Later, recalling his feeling that 'we couldn't go on like that any longer, and we had to change life radically, break away from the past malpractices,' he called it his 'moral position.'
>
> In a 1989 interview, the 'godfather of glasnost,' Aleksandr Yakovlev, recalled that, returning to the Soviet Union in 1983 after 10 years as the ambassador to Canada, he felt the moment was at hand when people would declare, 'Enough! We cannot live like this any longer ... There has come an understanding that it is simply impossible to live as we lived before – intolerably, humiliatingly.'
>
> To Gorbachev's prime minister Nikolai Ryzhkov, the 'moral [nravstennoe] state of the society' in 1985 was its 'most terrifying' feature: '[We] stole from

ourselves, took and gave bribes, lied in the reports, in newspapers, from high podiums, wallowed in our lies, hung medals on one another. And all of this – from top to bottom and from bottom to top.'

[...] Democratization, Gorbachev declared, was 'not a slogan but the essence of perestroika.' ... That reforms gave rise to a revolution by 1989 was due largely to another 'idealistic' cause: Gorbachev's deep and personal aversion to violence and, hence, his stubborn refusal to resort to mass coercion when the scale and depth of change began to outstrip his original intent. To deploy Stalinist repression even to 'preserve the system' would have been a betrayal of his deepest convictions. (Aron 2011)

This change in the Kremlin reflected a deeper and broader movement of disgust with the prevailing culture of corruption, lies, and assaults on the dignity of the individual: 'The weekly magazine *Ogoniok*, a key publication of glasnost, wrote in February 1989 that only the "man incapable of being a police informer, of betraying, and of lies, no matter in whose or what name, can save us from the re-emergence of a totalitarian state"' (Aron 2011).

However, democratisation had an unintended consequence: the revival of the demand for independence by Russia's colonies. Hoping to prevent the disintegration of the Soviet Union, Gorbachev drew up plans for a new treaty that would have created a truly voluntary federation, but on the eve of the signing of the new treaty, hardliners formed a 'State Emergency Committee' and launched a coup on August 19, 1991, putting Gorbachev under house arrest at his government 'dacha' in Crimea (Piskunov n.d.), and sending tanks into the streets of Moscow to storm the White House, where the Supreme Soviet of Russia was housed. The public responded by coming out onto the streets to defend their newly-won freedoms, and Boris Yeltsin made a speech condemning the coup from atop a tank outside the White House. In the words of a participant in the action: 'In the center of Moscow we saw that huge crowds were making their way to the White House with banners and flags. Opposition to the coup was already starting to form then. ... The crowd there was wonderful. There weren't any incidents, any fights, any brawls. There was a sense of victory, right from the beginning. And there was a sense that what was happening couldn't be reversed' (Bykov 2016).

As we saw in Chapter 1, the coup catalysed the disintegration of the Soviet Union by sidelining Gorbachev, who wanted a more democratic Union, and replacing him with Yeltsin, who had no interest in the survival of the Soviet Union and in fact inaugurated its demise by seceding from it; yet Stalinist hardliners continued to blame Gorbachev (RT 2014a). The

USSR was replaced by fifteen independent republics, including the Russian Federation. However, Russia's domination over many of the other republics persisted, and not all of its colonies succeeded in establishing their independence. For example, the people of Chechnya, which had been incorporated into the Russian empire in 1859 after decades of stiff resistance and had been subjected to mass deportation under Stalin, elected Dzhokhar Dudayev president in October 1991, and in November he declared Chechnya's independence from the Russian Federation. In 1994, Russian troops invaded Chechnya and in March 1995 took the capital city Grozny, but guerrilla resistance continued. In 1996 Dudayev was killed by Russian shelling. The following year, guerrilla leader Aslan Mashkadov was elected president, and in May 1997 signed a peace treaty with Boris Yeltsin, which postponed the determination of Chechnya's status (Encyclopædia Britannica n.d.).

This was the first Chechen war, and the carpet bombing of Grozny in early 1995 'took the lives of an estimated twenty-five thousand to twenty-nine thousand inhabitants – mostly civilians, especially older and disabled people and children, who had been unable to flee the city. As a point of comparison: the Allied bombardment of the German city of Dresden in February 1945 involved a civilian death toll of about twenty-five thousand people' (Van Herpen 2015, 164). Sergei Kovalev, a former dissident who was appointed by Yeltsin to chair the Presidential Human Rights Commission, pointed to the central role of the secret services (the FSB, successor of the KGB), which was in the forefront before and during the war, and stated that 'the true goal of the war in Chechnya was to send a clearcut message to the entire Russian population: "The time for talking about democracy in Russia is up"' (cit. Van Herpen 2015, 167).

By the spring of 1999, Yeltsin and his family were panicking. Duma (parliamentary) elections were due in December, and presidential elections – which Yeltsin could not contest since he had already served two terms – in spring of 2000. One of the possible winners of the presidential election, Yevgeny Primakov, threatened to sue all oligarchs who had illegally enriched themselves, while at the same time investigations being conducted by Swiss and US authorities were uncovering corrupt deals in which Yeltsin and his family members were involved. 'Members of the Family were not only afraid that the new leadership would strip them of their newly acquired wealth, but – even worse – they feared that they could end up in prison' (Van Herpen 2015, 173). This was the context in which Yeltsin decided that Putin, who was then director of the FSB, should be his successor, because he could be trusted to protect the interests of the Family. However, he was unknown to the public, and needed to be made electable. The second Chechen war was a means to that end.

Both Mashkadov's war of national liberation and his government thereafter had been marred by atrocities carried out by Islamists like Shamil Basayev, who had been recruited by Russia's military intelligence (the GRU) in order to undermine the secular democratic independence movement:

> Anatoly Kulikov, the former chairman of the Russian Interior Ministry and a former deputy prime minister under Boris Yeltsin, attested in the weekly newspaper *Argumenty i Fakty* in 2002 that he had a 'great deal of evidence' to suggest that Boris Berezovsky, then the most powerful oligarch in Russia and a key political adviser to the Yeltsin administration, was using the Russian Security Council to finance Chechen extremists, Basayev included. ... Even one of Berezovsky's closest friends and allies, Alex Goldfarb, conceded that by 1999, the goal in Moscow had become even more subversive than that: to prompt a guerrilla incursion into Dagestan, which would then green-light a short but popular Russian invasion ... In the Russian intelligence playbook, such a gambit is known as *provokatsiya*. (Weiss 2015a)

In other words, Basayev was being used as an *agent provocateur* to justify an invasion of Chechnya. On August 8, 1999, when

> jihadi rebel leader Basayev and his foreign mujahideen ally Umar Ibn al-Khattab led around 1000 Chechen fighters into neighbouring Dagestan, which was part of the Russian Federation, Yeltsin declared that Russia was under attack by international terrorism, and recommended that Putin should succeed him. ... Shortly afterwards, the investigative Russian weekly *Versiya* published a report alleging that some time before the Dagestan attacks, the head of Yeltsin's presidential administration, Aleksandr Voloshin, had met Basayev at a meeting arranged by Anton Surikov, a retired GRU officer, who had fought alongside Basayev against Georgia in 1992. (Van Herpen 2015, 175)

However, the Dagestan incursion failed to rouse Russian citizens to demand an invasion of Chechnya; something more was needed. In September 1999, a series of apartment bombings in Moscow and elsewhere killed hundreds of people, many of them children, and wounded hundreds more. These terrorist attacks were blamed on Chechens and played the same role in Russia that the 9/11 attacks did in the US two years later, arousing a fear of terrorism and a desire for revenge among the population. But did the Chechens actually carry out the bombings? The trail of evidence does not lead to them.

Achemez Gochiaev, who had been asked to rent the basements in which the Moscow bombs were planted, got cold feet after the second bomb went off and informed the police, as a result of which other explosions in Moscow were prevented. He wrote an open letter accusing the FSB of having organised the Moscow bombings and Dyshenkov, who had asked him to rent the basements, of being an FSB agent (Van Herpen 2015, 180). On September 22 in the city of Ryazan, about a hundred miles southeast of Moscow,

> residents of an apartment complex had reported unusual activity in the basement and observed that three people in a car with partially papered-over license plates had unloaded sacks whose contents they couldn't make out. A professional bomb squad arrived and discovered that the sacks contained not only sugar but also explosives, including hexogen, and that a detonator was attached. After the sacks were examined and removed, they were sent by the local FSB to Moscow.
>
> The entire apartment building was evacuated. Local authorities found the car used by the three who had planted the explosives, a white Zhiguli, in a nearby parking lot. To their astonishment the license plates were traced to the FSB. And when they apprehended two of the suspects, it turned out that they were FSB employees, who were soon released on orders from Moscow.
>
> [...] A central question involved the materials used in the explosives. The day after the first Moscow apartment bombing, an FSB spokesman said that both hexogen and TNT were discovered. ... But by March 2000 the FSB had changed its story and claimed that hexogen had not been used in the bombs. In fact, several Russian investigative journalists were able to demonstrate that hexogen was the key ingredient in all of the bombs and that hexogen can only be obtained from Russian government facilities under the control of the FSB. (Knight 2012)

At the time, the FSB was under the directorship of Nikolai Patrushev, whose ties to Putin dated back to 1975, when both joined the KGB and worked together. When Putin took over the FSB in 1998, Patrushev was his deputy, and he became the chief when Putin was appointed prime minister the next year; asked in an interview whom he trusted most, Putin named Patrushev among a few others. Shortly after the Russian interior minister Vladimir Rushailo congratulated the people of Ryazan for thwarting a terrorist attack, Patrushev announced on TV that the incident was only a training exercise and that the sacks contained only sugar (Knight 2012). However, when in 2002 the Duma established an independent commission of inquiry headed by Kovalev, a teleconference was arranged with Alexander Litvinenko, a defected FSB agent, and Yuri Felshtinsky, who had written a book, *Blowing Up Russia*, in which they claimed the FSB was behind the Moscow bombings. Commission member Sergei Yushenkov, who, after learning that the speaker of the house knew about one of the explosions before it took place, said that this was further proof of FSB involvement, was gunned down and killed in April 2003. Yuri Shchekochikhin, an investigative journalist who initiated the inquiry, died suddenly in July of that year of suspected poisoning (Van Herpen 2015, 180–82). Most famously, Alexander Litvinenko was assassinated in London in November 2006. Having proved that the poison was polonium – used in quantities that could only have been procured by a state organisation – investigators traced it to former KGB agent Andrei Lugovoi, who had had tea with Litvinenko the day he was poisoned.

When the British government sought Lugovoi's extradition, Putin refused, instead making him a Duma deputy and thus immune from prosecution. The secret services of Britain and Russia stopped cooperating, and then-chancellor Gordon Brown refused to meet Putin. Under the new government elected in 2010, there was a change of policy in favour of closer ties with Putin, but Litvinenko's widow Marina pursued the case despite obstacles placed in her way by David Cameron, William Hague, Chris Grayling and Theresa May. Robert Owen, the High Court judge carrying out the investigation, concluded on the basis of voluminous evidence that Lugovoi and his assistant Dmitry Kovtun killed Litvinenko in an operation most probably approved by Putin (Pomerantsev 2016a).

Kovalev described in graphic terms the disastrous effect these apartment bombings, blamed on Chechens by Putin and his associates despite a total lack of evidence, had on the public in Russia.[2] They helped to justify not just crimes against humanity in Chechnya in the name of the war on terror, but also a crackdown on human rights defenders, conscientious journalists, and human rights and democracy in Russia itself. As Kovalev (2000) put it, 'The Russian army is quite prepared for genocide. This was demonstrated in the previous war … What is new this time around is that Russian society as a whole is prepared to carry out genocide. Cruelty and violence are no longer rejected. … I fear, it is very likely that the year 2000 will someday be referred to as the "twilight of Russian freedom"'. This was the popular mood that swept Putin to power in the presidential election of 2000. It is worth noting that Putin conducted an imperialist war in the name of the 'war on terror' two years *before* the George W. Bush administration used this strategy in the wake of the 9/11 terror attacks, and also propagated the lethal combination of racism and anti-Muslim bigotry[3] that plagues the world today. As Emma Gilligan (2010, 5–6) argues,

> The Russian armed forces terrorized Chechen civilians in the hope of wearing down the material and psychological support base of the separatist movement. A principal objective of the Russian government was the subjugation of the population and the elimination of Chechnya's intellectual and political elite. The intent, it appears, was not to destroy the *entire* Chechen population but to exert control through fear and the military tactics of periodic summary executions, enforced disappearances, rape, torture, detainment, and humiliation.
>
> [...] The most ignored question of this conflict is the role of racism as a deep motivating factor. The excessive violence directed at the civilian population of Chechnya was, in fact, collective punishment. ... The state-controlled media in Russia conducted a virulent propaganda campaign against Chechens as a group. What began in 1994 as a conflict with national separatists was in 1999 reshaped by the Kremlin spin doctors, led by Sergei Yastrezhembskii, into a war against international terrorism. Chechens were dehumanized with racially bigoted language that depicted the enemy as 'blacks' (*chernye*), 'bandits' (*banditi*), 'terrorists' (*terroristi*), 'cockroaches' (*tarakany*), and 'bedbugs' (*klopi*). The identity of the Chechen people was reduced to a few repeated phrases, images, and concepts embodied in the repeated image of the 'bandit' or the 'terrorist'. The Russian propaganda machine was unfailing in its perpetuation of this image.

Gilligan goes on to chronicle the war crimes committed as a deliberate policy: murder of all kinds, rape, mutilation, torture and other cruel treatment, as well as loot and pillage, and the extortion of money for the return of detained civilians or combatants, dead or alive. She examines the claim by Chechens that what took place during the second war was genocide, conceding that it looks as if the intent was to 'destroy, in whole or in part', the Chechens as such: for example, the mass killing of men and boys between the ages of fourteen and sixty, the targeting of male genitals in torture, and systematic rape of women and girls to such an extent that a Russian soldier told a journalist, 'You should not believe people who say Chechens are not being exterminated.' Yet she concludes that there is no proof of *intent* to destroy the Chechens as a people, and that therefore the category of 'crimes against humanity' would be more legally sustainable (Gilligan 2010, 6–12).

Reports of what was going on in Chechnya certainly go beyond war crimes and conform to the definition of crimes against humanity. Here is an extract from one report that was scathingly critical of the British government's positive assessment of Putin, which begins by describing one of the victims:

Her face burnt almost beyond recognition, she lies prone on her hospital bed and tells in a child's whispers of the day her mother, father, her two brothers, her sister and her cousin – among 363 people from the same village – were wiped out. At eight years old, Taisa Abakarova is an eyewitness to the worst war crime in the savage campaign of Russia's acting President, Vladimir Putin, against the 'terrorist fighters' of Chechnya.

The village of Katyr Yurt, 'safe' in the Russian-occupied zone, far from the war's front line, and jam-packed with refugees, was untouched on the morning of 4 February when Russian aircraft, helicopters, fuel-air bombs and Grad missiles pulverised the village. They paused in the bombing at 3pm, shipped buses in, and allowed a white-flag convoy to leave – and then they bombed that as well, killing Taisa's family and many others.

The Observer, in a joint investigation with Channel 4's *Dispatches*, went to Katyr Yurt and saw what was left: a landscape as if from the Somme, streets smashed to matchwood, trees shredded, blood-stained cellars, the survivors in a frenzy of fear. The village was littered with the remains of Russian 'vacuum' bombs – fuel-air explosives that can suck your lungs inside out, their use against civilians banned by the Geneva Convention. (Sweeney 2000)

Mass graves continued to be discovered in Chechnya, bearing grim witness to the wholesale execution of civilians (Warren 2001). Gilligan (2010, 8) commented, 'When the Russian armed forces killed Maskhadov in 2005 they also killed the only man with the stature to conduct negotiations with the Russian government,' but negotiating was never the aim of the Russian government. After Russian forces took control of Chechnya in 2000, Putin loyalist Akhmad Kadyrov was appointed acting head of the administration and became president of Chechnya in 2003. When he was assassinated in 2004, his son Ramzan Kadyrov, even more slavishly loyal to Putin, was given a green light to stamp out any remaining resistance to Russian rule by 'whatever means he considered expedient', and in return was given vast sums of money to rebuild Grozny, which had been bombed into rubble, and for other infrastructure projects. He was appointed deputy prime minister in October 2004, and in February 2007, when he reached the statutory minimum age of thirty, he became president, giving him more or less absolute power in Chechnya and also a great deal of power in the rest of Russia (Fuller 2015).

The 'pacification' of Chechnya marked the advent of Russian neoconservative imperialism. A key ploy of Putin's escalating authoritarianism is to propagate Stalin's myth of the 'Great Patriotic War', glossing over the fact that Stalin was a Nazi collaborator for most of the first two years of the war, and would have remained one if Hitler's hubris had not led him to attack Russia in 1941 (Thoburn 2016; RT 2016a).

Chechnya is only one of the examples that show that the Russian Federation continues to be an empire incorporating twenty-one of Russia's former colonies (Batou 2015). Tatarstan, the homeland of the Kazan Tatars, the second largest nationality in the Russian Federation with around six million people, is another. In a March 1992 referendum certified as fully legitimate by international observers, 61.4 per cent of the population voted for independence. The Russian authorities refused to recognise the results of the referendum – which is not surprising, given that Tatarstan is situated in the oil- and gas-rich Middle Volga – and the leadership of the Kazan Tatars submitted to them (Goble 2014). However, when in 2014 this refurbished Russian imperialism led to the Russian annexation of Crimea and invasion of eastern Ukraine, an appeal was sent to the UN and the EU, signed by Fausziya Bayramova, president of the Milli Mejlis of the Tatar People. Paul Goble (2014) translates it as follows:

> 'Russia is being transformed into a totalitarian, militarist and extremely chauvinist state,' it says. 'Despite its multi-national population, the Russian state has put as its task to make all of its citizens into [ethnic] Russians and Russian speakers.' There is 'open discrimination toward all non-Russian peoples, national schools and newspapers are being closed, and the planned elimination of Muslims is being carried out. In such circumstances, we do not see a future for the Kazan Tatars in Russia.'
>
> In the course of its 'annexation of Crimea by means of a false referendum,' the appeal continues, 'Russia covered itself by making reference to the supposed oppression of ethnic Russians by the new authorities in Kyiv and frequently talked about double standards,' a reference to Kosovo. But it is Russia itself which is guilty of double standards, sometimes invoking the right of ethnic Russians to self-determination via referendum while denying that right to non-Russians like the Kazan Tatars.
>
> 'Tatar national organizations express their categorical disagreement with Russia's policy toward other peoples and Islam,' the appeal concludes, and that means that for the sake of survival, 'we must leave Russia.' To that end, they are appealing to the UN and the European Union to finally at long last recognize the results of the 1992 referendum.

Of course there was no response to this appeal, but it brings us to the domestic consequences of the turn to neo-Stalinist imperialism in Russia.

Crushing Dissidence

Michael Mainville (2006) recounts the story of Anna Politkovskaya, who joined the staff of the independent newspaper *Novaya Gazeta* in 1999, and

> became obsessed with exposing the killings, torture and beatings of civilians by Russian soldiers in Chechnya. She wrote two books on the conflict, 'A Dirty War: A Russian Reporter in Chechnya' and 'A Small Corner of Hell: Dispatches From Chechnya.' She made no secret of her contempt for Kadyrov or for Putin, and critics in Russia frequently accused her of lacking objectivity. In 'Putin's Russia,' a highly critical political biography of the president published in 2004, she accused Putin of failing to shake off his past as a KGB agent in East Germany. 'He persists in crushing liberty just as he did earlier in his career,' she wrote in the book.

On October 7, 2006, she was shot dead just outside her apartment in central Moscow. She had been working on a story describing the alleged torture of a young man by Kadyrov's security forces based on written testimony from the victim, writing that 'brutal torture was being widely used to extract false confessions from innocent civilians so that the pro-Moscow Chechen government could appear to be capturing rebel fighters' (Mainville 2006).

Politkovskaya's death was greeted with shock and horror by her friends and associates. As Tanya Lokshina (2016) remembers,

> That night, with dozens of others, we stood by Anna's apartment building for hours. Many brought flowers. People spoke quietly, moved slowly. ... Anna was and will always be a hero for ordinary Chechens. It is largely owing to her that the world knows about crimes against civilians in the course of that dirty war. Ramzan Kadyrov has been running Chechnya as his own fiefdom with the Kremlin's blessing for close to a decade already. ... But back in 2004 to 2006, when he was only consolidating his power, Anna published damning reportages about Kadyrovtsy, Chechen security officials under his control who effectively picked up the mantle of egregious abuse from federal forces. She described Kadyrov as the Kremlin's "little dragon" and called for his arrest.

Ten years later, memorial protests were held in Moscow under the slogan 'The sponsor is still at large'. *Novaya Gazeta's* deputy editor-in-chief Sergei Sokolov wrote, 'The journalists ask: what do we, *Novaya Gazeta* employees, feel on this day – October 7, 2016, 10 years after a fragile, courageous, beautiful and strong woman – Anna Politkovskaya – was shot at point blank range on the threshold of her building? I respond – rage.' The first trial had ended with acquittal of the accused due to lack of evidence; only in a second trial, in 2013, were six organisers and executors of the murder, including

Interior Ministry collaborators and FSB agents, convicted; but those who ordered the killing were not identified (Sinelschikova 2016). In the decade since Politkovskaya's death, the space for independent journalism in Russia has narrowed further. 'Since 2006, the Committee to Protect Journalists has recorded 20 journalists' killings, while Freedom House has counted 63 violent attacks on reporters. But for the most part, the threat of closure keeps publications in line and encourages self-censorship.' Yet courageous journalists battle on, trying to uncover and publicise the truth (Walker 2016).

Being a whistle-blower in corruption cases was equally life-threatening. Sergei Magnitsky, acting on behalf of Hermitage Capital Management, had exposed a scam in which government officials had stolen $230 million of tax revenue, but instead of arresting any of the alleged embezzlers, the police arrested Magnitsky, and he died in custody in 2009. Laurence Peter (2013) reports:

> In prison his pancreatitis went untreated and an investigation by the Russian Presidential Human Rights Council concluded that he was a victim of criminal negligence. There is evidence that a beating by prison guards may have killed the chronically ill prisoner, the council reported. His relatives said his body was bruised and finger bones had been broken. The council also condemned the fact that the same interior ministry officials whom Mr Magnitsky had accused of tax fraud were the ones who handled his arrest and prosecution.

Yet instead of being rehabilitated, Magnitsky was put on trial posthumously. Bill Browder, the financier who had hired Magnitsky to conduct the investigation, subsequently pushed the 2012 Magnitsky Act, which imposed sanctions on those held responsible for the murder, through the US Congress. He established that Putin was a beneficiary of the theft, and therefore had a direct interest in repeal of the act. Putin retaliated by suspending American adoptions of (disabled) Russian children and hired Russian lawyer Natalia Veselnitskaya to campaign in the US for repeal of the Act (Gray 2017).

In this context, it is not surprising that when Yulia Stepanova – the athlete who blew the whistle on state-backed doping in Russia – found that her Anti-Doping Administration and Management System account had been hacked to find out her location, she and her husband went into hiding, saying, 'If something happens to us then you should know it is not an accident' (Stubbs 2016).

Being a human rights defender, especially in Chechnya, was also almost certain to be a death sentence. That is what Natalya Estemirova was, attempting to help the family members of victims of public executions, as well as survivors of house burnings directed against the families of persons accused of being connected to the rebels. She was a board member of the Russian human rights organisation Memorial. In July 2009 Tanya Lokshina, afraid for Estemirova's life, tried to persuade her to move out of Grozny to a safer place and write up her experiences, but she refused, asking, 'If she leaves, then who'll do this work, who will these people who need help be able to turn to? … She was killed two days later, on 15 July. She was pushed into a car while running to catch a shuttle taxi early in the morning. They took her from Chechnya into Ingushetia, and shot her by the forest' (Lokshina 2009).

Opposition politicians too seem to have a tendency to drop dead. Boris Nemtsov, for one, had criticised Putin's regime for its authoritarianism and corruption, and strongly opposed what he called 'Putin's war' in Ukraine. On September 1, 2014, he wrote an op-ed, published in Ukrainian and Russian, in which he said,

> This is not our war, this is not your war, this is not the war of 20-year old paratroopers sent out there. This is Vladimir Putin's war. Why does he need it? Well, he has openly answered this question himself. 'We need to start negotiations about politically organizing a society and statehood in southeastern Ukraine.' He made this statement only now, but the sending of saboteurs-separatists, weapons, and a persistent desire of Putin to force Ukrainian President Petro Poroshenko to sit at the negotiation table with pro-Putin militants, many of whom are Russian citizens – all of this betrayed his intentions long before the public confession.
>
> [...] So, Putin is trying to dissect Ukraine and create in the east of the country a puppet state, Novorossiya, that is fully economically and politically controlled by the Kremlin. It's crucial for his clan to control metallurgy in the east of Ukraine, as well as its military-industrial complex. Moreover, southeastern Ukraine is rich in shale gas which would create real competition for the business of Putin's Gazprom.
>
> [...] To achieve these goals, Putin brought in his troops, including paratroopers and Chechen leader Ramzan Kadyrov's men. This is why he supplies weapons and heavy artillery to the east, and this is why he doomed Russia to isolation and sanctions. These are the paranoid goals for which Russians and Ukrainians are dying while Russia itself is sinking into lies, violence, obscurantism and imperial hysteria.
>
> [...] Ukraine became an example of an anti-criminal revolution, which overthrew a thieving president. Oh so you dared to get out onto the street and throw off a president? Ukraine needs to be punished for it to make sure that no Russian would get these thoughts. (Nemtsov 2014)

At the end of December 2014, he started collecting evidence for a book on the war, but did not live to complete the work; on February 27, 2015, he was shot dead on a bridge near the Kremlin. It was left to his friends and colleagues to complete the book.

> Juxtaposed against the massive propaganda and disinformation campaign mounted by the Kremlin as part of its 'hybrid war', the report is intended as an antidote to the narcotic effect that Russian state television has on the country. Several Russian printing plants refused to take the job, so in the end only 2000 copies were printed.
>
> [...] The report describes the abuses and atrocities committed by Russian-backed separatists against civilians who wished to remain part of Ukraine. ... A mass grave of civilians was discovered in Slavyansk, a separatist stronghold, after it was retaken by Ukrainian forces.
>
> The authors also provide evidence of Russian soldiers fighting and dying in eastern Ukraine, including special combat units from Chechnya. At a minimum, they estimate that 150 Russian soldiers were killed in fighting in the summer of 2014, and an additional 70 during early 2015. Regular soldiers were directed to resign their army commissions and travel to Ukraine as 'volunteers', to maintain the fiction of Russian non-involvement. The authors of the report calculate the direct cost of the war in the 10 months beginning in April 2014 at 53 billion roubles (about $1 billion), including subsidies for separatist fighters and compensation paid to 'volunteers' and Russian regular soldiers, as well as maintenance of military hardware. This does not include the costs of the annexation of Crimea (estimated at about 680 billion roubles). (The Economist 2015)

As in the other assassinations, the alleged killers of Nemtsov were arrested and tried, but the person who gave the order to kill was not identified. There was, briefly, what appeared to be a chance of a return to democracy in Russia when there were large protests against ballot-stuffing and fraud on the part of Putin's United Russia party in the parliamentary elections in December 2011, and again when Putin came to power in the presidential election of March 2012 (Barry 2011; The Guardian 2012), but the only outcome was protestors being arrested and detained. In February 2017 Alexei Navalny, who had announced his intention to contest the presidency against Putin in 2018, was convicted of embezzlement, disqualifying him from standing for election (Luhn 2017). What we see in Russia, then, is the rapid extinction of human rights, the rule of law, freedom of expression and association, and other democratic rights and freedoms. But what accounts for the acquiescence of a large section of the Russian population in this counterrevolution?

Incubating Racism

The theorist of the second counterrevolution in Russia is Alexander Dugin. As Andreas Umland (2008) writes:

> In the 1990s, this self-styled 'neo-Eurasian' joyously welcomed the imminent birth of 'fascist fascism' in Russia and praised the organiser of the Holocaust, Reinhard Heydrich, for being a 'convinced Eurasian.' Back then Dugin frankly described his ideology as 'conservative revolutionary,' asserting that the core idea of fascism is the 'conservative revolution.' Throughout the nineties the 'neo-Eurasian' made a whole number of similar statements, including various more or less qualified apologies for the Third Reich. In recent years, to be sure, Dugin's rhetoric has changed – if not in tone, then in style. He now, oddly, often poses as an outspoken 'anti-fascist,' and does not hesitate to label his opponents both in- and outside Russia 'fascists' or 'Nazi.'

This 'Eurasian' supremacism is easily traceable to the 'Aryan' supremacism of the Nazis, itself originating from a racist distortion of the classification of Indo-European languages (Encyclopædia Britannica 2015). Labelling opponents as 'fascist' or 'Nazi' is a tactic also employed by the Zionist right, despite the fact that 'Zionism is a European colonial movement that's as white as the snow in the Carpathian mountains' (Niv 2013); what Nazism, Eurasianism and Zionism have in common is white supremacism.

Dugin's influence is clearly visible in Putin's rhetoric about Russia's unique Eurasianism, and in his creation of a Eurasian Union in which Russia would continue to dominate its former colonies, using the dependence of their economies on Russia – which was built up during the period of tsarist and Soviet imperialism – as a means of blackmailing them into a neocolonial relationship (Kimball 2014; Standish 2015a). Starting with the second Chechen war, 'with every passing year the new century sees closer rapprochement between the rhetoric of Russia's extreme right and those at the very top, not least Putin himself. ... The Russian extreme right, including some of its crypto-fascist sections, is becoming an ever more influential part of Moscow mainstream public discourse. Its influence can be felt in Russia's mass media, academia, civil society, arts, and politics' (Umland 2008). Nowhere is the growth of fascism more evident than in the proliferation of racist attacks.

Neo-Nazi attacks on Black and minority ethnic citizens and foreigners were already taking place in the 1990s. Kester Klomegah, a Ghanaian writer living in Moscow, wrote in November 1997: 'If you are black in Russia, hardly a day goes by without having to confront racism' (cit. Reeves 1998).

However, the twenty-first century saw a significant rise in xenophobia, racism, and violence against non-Slavs within Russia. 'The reason, experts say, is widespread anger over economic stagnation and corruption. It is also a reaction to a surge of migrant workers from Russia's "near abroad" of the Caucasus and Central Asia. With foreign arrivals now totaling 13 to 14 million, Russia's migrant labor force ranks second only to the United States,' Ilan Berman writes (2013), adding that 'the rise of ethnic violence in Russia has been propelled by a surge in extreme right-wing nationalism', which has seen the growth of violent neo-Nazi groups and parties espousing an ethnonationalist agenda. The surge in migrant workers was largely a consequence of the underdevelopment of Russia's newly independent colonies. As Timur, a construction worker from Tajikistan, put it, 'Yes, we are *gastarbeiter* [a German term that means "migrant workers"]. But we clean their city, we build their houses. We are human, and [the Russians] treat us like beasts' (cit. Monteleone 2016).

The carnage during the second Chechen war was one of the ways this racism played itself out. As a result of the Russian victory, Chechens continued to be Russian citizens, yet they were treated as anything but equals; this reminded Dewaine Farria (2012), a Black American working in the North Caucasus, of the way African Americans were treated in the US during his parents' generation:

> The first time I heard a Russian call a person from the Caucasus a 'black ass' I was dumbfounded. Looking at my pale-skinned Chechen friends, I would be inclined to laugh at the term if it wasn't such an obvious symptom of the xenophobia in Russian society. In the West, Caucasian means white person, but in Russia, being Caucasian makes you a target for rampant racial discrimination. ... I never had to deal with the type of racism my father dealt with in the United States in the 60s and 70s. I had to travel to the former Soviet Union to get a taste of it.

Another American visitor, Cody Boutilier, who describes himself as 'of Mexican extraction', noted:

> Russia is a deeply racist country that holds minorities in open contempt – not quite the equivalent of Jim Crow, but still distressing. The default names for Central Asians and Caucasians are the derogatory churki and khachi, for Ukrainians khokhly and for Jews zhidy; but don't be surprised if you hear 'black a**es' [*sic*] to refer to swarthier ethnics, including Armenians ... Common graffiti include swastikas and slogans like Rossiya dlya russkikh. This means 'Russia for Russians,' but the American equivalent would be 'America for whites';

rossiyskiy refers to any national of the multiethnic Rossiya ... whereas russkiy means ethnic Russian (Boutilier 2014).

The link between Russian ethnonationalism and imperialism explains why Putin has encouraged the rise of neo-fascist groups carrying out violent attacks on minorities: 'The government of Vladimir Putin has sought to harness nationalist sentiment for its own ends, and so – even as it has cracked down on the most violent offenders – has nurtured and cultivated nationalist ideas among the Russian population. In the process, it has spawned youth groups ... whose members, experts say, tend to share a common vision with Russia's ultra-right' (Berman 2013). Indeed, it would be hard to tell state-sponsored and independent neo-fascists apart in incidents like the racist riots in Manezhnaya Square in December 2010, in which at least two people were killed following a five-thousand-strong rally of far-right football fans and nationalists. 'The demonstrators ... flashed the Nazi salute, chanted "Russia for Russians" and pelted riot police with flares, smoke bombs and metal fence posts. After the rally hundreds of protesters entered the Moscow metro where they continued their rampage, beating and stabbing passersby from Central Asia and the Caucasus' (Elder 2010).

The picture is not uniformly bleak, however. On the day of the riot, six schoolboys who went out for a birthday celebration were attacked by the mob because four of them were not 'ethnic Russians'. The two who were, fought back ferociously alongside their friends, and fortunately four young special police officers (also 'ethnic Russians') came to their rescue, refusing to hand them over to the crowd; as one of them said later, 'How could we have done such a thing? They were only kids, boys. If we had let the crowd have them, they would have just torn them to pieces.' This story of decency, hope and friendship, contend Andrei Loshak and Svetlana Reiter (2011), represents the real Russia.

Patriarchy and Homophobia

Putin has built a close relationship with the most right-wing Orthodox Christian church leaders like Patriarch Kirill and Archpriest Vsevolod Chaplin, intertwining ethnicity, church and state to such a degree that Russian nationalism could be described as Christoslav nationalism (Bennetts 2015; Sotiropoulos 2016). The church-state union has also had an impact on gender and sexuality legislation and policies, justifying the restriction of women's and LGBT rights in the name of national values and the national interest:

> Indeed, population growth and the well-being of the nation are explicitly linked to fertility and family values in two white papers ... issued by the Russian government, the *Concept on the Demographic Policy of the Russian Federation until 2025* (CDP 2007) and the *Concept on State Family Policy* (CFP 2013). ... Two of the six key aims of CDP concerned support for families and for 'traditional' family values: the growth of the birth rate on account of the birth of a second child or subsequent children in families, and the strengthening of the family as an institution ... Among family values worthy of state protection, CFP explicitly mentions marriage, understood 'solely as the union between a man and a woman ... and undertaken by the spouses with the aim of perpetuating their kin' (Stella and Nartova 2016, 21)

Russian Orthodoxy underpins this notion of the family. In 2013 the State Duma approved law N323–FZ, restricting free access to abortions by postponing them and providing counselling in order to reduce them; in parallel, there were consecutive reductions in the reasons for which a woman could obtain an abortion in the second trimester, until eventually there was only one: ending a pregnancy resulting from rape. Doctors were allowed to refuse to perform medical termination of pregnancy unless the patient's life was at risk. The fact that there was no attempt to promote contraception and sex education made it clear that 'the new abortion legislation was not intended to protect women's reproductive rights or health; rather, it was conceived as a measure to boost the birth rate' (Stella and Nartova 2016, 23–24). In February 2017, Putin signed into law an amendment decriminalising some domestic violence, leading to a doubling of such incidents in a country where domestic abuse already killed twelve to fourteen thousand women a year (Walker 2017a; Keating 2017).

Protecting children from information 'promoting the negation of traditional family values,' namely any suggestion that LGBT relationships are normal, was also a preoccupation of the Putin regime and Orthodox hierarchy, and resulted in the denial of adoption services to gay couples.

> The 'gay propaganda law' was eventually approved by an overwhelming majority of MPs and signed into law in June 2013 (N135-FZ). As critics have pointed out, the term 'propaganda' is legally ill-defined; nonetheless, the scope of what can potentially be punished as 'propaganda' is very broad. It includes any public discussion of same-sex relations (restricting, among others, the activities of school teachers and LGBT organisations), as well as representations of same-sex rela-

tions in the media and the Internet. 'Propaganda' is defined as the 'dissemination of information among minors' whose aim is ... 'making non-traditional sexual relationships look attractive, perversely presenting traditional and non-traditional sexual relations as socially equal', or creating an interest in 'non-traditional' sexual relations ... Both in the debates on the 'gay propaganda' law and in *RG*'s coverage of LGBT issues, same-sex sexualities are constructed as the 'Other' to Russian national traditions and family values. (Stella and Nartova 2016, 29)

The personal tragedies, including loss of life, resulting from the lack of contraception and sex education – especially if the right to free abortions is withdrawn altogether, as Patriarch Kirill and others have demanded (Lordkipanidze and Traktina 2016) – are too well known to need elaboration here. The concerted hostility towards LGBT people has also resulted in sickening homophobic violence, leading to a spike in LGBT asylum seekers fleeing Russia (Day 2014; Fitzgerald and Ruvinsky 2015). Combined with the othering of ethnic and religious minorities, this adds up to the construction of Russia as a far-right ethnoreligious nationalist state, which may not be fascist as such, but depends on fascist support for its survival. The opposition has been weakened by the fact that the 'radical left is today itself in a state of decline. Some of its well-known spokespersons, such as Sergei Udaltsov and Alexei Gasparov, are still in prison. The events in Ukraine have also led to a deep split in the left, part of which has effectively supported the Russian intervention' (Russian Socialist Movement 2016).[4]

Globalising Far-Right Authoritarianism

Given the far-right character of the Russian state, it comes as no surprise that it sponsors neo-fascist groups and parties around the world. The 'international observers' invited to endorse the 'referendum' in Crimea came overwhelmingly from European extreme-right parties and organisations:

Austria's Freiheitliche Partei (FPÖ) and Bündnis Zukunft, Belgian Vlaams Belang and Parti Communautaire National-Européen, Bulgarian Ataka, French Front National, Hungarian Jobbik, Italian Lega Nord and Fiamma Tricolore, Polish Samoobrona, Serbian 'Dveri' movement, Spanish Plataforma per Catalunya. They were invited to legitimise the 'referendum' by the Eurasian Observatory for Democracy & Elections (EODE) – a smart name for an 'international NGO' founded and headed by Belgian neo-Nazi Luc Michel, a loyal follower of Belgian convicted war-time collaborationist and neo-Nazi Jean-François Thiriart'. (Shekhovtsov 2014b)

Ex-members of the Front National run ProRussia.TV. The Paris-based Russian Institute of Democracy and Cooperation co-organised a conference in Leipzig on 'family issues' at which Frauke Petry of the German Alternative für Deutschland (AfD) was a speaker, and Dugin himself wrote a letter of support to Nikolaos Michaloliakos of the Greek neo-Nazi Golden Dawn party (Shekhovtsov 2014b). Petry held talks about possible cooperation with Russian officials in February 2017, and a large number of Russian-speaking Germans, who follow Russian media, supported the AfD in the September elections (Reuters 2017c; Meyer 2017).

In addition to these and many other concrete links (including financial ones), Anton Shekhovtsov (2014b) notes that 'in his manifesto, the notorious Norwegian mass murderer and terrorist Anders Breivik called Putin "a fair and resolute leader worthy of respect". Italian far-right Forza Nuova salutes Putin's Russia as "a new beacon of civilisation, identity and courage for other European peoples" ... Who praised Putin's Russia – after "observing" the unfair parliamentary elections in Russia in 2011 – for having "a robust, transparent and properly democratic system"? Nick Griffin, MEP and leader of the extreme-right British National Party'. When asked which current world leader he most admired, the UK Independence Party's Nigel Farage named Putin (The Guardian 2014). By supporting Assad and bombing Syria, Putin indirectly assisted UKIP's project by creating the huge outflow of refugees that neo-fascist parties have used to undermine the EU, with Farage using it in his successful campaign for Brexit (Judah 2016; Safdar 2016). A hacking attack against French presidential candidate Emmanuel Macron, evidently intended to boost the chances of his rival Marine Le Pen, had Russian digital fingerprints all over it, and was promoted by neo-fascists in the US (Scott 2017).

In other words, fascist groups and parties in Europe admire Putin and aspire to follow his example, while he encourages and supports them. As Shekhovtsov (2014b) sees it, 'the inherently anti-democratic extreme right [are] natural allies of Putin in his anti-democratic crusade against the EU. Although there is no reason to idealise EU mainstream parties, they are less prone to corruption than the extreme right, or – looking at Germany's former social democrat chancellor Gerhard Schröder, now the chairman of the board of Nord Stream AG and a top lobbyist for the Kremlin[5] – the extreme right may simply be less expensive to corrupt.'

There is a similar symbiotic relationship between Putin and Trump, who was supported strongly by the Ku Klux Klan and neo-Nazis (Berger

2016). Over the year leading up to the US presidential election, his debt load grew by $280 million, most of it coming from oligarchs close to Putin, and over the same period of time, Putin aligned all Russian state-controlled media behind Trump. On his side, Trump spoke very positively about Putin and went out of his way to change the Republican Party programme to remove any mention of assistance to Ukraine against Russian military operations; he also suggested that the US and NATO might not come to the assistance of Baltic states if they were invaded by Russia. These two policy changes would be of great value to Putin's agenda (Marshall 2016a). The seriousness of Putin's commitment to Trump is illustrated by the formal Russian complaint lodged with the UN against UNHCR High Commissioner Zeid Ra'ad al-Hussein's speech at The Hague in September 2016, in which he criticised Trump along with European right-wing leaders for seeking to restore a mythical ethnically pure past (Zeid 2016; Keaten and Klapper 2016). In addition, 'Russia's increasingly sophisticated propaganda machinery – including thousands of botnets, teams of paid human "trolls," and networks of websites and social-media accounts – echoed and amplified right-wing sites across the Internet as they portrayed Clinton as a criminal hiding potentially fatal health problems and preparing to hand control of the nation to a shadowy cabal of global financiers' (Timberg 2016). More than a year after Trump was elected, Putin continued to praise him (Hodge 2017).

The position of self-professed socialists who support Putin is more anomalous. Stalinists were never genuine anti-imperialists because they always supported Russian imperialism, but one could forgive socialist contemporaries of Stalin for supporting him: he did, after all, go to great lengths to portray himself as Lenin's closest comrade by killing off Bolshevik leaders, vilifying them as traitors, and chopping them out of photographs. Even so, sincere socialists drifted away as they became aware of the yawning gulf between precept and practice. But Putin makes no such pretence; on the contrary, he curses Lenin's anti-imperialism and glorifies tsarist imperialism (Craine 2015). We have to conclude, therefore, that neo-Stalinists who gravitate towards him do so because of their proclivity for authoritarian politics and support for Russian neoconservative imperialism. Unlike classical imperialism, which had benefits for the working class of imperialist countries, taxpayers in Russia paid billions to bribe Ukrainian oligarchs like Dmitri Firtash to back Putin's puppet Yanukovych (Grey et al. 2014).

The problem this poses in terms of a global assault on democracy is multiplied manyfold by the propaganda offensive of the Putin regime:

> Almost as soon as he came to power, Putin began taking control of Russia's TV stations. That process is now complete. What you see on television today is either sanctioned by or sympathetic to the Kremlin. News programmes serve up a diet of stories about war and crisis abroad, and of international double standards. The Ukrainian government has been accused of crucifying babies; the BBC of staging a chemical attack in Syria.
>
> Truth has become subordinate to political expediency. To support this difficult balancing act, a philosophical framework has been constructed. One of its chief architects is Alexander Dugin ... 'The truth is a question of belief,' he told me, when I visited him at his own religiously oriented TV station near the Kremlin. 'Post-modernity shows that every so-called truth is a matter of believing. So we believe in what we do, we believe in what we say. And that is the only way to define the truth. So we have our special Russian truth that you need to accept.'
>
> [...] Mr Dugin's bellicose doublethink is not aimed solely at the West. There is a message for internal consumption too. It is this: there is no such thing as universal liberal values; there is no inherent contradiction in a democracy that allows no dissent.
>
> In the shadow of the walls of the Kremlin, Russia's dwindling band of activists keep alive the memory of Boris Nemtsov, laying flowers on the spot where the opposition politician was gunned down last year. It's cold and lonely work. 'I still believe that truth exists,' says Mikhail Shneider, a former Soviet dissident and comrade of Mr Nemtsov. 'It is a fact that they killed Boris Nemtsov right here, 10m from where we're standing. It is a fact that Putin is in the Kremlin. It is a fact that Putin's TV lies.' (Gatehouse 2016)

Dugin's insistence that the truth is a question of belief underpins the barrage of fake news emanating from Russia. In the wake of the annexation of Crimea, *Russia Today* was renamed *RT* and its $300 million budget increased by 40 per cent; 'The channel broadcasts in English, Arabic and Spanish and can reach 600 million people. It claims to have surpassed a billion hits on YouTube, and will add German- and French-language channels' (Cohen 2014). *RT* is not the only state purveyor of fake news; *Sputnik* is another, and there are numerous other internet sites and blogs which spread lies. And although there was a huge increase in the propaganda output after the Russian annexation of Crimea and invasion of Ukraine, it actually started earlier, in the wake of the Syrian uprising:

> When experts published content criticizing the Russian-supported Bashar al Assad regime, organized hordes of trolls would appear to attack the authors on

Twitter and Facebook. Examining the troll social networks revealed dozens of accounts presenting themselves as attractive young women eager to talk politics with Americans, including some working in the national security sector. These 'honeypot' social media accounts were linked to other accounts used by the Syrian Electronic Army hacker operation. All three elements were working together: the trolls to sow doubt, the honeypots to win trust, and the hackers (we believe) to exploit clicks on dubious links sent out by the first two. The Syrian network did not stand alone. Beyond it lurked closely interconnected networks tied to Syria's allies, Iran and Russia. (Weisburd et al. 2016)

In fact, there are as many fake stories linked to the Syrian uprising as to the Russian war on Ukraine, and some are a bizarre combination of the two, such as reports that 'Ukrainian Banderites' are fighting in Syria, or that there are ISIS fighters in Ukraine (StopFake 2015).

Some of these lies are easily debunked: for example, the claim that Austria and Slovenia have announced the intention to close their borders with Serbia to stem the flow of refugees is refuted by a quick look at a map, which shows that Austria and Slovenia have no borders with Serbia; in another bloomer, the Russian Ministry of Defence boasted it had bombed ISIS headquarters in Idlib while misidentifying Idlib on the map. Some lies are contradicted by those to whom various remarks are attributed, for example the French ambassador to NATO dismissed as 'pure fiction' the claim that he had made the remarks condemning Turkey attributed to him by *Sputnik*. Statistics claiming to show that millions of Syrians are returning home thanks to Russia's bombing Syria, and that the majority of refugees in Europe are not Syrian, are contradicted by official statistics of the UN refugee agency. Other lies require more research to demolish, for example a photograph of Erdoğan's son with supposed ISIS warlords turns out to be a photograph of him with Turkish restaurateurs (StopFake 2015), and 'irrefutable evidence' of US support for ISIS consists of stills from a video game and footage of the Iraqi assault on ISIS near Fallujah (Walker 2017b).

These lies are picked up and repeated over and over again, not only by neo-Stalinists and neo-fascists spreading the Kremlin's propaganda, but also by writers and bloggers who have developed a healthy scepticism about Western politicians and media, but who naïvely swallow Russian lies, hook, line and sinker without bothering to perform even the most perfunctory fact check. The impact is amplified by an army of internet trolls supplemented by bots, as revealed by leaked documents. Max Seddon (2014) recounts:

The documents show instructions provided to the commenters that detail the workload expected of them. On an average working day, the Russians are to post on news articles 50 times. Each blogger is to maintain six Facebook accounts publishing at least three posts a day and discussing the news in groups at least twice a day. By the end of the first month, they are expected to have won 500 subscribers and get at least five posts on each item a day. On Twitter, the bloggers are expected to manage 10 accounts with up to 2,000 followers and tweet 50 times a day.

[...] Two Russian media reports partly based on other selections from the documents attest that the campaign is directly orchestrated by the Kremlin. Business newspaper *Vedomosti*, citing sources close to Putin's presidential administration, said last week that the campaign was directly orchestrated by the government and included expatriate Russian bloggers in Germany, India, and Thailand. *Novaya Gazeta* claimed this week that the campaign is run by Evgeny Prigozhin, a restaurateur who catered Putin's re-inauguration in 2012. Prigozhin has reportedly orchestrated several other elaborate Kremlin-funded campaigns against opposition members and the independent media.

[...] The group that hacked the emails, which were shared with Buzz-Feed last week and later uploaded online, is a new collective that calls itself the Anonymous International, apparently unrelated to the global Anonymous hacker movement. In the last few months, the group has shot to notoriety after posting internal Kremlin files such as plans for the Crimean independence referendum, the list of pro-Kremlin journalists whom Putin gave awards for their Crimea coverage, and the personal email of eastern Ukrainian rebel commander Igor Strelkov. None of the group's leaks have been proven false.

Some of the fake news and troll commentary is amusing in its ignorance and illiteracy, but this is no joke. Careless readers and writers who reproduce the content – including some in the mainstream media – assist anti-democratic counterrevolutions in countries like Ukraine, Russia and Syria, and they help to cover up the mass murder of civilians, including children, who are designated as 'fascists' and 'terrorists' and therefore fair game. The case of Syria is taken up in Chapter 7, but we will look briefly at Ukraine here.

Ukraine's Struggle for Democracy

While human habitation in Ukraine dates back tens of thousands of years, the first stable state was Kievan Rus, established by the Scandinavian Varangians who settled in Kiev in the late ninth century AD. The height of its prosperity occurred under Volodymyr the Great (980–1015 AD), who converted to Byzantine Christianity, and his son Iaroslav the Wise; but Kievan Rus was destroyed by the invasion of Genghis Khan's Golden Hordes in the thirteenth century, and was subsequently fought over, divided and dominated by Lithuania, Poland, Austria and Russia, until most of it was colonised by Russia (then called Muscovy) in 1654. Nonetheless there was a revival of Ukrainian culture in the nineteenth century, in the latter part of which both nationalist and socialist parties grew as Ukraine was integrated more closely into the Russian empire as a provider of food and raw materials such as coal and iron, and as a market for Russian manufactured goods (Subtelny 2000, 25; 32–41; 75–77; 134–35; 227–35; 268–69). This was a typical colonial relationship; as Lenin observed in 1914 at a talk in Zurich: 'What Ireland was for England, Ukraine has become for Russia: exploited in the extreme, and getting nothing in return. Thus the interests of the world proletariat in general and the Russian proletariat in particular require that the Ukraine regains its state independence, since only this will permit the development of the cultural level that the proletariat needs' (Subtelny 2000, 269; Kowalewski 1989).

Thus Ukraine has a history as a country in its own right, and is not simply an appendage of Russia; nor is Crimea, as we saw in the Introduction. It is therefore entirely understandable that it would have a national liberation movement. This movement succeeded briefly in establishing Ukraine as an independent Soviet Socialist republic from 1920 to 1922, before it was recolonised by Stalin. During World War II, the Organization of Ukrainian Nationalists (OUN), a formerly marginal right-wing ethnonationalist group, grew in importance. As Snyder (2014) describes,

> The OUN opposed both Polish and Soviet rule of what it saw as Ukrainian territories and thus regarded a German invasion of the east as the only way that a Ukrainian state-building process could begin. Thus the OUN supported Germany in its invasion of Poland in 1939 and would do so again in 1941, when Hitler betrayed Stalin and invaded the USSR.
>
> [...] Hundreds of Ukrainian nationalists joined in the German invasion of the USSR as scouts and translators, and some of them helped the Germans organize pogroms of Jews. Ukrainian nationalist politicians tried to collect their debt by declaring an independent Ukraine in June 1941. Hitler was completely uninterested in such a prospect. Much of the Ukrainian nationalist leadership was killed or incarcerated. [OUP leader] Bandera himself spent most of the rest of the war in the prison camp at Sachsenhausen.
>
> [...] In the province of Volhynia, nationalists established a Ukrainian In-

surgent Army whose task was to somehow defeat the Soviets after the Soviets had defeated the Germans. Along the way it undertook a massive and murderous ethnic-cleansing of Poles in 1943, killing at the same time a number of Jews who had been hiding with Poles. This was not in any sense collaboration with the Germans, but rather the murderous part of what its leaders saw as a national revolution. The Ukrainian nationalists went on to fight the Soviets in a horrifying partisan war, in which the most brutal tactics were used by both sides.

This is the fascist history of Ukraine Putinist propaganda refers to. What is left out of this picture is the fact that

far, far more people in Ukraine were killed by the Germans than collaborated with them, something which is not true of any occupied country in continental Western Europe. For that matter, far, far more people from Ukraine fought against the Germans than on the side of the Germans, which is again something that is not true of any continental Western European country. The vast majority of Ukrainians who fought in the war did so in the uniform of the Red Army. More Ukrainians were killed fighting the Wehrmacht than American, British, and French soldiers – combined. (Snyder 2014)

Thus, a more balanced picture would show that the vast majority of Ukrainians fought against the Nazis, while a minority collaborated with them – as did Stalin and many Russians.

The Putinist claim about Ukrainians dominated by fascism has also been used to vilify the Maidan movement against Russian-supported president Yanukovych. When Ukraine gained its independence in 1991 after a referendum in which more than 90 per cent of its inhabitants, including majorities in every province, voted for independence (Lalpychak 1991), its state-owned assets were grabbed by oligarchs, as in Russia. Its people wanted relationships with both Russia and the EU, but this clashed with Putin's goal of incorporating Ukraine into his Eurasian empire. Consequently, he arm-twisted then-president Yanukovych to go back on his promise to sign an Association Agreement with the EU, resulting in an uprising in which Yanukovych was overthrown (see the Introduction). According to the neo-Stalinist narrative, this was a fascist uprising, but the evidence proves the opposite. Although far-right nationalists were certainly part of it, and garnered a great deal of publicity, their performance in the 2014 presidential and parliamentary elections was pathetic, with the ultranationalist Svoboda and Right Sector parties getting around 1 per cent each of the votes cast in the May 2014 presidential election (Socor 2014), while Svoboda got 4.72 per cent of the votes and Right

Sector 1.81 per cent in the October parliamentary elections – both below the minimum 5 per cent required for representation in parliament (Olszański 2014). However, pro-Russian parties were also wiped out in the elections, which was reason enough for the Putinist media to term the winners 'fascists'.

Of course there are neo-fascists and anti-Semites in Ukraine, but there have been serious efforts to deal with Ukraine's anti-Semitic past. On September 29, 1941, almost 34,000 Jewish men, women and children of Kiev were taken by the Nazis out of the city to the ravine at Babi Yar and shot dead. There were many Ukrainian collaborators of the Nazi genocide, but there were also at least 2,500 Ukrainians recognised by the Yad Vashem Holocaust Memorial Center as 'righteous of the nations', who saved the lives of Jews. Just one month after Ukraine became independent, it built a holocaust memorial at Babi Yar, and in September 2016 it held a week-long commemoration of the seventy-fifth anniversary of the massacre. It was inaugurated by a youth conference in Kiev, with numerous other conferences, symposia, memorial gatherings, exhibitions, concerts and other events.

> On Tuesday afternoon, Ukraine's parliament, the Verkhovna Rada, held three hours of hearings on the events of Babi Yar, which were attended by dozens of MPs, dignitaries, and the patriarch of the Ukrainian orthodox church. The hearings consisted of short parliamentary style several-minute-long speeches given by various MPs and political dignitaries. Volodymyr Viatrovych, the controversial head of the government-funded Ukrainian Institute of National Memory, spoke, as did Ukraine's Brooklyn-born chief rabbi Yaakoc Dov Bleich. After the speeches, he informed me that it was the first time that the chief rabbi of Ukraine had ever spoken on the floor of the Ukrainian parliament. Also noteworthy was Rabbi Moshe Reuven Azman, of Kiev's Brodski Synagogue, blowing the shofar on the podium, likewise a first on the floor of the Verkhovna Rada.
>
> Jewish Ukrainian Parliamentarian Georgy Logvinsky, a member of the People's Will party who was one of the prime organizers of the hearings, gave an impassioned speech about the coexistence of the Jews and Ukrainians. (Davidzon 2016)

By contrast with Russia, where the state encourages homophobic violence with its anti-gay legislation, police defended a Kiev gay pride march from violence by the Right Sector, and twenty-five members of the anti-gay militant group were arrested. Alya Shandra (2015) of the *EuroMaidan Press* challenged the homophobia of the Right Sector, writing,

> It is fascists that divide people into real people and sub-humans, using definitions such as 'sodomites' and calling for harassment against certain groups in

our society because they are different. It doesn't matter much to me if I live in Russia's totalitarian society where the today's czar will decide how you think, dress, and what you write in social networks, or the totalitarian society based on nationalist ideology, which, apparently, you want to build in Ukraine. In both situations I will spend my life in helping those who are oppressed, humiliated, and exterminated by the limited and cynical regime. Right Sector, your threats of violent reprisals against people who think and behave differently than you do make you no better than Russian President Vladimir Putin in my eyes.

If charges of 'fascism' in Ukraine are false, however, charges of sky-high levels of corruption are all too true: 'The global corruption watchdog Transparency International lists it at 142nd place out of 175 countries, somewhere near Uganda and much lower than Nigeria. It's been estimated that officials on the take annually pocket about 20 percent of Ukraine's GDP' (Weir 2015). This is not surprising in a country where the president, Petro Poroshenko, is himself an oligarch. Yegor Sobolev, the head of the Ukrainian parliament's anti-corruption committee, 'cheerfully admits that most of his predecessors in the job, which has existed for two decades, have indeed turned out to be part of the problem. "We've never made any headway against corruption in the past because it totally pervades this society," he says. "It's the biggest problem in Ukraine. Not war, not economic crisis, but corruption. Every judge, cop, general, prosecutor, politician and teacher is accustomed to using his position to line his pockets. And they protect each other. We have a total kleptocratic state"' (Weir 2015). Yet, he was hopeful. Sobolev was a product of Samopomich ('self-reliance'), a grassroots anti-corruption and good governance movement in the West Ukrainian city of Lviv, which was so successful that it constituted itself as a political party, winning nearly 11 per cent of the vote in the 2014 elections and sending thirty-two legislators to parliament (Lozovsky 2015).

The reason for resistance to change, according to Lozovsky (2016), is that

> though Ukrainians managed to topple their strongman President Viktor Yanukovych and many of his enforcers, the 'deep state' – the mass of corrupt officials who run the country at the whims of its oligarchs – survived. That's why the reforms of the last two years have just barely limped along, each tentative step forward provoking a fierce counter-reaction. There's a fresh, Western-trained new police force, but its powers are useless in the face of the crooked courts. There's an independent new anti-corruption agency, but it's locked in fierce battle with the hugely powerful and utterly unreformed prosecutors' office, which is trying to check its every step.

Such an entrenched system cannot be changed without a high level of civil society activism; that is the real change taking place beneath the superficial stagnation in Ukraine. An example is the formation of the Reanimation Package of Reforms (RPR), an umbrella civic organisation, which involves the regular cooperation of over seventy members of parliament, and which boasts eighty-two bills from its agenda that have been adopted into law.

> Of course, that commitment has often been spotty, and some of the bills are worth more on paper than in reality. But consider what's been accomplished. Naftogaz, the notoriously crooked gas company that was bleeding the state dry, is now posting a profit. The state railroad company, now headed by a Polish crisis manger [sic], has turned the corner and is now also making money. The National Anti-Corruption Bureau, an independent new agency, is doggedly pursuing corrupt officials. And the beginnings of decentralization have returned more tax revenue to local communities, enabling cities across the country to invest in new infrastructure, from roads and buses to hospitals and kindergartens. (Lozovsky 2016)

It is in civil society that the greatest change has taken place, and that is connected to the newly won freedom of expression and association. "'People stopped being afraid, after [the] Maidan [demonstrations],'" says Ivan Kozlenko, the 35-year-old general director of Ukraine's national film archives. "'Nobody's afraid any more to say what they believe, to express their visions, their ideas. Young Ukrainians today – they are so free, and the revolution moved them, spurred them'" (Lepeska 2016). There has been a flowering of innovative theatre, music and film, as well as cafes, bars and street food festivals:

> Impressive street art has been popping up across the city. Pinchuk Art Centre, perhaps the country's top independent art space, now positions "mediators" in every room of its four-floor gallery space – young art students who speak Ukrainian, Russian, and English and answer questions from visitors. Last year's Kiev biennial, called School of Kyiv, commandeered a variety of unusual spaces – a shuttered factory, a stylish shop, an unused mall – to reach a broader audience … The Ukho Music Agency, founded by Eugene Shimalsky and Sasha Andrusyk, has in the past two years held 15 classical music concerts in unlikely spaces across the city … With tickets at $6-10, all the shows sold out. (Lepeska 2016)

Among those who have gained most from the new freedoms are left-wing academics, students and activists, who in November 2015, on the anniversary of the October Revolution, organised a highly successful international conference entitled 'Economic Crisis or Crisis of Neoliberalism? Alternative Development Policy for Ukraine'. There was a high level of debate among the economists, sociologists and trade union activists attending the conference, including reports of workers' struggles. 'Judging by the heated discussions and lots of questions, the conference helped bring together workers and students, academics and activists from Ukraine and abroad in sharing their experience, developing the agenda of a democratic socialist alternative, and finding a way for deeper cooperation' (Dudin and Pilach 2015).

A War Supported by Pseudo-anti-imperialists

It is hard not to agree with Boris Nemtsov that the real threat Ukraine poses to Putin is that it might become an example of a successful democratic revolution. If Putin feared NATO moving into neighbouring countries, the last thing he would have done would be to drive them into it with military threats and aggression as he has done in Ukraine, where there was no question of joining NATO before the annexation of Crimea and the war in the east. What is achieved by starting that war, however, is to hamstring all efforts to stabilise Ukraine. The critical Russian role in the war is revealed by the words of Russian right-wing ultranationalist Igor Strelkov, who claimed, as we saw in the Introduction, that he 'pulled the trigger of this war', and that 'the Ukraine has been and remains a part of Russia' (Dolgov 2014; Batou 2015); by the large number of Russians killed in the conflict, as discovered by Nemtsov and others including Ruslan Leviev (2015); and, of course, by the affair of Flight MH17.

When Malaysia Airlines Flight MH17 exploded over eastern Ukraine on July 17, 2014, killing all 298 people aboard, Russian media claimed it was shot down by an air-to-air missile fired by a Ukrainian fighter jet, and even named Ukrainian pilot Vladislav Voloshin as being responsible, while a Russian investigator claimed the CIA, Ukrainian secret service and Dutch security service planted bombs on the plane (Stephenson 2016). When a Dutch Safety Board investigation established that the plane had been brought down by a Russian-developed ground-to-air Buk missile, the official Russian story shifted to stating that it had been fired from Ukraine-controlled territory, and that commercial airliners should not have been flying above a war zone where separatist forces had already brought down more than a dozen Ukrainian aircraft and helicopters (Roth et al. 2015). Meanwhile, transcripts of phone conversations between rebel fighters and Russian intelligence released by the Ukrainian Security Service suggested that the rebels shot the plane down thinking it was a Ukrainian fighter jet (Masi

2014). In September 2016, a Joint Investigation Team reported in a press conference that on the basis of forensic evidence, radar evidence, questioning of two hundred witnesses, and analysis of hundreds of thousands of photographs and videos, they had been able to track the Buk missile system travelling to rebel-held territory from Russia before the plane was shot down, and travelling back to Russia afterwards (Campbell and Kitching 2016).

On October 16, 2016, Russian commander Arsen Pavlov, also known as 'Motorola', was assassinated in Donetsk by a remote-controlled bomb planted on his apartment-building's elevator. He was the latest among dozens of separatist leaders of the Donetsk People's Republic and Luhansk People's Republic to be targeted 'in apparently safe surroundings, far from the dangers of the battlefield' (Losh 2016). A video purporting to show Ukrainian neo-Nazis claiming responsibility was widely discredited even among separatists. So who would want Motorola dead?

> Many believe that it was one of his own. Feuds over the control of trade routes and contraband energy resources – namely Ukrainian coal and Russian oil – are common in the breakaway regions. Pavlov was said to have been involved in dealing scrap metal, a profession that the *Moscow Times* last week called 'one of the few growth industries in and around the destroyed Donetsk airport.' By removing rogue competitors, eastern Ukraine's ruling coalitions of rebel warlords and criminal syndicates could be seeking to tighten their grip on these underground and hugely profitable markets. [...]
>
> But privately some separatists acknowledge that the danger may be coming from as far away as Moscow. Pavlov's murder was sophisticated, efficient, and required close access – signs of tradecraft that suggest Russian involvement. Speaking on condition of anonymity due to security concerns, a well-placed source with links to key figures in the Russian-controlled separatist regime told me: 'Some are saying that handlers higher up the chain are cleaning up first-generation rebels to destroy any incriminating evidence and remove witnesses to war crimes. The Kremlin needs its proxies to have a more acceptable public face.' (Losh 2016)

Either way, Russia's imperialist war in eastern Ukraine, with ten thousand dead and counting (including Russian soldiers like the young men identified in Leviev's report), has brought nothing but death and destruction to Ukraine with no benefit to Russians apart from Putin. It has also cost the lives of 298 passengers and crew of Malaysia Airlines Flight MH17. How many deaths will it take until Putin supporters like Pilger (2014) know that too many people have died?

3. Bosnia and Kosovo

T
ito's authoritarian response to a nascent democratic revolution facilitated the growth of ethnic nationalism in the former Yugoslavia. The conflict in Bosnia in the 1990s, driven by Slobodan Milošević's drive to build a Greater Serbia, was the earliest post–Cold War example of sections of the left supporting right-wing ethnoreligious nationalism. After Bosnia-Herzegovina declared independence in 1992, it was surrounded and invaded by the Serb army and militias as well as by Croatian militias, all pursuing an agenda of ethnic cleansing and genocide, in which the UN and NATO colluded. Pseudo-anti-imperialists covered up the mass rape, torture and murder carried out by Serb nationalists, and instead of criticising the US and NATO for failing to protect Bosnian Muslims, attacked them when they belatedly stepped in to halt the genocide.

Socialist Yugoslavia

Unlike the Soviet Union under Stalin, the Socialist Federal Republic of Yugoslavia under Josip Broz Tito was not an empire but a voluntary federation; and unlike Stalin, Tito was not an ethnic nationalist. So why did Yugoslavia disintegrate?

In the early 1970s, both ethnic nationalism and pressure for democratic political reforms began to surface in Yugoslavia. Instead of democratising, Tito carried out a number of political purges of those who wanted reform: 'In Serbia, after 1972, more than 6,000 people lost their jobs in politics, the economy, the media and the cultural institutions. Their places were quickly filled with party *apparatchiks* loyal to old-fashioned communist values ... Ti-

95

to's second move was to create a new federal economic structure for Yugoslavia based on workers' self-management' (Guzina 2004, 18). However, 'Ethnic nationalism continued to gain ground while the only "success" proved to be a very effective prevention of the rise of democratic social movements that might cut across regional borders' (Guzina 2004, 18).

These changes were formalised in the 1974 Constitution, which designated Yugoslavia as a federation of the Republics of Bosnia-Herzegovina, Croatia, Macedonia, Montenegro, Serbia and Slovenia. As Roland Rich (1993, 38–39) outlined,

> The first Basic Principle listed in the Constitution begins with the formulation 'the nations of Yugoslavia, proceeding from the right of every nation to self-determination, including the right of secession' ... A distinction was made between the 'nations' of Yugoslavia and the 'republics' of Yugoslavia, the former being peoples like the Croats, Macedonians, Serbs and Slovenes without any necessary geographic connection and the latter being the six geographically defined federal units without any necessary ethnic connection. A second distinction was made between 'nations' and 'nationalities' with the latter being defined as 'members of nations whose native countries border on Yugoslavia' like the Albanians of Kosovo and the Hungarians of Vojvodina (both in Serbia), who were given autonomy but not the right to secede.

Thus, in principle, it was not the multiethnic republics that were given the right to secede but the 'nations,' which conform to what are today called ethnic groups. This formulation encouraged ethnic nationalism, which continued to gain ground.[1]

The decentralised workers' self-management system had a great deal of potential but was beset with problems because interests differed between constituents at different economic levels (federation, republics, communes, enterprises and Basic Organizations of Associated Labour or BOALs), as well as between different organisations at the same level. For example, an agreement with Czechoslovakia that around twelve thousand Yugoslav workers in that country would get health insurance there, provided that a much smaller number of Czech tourists in Yugoslavia got free health coverage, fell through because the communes where the tourists wanted health care did not want to supply it to foreigners who did not contribute to the local funds (Comisso 1980, 199). Again, it would have made sense for producers of household appliances, which suffered from low capacity utilisation and low profitability due to the fact that they were all producing the same wide range of products, to specialise in complementary product lines instead, but this never happened (Comisso 1980, 200). The contribution that individual firms might have made to overall planning was hampered by their narrow perspectives: 'Thus, while it was beyond the capacity of any individual firm to think in terms of a general solution to inflation, few collectives could resist seeking approval for price increases to combat inflation's effect on their own operations' (Comisso 1980, 205). Arriving at the plethora of agreements required to coordinate production was so cumbersome that most collectives charted their own course; common goals like raising productivity and reducing inflation fell by the wayside.

Consequently, self-management failed to boost the economy. 'Between 1974 and 1980, Yugoslavia borrowed 16,433 million US dollars from the IMF, western governments and a great number of western commercial banks. Inflation reached an annual rate of 45 per cent and unemployment rose to 800,000. Beyond the unemployment figures, nearly two million people became so-called technological surplus' (Guzina 2004, 19). While Tito was alive, his prestige as the leader of a multiethnic partisan force which had fought successfully against the Nazis, and as a leader of the Non-Aligned Movement, counteracted the centrifugal forces pulling the Federation apart. But after his death in 1980, the decentralised character of decision making 'deprived the last pro-Yugoslav federal government of [prime minister] Ante Marković the capacity to act in any legitimate fashion. Even though enjoying a great popularity at the time in Bosnia-Herzegovina, Serbia and Croatia, Marković's government soon fell prey to the orchestrated campaign of the republican elites of Serbia, Croatia and Slovenia to topple the government's program of economic and political reforms' (Guzina 2004, 19). The IMF imposed its usual austerity conditions for the loans it gave. As living standards plummeted, ethnoreligious nationalism took over.

Ethnoreligious Nationalism

Serbs, Croats and Bosniaks[2] are all Slavs with variants of the same language, differentiated mainly by the religion of the majority: Orthodox Christianity, Catholicism and Islam respectively. Kosovar Albanians are not Slavs, have a completely different language, and are mostly Muslims. Islam came to the Balkans mainly with the Ottoman conquest of the fourteenth century, and at the centre of Serb nationalist mythology is the battle of Kosovo in 1389, in which the Serb army led by Prince Lazar was defeated by the Ottoman Turk-ish forces of Sultan Murat, although both were killed in the battle. 'During the nineteenth century, Serbian nationalist writers transformed Lazar into an explicit Christ figure ... In this story, the Ottoman Turks play the role of the Christ killers. Vuk Branković, the Serb who betrays the battle plans to the Ottoman army, becomes the Christ killer within', who 'represents any Slavs who converted to Islam ... and any Serb who would live with them or tolerate them' (Sells 1998, 31).[3] These nationalists propagated three myths – that conversion to Islam was based only on cowardice and greed, that there were stable ethnoreligious groups down the centuries, and that Ottoman rule was completely depraved – which 'became the foundation for a new religious ideology, Christoslavism, the belief that Slavs are Christian by nature and that any conversion from Christianity is a betrayal of the Slavic race' (Sells 1998, 36). Serb nationalism is linked to Orthodox Christianity. Contempt for Muslims is shared by Croatian nationalists, with Croatian president Franjo Tudjman wishing 'to eradicate what he sees as contamination by the "Orient"' (Sells 1998, 95).

By the twentieth century, Christoslavism had put down deep roots. 'During the Balkan war of 1912, Leon Trotsky was a war correspondent for a group of liberal Russian and Ukrainian newspapers. He understood that pan-Slavic and Christian Orthodox chauvinism was a crucial element in Russian tyranny ... and he wrote of the atrocities committed in Kosovo that Russian indulgence made it much easier for Serbian and Bulgarian gangs "to engage in their Cain's work of further massacres of the peoples of the Cres-cent in the interests of the 'culture' of the Cross"' (Hitchens 1999). Christo-slavism might have been repressed during Tito's rule, but it was not rooted out; on the contrary, many self-professed 'communists' like Milošević made a seamless transition to Christoslavism in the 1980s and 1990s. Another example is Biljana Plavšić, former dean of the Faculty of Natural Science and Mathematics in Sarajevo, who claimed that 'it was genetically deformed material that embraced Islam. And now, of course, with each successive gen-eration this gene simply becomes concentrated' (cit. Sells 1998, xiv–xv). It is notable how similar this is to Nazi ideology, with Christoslav supremacism and demonisation of Muslims substituted for 'Aryan' supremacism and de-monisation of Jews.

Kosovo had been part of the Ottoman Empire and was inhabited pri-marily by Albanians for around three hundred years. In 1912, most of it was conquered by Serbia, which pushed out Albanians and settled Serbs in it during the interwar years. Serbian nationalists protested when Tito came to power and abandoned Serb colonisation, and were even more enraged at the enhanced autonomy granted to Kosovo by the constitution of 1974. By 1986, Serb nationalists were accusing the Albanians of engaging in 'genocide' against the Serbs, the main 'evidence' for this being their high birthrate, although this was easily explained by the fact that Kosovo was the poorest region of Yugoslavia, and birthrates of the poor are usually higher than those of the wealthier. Serb women were alleged to have been targeted for rape, while the Serb cultural heritage of Kosovo was allegedly being destroyed – charges that collapsed when set beside actual police records. That did not deter the nationalists, however: in January 1986, two hundred Belgrade intellectuals signed a petition to the Yugoslav and Serbian national assemblies that 'condemned the autonomy and majority rule in Kosovo, established in the constitution of 1974, as national treason' (Sells 1998, 56).

In 1987, at a meeting in Kosovo, an elderly resident complained to Slobodan Milošević that the Albanian-dominated police were beating Serbs in the crowd. '"These people will not beat you again!" The response by Milošević was shown throughout Serbia on all the major television networks. What the viewers were not shown was how the incident was staged. Serb nationalists, with Milošević's approval, had supplied the crowd with truckloads of heavy stones. At a given moment the crowd threw the stones directly into the face of police who had been standing by.' On June 28, 1989, at the six hundredth anniversary of the Battle of Kosovo, Milošević stood before a crowd of between one and two million Kosovo Serbs and 'consolidated three years of effort to instigate and appropriate radical nationalist sentiment' (Sells 1998, 67–68). The agenda of transforming Yugoslavia into Greater Serbia was out in the open.

The Slovenes and Croats, in 1991, were the first to declare independence from Yugoslavia, after their proposals for a looser federation were blocked by Milošević and his supporters. The Yugoslav army invaded Slovenia but soon retreated, since there were few Serbs living there. However, Croatia – where the new president, Franjo Tudjman, pursued an equally aggressive Croat nationalism and refused to acknowledge the atrocities against Serbs committed by the fascist Ustashe during World War II – was a different matter. There were around 600,000 Serbs in Croatia, and Milošević strongly opposed Croatian independence unless parts of Croatia like Krajina, where

Serbs predominated, were annexed by Serbia. Tudjman's government absolutely refused to agree (Sudetic 1991). War broke out between the Yugoslav army and Serb militias on one side, and the new Croat army on the other. Bosniaks were caught in the middle, threatened with being regarded as traitors if they did not fight in the Yugoslav army, and threatened with reprisals by the Croatian army if they did. This was the context in which Bosnians voted for independence in a referendum conducted on April 6 and 7, 1992, while Serb nationalists in Bosnia, armed and backed by Milošević, declared their own 'Republika Srpska' with Radovan Karadžić as president.

In March 1991, the warring Serb and Croat nationalists came to an agreement to partition Bosnia between Serbia and Croatia (Silber and Little 1997, 131–32). 'Tudjman helped overthrow the moderate Bosnian Croat leader, Stjepan Kljuić, who had been elected Bosnian representative of the HDZ [Hrvatska Demokratska Zajednica, or Croatian Democratic Union]. Kljuić was replaced with nationalist warlord Mate Boban. In May 1992, Boban had met with Radovan Karadžić in Graz, Austria, to draw up plans for dividing Bosnia between Croat and Serb nationalists' (Sells 1998, 96). Serb militias and the Yugoslav army, by this stage completely dominated by Serbs, invaded, and by August they occupied around two-thirds of Bosnia-Herzegovina (Silber and Little 1997, 205–56).

The Genocide of Bosnian Muslims

The first journalist to reveal the horror of what was going on in the Serb-occupied parts of Bosnia was Roy Gutman, who had been covering Yugoslavia since 1991. Hearing stories of Muslims being deported in cattle cars to camps where terrible things were happening, he asked the Serb authorities for permission to visit one of these camps, Omarska. Instead, he was taken to a prisoner of war camp in Manjača, where his photographer 'managed, despite the fact that ... he was surrounded all the time, to get some superb photographs which just showed the degradation that they were subjecting Muslim prisoners to' (Kreisler 1997). Still unsatisfied, on August 2, 1992, Gutman published a story entitled 'Death camps: survivors tell of captivity, mass slaughters in Bosnia', based on interviews with two survivors of camps at Omarska and Brčko:

> The Serb conquerors of northern Bosnia have established two concentration camps in which more than a thousand civilians have been executed or starved

and thousands more are being held until they die, according to two recently released prisoners interviewed by New York Newsday. [...]

In one concentration camp, a former iron-mining complex at Omarska in northwest Bosnia, more than a thousand Muslim and Croat civilians were held in metal cages, without sanitation, adequate food, exercise or access to the outside world, according to a former prisoner who asked to be identified only as 'Meho.' The prisoners at the camp, he said, include the entire political and cultural elite of the city of Prijedor. Armed Serbian guards executed prisoners in groups of 10 to 15 every few days, he said. 'They would come to a nearby lake. You'd hear a volley of rifles. And they'd never come back,' said Meho. [...]

In a second improvised camp, in a customs warehouse on the bank of the Sava River in the northeast Bosnian city of Brčko, 1,350 people were slaughtered between May 15 and mid-June, according to Alija Lujinovic, 53, a traffic engineer who was imprisoned at the camp. Guards at Brčko executed prisoners by slitting their throats or with firing squads, he said.

On August 6, a report by Penny Marshall and Ian Williams of ITN, whose crew was given a conducted tour of the canteen at the Omarska camp and allowed to film prisoners at the Trnopolje camp by the Serb authorities, was aired. These were sanitised images, released in order to counteract the even more damning reports of thousands of prisoners, almost all civilians, being starved, beaten and tortured to death in these camps; but even so, a still from their film, which was reproduced widely, was so strongly reminiscent of Nazi concentration camps that it created an international outcry (Iconic Photos 2009; Silber and Little 1997, 244–56).

The account of a survivor who was released in a prisoner exchange, Rezak Hukanović (who tells it in the third person, calling himself 'Djemo'), is all the more nightmarish because it starts with the elements of a normal life: a wife and two sons, a home in Prijedor, a job as a journalist, evenings in a bar, and occasional soccer games. When Serb nationalists took over in April 1992,

all the Muslims – along with the few Croats who lived there – were dismissed from their jobs. The schools were closed. The Serbs took control of all the radio and television transmitters and began broadcasting their own programs. The newspapers, except for the Serbian ones, stopped appearing or, at any rate, could no longer be found in town ... The local radio station announced that Prijedor had – as the announcers put it – been attacked by 'Muslim extremists.' This item was repeated a number of times. ... Djemo knew very well that, in a war such as this one, truth had to be killed first ... Every Friday the newsstands sold fresh lies. (Hukanovic 1996, 24–25)

Hukanović goes on to describe the sadistic treatment meted out to the prisoners: denial of food, water and sanitation, overcrowding to the point where they had to sleep standing up, constant humiliation and beatings, gruesome torture, and absurd confessions extracted under torture: an almost blind man forced to confess he was a sniper, a doctor without a basement forced to confess he had hidden stolen medicines in his basement. 'In the course of two days, more than 3,000 inhabitants of Prijedor and its outlying villages were arrested in their homes in these inconceivable raids and brought to the Serb prison at Omarska. Among the prisoners, whose only fault was being Muslim or Croat, were intellectuals, teachers, engineers, police officers, craftsmen. Djemo recognized the mayor of Prijedor, the Honorable Mr. Muhamed Cehajic' (Hukanović 1996, 28).

Numerous similar accounts of mass killings, with an emphasis on exterminating the intellectual and political elites, have been documented. The actions that accompanied these murders were equally chilling:

> Since April 1992 the Serb army has targeted for destruction the major libraries, manuscript collections, museums, and other cultural institutions in Sarajevo, Mostar, and other besieged cities. What the Serb artillery missed, the Croat nationalist militia known as the 'Croatian Defence Council' (HVO) took care of.
>
> Where the Serb and Croat armies have been able to get closer than shelling range, the destruction has been even greater. The Croatian Defence Council dynamited mosques and Orthodox churches throughout the regions controlled by the Croat military. Serb militias have dynamited all the mosques (over six hundred) in areas they have occupied, some of them masterworks of European architecture such as the sixteenth-century Ferhadija Mosque in Banja Luka and the Colored Mosque in Foča built in 1551. Between them, the Croat and Serb nationalists have destroyed an estimated fourteen hundred mosques. In many cases the mosques have been ploughed over and turned into parking lots or parks; every evidence of their existence has been effaced. Graveyards, birth records, work records and other traces of the Bosnian Muslim people have been eradicated. (Sells 1998, 3)

All these actions, along with the killings, constitute elements of genocide as defined by Lemkin: they were not just massacres but an attempt to wipe out a whole people. A new element was the rape camps, where Muslim women and girls were held and subjected to continual rape and other physical violence. Given the culture in traditional Mediterranean societies, where women who have been raped are often not accepted as wives, 'the organized rapes were meant to destroy the potential of the women as mothers' even if they survived (Sells 1998, 21–22; 32). Many did not. The Serbian Guard boasted of gang-raping a 13-year-old Muslim girl in the Bosnian town of Gacko, attaching her to a tank, and riding around until there was nothing left of her but the skeleton (Sells 1998, 172 n.33).

The neo-fascist character of the Serb nationalists was underscored by the way in which they treated dissenters. Often, the punishment was death:

> In a Serb-army occupied area of Sarajevo, Serb militants killed a Serb officer who objected to atrocities against civilians; they left his body on the street for over a week as an object lesson. During one of the 'selections' carried out by Serb militants in Sarajevo, an old Serb named Ljubo objected to being separated out from his Muslim friends and neighbours; they beat him to death on the spot. In Zvornik, Serb militiamen slit the throat of a seventeen-year-old Serb girl who protested the shooting of Muslim civilians. (Sells 1998, 73)

It is testimony to the courage and humanity of these dissidents that despite the risk of torture and death, many Serbs resisted by evading military service, helping Muslims to escape, or sheltering fugitives in their homes. 'Bogdan Bogdanoviç, the Serb former mayor of Belgrade, has spoken out courageously against the systematic annihilation of mosques and other cultural monuments ... In Bosnian government areas, the Serb Civic Council was formed to work for a multireligious society and to articulate the concerns of those Serbs loyal to a multireligious Bosnia-Herzegovina ... The council criticized the international community for treating the religious nationalist faction as the sole representative of the Serb people' (Sells 1998, 78–79). Indeed, the Serb Civic Council's criticism applies equally to the reaction of pseudo-anti-imperialists to the genocide in Bosnia.

International Complicity

The UN Security Council resolution of September 1991, which put an embargo on the delivery of all weapons and military equipment to Yugoslavia, locked in place a huge imbalance between the heavily armed Serb nationalists and the extremely lightly armed Bosniaks, effectively preventing the latter from being able to defend themselves and their communities. In May 1992, trade, political and financial sanctions against Serbia and Montenegro were passed, but, as *Economic and Political Weekly* argued, 'there is no escaping the harsh fact that the western powers, who dominate the UN, are disinclined to intervene in any meaningful way to protect the Bosnian Muslims' (1992). Without any efforts to enforce compliance, or any monitoring of goods entering Serbia on the Danube River, the sanctions against Serbia 'were evidently intended to fail' (Economic and Political Weekly 1992).

In 1993, Cyrus Vance, representing the UN, and David Owen, representing the European Community, formulated a peace plan dividing Bosnia into ten cantons, designating a dominant ethnic group in nine of them. The Croats and Bosniaks accepted it, but the Serb nationalists did not. After Vance was replaced by Thorvald Stoltenberg as UN negotiator, the Owen-Stoltenberg proposals, based on a map drawn by Croatian president Tudjman and Serbian president Milošević, were presented. 'The proposals, which were heavily loaded against the Bosnian Muslims, blatantly rewarded the militarily stronger and more aggressive parties, mainly the Serbs who now control 70 per cent of the territory. According to these proposals, the Serbs were under no obligation to return most of the ethnically-cleansed territories which they had taken by force' (Economic and Political Weekly 1993).

In an interview in 1993, Gutman expressed satisfaction that his stories had led to the release of thousands of Muslim prisoners, but immense frustration at the failure of the UN, the European Community, presidents George H. W. Bush and Bill Clinton, and NATO to halt what he called 'the worst genocide in Europe since the Holocaust' (Ricchiardi 1993). He was not the only Jewish commentator to make the comparison. The last surviving leader of the Warsaw Ghetto resistance, Marek Edelmann, at an event in 1994 at the former Buchenwald concentration camp attended by around three thousand people including Bosnian concentration camp survivors, said, 'Europe has learned nothing from the Holocaust. Nothing has been done to put an end to this slaughter. What is happening in Bosnia and Herzegovina is a posthumous triumph for Hitler.' Holocaust survivors Simon Wiesenthal and Elie Wiesel both urged action to stop the slaughter. Jewish-American writer Susan Sontag, who lived in Sarajevo during the years of starvation and bombardment that began in 1992 and ended only in 1995, declared: 'I have lost my faith in the ideals of the West. What is happening here in Bosnia is a stab in the back for western democracy and for my soul' (GFBV 2012).

By contrast, Western leaders persisted in referring to what was happening as a 'civil war', and refused to accede to the desperate pleas of Bosnian president Alia Izetbegović that the arms embargo be lifted. In fact, the UN distinguished itself by failing spectacularly either to protect Muslims or to allow them to defend themselves, and can therefore be seen as complicit in the genocide. Muslims fleeing Serb forces sought refuge in Goražde, Žepa and Srebrenica, which were designated 'safe areas' for Muslims by the UN, but were, like Sarajevo, allowed to be besieged, starved and shelled by Serb nationalist forces. British general Michael Rose of the UN Protection Force (UNPROFOR) – photographed sharing a laugh with Bosnian Serb general Ratko Mladić in 1994 (Srebrenica Genocide Blog 2010) – accused the beleaguered people of Goražde of '"exaggerating" their plight', even as its inhabitants 'struggled to find food, to stay warm, and to survive the constant Serb shelling' (Tanner 2000). Meanwhile, the UN special representative for former Yugoslavia, Yasushi Akashi, refused to grant permission to NATO troops preparing to undertake punitive airstrikes (Economic and Political Weekly 1994). It was only after thousands of Muslims in Srebrenica were exterminated in one fell swoop in 1995, while civilians in Sarajevo continued to be massacred, that action was finally taken (Hansen 2006, 107–8).

More than two decades later, the horror of what happened in Srebrenica has not diminished. It was one of the enclaves in which Muslim survivors of ethnic cleansing from other parts of Bosnia had fled because the Bosnian republican army in Srebrenica had resisted the relentless bombardment by Serb nationalist forces. In 1993 it was placed under the protection of UNPROFOR, and the Security Council passed a resolution that peace in Bosnia 'must be based on withdrawal from territories seized by the use of force and "ethnic cleansing"', while tabling a report warning of a potential massacre if Serb forces were to enter. Bosnian Serb president Radovan Karadžić promised that if his army entered Srebrenica, there would be 'blood up to the knees', while General Mladić declared that his intention with respect to Bosniaks in the enclaves was to 'have them vanish completely'. Instead of protecting the Bosniaks, UNPROFOR became a liability for them, because its presence – especially after its members were taken hostage by Serb nationalists – led to the UN ruling out airstrikes that might have helped to save the lives of the threatened population. Knowing that airstrikes would not occur, the Serb militias proceeded with their planned massacre. Florence Hartmann and Ed Vulliamy (2015) recount the events of July 1995:

> The UN's envoy, Akashi, sent a cable: 'The Bosnian Serb army is likely to separate the military-age men from the rest of the population, an eventuality about

which Unprofor will be able to do very little.' Indeed, Dutch soldiers watched Mladić's troops separate women and young children (for expulsion) from men and boys (for killing).

[...] Early on 12 July, the Dutch commander in Srebrenica, Colonel Ton Karremans, met Mladić, with orders to 'let the Serbs organise the transport' of civilians out of Srebrenica. But, says General Onno van der Wind of the Dutch defence ministry, the UN then provided 30,000 litres of petrol which proved necessary for the genocide. 'After Unprofor approval,' says Van der Wind, 'the fuel was delivered in Bratunac [the Bosnian Serb HQ outside Srebrenica] after the arrival of a logistical convoy.' The UN petrol was used, he says, to fuel transport of men and boys to the killing fields, and bulldozers to plough the 8,000 corpses into mass graves.

The mass murder was later described at The Hague by Judge Fouad Riad as 'written on the darkest pages of history'. A sole 'executioner' to turn prosecutor's evidence at the trials, Dražen Erdemović, described how death squads asked to sit down – they were so tired, killing wave upon wave, busload after busload, of men and boys.

Unbelievably, despite this incontrovertible evidence that UNPROFOR was not protecting the Bosniaks from genocide, the UN still refused to lift the arms embargo to allow them to defend themselves. In the US, outrage at what was happening led to overwhelming support for lifting the arms embargo in both houses of representatives, with several Democrats joining the attack on the Clinton administration's Bosnia policy, including Senator Joseph I. Lieberman, a Connecticut Democrat, who argued that it amounted to tolerating genocide (Hosler and Matthews 1995). It was popular pressure and the lethal shelling of a marketplace in Sarajevo in late August that eventually pushed the Clinton administration and NATO into providing air support to a Bosniak-Croat ground offensive that successfully reduced Serbian territorial gains from 70 per cent of Bosnia to less than 50 per cent. This was followed by the Dayton peace negotiations led by Assistant Secretary of State Richard Holbrooke, which resulted in an accord in November dividing Bosnia into a Bosniak-Croatian federation on 51 per cent of its territory and the Serb Republika Sprska on 49 per cent, which were associated in a loose confederation with an internationally backed high representative to oversee it. Effectively, in violation of the UN Security Council resolution in 1993, the perpetrators of genocide were rewarded with a Serbian statelet which included Srebrenica. EU special envoy Carl Bildt later wrote in his memoirs that the Bosnian leadership 'knew that the peace settlement would mean the loss of the enclave. So from this point of view what happened made things easier' (Hartmann and

Vulliamy 2015). The Clinton administration saw the massacre as 'a blessing in disguise', because it terrified the Bosnians into parting with almost half their territory (Hitchens 1999). Both saw the slaughter of around eight thousand Muslim men and boys, and rape and expulsion of the rest of the population, as a blessing!

One explanation for the reluctance of Western leaders to help the Bosnian Muslims was the fact that such an action 'promise[d] no visible economic, political or even strategic dividends' (Economic and Political Weekly 1994); by contrast with the Bush Sr. administration's alacrity in bombing Iraq when Saddam Hussein invaded Kuwait in 1991, the US was moved to action in Bosnia only when accused of complicity in genocide. Anti-Muslim bigotry, too, was clearly evident among many Western peacekeepers, including the Dutch soldier who handed over Muslims in Srebrenica to be slaughtered by Serb nationalists and 'expressed contempt for Muslims because they were "smelly." It evidently did not occur to him that people living in concentration-camp conditions are not able, as part of a deliberate policy, to practice normal hygiene' (Sells 1998, 186 n.13).

The UN was also hamstrung by the fact that support for Serbian nationalism from Russian nationalists blocked any decisive action (Economic and Political Weekly 1994). In February 1994, Russian ultranationalist Vladimir Zhirinovsky visited Bosnia. As the *Washington Post* reported at the time,

> To resounding cheers from a crowd of several thousand, who stood for several hours in [the] freezing rain to see him, Zhirinovsky praised the Serbs for waging war to 'save Orthodoxy'. 'Don't worry brothers,' he told the applauding throng, 'we will protect you … If a single bomb falls on Serbia, we will consider that an attack on Russia.' … Ultranationalist Serbs and Russians say that traditionally their two peoples have been allies, sharing the same religion and what they both call 'the great Slavic soul'. (Pomfret 1994)

Not only were there volunteers from Russia fighting alongside Serb militants in Bosnia, but there were also supporters of the Serbian cause among the UN peacekeeping forces. One was the Russian colonel Vicktor Loginov, who used his position to smuggle fuel and supplies to the Serb Volunteer Guard, the paramilitary unit supporting the army. In a 1992 interview, Loginov avowed, as Sells reports, that 'Russia and Serbia were brothers in a Christian Orthodox war' (Sells 1998, 195 n.18).

Only some combination of these elements can explain a botched UN operation that allowed its peacekeepers to be taken hostage by Serb nationalists and repeatedly handed over Muslim civilians it was supposedly protecting to be massacred by Serb militias. The International Criminal Tribunal for the Former Yugoslavia, established by the UN in May 1993 in response to reports of large-scale atrocities, did subsequently bring people of all ethnic groups in former Yugoslavia to trial for war crimes, crimes against humanity and genocide, but the complicity of the UN in these crimes was never acknowledged.

A Ticking Time Bomb

The Dayton Accord, which sacrificed justice in the interests of peace, could only be a stopgap solution. In the short term, it did indeed bring peace, the rebuilding of state institutions and incipient democratic reforms. However, almost immediately after High Representative Christian Schwartz-Schilling took over in 2006 and announced a more hands-off approach, things began to unravel. As James Lyon (2015) recounts, 'Sensing weakening international resolve, [Milorad] Dodik, then-prime minister of Republika Srpska, began using virulent nationalist rhetoric, speaking derogatorily of Bosniaks and the Bosnian state, and announcing that the state established at Dayton was temporary.' This was followed by a series of measures over the next nine years devised to weaken Bosnian state institutions, so as to systematically 'hollow out the Bosnian state that had been so painstakingly crafted by the international community'. Included in these institutions was the judiciary, Dodik's opposition to which, Lyon suspects, is related to 'his distaste for an independent judiciary and his personal fear of being indicted for corruption' (Lyon 2015).

The twentieth anniversary of the Srebrenica massacre brought all these tensions to the fore. When Serbian prime minister Aleksandar Vučić tried to join the commemoration ceremony in 2015, mourners hissed and shouted, some even throwing bottles and stones at him, as 136 victims, who continue to be found so many years later, were buried (Hanna et al. 2015). The US Embassy condemned the incident, but is it surprising that Vučić, who, in the wake of the Srebrenica massacre, gave an inflammatory speech pledging that 'for every Serb killed, we will kill 100 Muslims' (Lynch 2015), might have aroused the ire of those who had lost their loved ones? Meanwhile Russia vetoed a resolution in the UN Security Council condemning the Srebrenica massacre as an act of genocide, leading Munira Subašić, head of the Mothers of Srebrenica, to say, 'We are not surprised by such a decision ... Russia is actually supporting criminals, those who killed our children' (Al Jazeera 2015a).

Most ominously, Dodik, supported by Russia, threatened a referendum on independence from Bosnia. A few months later, High Representative for Bosnia and Herzegovina, Valentin Inzko, received death threats 'written on postcards that were distributed to the public by the party of Milorad Dodik ... [who] has long called for the departure of the [high representative] and other international officials' (Bosnia Today 2016b). These moves, potentially leading to a resumption of war, expose one of the fatal flaws of the constitution established by the Dayton agreement, which, as Borger (2015) argues, 'froze in place the ethnic politics that had fuelled the war. To this day, places at all levels of government are allocated according to affiliation to the three principal groups: Bosniak, Serb or Croat. If you are identified in any other way – Jewish, Roma, or "other", just Bosnian with no specific ethnic label – political leadership in Bosnia and Herzegovina is out of your reach, by law.' If war does break out, it is likely that support for ISIS – already threatening Bosnia's predominantly secular Muslim leaders with decapitation (Bosnia Today 2016a) – would expand.

James Lyon (2015) suggests that 'if Dodik moves ahead with the referendum, it will be a blatant violation of the Dayton agreement, upon which Republika Srpska's only legal legitimacy lies. If it chooses to renege on Dayton, then Republika Srpska legally loses all legitimacy and becomes a rogue entity founded on genocide. The international community should then act accordingly and abolish Republika Srpska, which, while extreme, would be enforceable via administrative and financial means.' This would allow Bosnia to become a republic in which all citizens have equal rights in all parts of the country, regardless of ethnicity. It would also help to reverse a situation in which, as Ed Vulliamy (2017) observes, Ratko Mladić is still adored despite having been convicted of genocide, war crimes and crimes against humanity by the International Criminal Tribunal for the former Yugoslavia. As Lily Lynch (2015) puts it, 'Those responsible for mass murder and the forced displacement of entire populations are celebrities, their faces inescapable on billboards, television and posters. Having refused to kill often means the opposite: being labeled a traitor, testifying under a pseudonym at The Hague, your face obscured.' A genuine peace would enable 'Balkan Schindlers' like 'Srdjan Aleksić, a Bosnian Serb who was beaten to death in 1993 for attempting to defend a Bosniak friend in the town of Trebinje in southern Bosnia' to be honoured as they deserve (Lynch 2015).[4]

Kosovo

Shortly after his speech in Kosovo in 1989, Milošević revoked the autonomy granted to it by the 1974 Constitution. He followed this with various measures denying Kosovar Albanians the liberty to use their language and develop their culture. This was at first countered by non-violent resistance:

> When the University of Pristina personnel were fired, the administration quickly threw together buildings for classes to be held for some 20,000 students in defiance of Milošević's move. The Belgrade regime then went a step further, determining the curricula for primary and secondary schools throughout Kosovo and forbidding ethnic Albanian personnel from entering the buildings. Albanian-language schools moved into garages, basement floors, barns and so on. At the same time, the Albanian-language press went into overtime, secretly printing and distributing opposition voices. When 38 state clinics in the Kosovo health system were forcibly shut down by Belgrade, it led to the birth of a parallel system run by the Saint Theresa Foundation, meeting the needs of some 350,000 Kosovars.
>
> By 1992 there were two stark political blocs in Kosovo. The first was one imposed by Belgrade, driven by the belief that force should be used when necessary to break down the political will of the Kosovars and push for the 'Serbification' of Kosovo. The other bloc was the separatist political movement, driven by the belief that Kosovo was in essence under occupation by Serbia. Throughout the 1990s, the country was to witness two separate but parallel political and social structures.
>
> The illegal Kosovar administration of that decade – referred to in political writings of the time as a 'parallel state,' 'shadow state' or even a 'parallel society' – wound up electing Ibrahim Rugova as its state president. It was now a substantial governmental structure led by Rugova, with his Democratic League of Kosovo; it included not only an education system but also culture, health and social security networks, political parties, financial institutions and a constitution. It was a collective and pacifistic political movement that had the support of 2 million Kosovo Albanians and which successfully brought civil disobedience to a functioning level. And so it was no surprise when the independence referendum in 1992 elicited an overwhelming 'yes' from society. (Aktar 2015)

Of course Serb nationalists were not prepared to recognise this non-violent independence movement; police repression continued to be used against the Albanians. Impatient young men began to feel, as one Kosovo Liberation Army (KLA) soldier interviewed by *Frontline* put it, that 'the so-called pacifist way failed, and finally Albanians were convinced that they had to organize armed resistance ... Under the permanent repression of Serbs, Albanians protested in a civilized way by protests ... conferences, cultural events and [so on], but it was not enough to resist Serb repression. It had to be more than that, which is why KLA had to be born.' Movements critical of Rugova's non-violent approach emerged from around 1996, eventually giving rise to the KLA. It began a guerrilla war targeting Serb security forces, knowing, as KLA leader Hasim Thaçi admitted, that 'any armed action we undertook would bring retaliation against civilians. We knew we were endangering a great number of civilian lives' (Little 2000).

He was right. Serb security forces responded to the guerrilla attacks with indiscriminate massacres of civilians. One of the earliest attacks was in Likosane, in the Drenica region. Chris Hedges (1998) reported on the event:

> The dead, some of the 24 people killed during the weekend in the most brutal sweep to date by the Serbian police and paramilitary units against armed members of the Kosovo Liberation Army, bore the signs of torture and summary execution, the hallmarks of the Serbian forces in Bosnia during the war there. The testimony of the survivors, many of whom were badly beaten, add weight to charges that the Serbian police and paramilitaries in black uniforms went on a rampage after four of their officers were killed over the weekend in two ambushes, lashing out with a blind fury at ethnic Albanians who live in areas where the rebels operate. ... 'I saw most of the bodies,' said Dr. Bajram Gashi, who works at the small village clinic run by the Sisters of Charity, 'and many of them had powder burns suggesting point-blank executions.'

In Prekraz, eleven-year-old Basorta Jashari was the only survivor in an attack that killed all the other members of her family, including her little sisters aged ten, eight and seven (Colvin 1998). Eighty-three people were killed throughout Drenica, most of them civilians (Krieger 2001, 93).

According to Human Rights Watch, 'The police attack in Drenica was a watershed in the Kosovo conflict; thousands of outraged Albanians who had been committed to the non-violent politics of Ibrahim Rugova decided to join the KLA ... there is no question that the brutal and indiscriminate attacks on women and children greatly radicalized the ethnic Albanian population and swelled the ranks of the KLA' (cit. Krieger 2001, 92–93). The massacres of Albanians multiplied, and hundreds of thousands fled. At the same time, Human Rights Watch reported that the KLA also 'committed serious violations of international humanitarian law, including the taking of hostages and extrajudicial executions', leaving 138 Serbs and an unknown number of Albanians and Roma unaccounted for (Krieger 2001, 92).

As the death toll and numbers of displaced Albanians mounted, NATO members, fearing a repeat of the Bosnian genocide, told Milošević that unless he pulled his forces back, they would bomb. Milošević complied, and international monitors moved in to verify implementation of the agreement. Seeing the KLA advance, however, Milošević resumed the war in January 1999. The NATO forces invited the warring parties to peace negotiations at Rambouillet near Paris, where the proposal was that Kosovo would regain the autonomy it enjoyed under the 1974 constitution, and that NATO forces would enforce implementation. At first, Thaçi refused to agree because he wanted full independence for Kosovo, but the threat of being abandoned by NATO finally persuaded him to accept. However, the Serbs refused to agree to the NATO implementation force.

As the fighting resumed, NATO leaders found they had been wrong to believe that the mere threat of force would deter the Serb security forces. International monitors were pulled out as the prospect of bombing loomed, leaving Albanians even more vulnerable when Serb forces attacked them. NATO did carry out bombing raids, but they were largely unsuccessful. It later turned out that prior information about them was being leaked to the Serb forces, allowing them to evacuate the military targets before they were bombed. Meanwhile, on the ground, '[commander of the Yugoslav army in Kosovo] General Pavković's units were in fact organising the biggest programme of forced deportation in Europe since the second world war. It was bound by the sheer force of the image to evoke memories of Nazi Germany ... The reality was stark – the air campaign could not stop this' (Little 2000). When the bombing was extended outside Kosovo, first to military and then to civilian targets, the motivation was as much to preserve the credibility of NATO as to rescue the Albanians, but this led to international condemnation. It was only after a Russian emissary told Milošević that they would not intervene on his side, and persuaded him to accept a joint NATO-Russian peace plan that left Kosovo in Serbia but put it under the administration of the UN Mission in Kosovo (UNMIK), that there was a cessation of hostilities in mid-1999, albeit marred by revenge attacks on Kosovar Serb civilians (Little 2000).

A year later, Richard Falk, a professor of international law, wrote,

> During my recent visit to Kosovo two strong impressions emerged. The first is that the curse of Serbian oppression has been definitively lifted from the majority-Albanian population. The NATO campaign achieved the removal of

Yugoslav military forces from Kosovo and, even more significant, the departure of the dreaded Serbian paramilitary units and police. This should be acknowledged by critics of the US/NATO war strategy, among whom I include myself. ... That is not a vindication of the NATO bombing campaign, but it is a tangible benefit to the Kosovars.

The unexpectedly rapid return of the Kosovar Albanians who had fled Serbian terrorism during the war, and their undisguised gratitude for the NATO intervention, further confirm such an interpretation. ... After decades of abuse, this de facto emergence of an Albanian Kosovo seems a reasonable outcome of the war, bringing relief to 90 percent of the Kosovar population, a result in accordance with the right of self-determination. [...]

The second strong impression I took away from Kosovo is that the UN Security Council has assigned UNMIK a mission impossible: establishing a multi-ethnic Kosovo subject to the sovereignty of Yugoslavia. ... At this point, an overwhelming majority of Kosovars are committed to full independence as a sacred cause. To deny this aspiration is to insure a return to violence in Kosovo. (Falk 2000)

As if to confirm Falk's analysis, the Kosovo parliament unanimously endorsed a declaration of independence at a session on February 17, 2008 which was, however, boycotted by the parliament's ten Serb MPs. The declaration promised to respect the rights of all communities, and despite Serbian and Russian objections, was accepted by several other countries on condition that it was supervised by an international presence. Subsequently, the Serbian government, backed by a majority in the UN General Assembly, appealed to the International Court of Justice on the legality of the declaration. The Court ruled that the declaration was legal, and in 2012 Kosovo moved to full independence: not an ideal outcome, given the human rights record of the new rulers, but probably the best that was possible after the withdrawal of Kosovo's 1974 status and the aggressive campaign of Serbification.

Genocide Denial by Pseudo-anti-imperialists

While pseudo-anti-imperialists easily acknowledged the fascist character of Croatian nationalism, Serb nationalism was measured by a completely different standard. Michel Chossudovsky (1996) claimed, 'It was not President Milošević but NATO that started the war in Yugoslavia,' an assertion that flies in the face of all the evidence. Shortly afterwards, in February 1997, *LM* (formerly *Living Marxism*), edited by Michael Hume, published an article by Thomas Deichmann alleging that Marshall and Williams had fabricated the images in their ITN News report on the camps at Omarska and Trnopolje in order to give the impression that these were concentration camps similar to those in Nazi Germany. ITN sued them for libel and successfully established that their footage was genuine, yet the allegations continued to circulate in pseudo-anti-imperialist circles. In the ensuing debate, Deichmann dismissed the testimony of US Congressman Tom Lantos, himself a Nazi concentration camp survivor, that the Bosnian camps were 'Nazi-style concentration camps, minus the gas chambers' as 'surely a contradiction in terms' (Campbell 2002, 151). According to this logic, as David Campbell (2002, 151) notes, 'the vast majority of the Nazis' concentration camps could not be so easily described, as only *six* were extermination centres with gas facilities'. Apart from their ignorance about Nazi concentration camps, Deichmann and Hume failed to understand that it was in the context of what was happening around them – rape camps for women and the destruction of homes, libraries, museums, mosques, and all evidence that Muslims had ever inhabited Bosnia – that these concentration camps gained their meaning. 'In this respect, the role the Bosnian Serb camps played as part of a systematic targeting of non-Serbian communities as a collectivity they intended to destroy conforms to the international legal understanding of genocide' (Campbell 2002, 157).

According to James Petras, former professor emeritus at Binghamton University, 'Most European and US progressives supported US-backed Bosnian fundamentalists, Croatian neo-fascists and Kosova-Albanian terrorists, leading to ethnic cleansing and the conversion of their once sovereign states into US military bases, client regimes and economic basket cases – totally destroying the multinational Yugoslavian welfare state' (Petras 2009, 117). The grotesque injustice of designating the Bosnian Muslims targeted for extermination as 'fundamentalists' and the Kosovar Albanians being expelled and murdered as 'terrorists', along with his deafening silence on the genocidal ethnic cleansing campaigns by Serb nationalists, makes it very clear where Petras stands. He also alleges that 'the break-up of Yugoslavia was initiated by Germany following its annexation and demolition of East Germany's economy. Subsequently it expanded into the Slovenian and Croatian republics. The US, a relative latecomer in the carving up of the Balkans, targeted Bosnia, Macedonia and Kosova' (Petras 2009, 125). All the evidence, on the contrary, points to a shameful failure of the Western powers to rein in Serb nationalists until they had effectively torn Yugoslavia to shreds.

The foregoing articles are worthy attempts at covering up the Bosnian genocide, but Edward S. Herman, professor emeritus at the University of Pennsylvania, surely takes the prize. In 'The Politics of the Srebrenica Massacre,' published by *ZNet* in 2005, Herman starts by warning that claims of a massacre in Srebrenica were 'extremely helpful to the Clinton administration, the Bosnian Muslim leadership, and the Croatian authorities', and therefore must not be taken at face value. He goes on to dismiss reports of concentration camps for Muslims run by Serb nationalists as 'propaganda lies', using arguments similar to those of *LM*, but goes even further than *LM* in accusing *Muslims* of 'the ruthless bombing of Sarajevo civilians in three massacres: in 1992 (the "Breadline Massacre"), 1994 (the Markale "Market Massacre") and a "Second Market Massacre" in 1995'. He follows up by questioning the numbers killed at Srebrenica and the claim that the men and boys were civilians, even while admitting that Bosnian Muslim soldiers had already left Srebrenica (he doesn't mention the fact that it was supposedly under the protection of UNPROFOR). He alleges one-sidedness and bias of the International Criminal Tribunal for the Former Yugoslavia (ICTY) in concentrating on Serb perpetrators, despite the fact that it also indicted Croat and Muslim war criminals. He concludes by saying, 'The "Srebrenica massacre" is the greatest triumph of propaganda to emerge from the Balkan wars ... But the link of this propaganda triumph to truth and justice is non-existent' (Herman 2005).

Herman seems unable to comprehend that extraction of false confessions under torture, monopolisation of the media, and the killing of Serb dissidents might have been potent means by which Serb nationalists manufactured consent for their policies. Julie Wornan (2005) analysed his method:

> Herman likes to put forth a highly questionable statement and then tell us that nobody else is talking about it. For example, 'even though only rarely discussed there is a major issue of how many were executed...' ... Z-Mag readers are sensitive to media bias, and so Herman imagines that they will swallow anything he cares to serve up, if he can say that the media are ignoring it. You can use this method to plant the idea that the moon is made of pineapple pudding: just say 'this question is rarely discussed...' ... This sort of pseudo-reasoning takes a particularly macabre turn when Herman turns his attention to the Bosnian Muslims: 'A remarkable feature of the Bosnian Muslim struggle to demonize the Serbs, in order to get NATO to come to Bosnian Muslim aid with bombs, was their willingness to kill their own people...' Of course it is 'not easy' to believe that the Bosnian Muslims would kill their own people – those allegations

are simply preposterous. But Herman would have us think that because such a grotesque accusation is 'not easy to believe', we must believe it.

Times journalist Oliver Kamm argues that such denials of the Bosnian genocide use many of the same techniques as Holocaust denial: 'Jewish campaigners immediately recognised in 1992 what was happening in the former Yugoslavia and appealed to the conscience of the world. Bosnia was no intractable civil war: it was a campaign of genocidal aggression launched by the Serb leader, Slobodan Milošević. Nobel Laureate and Holocaust survivor Elie Wiesel interrupted his own speech at the opening of the Holocaust Museum in Washington to implore President Clinton to protect Bosnian civilians. Tragically, it wasn't enough. The least we can do is ensure that the victims' stories are told' (Kamm 2015). Among the genocide deniers Kamm lists are right-wing extremists Robert Spencer and Pamela Geller (who alleged Obama is a 'muhammadan' who wants 'jihad to win' among other claims [Southern Poverty Law Center n.d.]); right next to them comes Herman.

Although less extreme than outright support for Serb nationalism, calling for 'working class opposition to all the main nationalist leaderships,' including the Bosnian leadership (Blackie 1995), was not a principled anti-imperialist position, because it allowed the genocide, ethnic cleansing and annexation of the victims' land to continue unchallenged; it is equivalent to calling for working-class opposition to the Palestinian Authority, Hamas and the Israeli state when Gaza is being bombed, Palestinians are progressively being driven out of their land, and the land is being annexed by the Israeli state. We can certainly criticise Islamists in Bosnia and Palestine, but that should not preclude recognising the imperialist character of the land grab by Serb nationalists and the Israeli state.

In a review of several books that touch upon the disintegration of Yugoslavia by people he calls 'left revisionists', Marko Attila Hoare exposes how the authors cite Western imperialist and Serb nationalist sources, use each other as sources, censor contrary evidence, are ignorant of Yugoslav history, support Hitler's policy of partition of Kosovo while opposing Tito's policy, and use double standards, half-truths and outright lies. He concludes his review, tellingly titled 'Nothing is Left', by saying, 'This, then is the face of the Western far left — with a few honourable exceptions — in the twenty-first century: intellectually superficial; morally bankrupt; callous about the suffering of foreign peoples; and cynical and hypocritical in its use of both facts and arguments' (Hoare 2003). This may be an exaggeration, but the problem he identifies is real.

The desire to condemn the West cannot explain the way in which pseudo-anti-imperialists acknowledge atrocities by Croats but only against Serbs, and refuse to acknowledge either atrocities by Serbs against Croats or the genocide of Bosnian Muslims: all the sources quoted above, who have stood firmly with victims belonging to all ethnicities, have been scathingly critical of Western leaders. What makes the reaction of the deniers even harder to explain is the fact that all three categories that they discriminate between so sharply are Slavs, and all were citizens of the Socialist Republic of Yugoslavia. Anti-Muslim bigotry, expressed in sweeping assumptions that all Muslims in Bosnia and Kosovo are 'fundamentalists' and 'terrorists', seems to be one of the reasons; the abhorrent doctrine of collective guilt, used to such devastating effect by the Nazis, also comes into play when characterising all Muslims as terrorists, and all Croats as fascists. Another motive for taking the side of Serb nationalists against their Muslim victims appears to be uncritical support for anyone supported by Russian imperialism. This is the first time in the post-Soviet world that such a clear convergence between neo-Stalinism and neo-fascism is discernible. If we specify that 'neo-fascism' refers to any variety of extreme right-wing ethnoreligious nationalism, and if 'neo-Stalinists' continue their uncritical support for Russian nationalism – regardless of the fact that it has by this stage abandoned all pretence of having anything to do with Marx or Lenin and openly flaunts its extreme right-wing Christoslavism à la Zhirinovsky – then this would account for the fact that Pamela Geller and Edward Herman are bedfellows on the issue of the Bosnian genocide.

4. Iran

Iranian Stalinists supported Khomeini because of his anti-imperialist rhetoric; but, having consolidated his power with their support, his regime proceeded to slaughter them, along with all dissidents. Since then, pseudo-anti-imperialists' support for the Islamic state of Iran goes well beyond objecting to threats of military attacks on Iran or to sanctions against the country which hurt ordinary citizens, which should certainly be condemned. In many cases it extends to implicit support for everything the regime does, including its attempts to export its right-wing jihadi project. The rationale is simple: Iran is opposed to the US, therefore supporting the theocratic regime constitutes 'anti-imperialism'. However, this position denies international solidarity to Iranians opposing Iranian imperialism and struggling for democratic rights and freedoms.

From Democratic Revolution to Islamist Counterrevolution

There is almost universal agreement on referring to the upheaval that resulted in the overthrow of Shah (King) Mohammad Reza Pahlavi in 1979 as an 'Islamic revolution', but in fact it was nothing of the sort. On September 4, 1978,

> several hundred thousand people demonstrated in Tehran at the end of the Muslim month of Ramadan. This was a peaceful demonstration in which the crowds, many of them women, appealed to the armed forces not to oppose them. Some called for the restoration of the constitution, and some for a republic. [...]
>
> A ban on further marches was then imposed, but on 7 September, the following Thursday, a similar demonstration took place in which an estimated

300,000 people took part. They defied the *mollahs'* appeals to stay at home and marched through central Tehran from morning to night. Again, appeals were made to the army. This proved too much for the régime, and on the morning of Friday, 8 September, martial law was declared in Tehran and eleven other cities. Troops clashed with demonstrators in Tehran's Jaleh Square, and … up to three thousand people were killed. (Halliday 1979, 292)[1]

The bulk of the demonstrators consisted of 'the urban poor, the people who had come to the cities and had experienced the rough face of the oil boom, enduring food shortages and inflation and paying up to 70 per cent of their income on rent … They were joined in their protests by the merchants of the bazaar, who were traditionally close to the mosque and who had felt their position threatened by the pattern of capitalist development in Iran' (Halliday 1979, 298). Oil workers, critical to the Iranian economy and foreign exchange earnings, went on strike in October; their demands included ending martial law, the release of political prisoners, and nationalisation of the oil industry (Bayat 1987, 60–81).

At the forefront of the uprising were writers, lawyers and opposition politicians demanding the restoration of civil and constitutional liberties. Among these was the new avatar of Mossadegh's National Front, which in August 1978 issued a twelve-point programme that included a demand for the dissolution of SAVAK (the dreaded secret police), the release of political prisoners, the right of political exiles to return, and the rights to freedom of expression and to form trade unions (Halliday 1979, 296). The religious leaders were split between those like Ayatollah Ruhollah Khomeini, who advocated an Islamic state, and liberals like Ayatollah Mohammad Kazem Shariatmadari, who had saved Khomeini's life by designating him a 'marja' (source of emulation) when the shah was about to execute him in 1963 (the constitution did not allow the execution of marjas), but who now demanded a return to constitutional rule.

Some sections of the left, which had faced extreme repression, also began to resurface. The Moscow-linked Tudeh (Masses) Party[2] and two guerrilla organisations – the People's Mujahedin (Mojahedin-e Khalq), an Islamic Marxist group, and People's Fedayeen (Fedayeen-e Khalq), inspired by Mao and Guevara – distributed their literature in the demonstrations (Halliday 1979, 236–38; 297). In addition to these and many smaller groups, including Trotskyists and anarchists, was the Unity of Communist Militants (UCM), formed in 1978 and led by Mansoor Hekmat, who criticised all of them for populism and nationalism, believed that state capitalism prevailed in the Soviet Union, and wished to go back to the theory and politics of Marx and Lenin (Hekmat 1987).[3]

This widely disparate coalition, united only by their opposition to the shah, disintegrated as soon as his regime started tottering. Most damagingly, not only did left groups compete with each other and liberal nationalists compete on the basis of personal rivalries, but the Tudeh Party aligned itself with Khomeini against the liberal democrats. A majority faction of the Fedayeen did likewise, while a minority faction, as well as the Mujahedin and smaller left groups, opposed the Islamists.

Why did the Moscow-affiliated Tudeh Party support an Islamist theocrat and oppose liberal democrats? Maziar Behrooz (1999, 137) explains that 'to some, like the Tudeh and the Fadaiyan Majority, the fact that the [Islamic Republic of Iran] was politically independent and that it (particularly its clerical wing) was often hostile to Western governments, political systems and cultural values, meant that the new state was anti-imperialist and able to pursue a course which might ultimately bring it into the Soviet camp'. They were not deterred by the fact that the theocracy's definition of 'anti-imperialism' simply meant support for an Islamic Iran, and included a commitment to stamp out socialism and Marxism. Support for the Islamic government by some Marxist groups, even after it had turned on the left with a programme of systematic repression, continued up until 1987. As Ali Rahnema and Farhad Nomani (1990, 5) argue, 'The left's support facilitated the régime's campaign against democratic rights and freedoms at home. The left's lack of theoretical analysis not only played into the hands of the clerical leadership, but provided it with a breathing space to prepare for the eventual liquidation of the left itself'.

In late December 1978, with strikes and street protests paralysing the country, the shah invited Shapour Bakhtiar to form a government. Bakhtiar had held the post of deputy labour minister in the Mossadegh government until it was ousted by the coup, and he spent almost six of the following twenty-five years in jail for activities such as printing anti-regime publications, supporting opposition candidates in elections, and campaigning for secularism and democracy as a member of Mossadegh's Iran Party and the National Front, of which it was a part. In June 1977, along with fellow National Front leaders Karim Sanjabi and Dariush Forouhar, Bakhtiar released an open letter to the shah demanding an end to despotism and the restoration of rights as mandated by

Iran's constitution and the Universal Declaration of Human Rights, and this was one of the sparks that ignited the revolution. However, he advocated keeping the shah as nominal head of state until a plebiscite had been held on what form the new government should take, leaving open the possibility of a constitutional monarchy. In 1978, he strongly opposed moves to align with Khomeini, at that time in exile near Paris; he is reported to have said that from the cracking of the clergy's sandals, he heard the sounds of fascism (Geist 2011).

Bakhtiar accepted the shah's invitation, on condition that he leave the country, and was sworn into office on January 6, 1979. He proceeded to oust the martial law governor of Tehran, lay the groundwork for prosecuting high officials close to the shah, begin to dismantle SAVAK, order the release of all political prisoners, end press censorship, reopen universities, exile the shah, and announce plans to hold elections for a constituent assembly. However, on February 1, he made the mistake of allowing Khomeini to return. Upon his return, Khomeini denounced Bakhtiar's government, warning, 'Do not provoke me to invite people to stage a jihad,' and declared his own government instead, establishing Mehdi Bazargan, a pro-democracy nationalist, as prime minister. Around the same time, clergy close to Khomeini formed the Islamic Republican Party (IRP). Bakhtiar went into hiding when his government collapsed on February 11 and later escaped to France. On March 30 and 31, Iranians voted in a referendum in which the only choice was 'yes' or 'no' to an Islamic state, implying that those who voted 'no' wished to retain a monarchy; with those who objected to both options boycotting the poll, the vote was overwhelmingly in favour. In May, Khomeini charged Bakhtiar with treason and he was sentenced to death. In 1980, Bakhtiar founded the National Movement of Iranian Resistance, and his followers in Iran staged an uprising that was crushed. In 1991, he became one of a large number of dissidents assassinated abroad by VEVAK, the secret police of the Islamic Republic (Geist 2011).

Hassan Habibi, a minister in the provisional government headed by Bazargan, prepared a draft constitution that drew on Iran's 1906 secular constitution (with the monarch replaced by a president) and Charles de Gaulle's 1958 French constitution. The government advocated a popularly elected constitutional assembly to complete the drafting and to finalise the constitution. Khomeini disagreed, instead calling on people to vote for an Assembly of Experts from a list heavily dominated by the clergy. This much-smaller body proceeded to redraft the constitution in accordance with the blueprint that Khomeini had been developing since the 1940s: an Islamic state where sovereignty belongs to God and not to the people; whose source of legitimacy is Islam, not the will of the people; and in which, since the government is to implement Islamic law, experts on Islamic law should rule (Hunter 2014, 108–11). Much of the original draft was, however, also retained.

Thus in the constitution finalised by the Assembly of Experts, supreme authority is vested in a just and pious jurist (*velayat-e faqih*), the first of whom is named as Khomeini (Iran Constitution, Preamble, Article 107). His duties and powers include appointing jurists to the Guardian Council; the chief judges; the joint chief of staff and commanders of the army, navy and air force; the commander of the Sepah-e Pasdaran-e Enqelab-e Islami (Islamic Revolutionary Guard Corps or IRGC); and the head of the radio and television network; and dismissing a president (Article 110). An elected president has a great deal of power, subordinate only to the supreme leader (Article 6). The constitution also allows for elections to the Islamic Consultative Assembly by secret ballot (Article 62) and to the Assembly of Experts, which selects a new supreme leader when the old one dies; but nominations to all elected posts are subject to the approval of the (unelected) Guardian Council (Article 99). There are also elements of what might be called socialism, such as the right to social security and welfare (Article 43), and state ownership of large-scale industry, foreign trade, major minerals, banking, insurance, power generation, dams and large-scale irrigation networks, radio and television, postal, telegraph and telephone services, aviation, shipping, roads, and railways (Article 44). The constitution is therefore a curious hybrid of republican democracy and theocracy, with theocracy in a dominant position and absolute power vested in the supreme leader. It was adopted by a referendum on December 2 and 3, 1979, which was boycotted by secularists, including the Mujahedin, who objected to the notion of velayat-e faqih.

The IRGC, which was established by Khomeini on December 4, but which had already existed in a less formal sense, played a crucial role as both a military force and a police force 'guarding the revolution' against internal and external enemies. On March 19, 1980, its official organ, Payam-e Enghelab, described its duties as 'cooperation with the government in military and security matters', while on July 25, 1981 it 'defined the two main tasks of the Guards' as 'guarding the principle of government of the supreme jurist and the principle of jihad' (Alfoneh 2008). In practice, this meant suppressing internal dissent: 'Khomeini actively employed the Revolutionary Guards to coerce and, when necessary, crush former political allies as he consolidated power within the revolution's broad coalition' (Alfoneh 2008). The Basij Force, a paramilitary force under the guidance of the IRGC, was also seen by IRGC chief Mohsen Rezai as having the duty not only of providing 'security and protection' but also of 'challenging counterrevolutionary forces' (Alfoneh 2008). After the end of the Iran-Iraq war in 1988, the IRGC gradually established a stranglehold on the Iranian economy, dominating the construction sector and large infrastructure projects, military production, personal computers, scanners, telephones and mobile phones, the oil and gas sector, telecommunications, and the import-export sector, including Iran's vast underground economy, smuggling billions of dollars' worth of goods per annum through the airports and 'invisible jetties' it controls (Alfoneh 2007). In addition, 'all of its finances stay off the budget, free from any state oversight or need to provide an accounting to Parliament' (Slackman 2009).

Assisting the IRGC and Basij to crack down on dissidents and demonstrators were the club-and-chain-wielding Hezbollahis, members of the Hezbollah (Party of God) with their distinctive chant: 'Only one party – of allah! Only one leader – Ruhollah!' 'Later, this shadowy organisation was found to have surreptitious links with the Islamic Republican Party. It was to play an important role in the street in crucial moments in the history of the revolution' (Hiro 1985, 113). Moojan Momen explains that 'Hezbollah' was only a new name for the street thugs (*lutis*) who had always had a close relationship with the religious scholars (*ulema*), listing among the other protagonists of the Islamist takeover the radical ulema controlling most of the mosques, the revolutionary committees, and the Islamic societies dominating many universities, factories and offices (Momen 1985, 293). From the mid-1990s, Ansar-e Hezbollah, an offshoot of the Basij, played a similar role.

On November 4, 1979, students stormed the US embassy in Tehran and took more than sixty Americans hostage after Carter allowed the exiled shah (who died shortly afterwards) to enter the US for cancer treatment. An interview with Seyed Muhammad Hashemi, one of the students involved in the hostage-taking operation, indicates that both left-wing and Islamist students took part (Hunter 2014, 104–5). Bazargan's inability to end the crisis – which was impossible once Khomeini decided it should continue – was used as a pretext to force him and his cabinet to resign.

Bazargan's government was not the only one to fall as a result of the hostage crisis. Carter's campaign for reelection in 1980 suffered irreparably from his failure to free the hostages, who were held for 444 days and released only on the day Ronald Reagan was inaugurated in January 1981. There is strong evidence from both US and Iranian sources that the Reagan campaign negotiated a deal with Khomeini to hold the hostages until he was in power (Ruiz-Marrero 2014). Moreover, 'Israel's Likud government of Menachem Begin moved quickly to reestablish secret ties with the "rogue" regime of Ayatollah Ruhollah Khomeini and became an important source for covert arms supplies to Iran after Iraq invaded Iran in September 1980' (Parry 2015). Assistant Secretary of State for the Middle East Nicholas Veliotes discovered that the arms originated in the US, the shipments to Iran via Israel began before the election in which Reagan came to power, and the operation was organised by neoconservatives Robert McFarlane and Paul Wolfowitz, who were to become part of Reagan's administration. Israel earned tens of billions of dollars from these transactions, with some of the profits going to fund Jewish settlements in occupied Palestine (Parry 2015). The Iran-Contra affair, in which the Reagan administration sold arms to the Islamic Republic in return for money to support the Contras in Nicaragua, was a continuation of this collaboration.

These examples of the Iranian regime's collusion with Reagan and Israel suggest that its opposition to Israel constitutes neither anti-imperialism nor support for the Palestinians, but is simply part of a struggle for regional dominance. As Oded Yinon's article, 'A Strategy for Israel in the Nineteen Eighties' (1982) argued, 'Iraq, rich in oil on the one hand and internally torn on the other, *is guaranteed as a candidate for Israel's targets* ... In the short run it is Iraqi power which constitutes the greatest threat to Israel. An Iraqi-Iranian war will tear Iraq apart and cause its downfall at home even before it is able to organize a struggle on a wide front against us.' The destruction of Saddam Hussein's regime, which guaranteed the unity of Iraq, was as much the goal of the Islamic state in Iran as of Menachem Begin and Yitzhak Shamir, so Khomeini had no compunctions about sacrificing the Palestinians and Sandinistas to the Israeli state and US imperialism.[4]

The fate of Mohammad Kazem Shariatmadari, who represented a strong but non-violent opposition to Khomeini, was tragic. When in February 1979 Khomeini described opposition to the provisional Islamic government as apostasy – which made it punishable by death – Shariatmadari countered by arguing that peaceful criticism or opposition should not be punished. During discussions on the constitution, he opposed the inclusion of the velayat-e faqih, arguing that it was contentious in Islam, and the Muslim People's Republican Party (MPRP) associated with him boycotted the elections to the Assembly of Experts tasked with finalising the constitution (Hiro 1985, 118–19). As pressure on him increased, his supporters demonstrated in Tabriz, Tehran and elsewhere, but their protests were crushed by the IRGC. He was put under house arrest, all of his communications were cut off, and in May 1982, he and his family members were tortured and blackmailed into making 'confessions' that they had been involved in a plot to carry out a coup against Khomeini – confessions that were later revealed to have been false (IHRI 2011). When Shariatmadari was diagnosed with cancer, Khomeini refused his doctors' request to allow him to be taken to the West for treatment – a request usually granted as a matter of course. 'In Shariatmadari's final, agonizing days, visitors were not allowed to pay their respects. And Khomeini's vendetta continued even after his rival died. His body was spirited out the back door ... and the regime permitted none of the funeral ceremony befitting the death of an eminent spiritual leader' (Anderson 1986).

In January 1980 Abulhassan Bani-Sadr, an independent who had been in Bazargan's cabinet but also helped to undermine him, was elected president, yet by June he was already facing attempts by the Islamic Republican Party (IRP) to reduce him to a figurehead without any real power. Parliamentary elections in March and May 1980, in which many secular candidates were disqualified by the Guardian Council, predictably returned an IRP-dominated Majlis (parliament), which designated Mohammad Ali Rajai as prime minister. In the ensuing struggle between Bani-Sadr and the IRP for control over state institutions, Bani-Sadr was defeated time after time. Cyrus Kadivar (2002) describes the situation:

> [Khomeini had] ordered Sadeq Khalkhali, a middle-ranking mullah, to execute the enemies of the revolution ... Iran's prisons overflowed with thousands of 'counterrevolutionaries' many unaware of the charges levied at them ... Prisoners fought each other for space and toilet facilities. That spring the International Red Cross was forbidden to visit or aid the prisoners. 'All these people should have been killed from the first instead of crowding the jails,' Khomeini declared. Khalkhali ... defended an Islamic judge who had brought back a horrible mediaeval form of killing: the judge had ordered that four sex offenders, two men and two women, be buried up to the neck and stoned to death. Drug addicts, homosexuals and prostitutes were also dispatched mercilessly ... President Bani Sadr charged that torture and rapes were taking place in Iranian prisons and that individuals were executed 'as easily as one takes a drink of

water' ... In June 1981 Khomeini impeached Bani Sadr who fled to Paris along with Masud Rajavi, the leader of the Mujaheddin Khalq.

What followed was qualitatively different from what had gone before. In an interview, Mansoor Hekmat (2000) gave a detailed account:

The two and a half years during 11 February 1979 ... and 20 June 1981 ... was still not strictly speaking, however, an Islamic rule. It was a period of relative open political activity, which the state was incapable of suppressing on a widespread scale, despite the existence of thugs and Islamicism. At that time, Khalkhali ... was the regime's executioner but even so, the regime did not have the power to completely suppress and neutralise the increasing people's movement. Political parties were flourishing; books of Marx and Lenin were sold everywhere; Communist organisations published papers; labour councils were established; various women's organisations were formed and the wave of protests continued to escalate, until an Islamic, counter-revolutionary coup d'état took place on 20 June 1981 ... They attacked and executed 300 to 500 people a day in Evin prison and all over the country; they closed down newspapers and crushed the opposition. This was what enabled the Islamic Republic to exist today. The point of the Islamic Republic's establishment was 20 June 1981 ... not 11 February 1979 ... 11 February ... was the people's revolution. [...]

The Islamic government's execution list was basically taken from the list of those who had been imprisoned during the Monarchy. A person who had been sentenced to two-month's imprisonment by the Shah's government was executed by the Islamic regime. They attacked and killed the very same people the Shah's regime wanted to but couldn't.

[...] They poured onto the streets and arrested anyone who did not look like a Muslim ... They arrested anyone who had recited a poem, who was known to be a Socialist or supporter of women's rights, anyone who was not veiled and anyone who looked Left wing and executed them that same night. Statistics, documents and witnesses proving these atrocities are ample. [...]

This was one of the greatest crimes of the 20th Century ... They attacked, suppressed, killed and buried in unmarked graves, innumerable people. They massacred many of the best, the most passionate and progressive people in order to remain in power.

Initially, the Tudeh Party was protected by its collaboration with the regime, but in February 1983 the government arrested Tudeh leader Nureddin Kianuri, along with other members of the party Central Committee, and over a thousand party members. 'Many of the rank-and-file were put to death. ... By the summer of 1988 ... the ailing Khomeini still found enough strength to order the wholesale massacre of an estimated 6,000 to 10,000 political prisoners including pregnant women and teenagers which continued until the autumn. Khomeini's death made no difference to the state of human rights in Iran' (Kadivar 2002).

If what happened on February 11, 1979 was a 'people's revolution' or a democratic revolution, how do we characterise what happened on and after June 20, 1981?

The Nature of the Iranian State

Extermination of all political opposition was an essential characteristic of the Islamic Republic. Mohammad Sahimi (2009), whose young brother was executed by the regime, writes of the forced 'confessions' extracted from prisoners and the terrible ill treatment and casual executions in prisons. These shocked Ayatollah Hossein Ali Montazeri, who was deputy to Khomeini and slated to succeed him. He told Khomeini that the crimes taking place in the jails of the IRI were even worse than those in the shah's jails, with many prisoners going blind or deaf or dying due to torture, or executed for trivial reasons, young women sexually abused and raped, and all prisoners, male and female, beaten regularly. In 1985, Montazeri took charge of prisons and began by ceasing the execution of female prisoners not directly involved in killings. Other improvements included

> sharp reduction in executions; release of many prisoners; general improvement of prison conditions (recreation, availability of books, family visits), and reduction in solitary confinement; lessening of torture as a form of punishment; abolition of compulsory ideological classes. A positive change in the condition of prisons throughout Iran had begun to take shape. More than a few ex-political prisoners have suggested that their lives were saved after Montazeri took over. (Behrooz 2005)

In 1988, Montazeri lost control over the prisons, and terror returned in full force: there is evidence that 'Khomeini had ordered the formation of a secret commission to look into the execution of the MKO [Mojahedin-e Khalq, or People's Mujahedin of Iran] prisoners, as well as secular leftists, and had secretly authorized their execution' (Sahimi 2009). Of the thousands executed in the bloodbath that followed, 'many had actually finished their sentences. Many were college or even high school students. Almost none had committed a serious offense' (Sahimi 2009). When Montazeri criticised what was happening, Khomeini made him 'resign' from his position, reportedly expressing a preference that Ali Khamenei, who was currently serving as president, should be his heir.

Even the fig leaf of a judicial process was abandoned in what came to be known as the 'chain murders' of dissidents between 1980 and 1998. Some were killed in Iran, but even those fleeing abroad could not escape. In a pattern reminiscent of Stalin's relentless extermination of dissidents, many of the victims (including Bakhtiar) were killed in countries as diverse as France, Austria, the United States, Germany, Cyprus, Switzerland, Turkey, Sweden, Iraq and Pakistan. They included members of the political opposition as well as Christians, Sunnis, and intellectuals like teachers, doctors, Islamic scholars, artists, poets, journalists and novelists critical of the regime; some were tortured and mutilated, as in the case of Fereydoun Farrokhzad, a popular Iranian singer, who had his tongue cut off and was beheaded (Sahimi 2011). The best-known case was the murder of a Kurdish leader and three colleagues in a terrorist attack at the Mykonos Greek restaurant in Berlin in 1992. The subsequent trial found that the killings had been ordered by the highest levels of the IRI leadership (Cowell 1997).

Oppression of Ethnoreligious Minorities

Enemies of the regime who had to be subdued included ethnic minorities like the Kurds, Baluchis, Arabs and Turkomans, who together add up to almost half of the Iranian population. The Kurdish Democratic Party (KDP) participated actively in the revolution to overthrow the Shah; it demanded the right to form a regional Kurdish government with control over internal matters, and that Kurdish should be recognised as an official language. Similarly, the Arabs in Khuzestan (where much of Iran's oil is located) demanded regional autonomy, a greater share of oil revenue, priority for Arabs in local jobs, and the teaching of Arabic as a first language (Hiro 1985, 111–13). Both movements were crushed militarily, and the KDP was banned; as Khomeini claimed, 'there is no difference between the nationalities' in Iran (Economic and Political Weekly 1979), and hence no need to recognise the languages used by minorities. Discrimination against and persecution of ethnic minorities, especially Kurds, persisted, such as large-scale expropriation of land, forced resettlement under very poor conditions, and a higher rate of incarceration, sadistic torture, and execution – including the execution of minors – in many cases simply for the crime of being Kurdish (Panah 2015). The repression spawned an armed struggle by the Free Life Party of

Kurdistan (PJAC), an offshoot of the Kurdistan Workers' Party (PKK) of Turkey (Pironti 2014).

The Iranian Constitution decrees that Zoroastrians, Jews and Christians 'are the only recognized religious minorities, who, within the limits of the law, are free to perform their religious rites and ceremonies' (Article 13), and they are entitled to elect their own representatives to the Consultative Assembly (Article 64). The same consideration is not extended to the Baha'i. An investigation into Setad, a state-owned enterprise worth an estimated $95 billion, reveals a pattern of systematic expropriation of Baha'is. Figures compiled by the United Nations office of the Baha'i International Community indicate that in 2003 Setad had confiscated seventy-three properties from its members, a 'figure captur[ing] only a fraction of the Baha'i properties taken by Setad' (Stecklow et al. 2013). *Reuters* journalists Steve Stecklow et al. (2013) report the story of one of the victims, Vahdat-e-Hagh, whose husband was arrested in 1981 after taking up a job with a company that helped unemployed Baha'i. 'According to Vahdat-e-Hagh, after five months, a cleric from the court sentenced him to death, with no chance to appeal. He was executed in 1982' (Stecklow et al. 2013). When Vahdat-e-Hagh protested, she was jailed for three months; after her release, Setad seized all her property and her children's property, forcing her to relocate abroad. Thirty years later, the government's position appears to have changed little, with Khamenei issuing an edict in July 2013 encouraging Iranians to avoid all dealings with Baha'is. 'An Iranian lawyer who represented more than half a dozen Baha'i clients in recent cases involving confiscated property says he was called in for questioning by intelligence agents last year and threatened. The lawyer, who is Muslim and spoke on condition he not be named, told *Reuters* he had to stop accepting Baha'i clients' (Stecklow et al. 2013).

Oppression of Women

After 1979, Leila Mouri (2012) argues, 'Iranian women covered by black chadors became the visual symbol of not only the Islamic government but also as a representation of the ideal type of Iranian wom[a]n.' This was accomplished due to a successful government project of 'disseminating distorted images of Iranian women's lifestyles by denying the existence of many others who did not wear chadors or believe in hijab. This state representation has been highly effective. Even today, the chador and hijab are the most common markers of Iranian women broadcast in both Western media and Iran's state-run television' (Mouri 2012). During the revolution against the shah, whose father had banned the veil in 1936, many women chose to wear the veil (including the tent-like black *chador*) as a symbol of protest against the Pahlavi regime. However, when on March 7, 1979 Khomeini made wearing the chador mandatory, the celebrations planned for International Women's Day morphed into huge demonstrations against the policy, with the same women launching massive protests against it (Afary 2009, 270–73). Khomeini, recognising that women had played a major part in the revolution against the shah, beat a tactical retreat, saying that the black chador was desirable but not compulsory; however, wearing at least a loose manteau (overcoat) and scarf covering all of a woman's hair not only remained mandatory, but was enforced by punishments like flogging, fines and imprisonment. One reason that protests against the compulsory hijab fizzled out was that socialists abandoned them, believing they could benefit the imperialists (Hoodfar 1999, 24–25), but left-wing women who formed the National Union of Women later regretted not having spoken out more forcefully against the reversals in women's rights (Afary 2009, 250). Khomeini made it clear, especially after the start of the Iran-Iraq war, that the main role of women was to produce sons who could fight for the IRI.

Compulsory hijab is only the tip of the iceberg of sharia laws discriminating against women. Women are supposed to be subordinate to men and can legally be beaten if they are not obedient; blood money for a woman is half that for a man, a woman's testimony is worth half that of a man, and a daughter inherits only half as much as a son; while both men and women can be stoned for sex outside marriage, stoning of women and girls is more common; girls can be married off by their fathers from the age of nine, and a woman cannot marry without her father's permission; women cannot get education or employment, leave the country, or even get a passport without the consent of their husbands or natural guardians; women can have only one marriage at a time whereas men can have an unlimited number under the provision for temporary marriages and can initiate divorce unilaterally; a woman has to be sexually available to her husband at all times; women are barred from many posts, including that of judges. Dissident women were attacked with knives and acid by Hezbollah goons, incarcerated, tortured, raped and executed (Afary 2009, 276–81; Rafizadeh 2014).

Jihadi Imperialist Counterrevolution

The preamble to Iran's constitution sets out an Islamic imperialist vision:

> With due attention to the Islamic content of the Iranian Revolution, the Constitution provides the necessary basis for ensuring the continuation of the Revolution at home and abroad ... In the formation and equipping of the country's defence forces, due attention must be paid to faith and ideology as the basic criteria. Accordingly, the Army of the Islamic Republic of Iran and the Islamic Revolutionary Guards Corps are to be organized in conformity with this goal, and they will be responsible not only for guarding and preserving the frontiers of the country, but also for fulfilling the ideological mission of jihad in God's way; that is, extending the sovereignty of God's law throughout the world. (Iran Constitution)

In other words, the IRI is engaged in a jihad to establish Khomeini's interpretation of Islam throughout the world. The Quds Force of the Iranian Revolutionary Guard Corps (IRGC) is specifically entrusted with this task.

The Israeli invasion of Lebanon on June 3, 1982, when Lebanese Islamist dignitaries were attending a conference in Tehran, provided an occasion for the IRI to send a delegation to Syria to discuss the possibility of offering support to the Lebanese. Syria allowed the IRGC troops to cross its territory on their way to Lebanon, while nine Islamist movement leaders met to form what would become the foundations for Hezbollah. The 'Iranian Islamic revolution in 1979 no doubt had a great and direct effect on the formulation of the party's ideologies, as well as providing it with academic and jihadist inspiration' (Harfoush 2013).

The Iran-Iraq war offered another opportunity. 'By June 1982, Iranian forces had pushed back Iraq's forces from almost all of Iran's occupied territories. When Khorramshahr, Iran's most important seaport on the Persian Gulf, was liberated, there were celebrations all over Iran. The war should have ended then. Saddam was ready to accept a ceasefire' (Sahimi 2009). Instead, Khomeini decided to invade Iraq, despite strong domestic opposition from many groups, including the Revolutionary Movement of the Iranian People (JAMA) led by Dr Kazem Sami Kermani, who was later hacked to death in his clinic (Sahimi 2011). When the first Iranian incursion into Iraq was repulsed in the summer of 1982 with heavy casualties, even the military leadership, supported by President Ali Khamenei, Prime Minister Mir Hossein Mousavi and Foreign Minister Ali Akbar Velayati, opposed the invasion; but a powerful hardline group, including mullahs on the Supreme Defence

Council headed by Ali Akbar Hashemi-Rafsanjani, insisted on continuing the invasion and were supported by Khomeini (Karsh 2002, 38–39). The war dragged on for six years longer, leading to hundreds of thousands more deaths; boys as young as twelve were brainwashed into joining the Basij and were used as 'little more than cannon fodder or human minesweepers sent in advance of Iran's other military forces' (Karsh 2002, 62).

More recently, in January 2015, Hojatoleslam Ali Shirazi, Khamenei's representative to the IRGC Quds Force, said, 'Hezbollah was formed in Lebanon as a popular force like Basij (Iran's militia). Similarly popular forces were also formed in Syria and Iraq, and today we are watching the formation of the Ansarollah in Yemen', the Ansarollah (God's Partisans) being the Houthi Shi'i rebels whose political slogans, 'Death to America, Death to Israel', are modelled on those of Iran. Ali Akbar Nategh-Nouri, head of the Office of Inspection of the House of the Supreme Leader, confirmed that 'we witness today that our revolution is exported to Yemen, Syria, Lebanon and Iraq' (ShahidSaless 2015).

Iranian Islamism

What is the ideology in the name of which all this has been done? Like all fundamentalists, Khomeini and his supporters seized upon the most regressive elements of their religion – those that support extreme patriarchy and legitimise inhuman punishments like flogging, amputations, public hanging and stoning – while ignoring 'the spirit of social justice and the revolutionary role Islam can play in redistribution of wealth' (Engineer 1981, 1093). However, there is not just selection, but also innovation. Mohammad Kazem Shariatmadari, who took the orthodox Twelver Shia position that the political supremacy of the clergy was invalid, had to be crushed.[5] Indeed, Islamic law was grossly violated by the regime; for example, 'a man who was certified as an imbecile by the judicial authorities was executed (Islamic law does not permit this); a man complained that his wife had been executed on charges of adultery although he never suspected her of any such misconduct (Islamic law demands that a husband must have been the litigant) ... The Islamic Guards, in many cases, are known to blackmail people and demand bribes for letting them go. There is rampant corruption' (Engineer 1981, 1091). Montazeri, who had been a full supporter of the IRI, was sidelined because his advocacy of justice and humanity in the prison system did not allow for the arbitrary exercise of power. Thus, the ideology of the state in Iran is a version of fundamentalist political Islam that legitimises the absolute power of one man and his close associates, and the unrestricted use of whatever cruelty and violence is required for this purpose.

It is apparent from all this that what happened on and after June 20, 1981 was an extreme right-wing counterrevolution that established a totalitarian Islamic state. How could this have happened? As Asef Bayat (2010, 163–64) explains,

> For over 25 years of autocratic rule, since the 1953 coup, all the effective secular political parties and nongovernmental organizations had been removed or destroyed. The United States-led coup crushed both the nationalist and Communist movements; trade unions were infiltrated by the secret police, SAVAK; publications went through strict censorship, and there remained hardly any effective non-governmental organizations (NGOs) … Student activism also remained restricted … In short, the secular groups, while extremely dissatisfied, were organizationally decapitated.
>
> Unlike the secular forces, however, the clergy had the comparative advantage of possessing invaluable institutional capacity, including its own hierarchical order, with over ten thousand mosques, *Husseiniehs* (informal and ad hoc religious gatherings), *Huwzehs* (theological seminaries), and associations that acted as vital means of communication … A hierarchical order facilitated unified decision making, and a systematic flow of both order and information ensured discipline … In short, the clerics' *institutional capacity*, in addition to the remarkable generality and *ambiguity* in their revolutionary message ensured their leadership.

These are major reasons for the victory of the Islamists, along with the disunity of the liberals and the left, and their naïvety, as contrasted with Khomeini's cunning and ability to exercise his authority over the various factions of Islamists.

Repression and Resistance

Although the rate of executions declined over time, even in the second decade of the twenty-first century the number of executions in Iran continued to be second only to China, and the rate per capita the highest in the world; flogging (for offences like not fasting during Ramadan), public hanging, amputations, mutilation and stoning to death continued to be used as punishments; and incarceration of labour activists, women's rights activists, child rights activists, and political and religious dissidents continued (UN 2015). The rise in executions was apparently due to the death penalty being awarded for drug-related offences; Shahindokht Molaverdi, vice-president for women and family affairs, revealed that the entire adult male population of a village in a poverty-stricken part of southern Iran had been executed for drug offences, and warned that unless their families were supported, their children too were likely to turn to drug trafficking (Dehghan 2016). Numerous juveniles continued to be executed, with laws permitting girls as young as nine and boys of fifteen to be sentenced to death (Amnesty International 2016a). In a grotesque inversion of justice, girls who had been victims of child sex abuse were being given sentences of a hundred lashes and executed for 'acts incompatible with chastity' (Secor 2016).

Imprisonment and torture of political dissidents too continued. 'In 2012, Iranian blogger Sattar Beheshti was arrested and murdered while in custody for online comments he made against the regime' (Panah 2016). Hossein Ronaghi-Maleki, another blogger and activist who founded Iran Proxy, a group helping journalists and activists to circumvent internet censorship, was arrested in December 2009 and charged with membership of an illegal organisation, posing a threat to national security, insulting the supreme leader and distributing propaganda against the regime – the usual charges making any dissent punishable – and received a fifteen-year sentence. As a result of torture and medical negligence in Evin prison, he developed a kidney ailment and related complications, and was granted bail for treatment in June 2015. But he was ordered to return to prison in February 2016, despite his deteriorating medical condition and eligibility for parole. Contradicting Foreign Minister Javad Zarif's denial that there were political prisoners in Iran, Ronaghi-Maleki tweeted, 'Mr Zarif, it is wrong of you to deny the truth and ignore issues. Look at political prisoners and imprisoned journalists with open eyes' (cit. Panah 2016). As Panah noted, 'Maleki's words are particularly haunting as he prepares himself to reenter a place he may never leave alive' (Panah 2016).

In addition to jailing, torturing and killing dissidents, the authorities use software that deletes censored content from websites and replaces them with acceptable alternatives. This has had some amusing results. One of the prohibited terms is 'anti-filtering software', and when Khamenei's website put up a *fatwa* (ruling) proclaiming that the use of anti-filtering software was not permissible, the offending term was deleted immediately! 'A few hours later, the operators of the religious leader's website noticed that by deleting the term, they had interfered with a legal ruling from the country's highest political authority and quickly took steps to reverse the process,' explains Faraj Sarkohi (2012), a writer who was sentenced to death for protesting against censorship, but later released following international protests. During the shah's repressive regime, writers and artists had been able to express their criticism through literature and art, but even this avenue of dissent was blocked by the Islamic government. The book reviews department of the Ministry for Culture and Islamic Guidance prohibited a long list of authors, including Sadegh Hedayat, modern Persia's greatest writer. Writers who were not prohibited were subject to censorship:

> Theoretical texts containing controversial philosophical or social theories or arguments, for example, have to be 'corrected' to fit in with official state ideology. In stories and novels, it is not just a matter of offending passages being deleted; in some cases, protagonists may well have to undergo alterations to their character, views or behaviour too. A paragraph may be inserted, which will suddenly and mysteriously transform the relationship between two characters by marrying them to one another ... Homosexuals either do not appear at all in the stories, or they change their inclinations in favour of the opposite sex.
>
> [...] The official censorship and self-censorship imposed by the climate of fear created by the imprisonment, expulsion and murder of writers, has existed for over three decades. In recent years, however, Iranian censorship has become so strict that most Iranian writers don't even bother to publish their books in the country. (Sarkohi 2012)

Yet, the very fact that political prisoners continued to be incarcerated shows that resistance persisted. Dissident bloggers continued blogging. Journalist, poet and human rights activist Asieh Amini investigated the execution of girls who had been victims of child sexual abuse, fought to have her story published, and secured the release of one young woman by finding her a good lawyer and publicising her case on her blog and the magazine *Zanan* (Women). She investigated stories of women and men being stoned to death according to sharia law despite Chief Justice Shahroudi having ordered a moratorium on stoning, and together with other women started a campaign called Stop Stoning Forever; she got documentary evidence of a court sentence to death by stoning and a forensic report confirming the cause of death, and published the story. The minister of justice responded by calling the story a lie, yet Amini continued to find cases of stoning and supplied evidence to groups like Amnesty International. Only after the outbreak of protests following the 2009 elections, when many of her colleagues disappeared or were shown on TV making forced confessions and she was warned she was on the hit list, did she escape to Norway (Secor 2016).

The most famous case is that of Shirin Ebadi, the first woman in Iran to become a judge in 1969, who was stripped of her position when the Islamists dismissed all women judges in 1979. She wrote several books and articles, finally obtaining a lawyer's licence in 1992. She took up many human rights cases, including those of the families of serial murder victims and of students killed during the 1999 police attack on a university dormitory; participated in some press-related cases; took on a large number of social cases including child abuse cases; and represented the mother of Zahra Kazemi, a photojournalist killed in Iran. She also taught at the university, with many students from outside Iran joining her human rights training courses (Ebadi 2003). In 2003, she received the Nobel Peace Prize and continued her work, but threats from the government also continued. As they escalated in the run-up to the presidential election in 2009, she took a vacation with her younger daughter to visit her older daughter in Atlanta. While she was away, intelligence agents hired a woman to seduce her husband, and they photographed and arrested him in the midst of his betrayal, before incarcerating him in Evin Prison and sentencing him to death by stoning. A few hours after the verdict, the agent who had arrested him came to the prison with his boss and offered to set him free if he agreed to denounce his wife in front of a camera, saying her work was not in the service of Iranians but in the interests of foreign imperialists. He complied, and in order to overturn the stoning sentence was required to get a backdated certificate of temporary marriage to the woman who had entrapped him (Ebadi 2016).

Both repression and resistance were most intense in the struggle over women's rights. In 2003 Zahra Eshraghi – the granddaughter of Khomeini, who had called the chador the flag of the Islamic revolution – admitted that she hated wearing it and only did so because of her family status (Sciolino 2003). However, women were advancing despite the constraints, pursuing education, the arts and music, seeking employment, practising sports, and encouraging their children to do the same. By 1997, their literacy rate had more than doubled to 74 per cent, and by 1998, more girls than boys were entering universities. Many women were forced to take up employment for economic reasons, while others chose to do so in order to be present in the public domain; with economic necessity forcing many men to take up multiple jobs and work long hours, women had to shoulder tasks like taking children to school, shopping, and dealing with the bureaucracy, giving them new confidence, social skills and city knowledge. There were daily battles between 'bad hijabi', young women showing inches of hair, and multiple official and unofficial agencies tasked with enforcing good hijab (Bayat 2010, 100–103). In addition to these unorganised 'nonmovements', there were more-organised efforts by magazines like *Zanan* to counterpose a feminist reading of the Quran to the patriarchal reading that was being used to deny women equal rights, and women participated in hundreds of NGOs, solidarity networks, rallies, meetings, lobbies, campaigns, book fairs, film festivals, seminars, women's magazines and websites (Bayat 2010, 109). In August 2006, women's rights activists launched the One Million Signatures campaign for the repeal of laws that discriminate against women (Secor 2016).

The backlash has been violent. Ansar-e Hezbollah has been especially active during Muhammad Khatami's reformist and Hassan Rouhani's moderate presidencies, forming motorcycle patrols to enforce hijab on women. They were instrumental in drafting the Plan to Promote Virtue and Prevent Vice, passed in parliament in October 2014, which designated the Basij as the agency entrusted with this duty (IHRI 2015a). The campaign was associated with acid attacks on women in Isfahan, but still women continued to resist, by, among other things, starting a Facebook page called 'My Stealthy Freedom' featuring selfies of a wide variety of bare-headed women defying the order to wear hijab (Aman 2014). Ansar-e Hezbollah's publication *Ya Lesarat* also featured verbal abuse of prominent women like Shirin Ebadi, lawyer Shadi Sadr and *Zanan* editor Shahla Sherkat, even describing Vice-President for Women and Family Affairs Shahindokht Molaverdi as 'worse than the most famous prostitute in the world' (IHRI 2015b). Like the systematic rape and sexual torture of women and girls in Iran's prisons (Iran Human Rights Review 2014), entrusting the promotion of virtue to misogynist thugs was intrinsic to the IRI's degraded interpretation of Islam, expressed by Khamenei's view that gender equality is a Zionist plot to corrupt the role of women in society (Dearden 2017a).

Finally, Iranian socialists like Omid Ranjbar and Azadeh Shurmand (2016) challenged Iran's imperialist role in Syria, Iraq, Lebanon, Yemen and Bahrain, calling for the regional solidarity of socialist and secular forces. An emotional appeal from an Iranian student at Amirkabir University in Tehran, calling for the questioning of the mass execution of political prisoners in

1988, of the continuation of the Iran-Iraq war after the liberation of Khor-ramshahr in 1982, of the US Embassy takeover of 1979–81, of the serial murders of 1988–98, and above all of Iran's role in the 'horrible genocide in Syria', was met with enthusiastic applause from the hundreds-strong student audience (Alliance of Middle-East Socialists 2016).[6] Shortly afterwards, 399 Iranian activists strongly condemned their government's intervention in Syria and apologised to the 'suffering Syrian people' for it (Alliance of Middle-East Socialists 2017a).

Reform or Revolution?

This brings us to the question: Can democracy be achieved by a process of reform in the IRI, or is revolution the only way?

The ruling clerics in Iran are seen as being divided into reformists, mod-erate conservatives, and hardline conservatives or 'Principlists'; all of them accept the dictatorship of the velayat-e faqih. A test case for the possibility of reform is provided by the presidency of Muhammad Khatami, who was first swept to power in May 1997, winning nearly 70 per cent of the popular vote on the promise of 'increased economic opportunities for Iran's youth, social justice, individual freedoms, political tolerance, greater rights for women and the rule of law'; while criticising Western imperialism, he also praised Western civilisation for advocating freedom from authoritarian rule and op-pressive traditions. His aim was not 'to do away with the Islamic Republic, but to make it democratic, tolerant, progressive, and in tune with the needs of the people' (Siddiqi 2004). Initially he faced opposition to his programme not only from the supreme leader and Guardian Council, but also from a hardliner-dominated Majlis. However, parliamentary elections in February 2000 brought to power a more reformist Majlis, which passed Khatami's bill aimed at encouraging foreign investment in order to boost employment. This was vetoed by the Guardian Council, so although the economy did improve slowly, Khatami was unable to fulfil his promise regarding employment (Sid-diqi 2004).

Khatami's initiatives in the field of democratic rights, especially free-dom of expression, fared no better. When he came to power, a plethora of reformist publications appeared; most were shut down by the hardline judi-ciary, but they often sprang up again under new names. Dissident clergy and intellectuals were arrested or disappeared and later turned up dead. In 1999, students protesting against the closure of a reformist newspaper, *Salam*, were viciously assaulted in their dormitories by police and Ansar-e Hezbollah thugs. In 2000, when the Majlis started debating a new law guaranteeing press freedom, Khamenei intervened and demanded the bill be withdrawn. Under these circumstances, Khatami was reluctant to run for a second term in 2001 and on the anniversary of the revolution made a speech sharply critical of the hardliners, yet ultimately he decided to run, and despite a lower turnout, won 77 per cent of votes cast. But with over fifty bills passed by the Majlis vetoed by the Guardian Council, he was unable to make any headway with his reform agenda. He attempted to regain the initiative by getting two bills drafted, one allowing him to reverse actions by the judiciary that violated the constitution, and the other limiting the rights of the Guardian Council. Both were passed by the Majlis, but were vetoed by the Guardian Council. Meanwhile, the judiciary sentenced Hashem Aghajari, a history professor in Tehran, to death for apostasy, and the universities erupted in protests that were crushed with the utmost brutality. With the Guardian Council disqualifying 3,600 candidates, including eighty-three sitting members of parliament, for the 2004 Majlis elections, and widespread boycott of the elections, the conservatives came back to power (Siddiqi 2004).

IRGC leader Yahya Rahim Safavi, who also controlled the Basij, played a major role in sabotaging Khatami's reforms, crushing student revolts and setting up special courts to silence dissenters. Under Mahmoud Ahmadinejad, who came to power in the 2005 presidential elections, IRGC officers occupied nine key government ministries out of twenty-one. Ahmadinejad also installed IRGC, Basij and prison administration personnel as governors of many provinces, while Khamenei installed former IRGC commander Ali-Reza Afshar to oversee elections, and another veteran, Ezzatollah Zarghami, to head Islamic Republic of Iran Broadcasting (IRIB). Mohammad Ali Jafari, who succeeded Safavi as commander of the IRGC in 2007, described the IRGC as not 'solely a military organization' but also a 'political and ideological organization' (cit. Alfoneh 2008). It played a key role in ensuring the victory of Ahmadinejad in the presidential elections of 2009, after which Khamenei appointed even more hardliners to its leadership, for example Mohammad Reza Naghdi, who had been deputy director of intelligence of the Quds Force during the chain murders and had played a key role in organising and financing Ansar-e Hezbollah when he was commander of the Basij (Abdo 2009). Whatever few reforms Khatami had managed to push through were reversed: 'The Ahmadinejad government is establishing a climate of fear, rolling back the opening created through the reform period of 1997–2005 and redrawing the boundaries of public space in Iran' (Postel 2006, 6).

With inflation at 25 per cent, unemployment at 30 per cent, and the number of those living in poverty at a record high, an end to economic sanctions and investment in Iran's oil and gas fields – both impossible under Ahmadinejad – were widely seen as essential to job creation; there were also complaints about corruption and nepotism (Abrahamian 2010, 63–65). By 2009, many Iranians had had enough. In the June 2009 presidential elections, Ahmadinejad was pitted against reformist candidate Mir Hossein Mousavi, whose supporters included the labour unions, the Association of Qom Seminary Teachers, Grand Ayatollah Montazeri, and relatives of Revolutionary Guards killed in the Iran-Iraq war, among many others (Abrahamian 2010, 64–65). With Mousavi gaining ground and a third candidate, Mehdi Karoubi, pledging to endorse him if there was a second round of voting, the interior minister, a millionaire friend of Ahmadinejad, forestalled that possibility. Having already purged 'unreliable' civil servants from the electoral commission, he proceeded to restrict the number of permits issued to poll observers, set up more than 14,000 mobile polling trucks (making the vote count easy to fiddle with), printed far more ballots than there were eligible voters, and broke precedent by not having the ballots tabulated on the spot at the end of election day, but instead rushed to the ministry where they were 'counted' by his aides. 'Within hours of the polls closing, the interior minister declared Ahmadinejad to be the winner with 66 per cent of the vote ... This decisive "victory" was intended to put an end to street demonstrations, but it had the opposite effect, outraging many who felt not only cheated but insulted – especially when Ahmadinejad described those who questioned the results as "specks of dirt"' (Abrahamian 2010, 66–67). In fifty towns, voter turnout exceeded 100 per cent; in one district, the number of votes was thirteen times the number of residents (Ansari 2010, 349–50). As the anomalies grew, so did the anger. There were massive protest rallies in many parts of the country, with millions demonstrating in Tehran alone. This was the birth of the Green Movement.

Shaken by the scale of the protests, the regime launched a massive crackdown. 'It banned all demonstrations, threatened to execute anyone participating in or calling for such protests, and sent out tens of thousands of

Revolutionary Guards and Basijis on motorbikes, armed with assault weapons, knives and truncheons' (Abrahamian 2010, 68). Vigilantes stormed university dormitories; more than 4,000 of Mousavi's and Karoubi's associates were arrested; the regime jammed foreign broadcasts, shut down newspapers and websites, expelled foreign journalists, disrupted telecommunications, broke into homes to arrest those suspected of shouting 'God is great' from rooftops, and 'tortured prisoners, including prominent public figures, who were made to confess before TV cameras that they had participated in a Western plot to launch a velvet revolution' (Abrahamian 2010, 69). In a bid to stamp out critical thinking in institutions of higher education, an educationally unqualified minister was put in charge of the centralisation of university administration under the regime's control, replacing dissident faculty with Islamist ideologues, expelling troublesome students, eliminating independent student organisations and banning their publications, strengthening Basiji student organisations and allowing them to engage in physical violence, shutting down whole fields of study, installing toadies as university administrators, attacking the autonomy of other educational and scholarly institutions, and facilitating the entry of a backward seminarian mentality into the universities (Salemi 2010).[7]

The opposition used the crackdown to fuel its own movement. Twenty-six-year-old philosophy student Neda Agha-Soltan, photographed being shot dead during the protests, became the face of the Green Movement. The regime's attempts to shame detainees of both sexes by raping and sexually abusing them backfired when the practice was exposed, mainly by Karoubi; 'One of Karoubi's witnesses, a male rape victim, refers to his decision to disclose what happened to him as "committing social suicide," which speaks to the power of the taboo – but then, once a taboo is broken, it loses its power' (Mir-Hosseini 2010, 145); similarly, when the regime sought to humiliate detained student leader Majid Tavakoli by publishing photographs of him allegedly trying to escape dressed in hijab, an Iranian photographer invited men to post pictures of themselves in hijab, and men responded en masse, asserting, 'We are all Majid' (Mir-Hosseini 2010, 140–41). Both were forms of resistance that challenged the perverted sexual politics of the regime.

Both inside and outside Iran, the dominant narrative has been that the protesters were mainly from the urban upper and middle classes, but more careful analyses contradict this perception. A large component of Mousavi's supporters 'are indeed university students, young faculty and the urban intellectual elite – such as filmmakers, artists and the literati. But the fact is that a major Mousavi constituency is the urban poor and particularly the war veterans ... Conversely, there is a significant segment of the traditional middle class, the *bazaaris*, that has benefited from Ahmadinejad's economic policies ... and thus supports him' (Dabashi 2010, 24). Nor would it be correct to assume that the students are mainly from the upper and middle classes. 'A simple glance at the background of Iran's prominent student leaders tells you that, by and large, they are not the children of affluent citizens of north Tehran, but instead come from provincial working-class families or are the children of rural schoolteachers and clerks' (Alavi 2010, 211).

Ascertaining the demands of the movement is more difficult. As Hossein Bashiriyeh (2010, 88) put it, in the first week, 'The focus on a single issue – the rigging of the election – polarized the population, leading to mass street demonstrations against the manipulations at the polls.' Thus Iran's Green Movement could be called an 'electoral fraud revolt', but after Khamenei endorsed the election results and initiated the brutal crushing of the revolt, there was potential for it to become a revolution. 'To become more offensive, however, the ideology needs to be differentiated from the dominant theocratic tendency in the constitution, and this is what the current oppositional leadership seems to be rather reluctant to propose' (Bashiriyeh 2010, 98). Bashiriyeh is right. The Green Movement Charter, released on June 15, 2010, starts defiantly: 'We are still standing tall and proud on the first anniversary of the tenth presidential elections despite our whipped body, which endures bruises and imprisonment. Our demands are the same: freedom, social justice and the formation of a [legitimate] national government'; yet it goes on to appeal to the legacy of Khomeini, and repeats more than once that the changes sought by the movement are 'within the framework of the Constitution' (Mousavi 2010, 332; 334; 336; 340): the very same constitution that allows the velayat-e faqih to negate all the rights granted to citizens.

The street protests gradually declined in the face of brutal repression by armed IRGC and Basij personnel because, as Azadeh Moaveni (2009) put it,

The people who respect Mousavi's determination are also wary of his strategy. He was challenging the Islamic system within its very confines ... Iranians' ambivalence about Mousavi's leadership has also been reflected on their Facebook pages. The personal sites that bore the green logo "What Happened To My Vote?" began to change tone in early July. Many posted a picture of

Mohammad Mossadegh, the democratically elected prime minister and national hero who was ousted in a CIA-backed coup in 1953 … He reappears
cyclically, at moments when Iranians despair of the leaders available to them,
and of any chance to shed the Islamic theocracy that many consider corrupt
and unaccountable.

Mossadegh surfaced again in the unlikely context of an immensely popular TV series called *Shahrzad*, centred on a love story between two university students set against the backdrop of Mossadegh's regime and the coup
against him in the early 1950s. With a license issued by the Ministry of
Culture and Islamic Guidance operating directly under Rouhani and not
the state broadcaster, IRIB, it managed to slip under the radar of the censors
(Lavasani 2015).

The Green Movement might have been crushed, with Mousavi and
Karoubi under house arrest, but the desire for democracy survived. It
emerged again in the 2013 presidential elections, which was won by the
moderate conservative Hassan Rouhani with the backing of Khatami
(Smyth 2013). At the top of Rouhani's agenda was a nuclear deal that would
put an end to sanctions. This goal had been sabotaged by hardliners in the
United States and Iran alike, and they continued to oppose it; but Rouhani's
resounding victory in the election allowed him more leeway (Milani and
McFaul 2015), while on the other side, Obama was determined to push it
through. With this momentum in its favour, the Joint Comprehensive Plan
of Action (JCPOA) was successfully concluded in 2015. However, opposition continued, especially from IRGC leaders, whose stranglehold over the
economy and lucrative import-export trade was threatened by the lifting of
sanctions. Khamenei, who had earlier backed the deal, criticised Rouhani's
talk of a second JCPOA for economic recovery and insisted on the necessity
to maintain the self-sufficient 'resistance economy' built up during the period
of sanctions; IRGC leader Jafari more explicitly advocated confrontation
with the West, since, he said, 'We have been building up our power for years
based on the presumption of a widespread war with the United States and
its allies' (EA Worldview 2016). Indeed, nostalgia for the sanctions regime
was so strong among Iran's extreme right that some of them openly endorsed
Donald Trump (who opposed the nuclear deal) for US president, hoping
that he would help a hardliner to win the 2017 presidential elections in Iran,
just as Bush Jr. and his 'axis of evil' rhetoric had helped Ahmadinejad to win
in 2005 (Faghihi 2016c).

This internal conflict was the background to the 2016 elections for parliament and the Assembly of Experts. In the run-up to the elections, attempts by the hardliners to dominate the conservative list led to most of the moderates splitting away and joining the reformist list (Faghihi 2016a) – which was campaigning on issues of human rights and freedom of expression – and calling on students in particular to come out and vote (Karami 2016b); meanwhile Rouhani called on women to play a greater role in politics (Karami 2016a), students and women being two constituencies likely to vote for reformists.

The conservative Principlists, knowing that a high turnout would favour the reformists, discouraged people from voting, even floating a rumour that the day after the election was a holiday so that people would plan outings over the election period (Faghihi 2016b). The Guardian Council disqualified 99 per cent of the reformist candidates, including all the women and moderate ayatollahs; in most of the provinces, they handpicked the only candidates who could run for the Assembly. The opaque disqualification process led to widespread outrage. After intense protests, some of the disqualified candidates were permitted to stand, yet around 40 per cent of the applicants, most of them reformist, remained disqualified (IHRI 2016).

The election results were a resounding victory for the reformist- and moderate-backed 'List of Hope', which won all thirty parliamentary seats and fifteen of the sixteen Assembly of Experts seats from Tehran, and wiped out the far-right majority countrywide (Alizadeh 2016). Jubilation over the victory among reformists was tempered with dismay over the tactics they had been forced to adopt:

> Sadegh Zibakalam, the reform-inclined professor of political science at the University of Tehran, said the mass disqualification of reformist candidates by the Guardian Council made compiling the lists difficult. 'We didn't have much choice left. Nearly 90% of reformist candidates, even the second- and third-rate ones, were disqualified. So we had to either boycott the elections and leave the political ground to the principlists, or change our strategy.'
>
> The reformists picked the latter. According to Zibakalam they decided to invest in a new, young generation of candidates who are not necessarily reformists and hope that if they get to the parliament and the Assembly, at least some of them will gravitate towards reformism. But he adds that … they were still short of candidates, so they had to approach some principlists. (Ajiri 2016)

The final list included candidates with dreadful human rights records. In response to criticisms, Zibakalam said, 'Unfortunately, we had to choose between bad and worse ... what other options do we have?' (Ajiri 2016).

The optimism surrounding the parliamentary elections of 2016 were also shadowed by an uncomfortable feeling of déjà vu. The same excitement and belief that 'Iran was heading down an irrevocable path toward internal reform, a process untainted by any Western intrusion, with citizens and progressive-minded leaders showing the way' had accompanied the election of Khatami in 2001, yet his efforts at reform had been blocked by unelected institutions (Moaveni 2016), and his second term was followed by the presidency of Ahmadinejad, who reversed whatever little he had managed to accomplish.

However, it would be wrong to conclude that voting and popular movements are pointless in Iran. In the presidential elections of May 2017, Rouhani was pushed to the left by the need to win support from reformists against his far-right opponent Ebrahim Raisi (one of the judges who sentenced thousands of dissidents to death in the 1980s, and enjoying the support of Khamenei and the IRGC), going so far as to attack the human rights record of the security forces and judiciary. The huge voter turnout and large numbers of young people and 'bad hijab' women in the crowds celebrating his landslide victory indicated that these sections, at least, rejected the far-right agenda in no uncertain terms (Hafezi and Dehghanpisheh 2017; Erdbrink 2017). Khamenei, probably having learned from the Green Movement that it would be unwise to rig the election, allowed him to take office for a second term.

In December 2009, the yearning for an alternative to the existing political system expressed itself in the massive crowds, both offline and online, attending the funeral of Ayatollah Montazeri, who in 2004 had said that 'the Iranian people did not go through a revolution in order to "substitute absolutist rule by the crown with one under the turban"' (Alavi 2010, 21). Dissident philosopher, theologian and cleric Mohsen Kadivar, who had been sentenced to time in jail for his writings, put forward the revolutionary (as opposed to reformist) position with even more clarity: 'The Iranian regime has shown that democracy and *velayat-e faqih* (rule of the Islamic jurist) are not compatible. Human rights and *velayat-e faqih* are not compatible. Republicanism and *velayat-e faqih* are not compatible. These are the contradictions that have come to light in practice' (Kadivar 2010, 116).

A state where an unelected supreme leader and his unelected Guardian Council control the executive, security forces and judiciary, select candidates for presidential and parliamentary elections, and override their decisions at will is not a genuine republic, because the republican legacy of the original democratic revolution has been crushed and stifled by an Islamic state. The image of sixteen-year-old child abuse victim Atefeh Sahaaleh, with the noose around her neck being hauled up by a crane in a square so that the public could witness her writhing in agony (Garnsey 2006), epitomises the velayat-e faqih, exposing it as the dictatorship of power-hungry men who use God as a cover for their own tyranny, misogyny and sadism. There is no way the Iranian people can be free until the republic is liberated from this incubus; reforms can always be reversed unless they lead to a democratic revolution. This is the lesson to be drawn from Khatami's reformist presidency, which failed to challenge the velayat-e faqih.

Condoning Counterrevolutionary Violence

In June 2003, as the Ansar-e Hezbollah assaulted non-violent student protestors with batons, chains and knives, and the government arrested over 4,000 people, banned meetings and closed university dorms, Jeremy Brecher (2003) commented, 'Normally, the global peace movement and political left would respond to repression by an authoritarian, theocratic regime with outrage and protest. But so far there has been a deafening silence.' In his exploration of why this might have been the case, Danny Postel (2006) argued,

> It's not that the [Iranian] students and other reformers are pro-imperialist. Quite the contrary ... But US imperialism is simply not the central issue for them – and this, I think, is a stumbling block for many American leftists, because it is the central issue for us ... Anti-imperialism can turn into a kind of tunnel vision, its own form of fundamentalism. Cases that fall outside its scheme simply get left out, and our solidarity with struggles around the world is determined by George Bush, rather than by our principles.

That would also explain some of the blatant double standards: condemnation of the Saudi regime for floggings and mass executions, but silence about the Iranian regime's use of the same punishments on a larger scale; condemnation of the Turkish regime's brutal treatment of its Kurdish minority, but not a word about the IRI's equally brutal treatment of its Kurdish and other minorities.

The EU has been more friendly to the Islamic Republic than has the US, and sections of the left have followed suit. When Iranian reformist participants in a German government–sponsored conference organised in Berlin by the Green Party–affiliated Heinrich Böll Foundation in 2000 were tried and jailed, Hekmat (2001) commented, 'Even the German officials and their shocked Iranian friends know very well that state terrorism, summary trials, Islamic retribution, execution and torture have not stopped for even one day during the last twenty years ... Even while the trials were in progress, 800 people have been sentenced to death by execution and stoning and the killings have already started.' There are even some who deny that human rights abuses are taking place, 'despite incontrovertible evidence from Amnesty International, Human Rights Watch and from Iran's underground left-wing, student and trade union movements. This shocking denialism is wholly divorced from reality and is a sordid betrayal of the Iranian people's struggle for liberty and justice' (Tatchell 2009a).

In Britain, following the vicious suppression of protests after the contested 2009 presidential election, Fariborz Pooya recounts that there was 'a surge in misinformation' propagated by the Islamic regime. This included Press TV, its English-language satellite channel, on which former UK MP George Galloway had his own show. Pooya (2009) comments: 'George Galloway is on the pay of the Islamic regime now ... He is supportive of Ahmadinejad and by association the policies of the Islamic regime and the current atrocities including the killings.' Similarly, the Bolivarian government of Hugo Chávez expressed full support for Ahmadinejad and hostility to the protests which, according to it, emanated from abroad (Bridges 2009). The Campaign for Nuclear Disarmament (CND) invited the Iranian ambassador to be the keynote speaker at its annual conference in 2009, while Stop the War Coalition (StWC) and the Socialist Workers Party (SWP) 'vetoed any protests against the Tehran regime' (Tatchell 2009b), and Jeremy Corbyn 'has spoken at the Iranian government's anniversary of the "Islamic revolution" despite the fact that Islamism in Iran is a counter-revolutionary force, which came to power by suppressing a Left-leaning people's revolution against the Shah' (Namazie 2015; Habibi 2016). The attitude of StWC is exemplified by its exclusion of the anti-imperialist, anti-war group Hands Off the People of Iran, evidently because its platform included 'opposition to the theocratic regime and solidarity with and practical aid to grassroots movements – of women, workers and students – fighting for democracy and freedom in Iran' (Hands Off the People of Iran 2007).

We cannot explain such positions simply by ignorance on the part of these foreigners, since Iranian Stalinists took similar positions in 1979. One explanation is that they feel duty bound to support a regime whose favourite slogans are 'Death to America' and 'Death to Israel'. But what exactly do these slogans mean? Islamists, including Ayatollah Behbehani and Ayatollah Kashani, were rabidly opposed to Mossadegh's secular, democratic anti-imperialism; the CIA and MI6 would not have been able to overthrow Mossadegh in 1953 without 'the distribution of CIA-provided "Behbehani dollars" among mullahs and knife-wielding mobs, in addition to Kashani's ability to summon in a short time a large contingent of his supporters to the streets' (Norouzi 2009). Khomeini openly endorsed this collaboration between Islamists and imperialism: 'I said [of Mossadegh] … he will be slapped and it did not take long that he was slapped and if he had lasted he would have slapped Islam' (Norouzi 2009). The IRI had no qualms when the money it paid for arms was used for Jewish settlements in the Israeli-occupied territories and for the US-backed, anticommunist Contra terrorists in Nicaragua. So it would be a mistake to interpret these slogans as opposition to US imperialism or support for the Palestinian struggle; rather, they mean 'Death to Democracy! Victory to the Islamic state!' It follows that pseudo-anti-imperialists who share platforms with representatives of the IRI or veto protests against it are guilty of appeasing an extreme right-wing regime.

Western left-wingers or liberals (including Michel Foucault) who support the Islamist theocracy in Iran seem to suffer from a postmodernist Orientalism, which holds that democracy is alien to Iranian culture (Afary and Anderson 2004). This, of course, is nonsense. 'Democracy is not a new idea in Iranian history and politics … The demand for democracy first surfaced more than a century ago at the latter part of the Qajar period to help produce Iran's first constitution in 1906. That constitution was notably a liberal and democratic document' (Gheissari and Nasr 2009, 6). There is an understandable fear that the exposure of human rights violations in Iran could be used to justify military attacks against the country or sanctions that hurt ordinary people. However, the correct response to such a danger is not to sweep the violations under the carpet but to argue against collective punishment of the Iranian population. Indeed, even if there is confirmation of the mounting evidence that – contrary to the belief that the Shia Islamist IRI and Hezbollah would never collaborate with the Sunni Islamist Al Qaeda – the groups in fact worked together on 9/11 (Rafizadeh 2016; El-Shenawi 2016), this would not justify sanctions that constitute the collective punishment of innocent people.

With campaigns against nuclear energy active in many countries, especially after the Fukushima disaster, it is not surprising that there are Iranians, too, who are 'against the production, storage, and use of any kind of nuclear weapons and energy by any state, including Iran' (Goya 2012, 14). For genuine anti-imperialists, therefore, it is entirely possible to oppose war on Iran and sanctions that hurt ordinary people, while at the same time opposing the oppression inflicted on its people by the Islamic state and supporting Iranian activists who believe that 'a true peace, freedom and equality in Iran is equivalent to the overthrow of the Islamic regime by a revolution' (Goya 2012, 17).

5. Iraq

While the 2003 US/UK invasion of Iraq is responsible for much of the chaos and slaughter that followed, the events that preceded and followed it are also implicated. Pseudo-anti-imperialists who blame everything on the US/UK invasion fail to recognise local and regional factors contributing to the crisis, particularly Iranian jihadi imperialism. Their blanket opposition to Western 'humanitarian' military interventions, absolutely justified in the case of the 2003 invasion of Iraq, would have allowed the ISIS genocide of Yazidis to proceed unhindered. Support or opposition should depend not on subjective factors but on the objective circumstances and the outcome of the intervention.

Saddam Hussein and the Baath Party

Saddam Hussein joined the Baath Party as a young man in 1956. The Arab Baath (Renaissance) Socialist Party was founded in the early 1940s by three French-educated Syrian intellectuals: Michel Aflaq, a Christian; Salah al-Din Bitar, a Sunni Muslim; and Zaki al-Arsuzi, an Alawite. A self-professed revolutionary party combining pan-Arab nationalism with a dedication to socialism, the Baath Party developed a serious following only in Syria and Iraq, despite its goal of encompassing the entire Arab world (Human Rights Watch 1990, 11). Communists, whose immediate objective was a democratic revolution, had a far stronger mass following in Iraq during this period.

Iraq had gained formal independence under King Faisal I in 1932, but British control continued. In July 1958, the monarchy was toppled by a military coup, establishing the republic which would eventually install

General Abd al-Karim Qasim as prime minister. It was a potentially revolutionary situation:

> The streets filled with jubilant Iraqis. Communists rallied tens of thousands of new members to support the new republic. Nine months later, on April 17, 1959, the communists gathered a million citizens and marched again in Baghdad … Marchers called for peace and for the army to hand power over to civilians … A local paper reported: 'All categories of people: the soldier, worker, peasant, wage-earner, intellectual, student, civil servant, merchants … Arabs, Kurds, Assyrians, Armenians and others, who flocked from every corner of Iraq. … The procession was rained with flowers, sweets and bouquets from balconies along both sides of the streets.' (Thompson 2013, 178–79)

Communism had 'arrived in Basra on British steamers from India, in books and magazines, and in the mouths of Indian soldiers, servants and employees of British firms', while Islamic socialist ideas had floated around the Arab world since the turn of the century (Thompson 2013, 183). Yusuf Salman Yusuf – a Christian Arab who was born in Baghdad in 1901, moved with his parents to Basra in 1908, and worked at an ice factory and then at the port from the age of fifteen – was attracted by these ideas. In 1927 he established a communist circle that grew to sixty members by the early 1930s; he was present at a meeting in the capital in 1934, where the communists formed the Committee against Imperialism and Exploitation, issuing 'a manifesto proclaiming workers … as the true basis of the nation. Their demands: cancellation of foreign debt and nationalization of oil, railways and banks. In 1935 the group became the ICP [Iraqi Communist Party] and published its first newspaper. A hammer and sickle with the slogan "Workers of the World Unite" adorned the masthead' (Thompson 2013, 185). Under the pseudonym 'Comrade Fahd', Yusuf built the ICP into a mass party. With a truly mixed and largely working-class leadership of Christians, Jews, Shiites, Sunni Arabs and a Sunni Kurd, they established the League Against Zionism, and in a booklet outlined their two-stage revolution, concentrating on the first stage, which was to establish a democratic regime in Iraq (the second stage was to establish a 'dictatorship of the proletariat'). Disturbed by the growing influence of the communists, the government subjected them to fierce repression, arresting and condemning Fahd and other leaders to death in 1947. The uproar with which the verdict was met led to their sentence being commuted to penal servitude; but in 1949 the Soviet Union's recognition of Israel created a pretext for the Iraqi state to accuse them falsely of Zionism and hang them (Thompson 2013, 189–98).

The ICP survived, however, and played a major role in shaping Qasim's secular social justice policies after he came to power. Qasim 'redistributed the land of royalist elites to 35,000 families, raised taxes on the landed rich, reduced housing rents and bread prices, issued labor regulations to improve workers' conditions, and built homes and schools for 10,000 families living in the slums around Baghdad'; but in late 1959 he openly turned against the ICP, ordering the arrest of hundreds of communists, shutting down their public branches, demobilising their popular militias, and removing communists from control of the peasant unions and the press (Thompson 2013, 202–3).

In 1959, Saddam Hussein was involved in an unsuccessful Baathist attempt to assassinate Qasim, after which Saddam fled the country, but in February 1963 Qasim was overthrown in a second Baathist coup and executed, along with his aides and thousands of communists. The Baathists installed Abd al-Salam Arif as president, but he ousted them from power in November of the same year, leaving the party in crisis. At this point, one of the original Baathist founders, Michel Aflaq, intervened in the organisation of the party, establishing a new leadership that put Ahmad Hasan al-Bakr and Saddam Hussein in key positions. Although jailed for two years after another failed coup in 1964, Saddam escaped and became deputy secretary general of the Baath party in 1966, when he was just twenty-nine (Sassoon 2012, 30).[1] In July 1968, the Baathists prevailed upon the military to withdraw support from Arif's brother, who had succeeded him as prime minister; after he was forced to resign and sent into exile, the Baath Party took power. By this time, there was an unbridgeable rift between the Iraqi and Syrian Baath Parties, and nationalism had replaced Pan-Arabism. R. Stephen Humphreys (1999, 121) outlines some of the ways in which the Baathist party leaders represented a significant change from Iraq's former political establishment:

1. They were much poorer – a full quarter of Baathist leaders were from peasant and working-class families.
2. They were markedly civilian rather than military by occupation ... Saddam Hussein's inexorable rise to sole power during the 1970s marked the definitive victory of the party apparatchiks over its military wing. Saddam Hussein reminds one of Stalin in more than one way.
3. They tended to come from the countryside rather than the city. Only four members of the RCC [Revolutionary Command Council] were Baghdadis by origin, while six were from Tikrit.

Indeed, there are striking similarities between Saddam and Stalin. Even before he became president in 1979, Saddam began to concentrate power in his own hands. And afterwards, aside from being president, Saddam was 'simultaneously the chairman of the RCC, secretary general of the Ba'th Party, prime minister, and commander in chief of the armed forces. Like his elaborate security apparatus, which had a systematic overlap in responsibilities in order to diffuse power, Iraq's bureaucracy had multiple organizational layers ... In essence, all major – and sometimes minor – issues percolated upwards to the presidential *diwan* and the president himself for a final decision' (Sassoon 2012, 227; 234). The Baath Party was similarly centralised, with all major decisions being taken by the Party Secretariat, and, 'in order to ensure that the party permeated and controlled every facet of life in Iraq, its members occupied most of the important positions in the country' (Sassoon 2012, 35).

The party had its own secret police, the *mukhabarat*, and a 'People's Militia', which reportedly numbered about 175,000 on the eve of the Iran-Iraq war and expanded to about 750,000 during the war. 'Civilian informers play a key role in surveillance. According to almost unanimous testimony, Iraq under the Baath Party has become a nation of informers. Party members are said to be required to inform on family, friends and acquaintances, including other party members' (Human Rights Watch 1990, 14). Loyalty was assured by liberal use of the death penalty; for example, any retired military or police personnel – which included the entire adult male population, since military service was mandatory – would be sentenced to death if they worked for any group or party other than the Baath Party, as would any former member of the Baath Party. Like Stalin, Saddam discovered plots against himself everywhere and executed officials suspected of them either secretly or after show trials involving torture to extract false confessions. The message was clear: dissent of any kind would not be tolerated. This was supplemented by an all-encompassing personality cult, which made it mandatory to have a picture of Saddam in every household, and made an insult to him punishable by life imprisonment or death (Human Rights Watch 1990, 15–20).

The Special Security Organization (SSO or Amn al-Khass) was the most powerful state security agency from 1980 onwards: 'It had a say in any significant promotion or demotion within the system ... documents indicate that it was involved in appointments of doctors in hospitals and of scientists in universities, property allocation, religious activities, archaeological digs, and even "Arabization" of Latin words' (Sassoon 2012, 109). A major part of its responsibilities was gathering information. The regime considered itself to have an extensive range of enemies: 'One of the Ba'th Party documents identifies at least eight opposition movements inside the country, among them the Communist Party, the two Kurdish parties (the Kurdish Democratic Party [KDP] and Patriotic Union of Kurdistan [PUK]), the Da'wa Party, the Muslim Brothers, any movement that had "a religious cover," groups that had split from the Ba'th Party, and any movements that pretended to be "nationalistic"' (Sassoon 2012, 113–14).

Like the Iranian secret services, the Iraqi secret services pursued 'enemies of the state' abroad and attempted – often successfully – to assassinate them in places as varied as Kuwait, Beirut, Cairo, London, Aden, Vienna, Berlin, Dubai, Sweden, Italy, Pakistan, Thailand, Khartoum and Lausanne (Human Rights Watch 1990, 23–25). The unelected Revolutionary Command Council could override decisions of the judiciary and the National Assembly, which was elected under strictly controlled conditions. The media were gradually brought completely under the control of the Baath Party; 'Failure to conform has brought imprisonment and torture, frequently ending in death, for hundreds of Iraqi writers and intellectuals' (Human Rights Watch 1990, 39–40).

The Baath Party proclaimed itself 'a socialist revolutionary party which considers socialism as a decisive necessity for liberating the Arab nation', but unlike Stalinist Russia 'there was no centralized economy, no forced industrialization, and no massive, state-run attempt to mould peasants into industrial workers'; nationalisation and land reform went along with encouragement of the private sector (Sassoon 2012, 236–37). Between 1972 and 1975, all oil companies were nationalised, and the quadrupling of oil prices after the 1973 October War allowed the regime to use the revenue to provide free healthcare and education, to expand the country's infrastructure, to organise large construction projects, and to invest in heavy industry. Per capita income rose from 97 Iraqi *dinars* in 1968 to about 825 Iraqi dinars by the end of the 1970s, while GDP increased more than fourfold, with the huge public expenditure stimulating private investment (Sassoon 2012, 238–39).

Although Saddam identified as a Muslim, he opposed officials attending mosques or praying during working hours in case it put pressure on others to do the same, and he told his cabinet that he had been completely oblivious to the differences between Sunni and Shi'i until he was exiled in Egypt; the preponderance of Sunnis among the political elite appears to be due to their Tikriti clan association with Saddam. While the regime was certainly hostile to the Shia Islamist Dawa Party, it was equally hostile to Wahhabism, which was prohibited as 'a deviation from the real Islam' (cit. Sassoon 2012, 261). In the 1990s, after the Iran-Iraq war, Saddam launched a faith campaign, building new mosques, repairing old ones, urging Iraqis to observe the Quran in his speeches, and adding the inscription 'Allahu Akbar' to the Iraqi flag (Sassoon 2012, 261; 265). Yet his hostility to Islamism remained. When relations between the IRI and Saudi Arabia warmed considerably after Khatami became president in 1997, with numerous meetings and Prince Abdullah praising 'the immortal achievements credited to the Muslim people of Iran and their invaluable contributions' (Cordesman 2001), a memo from the Iraqi regime warned that this might herald a future relationship between the Dawa Party and Wahhabists. 'Even throughout the 1990s, anyone showing an inclination toward Wahhabism was considered an enemy of the state'; as late as 'early September 2001, the minister of *awqaf* [charitable endowments] and religious affairs held a meeting attended by academics, religious leaders, and representatives from the different security organizations to discuss Wahhabism – how to fight it and how to show that its teachings had nothing to do with real Islam' (Sassoon 2012, 261).

Saddam was convinced that enabling women to access economic, social and legal rights was vital to the growth of Iraqi society; in a speech given to the General Federation of Iraqi Women (GFIW) in 1971, he said,

> We are all – in the Party and the Government, and in the social organisations – expected to encourage the recruitment of more women to the schools, government departments, the organisations of production, industry, agriculture, arts, culture, information and all other kinds of institutions and services. We are called upon to struggle tirelessly against all the material and psychological obstacles which stand in our way along this path. (Hussein 2009)

As a result, there was a significant increase throughout the 1970s in the number of girls attending primary and secondary schools, and the university attendance of women grew from about 9,000 in 1970 to more than 28,000 by 1979; there was a drive to combat illiteracy, which affected around 70 per cent of women, and there were significant achievements in the provision of healthcare to women (Sassoon 2012, 253). However, this began to change with the Iran-Iraq war.

The Iran-Iraq War

Saddam Hussein's downfall began with the return of Khomeini to Iran in February 1979. The Baathists had had problems with the shah; for example, in 1969 the shah unilaterally abrogated Iran's 1937 treaty with Iraq, which had fixed the frontier between the two countries at the low-water mark on the eastern edge of the Shatt al-Arab (the waterway through which the Tigris and Euphrates flow into the Persian Gulf), thus giving Iraq control over the entire waterway except near the Iranian towns of Abadan and Khorramshahr, where the frontier was at the median deepwater line; he also began providing military support to the Kurdish separatists in Iraq. With the Shatt al-Arab being Iraq's main outlet to the sea, and the loss of Kurdistan (where a substantial portion of Iraq's oil is located) threatening the country with disintegration, the Baathists had no option but to negotiate with their much bigger and more powerful neighbour; this resulted in the Algiers Agreement of 1975, which fixed the border at the median over the length of the Shatt al-Arab, while the shah agreed not to interfere in Kurdistan (Karsh 2002, 7–8). This was a loss for Iraq, but at least it was possible to negotiate with the shah. Hoping for a good relationship with the new rulers in Tehran, the Iraqi regime offered its friendship: 'The Iranian prime minister, Mehdi Bazargan, was invited to visit Baghdad, Iraq offered its good offices in case Iran decided to join the non-aligned movement, and ... shortly after his ascendancy to the presidency, Saddam Hussein reiterated Iraq's desire to establish relations of friendship and co-operation with Iran, based on mutual non-interference in internal affairs' (Karsh 2002, 13).

However, as the constitution of the Islamic Republic made clear, 'Khomeini wanted to export the Iranian revolution, and Iraq, with its large Shia population, was the obvious first destination. In the fall of 1979, the Iranian radio began openly inciting Iraqi Shias to rebellion. Terrorist attacks on senior figures of the Iraqi regime in April 1980 were attributed to an outlawed pro-Iranian Shia organization called the al-Dawa party, which received direct support from Tehran' (Human Rights Watch 1990, 7). The IRI also resumed support for the Iraqi Kurds. Sadeq Khalkhali (Khomeini's executioner) stated: 'We have taken the path of true Islam, and our aim in defeating Saddam Hussein lies in the fact that we consider him the main obstacle to the advance of Islam in the region'; Iran withdrew its ambassador and diplomatic staff from Iraq in March and April 1980 (Karsh 2002, 13–14). Having earlier been pragmatic enough to negotiate with the shah rather than enter into a military confrontation with a country whose territory was three times the size of Iraq and whose population in 1980 was likewise three times larger (39 million and 13 million in Iran and Iraq respectively),

> Saddam was gradually driven to the conclusion that the only way to deflect the Iranian threat was to exploit Iran's temporary weakness following the revolution and to raise the stakes for both sides by resorting to overt, state-sponsored armed force. On 7 September 1980 Iraq accused Iran of shelling Iraqi border towns from territories which, according to the Algiers Agreement, belonged to Iraq, and demanded the immediate evacuation of Iranian forces from these areas. Soon afterwards Iraq moved to 'liberate' these disputed territories and, on 10 September, announced that the mission had been accomplished. For his part, the Iranian acting Chief-of-Staff announced on 14 September that his country no longer abided by the 1975 Algiers Agreement on the land borders. Saddam responded three days later by abrogating the agreement. (Karsh 2002, 14)

On September 23, after having failed to destroy the Iranian air force by bombing airfields the previous day, Iraqi forces invaded Iran. The main thrust of the invasion in the southern province of Khuzestan aimed at gaining control over the Shatt al-Arab and capturing the strategic towns of Khorramshahr and Abadan, while supportive operations were carried out in the central and northern fronts. By October 24, after a bloody conflict in which about 7,000 had been killed or seriously injured on each side, Iraqi forces captured Khorramshahr. According to historian Efraim Karsh,

> Saddam's initial strategy ... avoided targets of civilian and economic value in favour of attacks almost exclusively on military targets. Only after the Iranians struck non-military targets did the Iraqis respond in kind. Nor did Saddam's territorial aims go beyond the Shatt al-Arab and a small portion of the southern region of Khuzestan ... Saddam hoped that a quick, limited, yet decisive campaign would convince Iran's revolutionary regime to desist from its attempts to overthrow him. (Karsh 2002, 27–29)

Instead of negotiating a settlement, as Saddam requested, the IRI counterattacked, targeting Basra and two oil terminals near the port of Fao with its navy, while the air force targeted 'oil facilities, dams, petrochemical plants and the nuclear reactor near Baghdad. By 1 October, Baghdad itself had been subjected to eight air raids. Iraq retaliated with a series of strikes against Iranian targets and the two sides became interlocked in widespread strategic exchanges' (Karsh 2002, 29). There was a stalemate for around eight months, after which Iran gained the initiative. Mobilising the IRGC and recruiting large numbers of child soldiers to the Basij, the IRI succeeded in driving Iraqi forces out of most of Iran, recapturing Khorramshahr along with a substantial amount of Iraqi military equipment and twelve thousand Iraqi troops in May 1982. Saddam announced on June 20 that he would withdraw his remaining troops from Iran within ten days, hoping that the war was over. Instead, on the very next day after Saddam's peace proposal, Khomeini announced that an Iranian invasion of Iraq was imminent, and in July a large-scale offensive was launched on Basra using around 100,000 fighters, including human wave attacks using Basiji as minesweepers. In response, the Iraqi forces used gas for the first time; while this was only non-lethal tear gas, its success would encourage them to use more-lethal chemical weapons, and much more widely, during the rest of the war (Karsh 2002, 36–37; Dunn 2009).

However, the factors which had earlier favoured the Iranian forces (defence of one's homeland and better knowledge of the terrain) now favoured the Iraqis, and the invasion was repulsed. 'Even many Kurds and Shia saw the war as their own: some 250,000 Kurds joined the Salah al-Din forces, a militia that helped the army in keeping the Iranians out of Iraqi Kurdistan; battalions with a majority of Shi'i soldiers mounted a similar defence in the southeast' (Jabar 1992). Neither side was in a position to defeat the other comprehensively, and the war dragged on for six more years, with each side bombing the other's cities, and an estimated million lives lost in total.

Iraq was financially supported by the Gulf countries, especially Kuwait, Saudi Arabia and the UAE, while the Soviet Union, the Eastern European countries, China and France were its main arms suppliers; the Netherlands provided a small amount of financial support to Iran, while North Korea, South Korea, Libya, Pakistan, Portugal, Syria and Sweden provided arms. However, many countries, including Brazil, China, West Germany, Spain, Switzerland and Turkey supplied arms to both sides, while Iran was also being armed clandestinely by Israel and the US, and by the Soviet Union and Warsaw Pact countries via North Korea. The United States, which had broken off diplomatic relations with Iraq after the 1967 Arab-Israeli war, normalised relations in 1982 and provided Iraq with financial and military aid. Only after the Iran-Contra affair was exposed and a US tanker was hit by an Iranian mine did the US take the initiative to pass UN Security Council Resolution 598 in July 1987, calling for an end to the conflict, and take action against Iran when it failed to comply. On July 17, 1988 President Khamenei finally sent a letter to UN Secretary-General Javier Pérez de Cuéllar accepting Resolution 598; three days later Khomeini accepted it under protest; and on August 8 the UN Security Council convened and declared a ceasefire effective from dawn on August 20 (Karsh 2002 58–61, 79–81; Dunn 2009). Saddam's decision to invade Iran and Khomeini's decision to continue the war for six years after Iraqi troops had been expelled resulted in massive death and destruction in both countries, and continued to have a devastating impact on Iraqi civilians even after the end of the war.

Fallout from the Iran-Iraq War

In the build-up to and during the war, Saddam expelled Shia Iraqis of Iranian descent and their families, regarding them as a fifth column of Iran; an estimated 250,000 people were affected (Jabar 1992). The war was an even greater catastrophe for the Kurds of Iraq. Their demand for independence or autonomy predated the Baathist regime and continued throughout. In 1970, the Baathist regime conceded them a far-greater measure of self-rule than Kurds in Syria, Iran or Turkey enjoyed; but the fourteen thousand square miles of the Kurdistan Autonomous Region was only half of what they claimed, and although it included the rich agricultural region producing half of Iraq's food, it excluded the oil wealth that lay below the fringes of the region. In 1974, Mullah Mustafa Barzani's Kurdish Democratic Party (KDP) launched a revolt, supported by the shah in neighbouring Iran as well as by Israel and the US; but when the shah signed the Algiers Agreement in 1975, he withdrew his support and the rebellion collapsed. After the KDP fled to Iran, tens of thousands of Barzani tribespeople were evicted from their homes and relocated to barren sites in the desert. Later, at least a quarter of a million Kurds on the borders with Iran and Turkey were also forcibly relocated to settlements in army-controlled areas of Iraqi Kurdistan; until 1987, they were paid a nominal cash compensation but were forbidden to return to their homes (Human Rights Watch 1993).

When the war began and troops were moved to the front, the Kurdish Peshmerga (military forces) emerged again. In 1983, Iranian forces in alliance with the KDP, now led by Barzani's son Masoud, captured the border town of Haj Omran. In retaliation, Iraqi troops abducted between five and eight thousand males from the relocated Barzani tribals, and they were never seen again. At this time, the rival Patriotic Union of Kurdistan (PUK) led by Jalal Talabani was in alliance with Saddam, but by 1986 it, too, concluded a formal political and military agreement with Tehran (Human Rights Watch 1993). The joint Kurdish-Iranian insurgency was so effective that in early 1987, Saddam launched counterinsurgency operations, appointing his cousin Ali Hassan al-Majid as overseer. In February 1988, as Joost Hiltermann (2016) recounts,

> the regime launched what it called the Heroic Anfal Operation, a six-month-long campaign in eight numbered stages designed to cover all of rural Kurdistan. Each stage was preceded by the extensive use of chemical weapons against Kurdish strongholds: this drove people out of the countryside and into the arms of the Iraqi military, which dispatched them in convoys to execution sites in the south. It's estimated that between eighty and one hundred thousand people, most of them civilians, died this way.
>
> In a separate operation, as part of the war, the Iraqi regime attacked the Kurdish town of Halabja with poison gas in March 1988 after it was captured by a combination of Iranian and Kurdish forces. The attack killed thousands of civilians, while leaving the fighters, who had protective clothing, mostly unscathed ... After Halabja, as chemical clouds wafted down in selective locations during the Anfal campaign, the merest rumour or hint of a gas attack would be enough to send people running, just as the army intended.

On September 6, 1988, by which time the Iran-Iraq War had ended, the Iraqi regime made a declaration of victory over the insurgency and announced a general amnesty for all Kurds. However, Kurdish populations continued to be relocated to barren camps, and survivors were not allowed to return to their villages (Human Rights Watch 1993). One is again reminded of Stalin, and in particular his treatment of ethnic minorities, especially Muslims, during World War II. In a judgement celebrated by survivors, in December 2005 a court in The Hague ruled that the mass killings of Iraqi Kurds in the 1980s was an act of genocide (BBC News 2005b).

Women's rights suffered a setback during the war. In an attempt to appease religious groups in Iraq and compensate for Iran's much-larger population, one year into the war, the RCC decided to provide interest-free loans to any man below the age of twenty-two who got married; if he was a student, he and his wife would get free accommodation in the university. A second law enacted in 1987 offered financial rewards to families who produced a fourth child after the law came into effect; and to those who already had four children, bonuses would be paid for future births. These measures ensured that more women would stay at home to look after their children, and women also lost jobs when soldiers returned after the end of the war. Worst of all, in 1990 the tribal practice of honour killings was legitimised (Sassoon 2012, 254–55).

War expenses, combined with a sharp drop in oil prices (from an average high of around $32 per barrel in 1981 to an average low of $12 to $14 in late 1988), depleted Iraq's foreign exchange reserves by 1983, forcing the country to borrow heavily, mainly from Gulf countries. A wide-ranging privatisation programme saw state-owned farms and factories being sold to private owners, and foreign investment being invited even into oil fields. Austerity measures were carried out, including the halting of all educational scholarships unless they were paid for by foreign governments (Sassoon 2012, 239–40). Trade unions were already dominated by the party, but additional measures were imposed to ensure they did not oppose privatisations: 'Labor Law no. 71 of 1987 dissolved the labor unions and confirmed that workers in the public sector would become members of the civil service', even while it 'guaranteed every worker the right to earn a wage that was adequate to meet his or her essential needs and those of his or her family and confirmed the rights of working hours and retirement' (Sassoon 2012, 250). The end of the war solved none of the economic problems. On one side, Saddam had to limit austerity measures and rebuild the country in order to portray the outcome as a victory; on the other, over the course of the war Iraq 'had accumulated a foreign debt of some $80 billion – roughly twice the size of its Gross National Product. This debt was extremely disturbing, since repayment arrears and the consequent reluctance of foreign companies and governments to extend further credits meant that the reconstruction of Iraq from the destruction wrought by the war would have to be shelved' (Karsh 2002, 89).

The most obvious way around this dilemma was to lean on the Gulf countries again, for a moratorium on wartime loans, additional funds, and adherence to oil quotas, so that prices would recover. But instead of acceding to his requests, Kuwait and the UAE continued to exceed the quotas imposed by OPEC (Organisation of the Petroleum Exporting Countries), putting a downward pressure on oil prices. Saddam was particularly frustrated and humiliated by the refusal of Kuwait, a major creditor, to respond to his desperate appeals. On July 16, 1990,

> the Iraqi Foreign Minister, Tariq Aziz, delivered a memorandum to the Secretary-General of the Arab League for distribution to the League's members. In this he accused Kuwait both of deliberately causing a glut in the oil market (allegedly costing Iraq some $89 billion between 1981 and 1990), and of directly robbing Iraq by setting up oil installations in the southern section of the Iraqi al-Rumaila oil-field and extracting oil from it ... Aziz demanded

the raising of oil prices to over $25 a barrel; the cessation of Kuwaiti 'theft' of Iraqi oil; a complete moratorium on Iraq's wartime loans; and the formation of 'an Arab plan similar to the Marshall Plan to compensate Iraq for some of the losses during the war'. (Karsh 2002, 91)

The Rumaila oilfield is mainly in Iraq, but its southern tip extends across the border into Kuwait. It provides around 60 per cent of Iraq's oil output, but during the war with Iran, Iraq's drilling operations declined while Kuwait's increased. The Kuwaitis did have the technology to drill across the border, but there is no conclusive evidence as to whether they did so or not. Of course they denied this charge, while refusing to accede to any of the other Iraqi demands. Having threatened that if negotiations failed, he would take 'effective action', Saddam invaded Kuwait on August 2, rapidly establishing Iraqi control over it. The Kuwaiti and US delegations to the UN immediately requested a Security Council meeting, which passed Resolution 660, condemning the invasion and demanding the withdrawal of Iraqi troops. The next day the Arab League had a meeting, which likewise demanded a withdrawal (with a few dissenters), but called for a solution from within the League and warned against outside intervention. UNSC Resolution 661 on August 6 placed economic sanctions on Iraq and was soon followed by Resolution 665, authorising a naval blockade that prevented the export of oil, on which the entire Iraqi economy was dependent. On August 23, the Iraqi Foreign Ministry sent a proposal to the US that Iraq would withdraw from Kuwait and allow foreigners to leave the country if in return UN sanctions were lifted, Iraq gained access to the Persian Gulf through the Kuwaiti islands of Bubiyan and Warbah which it had been trying to lease from Kuwait, and Iraq gained full control of the Rumaila oil field (Royce 1990).

The Bush Sr. administration rejected the proposal and instead continued with its military build-up in the Gulf, collecting money for it (including major contributions from Saudi Arabia and Kuwait) and pledges of military forces from thirty-three countries, including a large contingent from Syria's Hafez al-Assad. On November 29, the Security Council passed Resolution 678 authorising military action against Iraq if it had not vacated Kuwait by January 15, 1991 (Council on Foreign Relations 2011). In order to obtain the support of the American public for the war against Iraq, the government of Kuwait paid several law and lobby firms to sell it to them. Hill & Knowlton, run by Craig Fuller, a close friend and advisor of President Bush, masterminded the campaign as representative of 'Citizens for a Free Kuwait' and was paid $11.9 million for doing so. Its research arm, the Wirthlin Group, conducted daily opinion polls to 'identify the themes and slogans that would be most effective in promoting support for US military action'; they found that the story which had most impact was one about Iraqi soldiers removing scores of babies from their incubators and leaving them to die on the hospital floor – a story later found to be completely fabricated (Stauber and Rampton 1995). When Saddam failed to leave Kuwait by the January 15 deadline, the US and its allied forces began their assault. On February 27, allied troops entered Kuwait City, and on March 2, the UNSC passed a resolution establishing the terms of the ceasefire.

Ruthless control over journalists by the US as well as hindrance by Saddam Hussein prevented serious estimates of the Iraqi casualties at the time. More than ten years later, *BBC News* (2003) cited estimates of 60,000 to 200,000 soldiers and 100,000 to 200,000 civilians killed. Many of the soldiers (mostly peasant conscripts who were antagonistic to Saddam) were massacred from the air on the Mutla 'Highway of Death' on February 26 as they retreated from Kuwait in compliance with UN Resolution 660 (Chediac 2004). Apart from immediate civilian casualties as a result of airstrikes, future deaths were ensured by the destruction of grain and other food warehouses and of a dairy factory (which was particularly devastating given the concurrent sanctions and embargo), as well as of water-treatment facilities, including drinking water installations, and virtually the entire electrical system – which in turn exacerbated food shortages through causing a lack of refrigeration and the impairment of agricultural irrigation, crippling the surviving water-purification and sewage-treatment facilities, and causing the deterioration of vaccines and medicines requiring refrigeration. 'A UNICEF representative noted in late May the "vicious cycle" of "poor hygiene, contaminated water and poor diet," which he said left about 100,000 Iraqi children under one year of age vulnerable to diarrhea and dehydration' (Human Rights Watch 1991). Apart from electrical power plants, vital sectors of the economy were also destroyed, such as 'oil refineries, oil-pumping stations, industrial units, railway lines, airports, petrochemical plants, steel and cement plants, and so on' (Chalabi 2002, 150).

This destruction, combined with the sanctions, which continued until 2003, was to have a devastating impact on Iraqi civilians, especially children. A survey comparing the economy in 1991, one year after the imposition of sanctions, with the situation in 1996 argued that 'the main effect of sanctions has come through the complete closing off of oil exports and the barring of access to the international capital markets', which 'caused the abrupt ending of revenues from oil exports and also cut Iraq off from other sources of finance, such as foreign borrowing' (Gazdar and Hussain 2002, 33; 37). In an economy that had relied on oil revenues to fund the import of essential commodities, this led to the collapse of imports of food and medicines, rendering the UN's exemption of these commodities from the sanctions regime irrelevant. 'Before the sanctions, Iraq's imports per person were close to the average of those countries ranked as "high middle income" in the World Bank's *World Development Tables*. By 1996, they had declined to about a third of the level for the poorest countries in the world'; moreover, as the government tried to plug the resulting fiscal deficit by reducing expenditures and issuing money, the exchange rate, which had been around four Iraqi dinars per dollar prior to the invasion of Kuwait, dropped to 3,000 dinars per dollar in 1996 (Gazdar and Hussain 2002, 38, 39).

As Harris Gazdar and Athar Hussain (2002) write, 'All the evidence suggests that the government ... preserved employment levels in the public sector at the expense of the purchasing power of public-sector salaries, by not adjusting them with the rise in prices ... By 1996 public sector workers were commonly earning US$3–5 per month, compared to their pre-sanctions salaries of US$150–200.' By contrast with the public sector, where wages fell but employment was maintained, private sector employment declined sharply as production was hit by the steep fall in purchasing power. 'For the unemployed or those earning low wages, the most common means of gaining additional income was to find self-employment or casual labor', with child labour increasing (Gazdar and Hussain 2002, 41; 43). The other solution was to return to agriculture, the only sector where incomes were maintained; while in 1987 only 12 per cent had been engaged in agriculture, by 1996 this had shot up to 40 per cent. 'In the context of this dramatic collapse of private incomes in 1990–1 and their continuing decline since then, the state ration system proved to be a crucial source of sustenance. Early assessments of the humanitarian impact of sanctions identified the importance of the state ration as the main factor in preventing the onset of large-scale hunger and starvation in Iraq,' and its importance as a lifeline increased as time went on (Gazdar and Hussain 2002, 48). Even so, UNICEF surveys found that in government-controlled central and southern areas, under-five child mortality rates increased from 56 per thousand during 1984–89, to 91.5 during 1989–94, and 130.6 during 1994–99 (Graham-Brown 2002, 283).

In 1991, UNSC Resolutions 706 and 712 had allowed Iraq to sell $1.6 billion worth of oil every six months under UN supervision, with 30 per cent of the proceeds to go to a Compensation Fund for other parties damaged during the war, further appropriations for UN expenses in Iraq including the Special Commission dealing with weapons of mass destruction, and the rest for humanitarian relief. Saddam had refused to accept this. In 1995, probably in response to pressure for lifting sanctions completely as evidence of civilian suffering mounted, Resolution 986 was adopted, raising the amount to $2.2 billion worth of oil and accepting some of Saddam's objections to the original resolution. This was finally accepted by Saddam in May 1996 (Graham-Brown 2002, 268–70) and implemented in March and April of 1997. However, the extra amount was used mainly for food and medicines; the Sanctions Committee had placed numerous obstacles to the use of funds in the telecommunications, electricity, water and sanitation sectors, making it difficult to repair damaged infrastructure (Graham-Brown 2002, 284).

The revelation that, as Barton Gellman wrote for the *Washington Post* in 1991, 'preliminary planning for the bombing campaign began before Iraq even invaded Kuwait last August 2', along with the deliberate destruction of infrastructure and the persistence of sanctions long after Iraqi forces had withdrawn from Kuwait, make it clear that the real purpose of the war, as one US Air Force planner admitted, was 'to let people know, "...We're not going to tolerate Saddam Hussein or his regime. Fix that, and we'll fix your electricity."' In other words, civilians were deliberately targeted in the belief that this would induce them to overthrow Saddam, and this continued throughout Bill Clinton's two terms as president. The strategy was not only foolish but also criminal, and the central role played by the UNSC in implementing it puts a huge question mark over that institution's commitment to human rights. An assessment by economist Abbas Alnasrawi (2002, 347) of the long-term consequences of the sanctions regime concludes:

> Some ten years later, and after well over a million Iraqi deaths, the sanctions are still in place, performing their grisly task of what has been described as silent slaughter ... In addition to death, the sanctions regime has led to poverty, underdevelopment, stunted growth, social disintegration and the unprecedented emigration of huge numbers of professionals and skilled workers. [...]
> It is true, of course, that the government of Iraq has exhibited callous indifference to the plight of its own people, but this indifference cannot justify the UNSC's own violation of the human rights of an entire population ... In

effect, the UNSC has given itself the liberty to impose collective punishment on an entire population simply for the decisions of its leader.

It is important to keep in mind that, in the case of Iraq, the destructive impact of the sanctions regime has been intensified because of the war damage to the infrastructure, and that it has disproportionately affected children. As is well known, hundreds of thousands of children have died because of the sanctions. Such a tragic loss of life constitutes an outright violation of the most fundamental human right – the right to life.

When George Bush Sr. ordered an end to the military assault on Iraq at the end of February 1991, he called on the Iraqi people to rise up and overthrow Saddam. In response, the Kurds in the north and the Arabs in the south rose up against the Baath regime in March 1991. 'For two brief weeks, the uprisings were phenomenally successful. Government administration in the towns was overthrown and local army garrisons were left in disarray. Yet by the end of the month the rebellions had been crushed and the rebels scattered, fleeing across the nearest borders or into Iraq's southern marshes. Those who could not flee did not survive summary executions' (Jabar 1992). US forces did nothing as tens of thousands were slaughtered by Saddam's forces in the south; indeed, there are allegations that the Bush Sr. administration colluded in the slaughter by ordering that huge caches of arms and ammunition captured from Iraqi forces should not be turned over to the rebels (Lando 2007). But would the uprisings have been successful if US forces had thrown their weight behind them?

During the war with Iran, the opposition to Saddam had been severely damaged by popular support for his patriotic posture of defending the homeland. They were also 'cut off from the major urban centres – Baghdad, Basra and Mosul – that contain almost half of the Iraqi population', and their organizational structures in the cities were largely destroyed. 'The Kurds and the Communists retained bases in the northern mountains, with some ties to small towns and to the Kurdish cities of Suleimaniya and Erbil. The Islamists' only organized bases were in Iran' (Jabar 1992).

In 1991, all the Shia Islamist parties belonging to the Supreme Council for the Islamic Revolution in Iraq (SCIRI), including the Dawa party, took a pro-Iranian position. This was not shared by the majority of Shi'is, who were not sympathetic to radical Islamism. And although the Iraqi Shia Islamists living in Iran were only one element of the forces that seized cities in the south, they acted as if they were the decision makers, with SCIRI leader al-Hakim saying that all Iraqi armed forces should follow their orders, and that no ideas except Islamic ones should be disseminated. 'According to Muwaffaq al-Ruba'i, a Da'wa Party leader based in London, those who returned to the south bearing posters of al-Hakim and Khomeini achieved only the abortion of the *intifada*' (Jabar 1992).

The uprising in the north was more successful, with Masoud Barzani of the KDP winning over Salah al-Din forces and many soldiers, including high-ranking officers; the Peshmerga would withdraw once a town had been seized, leaving it to the locally selected administration, and refrain from revenge killings except in the case of security servicemen and top Baath officials. Although here too Saddam massacred some twenty thousand Kurds, in April a no-fly zone was imposed over the north, and the UN later took over the administration of aid (Jabar 1992).

The Bush Sr. administration failed to offer any support for the uprisings; as then–secretary of state James Baker described it, they feared a 'Lebanonization of Iraq', that Iranian-backed Shias would assume power in Baghdad, or that more US soldiers would lose their lives in 'another Vietnam' (cit. Zenko 2016). Twelve years later, prodded on by the same neocons, George W. Bush rushed in where his father had feared to tread, despite the fact that this time there was no ongoing uprising.

The brutal, totalitarian character of Saddam's regime is undeniable, but the US use of his invasion of Kuwait as a 'humanitarian' pretext to kill over a million Iraqis, including hundreds of thousands of children, was a crime which anti-imperialists quite rightly opposed.

Regime Change by Foreign Powers

As we saw in Chapter 1, in July 2016, the Chilcot Report confirmed officially that evidence for Saddam Hussein's weapons of mass destruction had been fabricated, and by then it was abundantly clear that it was the US/UK invasion that had brought Al Qaeda into Iraq, not Saddam. However, humanitarian arguments for the invasion, put forward by some liberals and a few socialists, notably Christopher Hitchens, do need to be considered briefly. In the introduction to a collection of these arguments, Thomas Cushman (2005, 2) takes the position that 'the war can be seen as morally justifiable ... Coming to the rescue and aid of a people who had been subjected to decades of brutality and crimes against humanity is entirely consistent with the basic liberal principle of solidarity with the oppressed and the fundamental humanitarian principle of rescue.' One can agree that coming to the aid of a people subjected to decades of brutality is consistent with solidarity with the oppressed, but is this what happened during and after the March 2003 invasion of Iraq?

It is hard to square this rosy view of what US/UK forces were doing with what was actually going on: 'The wailing children, the young women with breast and leg wounds, the 10 patients upon whom doctors had to perform brain surgery to remove metal from their heads, talk of the days and nights when the explosives fell "like grapes" from the sky. Cluster bombs, the doctors say – and the detritus of the air raids around the hamlets of Nadr and Djifil and Akramin and Mahawil and Mahndesin and Hail Askeri shows that they are right' (Fisk 2003a). Most victims died at once; sixty-one died after being brought to the Hillah hospital, which received over two hundred of the wounded (Fisk 2003a). Can killing civilians be described as coming to their aid?

> After the bombings, the ambushes and assaults, the news readers' voices lighten as they reach the humanitarian aid slot in the story running order. The images of bloodied limbs and bombed buildings are replaced by jostling crowds being roughly corralled by British troops distributing bottles of water. This is the battle for hearts and minds, we are repeatedly told ... [W]hose heart and mind are won by such images of angry desperation? Certainly not the Iraqis, bewildered by the invader who has deprived them of the water in the first place. (Bunting 2003)

Is it morally justifiable to destroy people's access to water and then dole out 'enough to last one person a couple of hours' (Bunting 2003)? Then there was the vandalisation of the Iraq Museum and its archaeological treasures dating back millennia (Steele 2003), and the murder of journalists reporting on civilian casualties (Fisk 2003b). It strains the imagination to think of all this as 'solidarity with the oppressed', and it is just a minuscule sample of the death and destruction meted out by the occupation forces in Iraq.

The criticisms Cushman and other contributors to the volume make of the UN's failure to stop the genocides in Bosnia and Rwanda are valid, and they would be relevant if the US had intervened in Iraq during the Anfal campaign or the uprisings of 1991 in order to halt or avert massacres; but there was no such justification in 2003. Most importantly, what these so-called humanitarian interventionists failed to do was to listen to the voices of democracy activists within Iraq. That the invasion would victimise Iraqi civilians was obvious to them. Take, for example, trade unionist Hadi Saleh and the Workers' Democratic Trade Union Movement (WDTUM) he helped to form, an underground organisation made up of intellectuals, liberals, communists, women, youth and student advocates. Hunted by the regime, Saleh himself escaped abroad, but WDTUM activists continued to organise in Iraq, at great risk to themselves. 'In early 2003 WDTUM activists marched against the planned military invasion of Iraq. In Britain, Italy, Denmark, Sweden, Canada and the USA, WDTUM militants who had long fought for regime-change from below spoke out against the invasion, conscious that the victims would be once again Iraqi workers and innocent civilians' (Muhsin and Johnson 2006, 25; 27). Women's organisations too opposed the invasion, anticipating that it would empower the Islamists (Susskind 2007). To pretend that you are trying to 'rescue' people who are desperately trying to prevent your intervention is a particularly vile form of hypocrisy.[2]

As post-invasion Iraq descended into chaos and bloodshed, with Shia and Sunni Islamists free to gain a foothold there, the neoconservatives who had orchestrated the invasion chose Paul Bremer (who was clueless about the Middle East and knew no Arabic) to sort out the mess as proconsul of the Coalition Provisional Authority. Appointed in May 2003 for fourteen months, Bremer carried out three policies (with the backing of his bosses) which catapulted Iraq into civil war. On just his fifth day in Iraq, he issued the 'De-Baathification of Iraqi Society' order, banning hundreds of thousands of Baath Party members – many of whom had joined the party for pragmatic reasons and had played no part in Saddam's atrocities – from public sector employment, thereby condemning them and their families to penury; a week later, a second order disbanded the Iraqi army, creating a huge number of embittered and unemployed veterans (Swidey 2016). With these two orders, Bremer sacked literally everyone who had any experience running the country or ensuring its security. The third policy was the imposition of ethnosectarian quotas on the government he set up before leaving, increasing the power of Shi'is and Kurds and discriminating against Sunnis. As a critic puts it, referring to an article Bremer wrote in 2007,

> Time and again, he refers to 'the formerly ruling Sunnis,' 'rank-and-file Sunnis,' 'the old Sunni regime,' 'responsible Sunnis.' This obsession with sects informed the U.S. approach to Iraq from day one of the occupation, but it was not how

Iraqis saw themselves – at least, not until very recently. Iraqis were not primarily Sunnis or Shiites; they were Iraqis first, and their sectarian identities did not become politicized until the Americans occupied their country, treating Sunnis as the bad guys and Shiites as the good guys. [...]

Despite Bremer's assertions, Saddam Hussein's regime was not a Sunni regime; it was a dictatorship with many complex alliances with Iraqi society, including some with Shiites. If anything, the old tyranny was a Tikriti regime, led by relatives and clansmen from Hussein's hometown. ... Local Sunni movements that were not pro-Hussein were repressed just as harshly as the Shiites.

Many Iraqis saw the Americans as new colonists, intent on dividing and conquering Iraq. That was precisely Bremer's approach. When he succumbed slightly to Iraqi demands for democracy and created [the] Interim Governing Council, its members were selected by sectarian and ethnic quotas. Even the Communist Party member of the council was chosen not because he was secular but because he was a Shiite. (Rosen 2007)

The first prime minister appointed to the Interim Governing Council (IGC) was Ayad Allawi, a former Baathist who had broken with Saddam in the 1970s and survived an attempt on his life. Exiled in Britain, his close ties to the Blair government discredited him with many Iraqis, but as a secular Shi'i he gained respect for fighting Sunni and Shia militants equally (Freeman 2010). Ibrahim al-Jafari, who served as prime minister from April 2005 to May 2006, was very different. A member of the Shia Islamist Dawa Party, he had spent almost a decade in Iran and established a strong relationship with the Supreme Council for the Islamic Revolution in Iraq (SCIRI) before moving to London in 1989 as a Dawa Party spokesman (Institute for the Study of War 2010).

During Jafari's period in power, members of the Badr Organization – the military wing of the SCIRI, which in 2007 changed its name to the Islamic Supreme Council of Iraq – flooded into the police and commando units under the Interior Ministry, which was headed by Bayan Jabr, a member of the organisation. There were reports of Shia death squads run by them, and a scandal when one of many secret prisons was discovered in which Sunnis, picked up illegally, were subjected to the same kind of torture used by Saddam's regime (Wong and Burns 2005). Created, trained and armed by the IRGC in 1982, the Badr Organization fought alongside Iran in the Iran-Iraq War and remained headquartered in Iran until 2003. Under instructions from Tehran, from 2005 its death squads carried out a wave of assassinations of former Baathists and Iraqi veterans of the Iran-Iraq

War. Captured IRGC documents showed that it was paying the salaries of up to 11,740 members of the Badr Organization (Musings on Iraq 2015). At the same time,

> wary of Iran, but seeing little alternative to the turban-wearing clerics of SCIRI and Badr, US and British occupation authorities put the party's officials into top positions … They were viewed by the United States and Britain as natural allies in the struggle against remnants of the Baath Party and the burgeoning Sunni resistance … Virtually en masse, Badr officers were recruited to the fledgeling Iraqi police and army that were being assembled by the United States. (Dreyfuss 2008)

The leader of Badr, Hadi al-Ameri, admitted being funded by the IRI at the same time that the organisation was using equipment and vehicles supplied by the United States (Lasseter 2005): a de facto alliance between the US and the IRI, even while Bush Jr. denounced Iran as being part of an 'axis of evil'. No wonder, as Patrick Cockburn (2015, xv) notes, 'Iraqis have always said cynically that when it comes to Iraq, "the Iranians and the Americans shout at each other over the table, but shake hands under it"'. In fact, according to Ryan Crocker, who was deputy chief at the American Embassy in Kabul in 2002, Iran was assisting the US in its attacks on the Taliban after 9/11, and the US even consulted Qassem Soleimani, head of the international jihadi Quds Force of the IRGC, about invading Iraq. Although relations were soured by Bush's 'axis of evil' speech, their alliance was revived after Saddam was toppled, with Crocker allowing Soleimani to vet every Shi'i member of the Iraqi Governing Council. By this time Soleimani was calling the shots, using Shi'i militias under his control to detonate 'explosively formed projectiles (EFPs)' targeting the Americans in Iraq; sheltering Al Qaeda fighters in Iran, including those who planned and executed the bombing of three residential compounds in Riyadh in 2003, killing thirty-five people including nine Americans; encouraging the Assad regime to facilitate the movement of Sunni extremists through Syria to fight against the US in Iraq; controlling Iraqi Shi'i and Kurdish leaders whom he met in Tehran, Baghdad or Erbil; and sometimes attacking American forces, while at others negotiating with them (Filkins 2013).

After an Islamist constitution drafted under the chairmanship of a SCIRI activist was passed in 2005, Jafari was replaced by an equally hardline Dawa Party Islamist, Nouri al-Maliki. As Saad N. Jawad and Sawsan I. al-Assaf describe,

> The Iraqi identity was totally erased from the dictionary of the occupiers. The

socio-political division of Iraq was further exacerbated by other decisions built on the understanding that the Shiites and Kurds were oppressed and marginalized. Eventually they were given further power and preference ... Thus instead of building a state with equal rights and responsibilities to all citizens, the Sunni Arabs were marginalized and left under the mercy of the ruling Shiite and Kurdish parties. (Jawad and al-Assaf, 2013)

Maliki disarmed Sunni militias in Baghdad while giving a free hand to Shi'i militias to carry out an ethnic cleansing drive. Consequently, 'Baghdad went from some 45% Sunni in 2003 to only 25% Sunni by the end of 2007. Al-Maliki's sectarianism led to the transformation of Baghdad into a largely Shiite city' (Cole 2014).

If we are looking for a 'smoking gun' that implicates US imperialism in the genesis and spread of ISIS, this is it. In post-invasion Iraq, the US (1) opened up Iraq to Al Qaeda, which had rigorously been excluded by Saddam Hussein; (2) sacked every Baathist and the entire army, and allowed death squads to target officials and veterans, thus creating a massive embittered cadre with intimate knowledge of Iraq; and (3) installed in power Iran-backed Shia Islamists, who proceeded to persecute, ethnically cleanse and kill Sunnis indiscriminately. Documents discovered after Samir Abd Muhammad al-Khlifawi, aka Haji Bakr, was killed in 2014 confirmed what had been suspected for some time: that former Baathists like Haji Bakr had formed an alliance with Al Qaeda in Iraq against their common bitter enemies, the Americans and Shia Islamists. Imprisonment in Camp Bucca and Abu Ghraib from 2006 to 2008 enabled Haji Bakr and other officers to establish a large network of contacts before they shifted their attention to Syria in 2012 with the intention of returning to Iraq in a stronger position (Reuter 2015).

The absence of religious language or books – even a Quran – among the documents recovered after Haji Bakr's death confirms his identity as a secular Baathist. How plausible, then, is it that 'Bakr and a small group of former Iraqi intelligence officers made Abu Bakr al-Baghdadi, the emir and later "caliph," the official leader of the Islamic State'? (Reuter 2015). Could a secular Baathist possibly have the authority to appoint the leader of an Islamist group? An independent investigation into the life of Sheikh Ibrahim, as the future 'caliph' was known before he became famous, found that he took up arms against the US occupation and was arrested in 2004 and incarcerated in Camp Bucca, where he was impressed by members of Al Qaeda and joined the group after being released; he reportedly also met Haji Bakr and other

Baathists (Hashem 2015). After Al Qaeda in Iraq (AQI) leader Abu Musab al-Zarqawi was killed by an airstrike in 2006, the Islamic State in Iraq was created, with Abu Omar al-Baghdadi as its emir and Abu Hamza al-Mohajer as his deputy and minister of war; but both were killed by a joint US-Iraqi operation in April 2010, and the top spot was vacant again. 'Haji Bakr backed Sheikh Ibrahim to be the next emir of Al Qaeda in Iraq. But bin Laden wanted a different man – Haji Iman – to be the successor. This made Haji Bakr's task difficult; he had to convince the key players that the man he supported was the best choice. Eventually, he succeeded, and nine members of the Shura Council voted for Sheikh Ibrahim,' who was descended from the Quraysh (the same tribe as the prophet Muhammed) and subsequently chose the name Abu Bakr al-Baghdadi (Hashem 2015).

A fourth way in which the US occupation contributed to the rise of AQI was by its clampdown on the democratic mass organisations which opposed it. For example, on May 16, 2003, a national preparatory committee attempting to form a 'proper base for a free and democratic trade unionism' convened a meeting in the main office of the Transport Union in Baghdad, in which '400 trade unionists known for their opposition to the Saddam regime crammed in, including leading members in the WDTUM … The meeting formed the Iraqi Federation of Trade Unions (IFTU) … Hadi [Saleh] was elected a member of the executive committee and given the task of consolidating its external relations' (Muhsin and Johnson 2006, 28). IFTU campaigned for a new labour law based on International Labour Organization (ILO) principles and opposed the privatisation of the oil industry, whereas Bremer retained Saddam's 1987 anti-union law and was intent on pushing through privatisation and foreign ownership of the oil industry. Consequently, on December 6, 2003, 'dozens of soldiers and armoured vehicles surrounded the IFTU headquarters. The troops stormed the building … ransacked the offices, destroyed documents, smashed windows, smeared the banner carrying the name of the IFTU with black paint and even tore down union banners that condemned terrorism. The raid ended with the arrest of eight IFTU leaders' (Muhsin and Johnson 2006, 45). Although the leaders were released without charge the following day and union militants reclaimed their building eight months later, these actions display hostility to democratic unionism: a hostility shared by Al Qaeda, which in January 2005 abducted, tortured and killed Hadi Saleh (Muhsin and Johnson 2006, 65).

Arguing against the post-invasion position of some sections of the left, who had cheered on the Al Qaeda–Baathist terrorist campaign against the US occupation as the 'Iraqi resistance to US imperialism', anarchist Wayne Price (2005) pointed out:

> The jihadis, theocrats, semi-ex-Ba'athists, and Sunni supremacists are a pro-capitalist enemy of the Iraqi working class. They would settle a heavy yoke on the Iraqi workers and peasants. The same is true of the leaders of the opportunist wing of the Iraqi movement, those who use the structure of the occupation to set up their own state, so they think. While their followers (just as the ranks of the armed resistance) seek to expel the U.S. forces, these opportunist leaders also seek to set up a theocratic, capitalist, state, with a revised relationship to U.S. imperialism. While we should defend any Iraqis against the occupation, both groups of leaders, of would-be new rulers, should be politically opposed as enemies of the working class.

The Islamist Takeover of Iraq

Four years after the invasion, the US occupation had led to a complete breakdown of Iraqi society, with Al Qaeda suicide bombers, Shia death squads and criminal gangs taking over the streets. As concrete barriers sprung up everywhere, Iraqis had to construct mental maps of where they could or could not go: Sunnis were compelled to stay away from a number of places, including 'certain hospitals, the Baghdad city morgue, the Ministry of the Interior, even petrol stations, for fear of the Shia militias' (Beaumont 2007a). As Peter Beaumont argued, Iraq met all the conditions of a failed state: 'A failed state is one that can no longer provide security and social requirements for its citizens; that has descended into factionalism and warlordism; that cannot guarantee the integrity of its own borders, and lacks the ability to sustain itself. All of which perfectly describes large areas of today's Iraq. Four million of its people have been displaced, with no indication that this is slowing' (Beaumont 2007a). The consequence of the US/UK 'democratization' process had,

> with bitter irony, been to concentrate power in the hands of those Shia parties whose supporters have been behind the worst of the violence. ... Billions of dollars were allocated for reconstruction, but in the end, you have to ask, what has been achieved? I look around searching for the grand projects: new hospitals, electricity grids, modern new universities. And I come away baffled by the waste and maladministration. But it is in terms of human rights that the Bush-Blair experiment in Iraq has failed most completely. How many people have died is

the subject of rancorous debate – but 150,000 is a low estimate in a range that some research [by *The Lancet*] has claimed could top 655,000. You see the bodies dumped on the streets, on rubbish dumps, in canals and in sewers – sometimes beheaded, at other times bearing the marks of torture. (Beaumont 2007b)

It was not just Sunni men who were the victims of state-sponsored violence. 'In spring 2003, as the smoke began to clear from the US invasion of Iraq, a wave of kidnappings, abductions, public beatings, death threats, sexual assaults and killings gripped the country. The targets were women' (Susskind 2007). In the words of the director of the Organization of Women's Freedom in Iraq (OWFI), Yanar Mohammed: 'We used to have a government that was almost secular. It had one dictator. Now we have almost 60 dictators – Islamists who think of women as forces of evil' (Susskind 2007). One of the first acts of the Iraqi Governing Council (IGC) assembled by Paul Bremer was to replace International Women's Day with a celebration of the birthday of the daughter of Prophet Mohammed. On December 29, 2003, it resolved to replace Iraq's 1959 family law – the most progressive in the region, with divorce proceedings heard only in civil courts, women divorcees having equal rights to custody of their children, women's income recognised as independent from their husbands', restrictions on child marriage, and women and men having equal inheritance rights – with Sharia law and religious courts, which would result in a loss of all these rights, impose compulsory hijab and legalise domestic violence. Iraqi women took to the streets in protest, and with women's organisations and Congress members in the US joining in, Bremer was forced to withhold ratification of the resolution (Susskind 2007). However, as Yifat Susskind (2007) writes,

> Under Bremer, the US refused to honor a series of demands by women's organizations, including calls to create a women's ministry; appoint women to the drafting committee of Iraq's interim constitution; guarantee that 40 percent of US appointees to Iraq's new government were women; pass laws codifying women's rights and criminalizing domestic violence; and uphold UN Security Council Resolution 1325, which mandates that women be included at all levels of decision-making in situations of peacemaking and post-war reconstruction.
>
> Indeed, rather than support progressive and democratically minded Iraqis, including members of the women's movement, the US threw its weight behind Iraq's Shia Islamists.

The occupation presided over the passing of an Islamist constitution that legalised discrimination and violence against women and girls. Meanwhile, the US military did nothing as Islamist militias unleashed an orgy of violence against women. 'Punishment committees' manned by SCIRI's Badr Organization and Muqtada al-Sadr's Mahdi Army made it impossible for women to leave their homes safely. 'By early 2005, two facts were clearly established. First, the US was arming and training Islamist militias in Iraq. Second, these same militias were using gender-based violence to impose a theocracy' (Susskind 2007). Ayatollah Sayyid Ali Sistani, usually seen as a 'moderate', issued an edict that women must wear hijab, and another that lesbians and gays be killed (Susskind 2007). Human rights group Iraqi LGBT–UK waged a campaign that ultimately prevailed upon Sistani to withdraw from his website the fatwa to murder gay men, but he did not issue a contrary fatwa, nor rescind the directive to punish lesbians. As Ali Hili, head of LGBT–UK, notes, Sistani is 'the spiritual leader of all Shia Muslims in Iraq and around the world', as well as of the SCIRI and Badr. In a statement on behalf of LGBT–UK, he said,

> Badr agents have a network of informers who, among other things, target alleged 'immoral behaviour'. They kill gays, unveiled women, prostitutes, people who sell or drink alcohol, and those who listen to western music and wear western fashions … Males who are unmarried by the age of 30 or 35 are placed under surveillance on suspicion of being gay, as are effeminate men. They will be investigated and warned to get married. Badr will typically give them a month to change their ways. If they don't change their behaviour, or if they fail to show evidence that they plan to get married, they will be arrested, disappear and eventually be found dead. The bodies are usually discovered with their hands bound behind their back, blindfolds over their eyes, and a bullet wound in the back of the head. (Iraqi LGBT 2006)

It would not be fair to blame Sistani for all the anti-gay violence of the Badr corps, which was also practised by their Iranian sponsors, but a gay activist in Iraq reported that the killings had indeed accelerated after Sistani's fatwa and complained that the US occupation forces did nothing to protect the victims (Ireland 2006). A later report named two other Shia militias – Asaib Ahl al-Haq (League of the Righteous) and Jaish al-Mahdi (the Mahdi Army) as responsible for homophobic 'pogroms' (OWFI et al. 2014, 2; 5). In June 2014, the former attacked a group of four men and boys, killing two boys aged 15–17 years, beheading them and throwing their heads in the garbage; in July they attacked a brothel, killing thirty-four – all as part of a cleansing drive against 'sexual deviance' (OWFI et al. 2014, 7).

All of these militias were linked to the state.

Commenting on the direct involvement of the Iraqi state in the abuse of women and girls after the US withdrawal in 2011, a human rights activist said, 'What's happening to women shows that no one is safe' (HRW 2014a). Nothing could illustrate this more vividly than the arbitrary arrest, torture and execution of women (both Shia and Sunni), so reminiscent of the treatment of women in the IRI. The Human Rights Watch (2014a) report found that

> security forces carry out illegal arrests and other due process violations against women at every stage of the justice system, including threats and beatings. Israa Salah (not her real name), for example, entered her interview with Human Rights Watch in Iraq's death row facility in Baghdad's Kadhimiyya neighbourhood on crutches. She said nine days of beatings, electric shocks with an instrument known as 'the donkey,' and *falaqa* (when the victim is hung upside down and beaten on their feet) in March 2012 had left her permanently disabled. A split nose, back scars, and burns on her breast were consistent with her alleged abuse. Israa was executed in September 2013, seven months after we met her, despite lower court rulings that dismissed charges against her because a medical report documented she was tortured into confessing to a crime.

> The report also finds that women are subjected to threats of, or actual, sexual assault (sometimes in front of husbands, brothers, and children.) Some detainees reported a lack of adequate protection for female prisoners from attacks by male prison guards, including those from adjoining male prisons. Two women reported that sexual assault by prison guards resulted in pregnancy. Women and officials reported that the likelihood of a woman being subject to sexual assault is far higher during arrest and interrogation, prior to a woman's confinement in prison. 'We expect that they've been raped by police on the way to the prison,' Um Aqil, an employee at a women's prison facility told Human Rights Watch.

> For example, Fatima Hussein (not her real name), a journalist accused of involvement in the murder of a parliamentarian's brother and of being married to an Al-Qaeda member, described physical and sexual torture in early 2012 at the hands of one particular interrogator in Tikrit, Colonel Ghazi. She described Ghazi tying her blindfolded to a column and electrocuting her with an electric baton, hitting her feet and back with [a] cable, kicking her, pulling her hair, tying her naked to a column and extinguishing cigarettes on her body, and later handcuffing her to a bed, forcing her to give him oral sex, and raping her three times. 'There was blood all over me. He would relax, have a cigarette, and put it out on my buttock, and then started again,' she said.

> Women who spoke with Human Rights Watch, who all explicitly denied involvement in alleged crimes, also described being pushed towards confes-

sions by interrogators threatening to hurt loved ones. Fatima described Ghazi passing her the phone, with her daughter at the end of the line, before threatening: 'I'll do to your daughter what I did to you.'

The US/UK occupation replaced Saddam's torture with its own equally barbaric techniques (Conrad 2005), then handed over power to IRI-sponsored Shia Islamists, who also used torture and added the elements of sectarian cleansing and misogyny. There was competition and conflict between the Badr Organization and Muqtada al-Sadr's Mahdi Army, but when the latter was facing sustained assaults and huge losses from joint US-Badr forces in 2007, Sadr declared a ceasefire, moved to Iran, and considerably toned down his anti-Iranian Iraqi nationalist rhetoric (Dreyfuss 2008).

The pattern of state-sponsored – as distinct from oppositional – violence in the 'new' Iraq suggests the formation of an extreme right-wing Shia Islamist state, which contributed to the spread of ISIS by its persecution of Sunnis. The fate of the Sunni tribal Sahwa or Awakening Councils illustrates this dynamic. In 2006, US forces were finding that Shia militias alone could not beat back Al Qaeda. At the same time, Sunni tribes, who had started by supporting the insurgency against the occupation, were getting disgusted with the Al Qaeda brand of radical Islam. Sam Collyns (2010) spoke to Sheikh Jabbar, a tribal leader:

> 'First of all we started seeing bodies filling the streets. Then they managed to capture five of my people and slaughtered them. Then they killed my brother'. ... For Sheikh Jabbar, desperate times required desperate measures, and this was the moment he triggered what would become the Awakening, a military counter-offensive in which he and his supporters joined forces with their former enemies, the Americans, to confront al-Qaeda. In late 2006, he arranged a meeting with Col John Tien of the US army in which he asked for weapons and ammunition for his men to take on al-Qaeda.

There are other accounts of the genesis of the tribal Sahwa movements, some tracing it back to 2005, but in broad outline the story remains the same: an alliance between tribal councils and US forces to chase Al Qaeda out of predominantly Sunni areas of Iraq. Myriam Benraad (2011) recounts the surprising success of the Sahwa movement:

> In the backdrop of the 2007 U.S. 'surge,' the Sahwa quickly took ground, with many tribal figures and imams rallying their ranks and setting up other councils (Majalis al-Sahwa) in al-Anbar localities and beyond. The movement, moreover, enjoyed the additional mobilization all across the country of thousands of Sunni

Arab fighters, mostly former insurgents – also referred to by the coalition as 'Concerned Local Citizens' or 'Sons of Iraq' (*Abna al-Iraq*). In less than a year, the Sahwa had become a major armed force comprising over 80,000 members. Tribes were provided arms and significant financial resources to fight al-Qaeda and delegated important authority prerogatives in their areas to reestablish order ... By mid-2007, insurgent hotbeds such as Ramadi and Fallujah had been cleansed and relatively pacified, to the surprise of the most skeptical.

The US forces paid the tribal fighters a salary of around $300 and promised that they would be absorbed into the regular Iraqi security forces. However, Prime Minister Nouri al-Maliki had no intention of honouring this promise. Very few were incorporated into the regular forces; only a minority were given public sector employment, mostly in temporary or menial jobs; the majority were disarmed and left unemployed; and some were arrested and detained by the Iraqi government (Benraad 2011). Worst of all, after Iranian ambassador Hassan Kazemi-Qomi warned the US against arming Sunnis, the Badr Corps carried out a wave of assassinations of Awakening leaders (Dreyfuss 2008). Simultaneously facing massive retaliatory attacks by the Islamic State in Iraq, large numbers defected to Al Qaeda/ISI, who undertook to pay them. For them, it was a matter of survival (Benraad 2011).

There was sufficient dissatisfaction with Maliki's government for the electorate to give candidates of Allawi's secular Iraqiya bloc ninety-one seats in parliament in the 2010 elections: far short of an absolute majority, but two more than the eighty-nine seats won by Maliki's State of Law coalition. The results were widely celebrated by secular Iraqis, like 23-year-old university student Mohammed Hassan, who said, 'We want to be proud of being Iraqis when we travel outside Iraq and not be asked if [we] are Shiite or Sunni. This is a blow to those who think in terms of sect' (Fadel and DeYoung 2010). However, Maliki rejected the results and the IRI swung into action, brokering a deal between Maliki and Muqtada al-Sadr with the blessings of Ayatollah Ali Khamenei and Hezbollah's Hassan Nasrallah, while Ahmadinejad persuaded Bashar al-Assad – who had broken off relations with Maliki fifteen months previously, when the latter accused him of harbouring terrorists who destroyed four ministries in Baghdad in a devastating bombing campaign – to support Maliki (Chulov 2010). The IRGC's Qassem Soleimani played a key role in putting together the government that emerged months after the 2010 elections:

In the months before, according to several Iraqi and Western officials, Suleimani invited senior Shiite and Kurdish leaders to meet with him in Tehran and Qom, and extracted from them a promise to support Maliki, his preferred candidate. The deal had a complex array of enticements. Maliki and Assad disliked each other; Suleimani brought them together by forging an agreement to build a lucrative oil pipeline from Iraq to the Syrian border. In order to bring the cleric Moqtada al-Sadr in line, Suleimani agreed to place his men in the Iraqi service ministries. ... Suleimani exerts leverage over Iraqi politics by paying officials, by subsidizing newspapers and television stations, and, when necessary, by intimidation. Few are immune to his enticements. 'I have yet to see one Shia political party not taking money from Qassem Suleimani,' [a] former senior Iraqi official told me. 'He's the most powerful man in Iraq, without question.' (Filkins 2013)

It is hard to escape the conclusion that Soleimani and the IRI completely outwitted the US, first by letting it take the brunt of the insurgency – indeed, contributing to it – and then, when the US withdrew in 2011, by grabbing the prize they had coveted since 1979: Iraq.

Although the constitution said that the coalition winning the majority in the elections should have the first chance to form the government, a pliant judiciary allowed Maliki's post-election coalition this privilege. He subsequently moved to consolidate power in his own hands, gaining control over the military, the courts and key ministries, including the interior ministry with its bloated intelligence apparatus. The head of the independent commission that had overseen relatively free and fair elections was arrested on corruption charges, Deputy Vice-President Tareq al-Hashemi, a Sunni Arab, was arrested on charges of plotting a coup in 2006 and 2007, and Iraqiya leaders were threatened (Yaphe 2012). Deprived of power, the Iraqiya bloc fragmented, as individuals within it tried to salvage some semblance of political influence by making compromises with the government (ICG 2013, 10), but this did not provide immunity from persecution.

In December 2012, when security forces stormed the residence of Rafi al-Issawi, Iraq's (Sunni) finance minister, arresting several of his security guards and staff members on charges of terrorism, peaceful protests broke out in Issawi's hometown of Falluja. 'Within days, they had spread to Ramadi, where thousands reportedly poured into the streets, blocking the highway linking Baghdad to Syria and Jordan, then to adjacent, predominantly Sunni provinces of Ninewa, Salah al-Din, Kirkuk and Diyala, as well as Baghdad's Sunni neighbourhoods' (ICG 2013, 1). The protests began by demanding the release of female prisoners but ended up with a much broader set of demands, including the abolition of anti-terror laws, house raids, and widespread corruption (GICJ 2013).

Instead of acceding to the demands, or even entering into negotiations, the government attacked, arrested and detained hundreds of protesters. Police gunfire in Fallujah in January 2013 left nine demonstrators dead, leading a resident of Baghdad's Adhamiya neighbourhood to comment, 'The US occupier left and enabled a new authority, Maliki, to kill, imprison our people and take our women away' (ICG 2013, 2). The outbreak of the war in Syria, and Iran's use of Iraq to send Assad both material aid, including weapons, and Iraqi Shi'i fighters, sharpened the antagonism, prompting one protester from Anbar Province to say, 'We [Sunnis] are not opposing the government only, but an alliance that extends from Teheran to Damascus' (ICG 2013, 13, n.57). Former Baath Party members also participated in the protests, finding in them a place where they could express their sense of injustice; former members of the insurgency participated too, prime among them the Naqshbandi Army, named after a Sufi sect in order to distinguish themselves from the Salafis. Although their leader was a former Baathist, the organisation explained: 'We do not belong to the Baath Party. The only thing connecting us to the Baath is Izzat Ibrahim al-Duri, who is our Supreme Commander in his personal capacity, not as Baath Party leader. We only follow the principles of our religion according to the teachings of the Naqshbandi. We seek to liberate the country from the U.S. and Iran and defend its unity and sovereignty' (ICG 2013, 22–23).

The confrontation between the government and peaceful protesters came to a head in Hawija, Kirkuk, where on April 19, 2013 around four thousand demonstrators were surrounded by army troops, blocking all access to food, water and medical aid. At around 5:00 a.m. on April 23, the troops stormed the camp, shooting indiscriminately, using live ammunition, tanks and helicopters, as well as boiling water, and killing at least fifty demonstrators (including children), injuring around 150, and arresting more than four hundred (GICJ 2013). As the International Crisis Group reported (2013, i), the assault on Hawija 'sparked a wave of violence exceeding anything witnessed for five years', adding: 'Belittled, demonised and increasingly subject to a central government crackdown, the popular movement is slowly mutating into an armed struggle.'

This is the backdrop against which ISIS, recently formed by ISI in Syria, returned to Iraq, its triumphant onslaught greatly facilitated by Maliki's sectarianism and subordination to the IRI.

Between ISIS and Iranian Imperialism

The fall of Mosul to ISIS in July 2014 illustrates how Maliki's regime had continued, rather than reversed, the destruction of Iraq wrought by the US occupation. The ISIS assault on Mosul began with multiple suicide bombings backed up by mortar fire in early June, and as Patrick Cockburn (2015, 14–15) reported, 'defeat became irreversible on July 9, when three top Iraqi generals ... climbed into a helicopter and fled to Kurdistan'. This was a huge army, into which the US had sunk billions of dollars, collapsing ignominiously before a much smaller number of terrorists. How did it happen?

> Asked about the military's cause of defeat, one recently retired Iraqi general was emphatic: 'Corruption! Corruption! Corruption!' It started, he said, when the Americans told the Iraqi army to outsource food and other supplies around 2005. A battalion commander was paid for a unit of 600 soldiers, but had only 200 men under arms and pocketed the difference, which meant enormous profits. The army became a money-making machine for senior officers and often an extortion racket for ordinary soldiers who manned the checkpoints. On top of this, well-trained Sunni officers were sidelined. (Cockburn 2015, 64–65)

A corrupt and sectarian army was one reason for the defeat; equally important were popular perceptions of the regime as a puppet of Iranian imperialism. Cockburn (2015, 15–16) recounts the testimony of a private soldier serving in the Iraqi army, Abbas Sadam, who had recently been transferred to Mosul:

> The fighting started not long after he got there. But on the morning of June 10 his commanding officer told the men to stop shooting, hand over their rifles to the insurgents, take off their uniforms and get out of the city. Before they could obey, their barracks were invaded by a crowd of civilians. 'They threw stones at us,' Abbas recalled, and shouted: 'We don't want you in our city! You are Maliki's sons! ... You are the army of Iran!' The crowd's attack revealed that the fall of Mosul was the result of a popular uprising as well as a military assault. The Iraqi army was detested as a foreign occupying force of Shia soldiers, regarded in Mosul as creatures of an Iranian puppet regime led by Maliki.

This perception of Maliki's government as an Iranian Quisling regime recurs again and again, and was reinforced in the eyes of Sunnis by the treatment they received. When Mosul was bombed in September 2014 by the Iraqi air force, killing and injuring civilians, a Sunni woman wrote, 'I have just heard from a relative who visited us to check on us after that terrible night. He says that because of this bombardment, youngsters are joining ISIS in tens if not in hundreds because this increases hatred toward the government, which doesn't care about us as Sunnis being killed' (Cockburn 2015, xvii–xviii). Those who joined or collaborated with ISIS in the belief that it promised liberation from foreign occupation were soon disillusioned, but in the meantime, ISIS successes bred disillusionment with Maliki's leadership among Shi'is. His State of Law coalition had won ninety-two seats in the elections of April 2014, the largest number scored by any party or coalition, and he wanted a third term as prime minister, but not everyone agreed; indeed, as the crisis dragged on, even Sistani began dropping hints that Maliki should quit (al-Salhy and Otten 2014; Middle East Monitor 2014).

At the end of June, as the Iraqi army and Iran-sponsored militias failed to halt the advance of ISIS, Iraq's ambassador to the US, Lukman Faily, requested American airstrikes. 'We desperately need United States assistance to turn the tide,' he said. 'We believe that immediate and increased military assistance, including targeted airstrikes, are crucial to defeat this growing threat' (cit. Capaccio 2014). The Obama administration agreed but stated that the situation required more than military intervention, thus adding its voice to those of Iraqis calling for Maliki to step aside. In September, Maliki eventually stepped down to allow Haidar al-Abadi to become prime minister. A member of the same Islamic Dawa Party as Maliki, but having spent his exile in Britain rather than Iran and Syria, Abadi was seen as a moderate within the party and as more willing to listen to the grievances of minorities (Madi 2014).

In early August, ISIS attacked the Kurdistan region, defeating the Peshmerga and taking Sinjar after heavy fighting. The majority of inhabitants, who belonged to the Yazidi faith, were regarded by ISIS as infidels, and although tens of thousands fled, up to 200,000 were stranded on a mountain with little food or water, threatened by ISIS with genocide (Salih 2014). With the UN Children's Fund estimating that 25,000 children were among those on the besieged mountain, and that dozens had already died, foreign minister Falah Mustafa of the Kurdish Regional Government (KRG) told foreign diplomats and international organisation representatives in Irbil: 'It is now time for the international community to step forward, urgently, and provide the KRG with humanitarian assistance and military support – particularly air support' (Goodenough 2014). In a CNN interview, Mustafa said that the Kurdish forces were largely up against ISIS on their own: 'This is something that is way beyond the capacity of the Iraqi air forces ... We need the United States and NATO to interfere' (Goodenough 2014).

These are the circumstances in which the United States, having withdrawn from Iraq at the end of 2011, stepped back in. Antiwar groups like Code Pink and Veterans for Peace in the US, and the Stop the War Coalition (StWC) in Britain, immediately organised protests against military intervention, warning that it could only make matters worse (Popular Resistance 2014a, 2014b; RT 2014b). There is an element of truth in this argument: bombing ISIS, if it entailed killing Sunni civilians, could indeed make matters worse in a sectarian war. However, it is also necessary to consider the alternative. Almost exactly two years later, the UN published a report confirming that ISIS was committing genocide against Yazidis (Reuters 2016). The anti-interventionists were in effect demanding that the genocide be allowed to continue, since the KRG and the Iraqi government had declared themselves helpless to halt it. The Genocide Convention, which asks the international community to prevent and punish the crime of genocide, required an intervention at that point. A position that took into account the human rights of all Iraqi civilians would have supported a military intervention which rescued Yazidis without killing civilians of other ethnoreligious groups.

Militarily, the intervention was somewhat successful; by the end of 2015, ISIS had lost 14 per cent of the territory it had controlled, including Sinjar, Tikrit, the Beiji refinery complex, the transit route connecting Mosul to Raqqa, and Ramadi (Alami 2015). However, the broader aim of encouraging a more inclusive government in Baghdad while avoiding a disintegration of Iraq remained elusive. After Sinjar was liberated from ISIS in November 2015 by a combination of Peshmerga fighters affiliated to the KDP, PKK-affiliated units including a Yazidi force trained by the PKK, and a unit that was briefly affiliated with the government in Baghdad, there were disputes over whether Sinjar should be administered from Baghdad or become part of Kurdistan's territory assisted directly by the US (Salih 2015). Subsequently, there were disturbing reports of Kurdish and Yazidi forces subjecting Arab communities to collective punishment by razing whole villages to the ground and expelling their inhabitants (Amnesty International 2016b), and reports that Kurdish authorities were refusing to allow Arabs displaced by the fighting to return to their homes in areas, previously under the government in Baghdad, that the KRG was seeking to incorporate into Kurdistan – either by destroying their homes or by giving them to Kurdish families. Kurdish officials justified these policies by claiming that most Arabs supported ISIS, but Kurdish neighbours testified that inhabitants of three destroyed homes were not linked to ISIS. One of the displaced Arabs, Thaer Hamdi, said, 'All my savings, all my life's work, went into my house ... My son doesn't even speak Arabic. He speaks Kurdish. He sings Kurdish songs. As a teacher in Makhmour I taught in Kurdish. We are not extremists. We are poor, decent people who want to live peacefully with others' (HRW 2015).[3]

In August 2014, Sunni tribal leaders offered to share with the US military information concerning hostages, ISIS supply routes, and recruitment efforts – on condition, however, that the US deal directly with them rather than the Iraqi government. 'The US needs to work hand in hand with the Sunnis that have on-the-ground intel[ligence] and that are being targeted by ISIS,' said a spokesman, but at that point, the Obama administration refused because it was pressing for the creation of an inclusive government (Pecquet 2014). By December 2015, however, as Sunni tribal leaders renewed their lobbying, arguing 'that Iranian influence runs deep in Baghdad and that Abadi's hands are tied,' they were heard with much more sympathy by lawmakers of both parties (Pecquet 2015). US pressure on the Iraqi government to rein in Iran-backed Shia militias and to incorporate Sunni fighters in battles for predominantly Sunni areas paid off in the liberation of Ramadi from ISIS, which was achieved by the Iraqi army backed by US airstrikes (McLeary 2015). This was a boost to the morale of the Iraqi army (Economist 2016), even while it provoked bitter complaints from the Iran-backed militias (Press TV 2016a).

It was clear by then that the Dawa Party was deeply split. Ali Mamouri (2015) summarised the division: 'Abadi's bloc wants to preserve close relations with the United States, keep some distance between Baghdad and Tehran, avoid hostile relations with Saudi Arabia and bring about national reconciliation, including good relations with the Kurds and Sunnis.' Maliki's bloc, on the other hand, 'has explicitly aligned itself with Iran, is hostile toward Saudi Arabia and the United States to the extent of suggesting Abadi approach Russia and is unwaveringly pro-Shiite, including backing for Shiite militias'. Sistani supported Abadi, while Maliki moved decisively into the camp of Ayatollah Ali Khamenei. This alignment was revealed when Abadi and Sistani condemned the mass killings of Sunnis, and the terrorist attacks on Sunni mosques and businesses in Diyala Province, by Iran-backed Shia militias after an ISIS suicide bombing of a cafe popular with Shi'i militia members in Muqdadiyah (HRW 2016a, Rudaw 2016a, DPA 2016). Tension between the two factions of Dawa surfaced in a joint statement by the Iran-backed Hezbollah Brigades, Badr Organization and League of the Righteous, all part of the Popular Mobilization Units, calling on the government 'not to seek help from US forces'; a spokesman for Abadi responded in an interview that 'the stance of the Iraqi government vis-à-vis US troops and the international coalition lies in the framework of communication and coordination in the war against terrorism,' while Abadi later made it clear that this did not include clearance for US ground troops (Saadoun 2015).

At bottom, this was – and still is – not a fight between Shi'is and Sunnis but between secular Iraqi nationalists and jihadi Iranian imperialism, with Maliki's faction and the IRGC-linked Shia militias widely perceived as agents of a Quisling regime (Chulov 2016). Seen from this point of view, as Ibrahim al-Marashi (2016) argues,

> the role played by national Iraqi forces in the fall of Ramadi also has implications for the creation of an inclusive sense of Iraqiness. A debate has ensued since the summer of 2014 as to whether one can claim that the Iraqi nation still exists. Iraqi nationalism persists if one were to watch the Iraqi-state sponsored Al-Iraqiyya TV station, which features almost continuous coverage of the war front, along with images of the Iraqi military in action with nationalist songs playing in the background … With the fall of Ramadi, the Iraqi military, which is featured prominently on this channel, can now also claim that it represents the national aspirations of Iraq.

In January 2016, Abadi approved of the appointment of forty thousand Sunni fighters to the Popular Mobilization Units (Hashd al-Shaabi), which were once almost exclusively Shi'i (Saadoun 2016a). However, Abadi's control over Iran-controlled Shia militias and state security forces remained extremely limited even in Baghdad, where abductions and disappearances still occurred (Saleh 2016). In the battle to reclaim Fallujah from ISIS, he promised to investigate violations to his instructions to protect civilians and to hold back the Shia militias from the final assault (BBC News 2016), and fears of a massacre led him to halt the assault on Fallujah temporarily (Vice News 2016). Yet when it finally took place, concern was expressed by the provincial council and in parliament at credible reports that hundreds of Sunni civilians had been detained and tortured – in some cases to death – by Shi'i militias. Disappearances and mass killings of civilians were reported, and a Shi'i militia commander spoke of local civilians in terms that would justify genocide: Human Rights Watch reported viewing a video 'in which a commander tells a room filled with fighters that Fallujah had been a bastion of terrorism since

2004 and that no civilians or true Muslims were left inside the city. The video bore the logo of Abu al-Fadhl al-Abbas, one of the brigades within the Leagues of the Righteous militia' (HRW 2016b). This was at a time when civilians remaining in Fallujah – including at least twenty thousand children – were being held as human shields by ISIS. Other Iran-backed militias involved in the atrocities were the Badr Organization and Kataib Hezbollah. Underscoring the priority Tehran attached to its militias' participation in the Fallujah operation, Qassem Soleimani visited the militia fighters at the end of May, and although 'the US was pledging air support only to the Iraqi army and on condition that the Iran-backed militias stay out of the city', it was unable to exclude the militias altogether (De Luce and Johnson 2016).

In August 2016, meetings were reported between the Shia National Alliance and Iran's Supreme Leader Khamenei to ensure that Maliki would return to power at the parliamentary elections in 2018, denying Abadi a second term (Naser 2016). At around the same time, a 'Reform Bloc' formed within Maliki's State of Law Coalition started gunning for members of Abadi's cabinet. A source from the State of Law Coalition said to *Al-Monitor* that 'Abadi's key ministries w[ould] be gradually brought down, which would hamstring his Cabinet, reduce his chances for a second term and thus pave the way for the nomination of his rival' (Mamouri 2016b). Khamenei also praised Maliki's role in Iraq, despite never doing the same for Abadi; it seemed that Khamenei was pushing for Maliki's nomination for the 2018 election (Mamouri 2016b).

In this context, there is symbolic significance in the fact that the battle for Mosul, which had been lost to ISIS as a consequence of Maliki's sectarianism, was initiated by Abadi in October 2016. Despite initial insistence by the Iran-affiliated Hashd al-Shaabi that they would spearhead the assault on Mosul, Abadi managed to extract an agreement that the operation would be conducted mainly by the Iraqi army and the Kurdish Peshmerga with US coalition air support, while the Hashd al-Shaabi would play a supporting role, cutting off ISIS to the west in the direction of Syria, and refrain from entering Mosul. A possible obstacle to the sectarian abuse of Sunnis in Mosul were the Turkish-trained Nineveh Guards, composed of locals who knew the city and could be trusted not to carry out reprisals against the residents (Al Jazeera 2016g), and the Sunni Liwa Salahaddin battalion of the Hashd al-Shaabi, led by Yazan al-Jabouri (Samaha 2016). As the fighting progressed, amid heartwarming stories of civilians overjoyed at their liberation were disturbing reports that thousands of men and boys had been subjected to arbitrary detention, many ill-treated, and some forcibly disappeared or executed (Wille 2016). A catastrophic escalation in civilian casualties was also reported in the battle for western Mosul (HRW 2017b).

Abadi's declaration of victory over ISIS in a devastated Mosul on July 9, 2017 (Arango and Gordon 2017) could be seen as an attempt to claim authority as prime minister; but that authority was challenged a few days later, when one regiment of the Hashd al-Shaabi wore what appeared to be the uniform of the IRGC at the victory parade in Baghdad. This was widely perceived as a gesture of defiance from the Iran-controlled militia: a reminder that Khamenei would like Abadi to be replaced by a more subservient prime minister who, unlike Abadi, would not object to a full Iranian takeover of the country or to Iraqi Shia militias being dispatched to fight for Assad in Syria (Saadoun 2017).

Abadi was not the only Shi'i political leader trying to escape the embrace of Iran's jihadi imperialism. On July 24, 2017, ISCI (Islamic Supreme Council of Iraq, formerly SCIRI) leader Ammar al-Hakim split from his party to found the National Wisdom Movement, taking many members and assets of his old party with him; it is notable that 'National' replaced 'Islamic' in the name of the party, that there were eight Iraqi flags behind him as he announced the new party, and that its founding declaration announced it would be open to anyone from the diverse Iraqi ethnosectarian population who chose to join (Kadhim 2017). At around the same time, Muqtada al-Sadr, a Shi'i leader with a large urban working-class base, visited Saudi Arabia and had cordial talks with Crown Prince Mohammed bin Salman; during the visit, the Saudi regime agreed to provide Iraq with $10 million in reconstruction aid and to award Sadrist officials with special visas for the upcoming Hajj (the Islamic pilgrimage to Mecca). Sadr followed this up with a visit to the UAE, where he met Sheikh Ahmed al-Kubaisi, an Iraqi Sunni cleric living in the UAE, to discuss the future of Iraq and the Middle East, agreeing on the need for unity among Arabs and Muslims across sectarian divisions (Malik 2017; Cafiero 2017). Both visits could be seen as attempts to challenge Iranian control over Iraq.

The Struggle for National Liberation and a Democratic Revolution Continues

Although hardly reported in the rest of the world, on February 25, 2011 the 'Iraqi Day of Rage', a weekly Friday protest inspired by the Arab uprisings began in several Iraqi cities. At that time, unsurprisingly, the foremost demand of the protestors was the departure of the US forces who had occupied Iraq for over eight years; but less obviously, this was combined with protests against 'a clear Iranian influence on the Maliki-led coalition government, [making] Maliki's regime especially glaring in its lack of legitimacy' (Issa 2015, 7; 20). As Uday al-Zaidi, brother of Muntazer al-Zaidi (who threw shoes at Bush), put it, this was a struggle 'for freedom and for booting out our two occupations, the US and Iranian' (Issa 2015, 23).

The US occupation ended when US forces withdrew from Iraq at the end of 2011, but, more than four years later, the struggle against the Iranian occupation still continued. The huge Iraqi flag displayed by demonstrators in Baghdad protesting against corruption, poor services and power cuts in January 2011 showed, in spite of political fractures, 'a resilient commitment to the Iraqi state' (Natali 2016). Shi'i leaders, especially Ayatollah Sistani and Muqtada al-Sadr, were prominent in the struggle for independence and sovereignty. For example, Sistani's spokesperson, Sayyid Ahmad al-Safi, said in 2015, 'We are proud of our country, our identity, our independence and our sovereignty. While we welcome any help offered today from our brothers and friends in our fight against terrorism and thank them for it, it doesn't mean that we would ignore our identity and independence in any way' (Mamouri 2016a). As Al-Monitor columnist Ali Mamouri reports, in an interview in December of 2013, Muqtada al-Sadr had criticised Iran's role in Iraq, calling Qassem Soleimani 'the most powerful man in Iraq, who implements an Iranian agenda in the country' (Mamouri 2016a).

In an interview in February 2016, Sadr's spokesperson, Sheikh Salah al-Obeidi, stated that 'Muqtada al-Sadr does not want Iranians to speak on behalf of Iraqi Shiites', adding: 'Muqtada al-Sadr has repeatedly said that we are with Iran, as a neighbouring country that we respect, but we categorically reject any Iranian interference in the Iraqi internal affairs' (Mamouri 2016a). Criticisms of Iran's role in Iraq centred on its support for corrupt Shi'i officials; as one of the protest leaders, Ahmad Abdul Hussein, wrote in a Facebook post, 'Iran's insistence on embracing corrupt thugs and thieves, desperately defending them, assisting them during crises and covering up for their disastrous corruption and failure will drive Iraqis to hate Iran, in case it continues to sponsor these thugs' (Mamouri 2016a).

The dispute was sharpest with respect to the presence of Quds Force commander Qassem Soleimani in Iraq. Some Shia militias raised the Iranian flag in his support, while others objected strongly:

A number of activists in the province of Basra organized a protest against the raising of the Iranian flag in their province, fighting back by hoisting the Iraqi flag. Asked to comment on the appearance of the Iranian flag in Iraqi cities, an Iraqi parliamentarian for the Sadrist movement, whose followers chanted slogans against Soleimani in Baghdad during the demonstrations against the Iraqi government, told *Al-Monitor*, 'In Iraq, only the Iraqi flag that represents the Iraqi state should be raised. Iraq is a sovereign country, and no other flag should be raised.'

[...] Blogger Saadallah al-Majid, an opponent of Soleimani's presence in Iraq, told *Al-Monitor*, 'Iraq has turned into an Iranian province, as Iran is dominating the political and security scene in Iraq ... The raising of the Iranian flag in Iraq as well as Soleimani's presence in the country are intended to convey the message to the world that Iraq is under the control of Iran.' (Saadoun 2016b)

The intention of the IRI, and the Iraqi Shia militias collaborating with it, to convert Iraq into a Shia Islamic state ruled by the supreme leader of Iran is visible in the fact that the leadership of Iraq's 80,000- to 100,000-strong Hashd al-Shaabi (Popular Mobilization Forces) is in the hands of Iran's IRGC (Bruce 2016). The boast by Hojjat al-Eslam Ali Saidi, the supreme leader's representative in the IRGC – that 'The Islamic Republic's borders ... are now transferred to the farthest points in the Middle East. Today, the strategic depth of Iran stretches to Mediterranean coasts and Bab al-Mandab Strait [southwest of Yemen]' (ShahidSaless 2015) – projects a distinctly imperialist vision, albeit on a regional rather than a global scale.

The Islamist character of Iranian imperialism is particularly dangerous for women. In 2013, placards at a demonstration in Samarra read: 'Obama, if you cannot hear us, Can you Not See Us?'; 'Iraqis Did not Vote for an Iranian Dictatorship'; 'Wake Up, this is an IRAQI REVOLUTION Not a Sectarian One!'; and 'Women Rights in Democratic Iraq Are NON-EXISTENT!' (Iraqi Spring 2013). On March 8, 2014, women, men and girls demonstrating in Baghdad called International Women's Day a 'day of mourning' in protest against a new draft Jafari Personal Status Law modelled on Iran's law and put forward by Maliki's government, which attacked women's inheritance rights and their parental and other rights upon divorce, made it easier for men to have multiple wives, and allowed girls to be married off from the age of nine and raped by much older husbands (HRW 2014b): a huge leap backwards from the existing secular law. The protests managed to get it withdrawn, but Shia Islamist parties proposed a similar bill in November 2017

(Sattar 2017). In August 2016, six cafes in Basra employing young women were bombed; flyers were found nearby calling for the women workers to be sent back to their homes and accusing the cafes of turning into 'homes for demons and the practice of adultery and sodomy' in language reminiscent of Al Qaeda and ISIS, although neither was present in Basra. The leaflets were associated with the Hashd al-Shaabi, who were distributing pictures of Khomeini in the streets of Basra and banning the sale of alcohol and modern hairstyles for men (Taher 2016).

On April 25, 2011, the chants against Maliki at a sit-in in Mosul were for the first time interspersed with the key slogan of the Arab uprisings: *al-Shaab Yureed Isqat al-Nizam* (the people want the downfall of the regime) (Issa 2015, 17). As Ali Issa (2015, 20) notes: 'The demands for political freedoms, transparency, an end to corruption, and due process rather than the arbitrary force exercised by police are similar to the demands of other pro-democracy movements in the Arab world.' One of the most hated aspects of 'the regime' was the system of ethnosectarian quotas introduced by Paul Bremer, and enthusiastically supported by Iranian officials because it gave them a means of control over Iraq so long as they could dominate the Shia parties. Falah Alwan, president of the Federation of Workers' Councils and Unions in Iraq, pointed out that the quota system not only exacerbated ethnosectarian conflicts but also resulted in incompetence, misgovernance and massive corruption, as ministries were given to politicians according to their ethnicity rather than their competence and integrity. Instead, he felt, 'putting out a societal understanding of "unity" based on an objective class analysis is a serious political goal' (cit. Issa 2015, 53).

A huge popular protest movement demanding 'the formation of a government without consideration of the sectarian quota system, reducing the number of ministries and positions in the government, fighting financial and administrative corruption in the country and calling for the provision of services and reform in the judiciary' was disappointed in February 2016 when Abadi failed to deliver the promised reforms due to opposition in parliament, especially from his own party (Sattar 2016). Then Muqtada al-Sadr jumped on the bandwagon, vastly increasing the size of the protests and putting more pressure on the Abadi government, but also leading to a split in the original movement. The Moustamerroun (We Will not Back Down) faction welcomed cooperation with Sadr, while Madaniyoun, the peaceful Civil Society Movement, split away, seeing Sadr – who had been in government, was associated with a militia, and was an Islamist – as part of the problem, not of the solution. In their launch statement, Madaniyoun stated, among other things:

- Madaniyoun places the protection of civil freedoms as a basic goal and one of its priorities. We call for expanding the margin of these freedoms in Iraqi society in the context of the constitution, and support for these freedoms through appropriate legislation, and oversight of the implementing organs and the extent of their commitment to this legislation. It is necessary to stand against any measures which seek to reduce the margin of these civil freedoms which represent one of the rare gains for Iraqi citizens under the current regime. [...]
- It is necessary to warn that the current economic crisis and the fight against terrorism do not exempt the government from carrying out urgent reforms, especially with respect to the judiciary ... [including] the serious effort to eliminate the sectarian and ethnic quotas for the high offices of state. [...]
- The individuals of the groups which make up Madaniyoun are secularists, and they are an integral part of the civil protest. Their aim is to strengthen its power and momentum, and to ensure its fundamental shared goals. (Robin 2016)

Shortly afterwards, Abadi finally appointed qualified persons who did not belong to any party or political bloc to fill vacant ministerial positions in his cabinet, including Ann Nafaa Awsei as minister of construction, housing and public municipalities. However, unidentified gunmen attacked Awsei's home shortly afterwards; along with the murder of officials exposing corruption, this suggested that eliminating the corrupt quota system would not be easy (al-Jaffal 2016).

Sections of the clergy, too, have challenged Islamism and sectarianism. An initiative by the ayatollahs of the holy city of Najaf included a welcome to a delegation of women from religious minorities (Melkite and Orthodox Christians, Sunni Muslims, and members of smaller minorities like Yazidis and Mandaeans) into the Imam Ali Shrine; Jawad al-Khoei, a senior lecturer at the seminary in Najaf and follower of Sistani, discussing a papal visit to Najaf; another follower of Sistani in Lebanon giving sermons in Beirut's churches; and the building of the al-Balaghi Interfaith Academy in Najaf where the teaching staff were to be mainly non-Muslim. Khoei explained, 'We want Yazidis to teach the Yazidi faith, Sabaeans to teach about Sabeans, and Christians to teach about Christianity ... The ayatollahs are resolute in their determination to see equal rights for all, regardless of sect ... If the people elect a Christian as leader, he should lead' (N. P. and Erasmus 2015).

Perhaps the biggest victories have been registered by the trade union movement. Hashmeya Muhsin al-Saadawi, president of the Electrical Utility Workers' Union in Iraq and the first female vice president of the General Federation of Iraqi Workers in Basra, recounted how despite both the 'terrible Labor Law 150 of 1987', which had outlawed unions in the public sector, and the US occupation with its own anti-union agenda, the General Federation of Trade Unions in Iraq had launched a campaign to pass a labour law that incorporated international labour standards (Issa 2015, 39–41). This finally came to fruition in late 2015, when a labour law covering employees in both the public and private sectors, and guaranteeing all the rights in the Core ILO Conventions (freedom of association, the right to unionise and bargain collectively, abolition of forced labour and child labour, freedom from discrimination in employment and occupation) was passed (US Labor Against the War 2015). Women workers and unionists played a major role in drafting the law, ensuring that in addition to ruling out discrimination, it prohibits sexual harassment at work, requires employers to provide onsite childcare, and increases paid maternity leave to fourteen weeks, with the option of unpaid leave for up to a year (Connell 2016).

The ability of Iraqi civil society to continue struggling for national liberation, democracy and social justice despite decades of a brutal dictatorship, sanctions, occupation, war, and communal violence is an admirable example of courage, resilience and creativity which deserves unstinted solidarity.

6. Syria: The Assad Regime

This chapter examines the historical background to the 2011 uprising, including the social forces and political currents active in the conflict, Hafez al-Assad's authoritarian regime and sabotage of the Palestinian struggle, the occupation of Lebanon, the transition to his son Bashar, Bashar al-Assad's role in sponsoring Islamists during the Iraq war, and the USSR support for the Assad regime.

Hafez al-Assad and the Baath Party

When twenty-year-old Hafez al-Assad joined the newly founded Syrian air force academy in 1951, he had already been an activist of the Baath Party since the late 1940s. As Humphreys (1999, 123) writes,

> He belonged to the Alawis, the largest, poorest, and most isolated of Syria's radical Shi'ite sects, who lived in the coastal mountains of the northwest. For Asad, the first member of his impoverished peasant family to gain a formal education, a military career represented great opportunities – a free education, vastly enhanced social status, and of course a chance to be at the forefront of the nationalist struggle ... It would not be correct to say that the Shi'ite sects dominated the Syrian officer corps, but they were certainly overrepresented. Moreover, their regional solidarity, class resentments, and sense of religious apartness made them an exceedingly cohesive group within the army.

In 1951, a democratic revolution was in full swing. When Akram al-Hourani, leader of the Arab Socialist Party (ASP), addressed the first peasant congress in the Arab world in Aleppo that year, he encouraged the poorest citizens of Syria to rise up against the landowners' domination of

Syrian politics and to call for equal political rights for all citizens (Thompson 2013, 207). During the 1940s, Hourani had been forging alliances with opposition leaders who shared his concerns, including the leaders of the Syrian communist party and the Syrian Muslim Brotherhood, but especially the leaders of the Baath Party, Michel Aflaq and Salah Bitar. In 1947, he allied with the Baath Party (Thompson 2013, 215; 216). Hourani established the ASP in 1950, calling for land reform, agricultural development, republican government, religious tolerance, and women's rights. The response was overwhelming:

> The ASP opened its Hama headquarters with a big party ... Literate peasant-gardeners rubbed shoulders with wage workers, soldiers, civil servants, shop owners, students and professionals ... In June 1950, the ASP began organizing peasant revolts. Hourani toured villages near Hama, where even women and children came to cheer him and beat drums ... Slowly, a powerful peasant leadership emerged northwest of Hama, altering the balance of power in the city's rural hinterland. Christians, Alawis, Druze and Sunni Muslims joined the movement. No other party in Syria could claim such a grassroots following; no other single personality wielded more power in politics.
>
> Hourani used the momentum of the peasant revolts to achieve a second victory: a new constitution. Syria's September 1950 constitution stands as one of the most democratic ever adopted in the Arab world. It included a twenty-eight-article bill of rights that guaranteed freedoms of speech and assembly as well as economic and social rights. (Thompson 2013, 221–22)

The adoption of a new constitution was followed by the hugely successful peasant congress in Aleppo, at which Hourani issued his call for a socialist revolution against feudal lords, imperialism and capitalism. As Thompson (2013, 224) argues, 'His socialism was rooted not in Marxist theory but rather in personal experience, Arab culture, and Islamic morals.' The irony is that all of this revolutionary ferment was taking place against the background of a military dictatorship: that of Adib al-Shishakli, an old friend of Hourani who, however, turned against the peasant movement in 1952. With the exception of four years of civilian rule between 1954 and 1958, the following decades saw a succession of military dictatorships, including that of Nasser, during the period when Syria and Egypt were merged into the United Arab Republic; this ended with a neo-Baathist military coup in March 1963, after which Hourani was imprisoned and then forced into permanent exile in 1965 (Thompson 2013, 224; 226–27; 232).

That was, effectively, the end of Syria's mid-twentieth-century democratic revolution. 'Although the coup was carried out by a coalition of several groups, made up of both military and civilian members, a very secretive, tight-knit military bloc within the Baath party was decisive to its success. By 1966, this military bloc had uncontested control of the government' (Humphreys 1999, 123–24). The new regime, often described as neo-Baathist, was led by Hafez al-Assad and Salah Jadid, and proceeded to carry out nationalisations and land reforms. An internal power struggle proceeded in parallel, with the losers being exiled, imprisoned or killed. In November 1970, Assad seized full control in an internal coup; he became president and Jadid was incarcerated in Mezzeh prison in Damascus until his death twenty-three years later (Yassin-Kassab and Al-Shami 2016, 10–11).

Assad's regime was heavily Alawi and became almost immediately a single-party police state. With an extremely complex party and governmental apparatus reaching into every nook and cranny of the country, power became 'as personalized, as focused on the kinsmen and clients of one man, as Saddam Hussein's regime in Iraq' (Humphreys 1999, 124). Hinnebusch (2001, 5; 67) describes how the personal authority of Assad was institutionalised in 'a virtual "Presidential Monarchy"' in which Assad controlled 'the three major power institutions' – the party, the military, and the government – through his combined roles as general secretary and president. Unlike Hourani, whose support base had been among the rural poor, the trade unions and left-wing intellectuals, Assad's base was among senior army officers and the bourgeoisie (Hinnebusch 2001, 65).

However, even as Assad centralised power by carrying out a savage purge of party and army, targeting left-wingers and replacing them with Alawis loyal to himself, he sought to broaden the regime's narrow base by wooing Sunnis, on one side, and pursuing more liberal economic policies to win over the old and new bourgeoisie, on the other. Peasants were placated by land redistribution, and the urban working class and middle classes by subsidised goods. Membership of the Baath Party offered job opportunities and better chances of promotion and access to state funds, although the patronage system also led to deep-seated corruption and incompetence (Yassin-Kassab and Al-Shami 2016, 12–13). This 'incorporation of a significant array of interests – the army and the minorities as well as sections of key social forces, including the bourgeoisie, the salaried middle class, the peasantry and the working class, gave the regime a cross-class, urban-rural social base' at the top of which 'Asad achieved relative Bonapartist-like autonomy, balancing between competing groups and social forces' (Hinnebusch 2001, 88).

At the same time, all dissent was wiped out. 'The security forces and intelligence services (*mukhabarat*) are multiple, pervasive in surveillance of society, and feared for the arbitrary arrest, imprisonment and torture of dissidents which they have practised', while the army, 'by virtue of its massive size and firepower makes rebellion very futile'; it was used to put down more than seven rebellions between 1963 and 1982 (Hinnebusch 2001, 85). Despite the totalitarian character of the state, Stalinists supported it because it dominated over the economy and was linked to the USSR, and their support continued even when the economy morphed into a neoliberal oligarchy (Hassan, O. 2017).

Initially, there was opposition from both socialists and Islamists, but this 'degenerated under harsh repression into a sectarian assassination campaign by the armed wing of the Muslim Brotherhood which alienated the minorities and most Sunnis' (Yassin-Kassab and Al-Shami 2016, 14). In response to the Brotherhood's ambush of soldiers and attacks on officials in 1982, six to eight thousand soldiers were sent to Hama. Amnesty International reports that in the weeks that followed, 'food and energy supplies to the city were cut off, and the incessant gunfire kept the besieged residents in constant fear ... Three weeks into the assault on Hama, the military called a pro-government rally. According to Abd al-Hadi al-Rawani [a former Hama resident who now lives in London], the security forces killed large numbers of those who stayed in their homes rather than attend the demonstration' (Amnesty International 2012). Estimates of the civilian death toll in the Hama onslaught range from ten to forty thousand, with most in the vicinity of twenty thousand.

As fearsome as the regime's willingness to engage in massacres of civilians was its systematic use of gruesome torture. Robert Fisk (2001, 178-79) detailed some of the macabre methods:

> As long ago as 1974, Amnesty International had been reporting on torture in Syria, and the details of the systematic ill-treatment of prisoners in Damascus and other locations – including cities under Syrian control in Lebanon – had become a constant theme of their reports. Beating on the soles of the feet, caning, whipping with steel cables, sexual assault, suspension by the wrists, the breaking of bones and secret executions were repeatedly catalogued. Some prisoners had been incarcerated since 1963.
>
> An Aleppo student who was imprisoned from July 1979 to March 1980 told Amnesty that the torture room in the military security prison in Aleppo

was a sound-proofed booth built inside a room where torture instruments included 'a Russian tool for ripping out fingernails, pincers and scissors for plucking flesh and an apparatus called *al-Abd al-Aswad* [the black slave] on which they force the torture victim to sit. When switched on, a very hot and sharp metal skewer enters the rear, burning its way until it reaches the intestines, then returns only to be reinserted.'

By 1984, one branch of the *mukhabarat* had acquired a machine known as the 'German chair', which slowly broke the vertebrae of the victim strapped into it. It had allegedly been manufactured in East Germany, although there was later a less refined instrument which was locally produced and thus called the 'Syrian chair'.

On December 10, 1989, activists formed the non-party-affiliated Committee for the Defense of Democratic Freedoms and Human Rights in Syria (CDF), which in April 1990 started publishing a regular bulletin, *Sawt al-Democratiyya* (Voice of Democracy). However, in late 1991 and early 1992, the government arrested members of the group and sentenced ten of them to prison sentences ranging from two to five years, leading to its collapse (HRW 2007).

The Push for a 'Greater Syria'

The background to Hafez al-Assad's intervention in Lebanon in 1976 was the fact that after the defeat of the Arab forces in the 1967 Arab-Israeli War, the Palestinian leadership decided to make their bases in southern Lebanon the main platform for attacks against Israel. In response, and to punish the Lebanese state, Israel targeted Lebanese infrastructure. While the Palestine Liberation Organization (PLO) had the support of Muslim and progressive or leftist forces in Lebanon, conservative and Christian groups armed themselves against the PLO. It was on the basis of this split that Lebanon's civil war broke out. Given Syria's claim that it supported the Palestinian cause, one would have expected Assad to side with the left-PLO alliance, but on the contrary, 'Syrian President Hafiz al-Asad intervened in support of the Christian coalition in 1976. By doing so, he saved the latter from an impending defeat that could have ended the war' (Haugbolle 2010, 17; 18). Fisk concurs: 'Just like the French 116 years earlier, the Syrians had entered Lebanon to save the [Christian] Maronites from defeat ... They also wanted the Palestinians crushed' (2001, 78).

Given that the Lebanese Maronite Christians had formed an alliance with Israel when it invaded southern Lebanon in 1978, before staging an all-out invasion of Lebanon in 1982 with the purpose of driving out the PLO and establishing a pro-Israeli government (Haugbolle 2010, 17), what could explain Assad's alliance with the same forces? One explanation is that, as Raymond Hinnebusch (2001, 156) writes, 'Lebanon was, given the PLO presence there, key to Asad's drive to control the "Palestinian card" … Whoever controlled Lebanon was in a strong position to control the PLO.' A similar explanation is that Assad's long-term policy was to impose a solution to the war that would secure enduring Syrian control over Lebanese affairs, and the war ended only when Syria broke the last resistance to a Syrian postwar order in Lebanon (Haugbolle 2010, 18). The Tripartite Accord, which legitimated the presence of Syrian armed forces in Lebanon, soon broke down, but the Syrian military remained in Lebanon, finally defeating General Michel Aoun's 'war of liberation' from Syria in 1991.

In other words, this was a drive by Assad to control both the Palestinians and Lebanon. Given Israel's drive to do the same, this has been described as 'a contest between Greater Syria and Greater Israel' (Hinnebusch 2001, 141). As in the case of Khomeini's alliance with Israel and the US during the Iran-Iraq war, this should alert us to the possibility that the attempt to establish a country (Iran, Syria) as a regional power is by no means synonymous with support for the Palestinian cause or 'resistance' to the US and Israel. Assad's absolute power and freedom from democratic control in Syria allowed him to take a number of unpopular foreign policy decisions: aside from the 1976 intervention in Lebanon, he also chose to side with Iran in the Iran-Iraq war, and with the Western forces against Iraq after its invasion of Kuwait (Hinnebusch 2001, 148). Both these latter two decisions were driven by his hostility to Saddam.

The New 'Presidential Monarch'

When Hafez al-Assad died in 2000 and was succeeded by his son Bashar, there were high hopes that the latter, who was young and not a military man, would introduce a period of democratisation. A report from Human Rights Watch (2007) describes the mood at the time:

> A number of informal groups began meeting in private homes to discuss human rights, reform efforts, and other topics, leading to a period of relative openness often referred to as the 'Damascus Spring.' The 'Damascus Spring' was characterized by the emergence of numerous *muntadat* (referred to in En-

glish as 'forums') where groups of likeminded people met in private houses to discuss political matters. [...]

Soon thereafter, intellectuals and activists mobilized around a number of political demands, expressed in the 'Manifesto of the 99': the cancellation of the state of emergency and abolition of martial law and special courts; the release of all political prisoners; the return without fear of prosecution of political exiles; and the right to form political parties and civil organizations.

Human rights activists seized the new-found openness to resume their activities. ... Many of the human rights activists at the time were former political activists who had previously spent time in jail. For example, Haytham al-Maleh, the then-president of HRAS [Human Rights Association in Syria], had spent seven years in jail for his activities in the Freedom and Human Rights Committee of the Syrian Lawyers Union; Salim Kheirbek, another activist in HRAS, had spent 13 years in jail because of his involvement with the workers' movement; Dr. Ahmad Fayez al-Fawaz, representative of HRAS, had spent 15 years in jail for his activities with the communist party; and Aktham Nu'aissa, had been sentenced in 1991 to nine years in jail for his activities in CDF. (HRW 2007)

Razan Zaitouneh, who was a young human rights lawyer at the time, was also a founding member of HRAS. The 'Statement of the 1000', released in January 2001, was bolder than the Manifesto of the 99, declaring that in Syria, 'citizenship was reduced to the narrow concept of belonging to one party and to personal loyalty ... Patronage replaced law, gifts and favours replaced rights, and personal interests replaced the general interest' (cit. George 2003, 183). It challenged authoritarianism, calling for a multiparty system, social justice, a more equitable distribution of national wealth, and the abolition of legal discrimination against women, who were subject to sharia-based Personal Status Laws regarding the marriage age, the right to divorce, inheritance and child custody (Yassin-Kassab and Al-Shami 2016, 18).

The 'Damascus Spring' came to an abrupt end in August 2001, when the government cracked down on civil society advocacy groups and arrested opposition leaders after they participated in a seminar during which they called for political reform, democratic elections, and a change in the constitution. It was back to the old police state, although human rights activists, including some Kurdish groups, continued to operate (HRW 2007). The arrest, incarceration and torture of political dissidents acted as a warning to the rest of the population of what would happen to them if they dissented:

Perhaps the most significant event of the extended aftermath of the Damascus Spring was the re-imprisonment, for varying periods of time, of prominent political activists including Riad Seif, Riyad al-Turk, Michel Kilo, and Mamun al-Humsi. These well-known, outspoken figures and others are only some of the thousands of political prisoners who filled Syria's notorious prisons and whose lives refracted the conditions of the virtual political imprisonment of millions of civilians who could not speak or write in protest against the situation of the silenced country. (Sakr 2013, 75)

This striking metaphor of the whole country as a prison is a recurrent theme in Syria's prison writings, from which we learn that, as Miriam Cooke (2012) writes, 'the more Syrian people were punished the more determined they were to stay the course. Those who survived the cell realised that the sense of suffocation and imprisonment they experienced there was much like life on the outside, except that prison produced a political subjectivity otherwise forbidden'. What Syrians rose up against in 2011 was, as political geographer and literary thinker Rita Sakr (2013, 72) puts it, 'a closed security system that, for several decades, has been transforming citizens into prisoners whether physically and/or psychologically … The majority of the Syrian population was compelled … to ignore the situation of the country that had become a large prison and, more seriously, to turn a blind eye to the actual prisons in which dissidents and militants who challenged the Baathist regime found themselves incarcerated, tortured, and sometimes executed.'

In terms of foreign policy, Bashar al-Assad colluded with the 'war on terror' (and the US colluded with his regime) by allowing Syria to be used as a destination for 'extraordinary renditions' where prisoners were tortured. However, he did not support the US invasion of Iraq in 2003, fearing that Syria would be next on the list of neocon targets (Yassin-Kassab and al-Shami 2016, 25–26).

In Lebanon, opposition to the Syrian occupation emerged even before the Damascus Spring; as early as March 2000, Gebran Tueni, the editor of Lebanese daily An-Nahar who would be assassinated in December 2005, published an open letter to Assad demanding Syrian troops be withdrawn from Lebanon; by spring of 2001, thousands of students throughout the country were demonstrating against the occupation, while Lebanese human rights groups launched campaigns on issues like the detention of hundreds of Lebanese political prisoners in Syrian prisons (Gambill 2001). When, in the summer of 2004, the Syrian leadership forced an amendment to Lebanon's constitution in order to allow pro-Syrian president Émile Lahoud's term to be extended by three years, several Lebanese politicians openly challenged the move, while the UN Security Council passed Resolution 1559, calling for the withdrawal of Syrian troops from Lebanon.

> The SCR 1559 led to a remarkable cross-sectarian rapprochement between leftist and Christian groups. As a result, cross-sectarian nationalist slogans became more and more prominent in oppositional discourse. The alliance was not just forged at the highest level … [It] also included student movements, women's groups, the Lebanese Bar Association and syndicates of writers, journalists, artists, workers and industry groups … On 15 December 2004, the *mur'ada* (opposition) was formalised in a meeting held at the Bristol Hotel in Beirut. The meeting was attended by political parties representing the Druze and Christian communities, as well as some leftist groups. The so-called Bristol Declaration produced by that meeting … presents the crisis of postwar Lebanon as a moral crisis related to the failure of dealing with the legacy of the civil war. (Haugbolle 2010, 203–4).

Prominent among those who called for the Syrian occupation to end was rags-to-riches billionaire businessman-turned-politician Rafiq Hariri, who was responsible for much of the postwar rebuilding of Beirut. But his punishment was fearsome. On February 14, 2005, Hariri and twenty-two others were blown to bits by a massive truck bomb, which also injured hundreds in the vicinity. In response,

> for the first time since the civil war, people from all sectors of Beirut felt compelled to take to the streets and show their anger and grief. The demonstrators blended serious demands of an immediate investigation into the murder with wry humour in their signs and banners, singing and chanting catchy anti-Syrian slogans that added to the atmosphere of pent-up emotions and opinions finally being allowed an expression … All political parties of the anti-Syrian opposition, the *mu'arada*, were present, including former enemies. (Haugbolle 2010, 206)

However, the Shi'i parties, Hezbollah and Amal, remained loyal to Assad and organised a major pro-Syrian rally on March 8. Leading the rally, Hezbollah leader Hassan Nasrallah thanked Syria for securing stability in Lebanon and warned against American interference in the region. Pictures of Lahoud, Nasrallah and Bashar al-Assad were carried by demonstrators. In response, the opposition organised an even bigger demonstration on March 14:

> The sheer scale of the crowd, which had come from all parts of Lebanon, and the carnival-like atmosphere that manifested itself, captured the attention of international media and made it a globally televised exhibition of the changes

taking place in Lebanon. From above, the usual landmarks in the downtown area appeared to be drowned in a sea of Lebanese flags. If the 8 March demonstration underlined that not all Lebanese supported the opposition, the 14 March demonstration showed that an even greater number of people backed its call for a speedy investigation into Hariri's death and a full withdrawal of Syrian troops. [...]

The slogans also changed. What had started as a spontaneous outcry against Hariri's death grew in scope to encompass a program for political reform, national unity and full sovereignty. This agenda was first formulated in the Bristol Declaration. Now, the truth (*al-haqiqa*) about Hariri's death was linked to the declaration's calls for freedom (*huriyya*) in the political system and independence (*istiqlal*) from Syria. Out of this trinitarian slogan, 'haqiqa, huriyya, istiqlal,' reminiscent of the French 'liberté, égalité, fraternité', came the expression *intifadat al-istiqlal*, or the Independence uprising. (Haugbolle 2010, 208, 209)

The Syrian army withdrew from Lebanon by the end of April, but the militias were not disbanded (UNSC 2005). Some weeks after Hariri's murder, a UN commission was constituted to investigate it in light of concerns about Syrian influence in the Lebanese criminal justice system. The UN investigation took place against the backdrop of violent intimidation: by 2008, twenty-four prominent Lebanese opponents of Syria had been killed or injured in car bombs or attacks. As Hammer (2008) reports, 'The first team leader, German prosecutor Detlev Mehlis, stepped down from his post and fled Beirut in January 2006; after implicating senior Syrian officials in Hariri's murder, he had been informed by Western intelligence officers of two assassination plots against him.' Wissam Eid, a high-ranking Lebanese intelligence official who was working closely with the UN commission, was killed by a car bomb in January 2008. Under Mehlis, the commission established that 'six anonymously purchased mobile phones were used on the day of the attack to keep the bomber informed of Hariri's movements; ... that the suicide truck moved into position one minute and 49 seconds before Hariri's convoy passed by; and that the truck itself had been stolen on October 12, 2004, in Sagamihara City, Japan' (Hammer 2008). The report exonerated the young Palestinian, Ahmed Abu Adas, who had been forced to read a statement confessing to the murder – the video of which was sent to *Al Jazeera* in Lebanon – and had then been killed. It also dismissed the authenticity of phone calls from a person with a non-Lebanese accent, purporting to be from an unknown group called 'Victory and Jihad in Greater

Syria', claiming responsibility for the assassination, which were received by both Ghassan bin Jeddo, *Al Jazeera*'s chief, and Laila Bassam, the *Reuters* Bureau Chief in Lebanon (Asharq al-Awsat 2005).

Mehlis was succeeded by Serge Brammertz, a Belgian lawyer who had served as deputy prosecutor in the International Criminal Court. During his two years in charge, the investigation moved more slowly. This was partly because the idea of prosecuting the case in a Lebanese court had been given up due to the numerous killings of anti-Syrian critics; instead, the UN Security Council created a special tribunal, which required very high evidentiary standards. Brammertz made headway in tracing the cellphone traffic and identifying the spotters who had tracked the route of Hariri's convoy, and also investigated and demolished alternative theories of the crime, including suggestions that it had been carried out by Al Qaeda. In January 2008, he was replaced by Daniel Bellmare, a Canadian prosecutor, and the pace picked up. However, by this point, French president Nicolas Sarkozy was inviting Assad to Paris, and the US appeared to have got cold feet about indicting the Syrian leadership. As Paul Salem, director of the Carnegie Middle East Center, put it, 'Israel and the United States are not eager to see this regime collapse ... They are afraid of the consequences' (cit. Hammer 2008).

When the trial finally commenced in January 2014 – after yet another investigator had been killed by a car bomb at the end of 2012, and Mohammed Chatah, one of the chief advisors of Hariri's son Saad, had been similarly blown up the previous month – charges were brought against four Hezbollah operatives – Salim Ayyash, Mustafa Badredine, Hussein Onessi and Assad Sabra – who were tried in absentia since Hezbollah refused to give them up (Chulov 2014a). This appears to have been a compromise between not pursuing charges at all, and targeting those with command responsibility for the bombing. A conversation with Hariri reported to the tribunal by Druze leader Walid Jumblatt – which Robert Fisk confirmed Jumblatt had conveyed to him at the time – revealed that Assad had threatened Hariri, and that the latter was terrified (Fisk 2015). Evidently the reason why Hariri was targeted was because this charismatic leader opposed the Syrian occupation of Lebanon, which Assad was determined to continue, but the tribunal did not present this argument. And, while it is inconceivable that Hezbollah would have carried out the killing without the go-ahead from their bosses in Tehran, there was no attempt to link it to the IRI leadership.

This episode provides a striking example of the ruthless manner in which

Assad destroyed anyone who stood in his path. It also illustrates that despite his pretensions of being a secular leader, there were deep links between his regime and the Islamists of Iran and Hezbollah, who sabotaged every attempt to create a secular, democratic state in Lebanon. Thirdly, it contradicts the popular misconception that the US and Israel have always been hostile to Iran and Syria; in this case, they made sure that neither state was indicted, just as after the suicide bombing of the US barracks in Beirut in 1983 that killed 241 Marines, none of the voluminous evidence of Iranian and Syrian involvement was acted upon by the Reagan administration (Timmerman 2003). The spate of terrorist attacks on Lebanese politicians like Hariri, journalists like Tueni, and other activists who opposed the Syrian occupation demonstrate that suicide bombings are not the hallmark of Sunni terrorism alone.[1]

Assad's Use of Sunni Islamists

In 2001, Assad allowed a Salafi agitator named Mahmoud Gul al-Aghasi (known as Abu al-Qaqa) to hold a large festival celebrating the 9/11 attacks, showing off the training his paramilitary Ghuraba al-Sham was receiving and playing Al Qaeda videos on large screens; clips from the festival were even shown on state television. According to Muhammad Habash, a former Syrian MP, 'Aghasi had been allowed to recruit without the state interfering because he wasn't "*saying anything against the government*" and had focused his wrath on the West. Al-Aghasi's collusion with Assad's intelligence services allowed the regime to monitor the jihadi networks on its territory, and ultimately to coopt them' (Orton 2014).

The collaboration was activated when the US invasion of Iraq in 2003 prompted Assad to funnel jihadi fighters into Iraq. In Aleppo, one of al-Aghasi's recruits, Abu Ibrahim, 'went door to door encouraging young men to cross the border. Volunteers boarded buses that Syrian border guards waved through wide-open gates' (Abdul-Ahad 2005). US intelligence discovered that another fighter, Badran Turki al-Mazidi (known as Abu Ghadiya) was put in charge of funnelling explosives and foreign fighters into Iraq through Syria; most of the recruits landed in Damascus on commercial flights, and, as one military report noted, 'once in Syria they seek accommodations in hotels typically located near large markets or mosques frequented by foreigners, allowing [them] to blend into the general population ... Within a few days facilitators contact the recruits and escort them to safehouses where they await onward movement into Iraq' (Gordon and Morgan 2012). This was confirmed by ISIS militant Abu Ahmed. 'The mujahideen all came through Syria,' he said in an interview with the *Guardian*'s Martin Chulov (2014b). 'I worked with many of them ... A very small number had made it from Turkey, or Iran. But most came to Iraq with the help of the Syrians.' Documents recovered after ISIS leader Haji Bakr was killed also confirm that 'Syrian intelligence officials organized the transfer of thousands of radicals from Libya, Saudi Arabia and Tunisia to al-Qaida in Iraq. Ninety percent of the suicide attackers entered Iraq via the Syrian route' (Reuter 2015).

In 2009, when Nouri al-Maliki was Iraq's prime minister, Major General Hussein Ali Kamal, director of intelligence in the Interior Ministry, was in charge of counter-terrorism. Kamal had discovered through a spy, who had attended meetings between Iraqi Baathists, Syrian military intelligence officers and senior members of the Islamic State in Iraq, that major attacks in Baghdad were being planned. However, he was unable to find out exactly where, and therefore failed to prevent them.

> On the morning of 19 August, the first of three flat-bed trucks carrying three large 1000-litre water tanks, each filled with explosives, detonated on an over-pass outside the Finance Ministry in south-eastern Baghdad ... Three minutes later, a second enormous bomb blew up outside the Foreign Ministry on the northern edge of the Green Zone. Shortly after that, a third blast hit a police convoy near the Finance Ministry. More than 101 people were killed and nearly 600 wounded; it was one of the deadliest attacks in the six-year-old Iraqi insurgency. The prime minister was livid ... Iraq recalled its ambassador to Damascus, and Syria ordered its envoy to Baghdad home in retaliation. Throughout the rest of the year, and into early 2010, relations between Maliki and Assad remained toxic. (Chulov 2014b)

By this time, ISI was on the retreat in Iraq (see Chapter 5), and as Islamist militants flowed back into Syria, Assad either redirected them into Lebanon, or took them into regime custody (Orton 2014).

7. The Syrian Uprising

The peaceful democratic revolution of 2011 sparked off by the Arab uprisings later became militarised in response to the brutal repression carried out by the state. Syria typifies the moral and political degeneration of pseudo-anti-imperialists who support, or fail to oppose, the genocidal crushing of a democratic uprising by a totalitarian state allied with Iranian and Russian imperialism.

A Democratic Revolution Crushed

There are always dissidents in authoritarian police states – people who risk torture and death to uncover the truth or fight for justice – but often the majority keep their heads down in order to survive. It is only when discontent builds to intolerable levels that a single spark can galvanise a large section of the populace to try to break out of the prison they have hitherto endured. This is what happened when Mohamed Bouazizi set himself ablaze on December 17, 2010 in Tunisia to protest against the impossibility of making a livelihood with dignity, setting off uprisings not just in Tunisia but also in other Arab countries.

> The slogan 'al-Shaab Yureed Isqat al-Nizam' ('The People Want the Fall of the Regime') reverberated through the region's streets and squares. The moment of insurrection entailed the temporary suspension of absolutist ideology, and what exactly was to follow the regime was not articulated – but civil disobedience, strikes, protests and the occupations of public space spread, networks and alliances were built, and tactics of struggle shared. (Yassin-Kassab and al-Shami 2016, 36).

The first two chapters of Gilbert Achcar's *The People Want* (2013b) describe how an explosion of poverty, inequality and precarity – food crises, unemployment, declining public investments, high military expenditures and financialisation superimposed on neopatrimonial, rentierist states – prepared the ground for the uprisings. Historian Fawwaz Traboulsi (2013, 2) argues that it is impossible to separate political and economic causes: 'These are revolutions that do not hide their causes: unemployment, dictatorship, social divides, the citizen's abused dignity. To which they roar back: Work! Freedom! Social justice! Human dignity!'

In Syria, too, 'when the revolution erupted, it broke this contradiction between the quiet, normal appearance on the surface that was a falsity ... and the real volcano that was brewing underneath' (Al-'Azm 2013). Bashar al-Assad's economic reforms included privatising state farms and introducing commercial farming, peasant evictions, and cutting subsidies which had been a lifeline for the poor. At the other pole, among the beneficiaries of the liberalisation were Bashar's maternal cousin Rami Makhlouf (estimated to control some sixty per cent of the economy), the Shaleesh family (related to Bashar on his father's side), and other Assad family members and loyalists. Thus, as is now a familiar story, the neoliberal policies implemented by Bashar al-Assad intensified the divide between the rich and the poor, with a 'gilded circle' reaping the benefits while most of the country suffered; in this respect, Assad's regime looked much like those of Mubarak in Egypt, Ben Ali in Tunisia and Saleh in Yemen (Rafizadeh 2013).

On February 17, 2011, in response to the son of a local trader being beaten up by traffic police, 1,500 people protested in Damascus, chanting, 'The Syrian people won't be humiliated'. Following the call for a Day of Rage on March 15, thousands demonstrated across the country. Among other slogans, the words *Selmiyyeh, Selmiyyeh* (peaceful, peaceful) were chanted, and continued to be chanted in other demonstrations, to underline the peaceful character of the protests; yet demonstrators were violently dispersed and the mukhabarat made many arrests. The next day, a demonstration outside the Interior Ministry calling for the release of political prisoners brought together families of detainees and activists of the 2005 Damascus Declaration – which had criticised the Syrian government and called for peaceful reform – and new human rights organisations. This protest led to the formation of Local Coordination Committees (LCCs) dispersed around the country. Protests demanding reforms continued and were met by assaults and arrests (Yassin-Kassab and al-Shami 2016, 37).[1] What catalysed the protests into an uprising, however, was an episode in the southern city of Deraa:

> Fifteen schoolboys, all under the age of fifteen and all from prominent families, had been arrested on 6 March for graffitiing walls with the revolutionary slogans they'd heard chanted on Tunisian and Egyptian streets. The children were tortured in detention, their fingernails ripped out. When their parents went to plead with the local head of political security, a cousin of the president called Atef Najib, they were told: 'Forget your children. Go sleep with your wives and make new ones, or send them to me and I'll do it.' Several thousand family members and their supporters responded by gathering in front of the Omari Mosque in the city's Balad district on 18 March, demanding the children's release and the resignation of Atef Najib and the city's mayor. Security replied with water cannons and live ammunition, killing at least four people, the first deaths of the uprising. The next day, the funeral for the victims turned into a mass demonstration chanting 'He Who Kills His People is a Traitor'. More were killed. In a tactic which would become routine, security forces occupied the nearby hospital, and any wounded who arrived there were detained or shot. Residents used the Omari Mosque as a makeshift hospital instead.
>
> Briefly, the regime adopted a conciliatory tone. On 20 March, Assad sent a delegation to offer condolences to the bereaved families and to promise that those responsible would face justice. On the same day, thousands gathered again at the Omari Mosque. Now their demands were somewhat more expansive: an end to corruption, the release of all political prisoners and the repeal of the Emergency Law. This time 15 were killed, immediately proving the emptiness of Bashaar's words. [...]
>
> The regime's violent repression outraged Syrians; as a result, the protests grew rapidly in numbers and in geographical spread ... Everywhere protesters chanted their solidarity with the people of Deraa. (Yassin-Kassab and al-Shami 2016, 38–39)

Syrian American Yasmeen Mobayed, a member of a group who visited Syria to find out what was happening there, notes in a well-illustrated blogpost (2013) that 'at first the revolution's demand was for mere reforms, but after experiencing the regime's hostile and vicious response, the people demanded the downfall of the regime in its entirety'. Yet the uprising remained peaceful for several months, despite the mounting death toll, and local councils were organised as well as field hospitals to care for the wounded. Mobayed continues,

> Immediately after the uprisings, the regime swept revolutionary cities and detained thousands and thousands of men and women who showed even the slightest bit of dissent. in detainment, the regime uses unthinkable methods of torture, violently assaulting and sexually abusing both men and women in count-

less ways. assad forces commonly use rape and molestation as a weapon to incite fear and terror in dissidents, their families and their communities. thousands of documented political detainees have been tortured to death at the hands of assad forces. recently, a defected regime photographer, who goes by the pseudonym 'caesar', leaked 55,000 images of over 11,000 tortured civilian detainees. Many peaceful revolutionaries, such as the civil activist giyath matar and the palestinian activist and filmmaker hassan hassan, have been tortured to death in syrian prisons. revolutionary artists, such as ali ferzat (an anti-regime alawite political cartoonist), are also abused, detained, and tortured for their anti-regime activist work. A renowned protest singer from hama, ibrahim qashoush, was kidnapped by regime thugs and found near a river with his throat cut open and his vocal chords pulled out ... since the beginning of the revolution, the regime continues to massacre innocent civilians, execute dissidents, shell protests, bombard residential neighbourhoods, torture detainees, and more. The regime commonly detains young children (which is no surprise, as the revolution began due to the detainment of young boys). (Mobayed 2013)

Anyone participating in demonstrations or seen filming them was liable to be detained and subjected to barbaric torture, as were activists, students and community leaders. Wissam Tarif, director of Syrian human rights organisation Isan, reported that the security forces were releasing detainees with unhealed torture wounds in an attempt to sow fear and deter protestors. Figures compiled by activists indicated that over seven thousand Syrians had been imprisoned between mid-March, when the demonstrations began, and mid-May, while hundreds more were documented to have disappeared during protest marches (Macleod and Flamand 2011a).

The gruesome torture, mutilation and murder of thirteen-year-old Hamza al-Khateeb in May 2011 after he participated in an anti-regime demonstration was, like the torture, rape and murder of adult dissidents, meant to cow the opposition into quiescence, but instead sparked further protests. 'After Hamza's body was filmed so the world could see how he died, the boy was buried in Jizah after last prayers for his soul in the local mosque. Following the ceremony, children walked through the streets of Jizah holding up a photo of Hamza and a banner that said he died a martyr, 13-years-old, under the brutal torture of the security forces' (Macleod and Flamand 2011b). In a pattern that has since become routine, the same regime that sought to terrorise the population with its brutality claimed on the pro-regime TV station Al Dunia that 'the marks on Hamza's body had been caused by natural decomposition' (Macleod and Flamand 2011b).

The Islamist Opposition Is Created;
The Democratic Opposition Militarises

The regime needed to fabricate an excuse to use military force to crush this unarmed civilian uprising. It began by systematically attempting to turn it into a sectarian conflict by targeting Sunnis and their sacred sites:

> Regime forces fired anti-aircraft guns at minarets until they crumbled. The Umawi Mosque in Aleppo burned, its thousand-year-old minaret fallen, and the minaret of Deraa's Omari Mosque, erected in the seventh century by Caliph Omar ibn al-Khattab. The Khalid ibn al-Waleed Mosque in Homs, built around the mausoleum of the famous Muslim general and companion of the prophet, was shelled and burned. In the regime's cells, meanwhile, in a parody of the Muslim profession of faith, detainees were forced to swear that there was no god but Bashaar. (Yassin-Kassab and al-Shami 2016, 110–11)

Appalling massacres were carried out in Sunni areas. One was in Houleh, where 108 residents were murdered on May 25, 2012. 'The victims – almost half of them children – had their throats cut, their skulls split open and were riddled with bullets'; a few weeks later, on June 6, up to a hundred people were murdered in al-Qubeir; and at Tremseh, between 60 and 150 people were killed on July 10 (Yassin-Kassab and al-Shami 2016, 12). Houleh and al-Qubeir are both surrounded by Alawi and Shia villages; in these areas the members of the regime's Shabeeha militias, who carried out the massacres, are purely Alawi and Shia. As Yassin-Kassab and al-Shami (2012, 12) explain, 'Using locally recruited gangs as death squads transforms neighbouring communities into bitter enemies. The strategy … incites the victims' community with a generalised thirst for revenge, while exploiting the spectre of this revenge to frighten even dissenting members of the "perpetrator community" into redoubled allegiance.'

At the same time, the regime embraced the Alawi community, attempting to make it complicit in its crimes. The Zahra neighbourhood of Homs, for example, was 'a visible affront to the besieged and shelled areas surrounding it. An Alawite community brimming now with soldiers, with rocket launchers set up in the square, the whole area was lit up while the rest of the city was dark' (Yassin-Kassab and al-Shami 2016, 111). The neighbourhood even had goods looted from opposition homes displayed in its shops and market.

However, even this divide-and-rule strategy did not serve to justify airstrikes against the democratic opposition. The imprisoned Salafi jihadis had to be called into play. 'From March to October 2011, at the same time that it was targeting thousands of non-violent, non-sectarian revolutionaries for death-by-torture, the regime released up to 1,500 of the most well-connected Salafist activists from its prisons,' and, according to a defected intelligence officer, assisted them to form armed brigades because 'the regime wanted to tell the world it was fighting al-Qaida but the revolution was peaceful in the beginning so it had to build an armed Islamic revolt' (Yassin-Kassab and al-Shami 2016, 120). Some of those released included Zahran Alloush, commander of Jaysh al-Islam (or Army of Islam); founding members of Jabhat al-Nusra; Hassan Aboud of Ahrar al-Sham; and key ISIS figures Abu Athir al-Absi and Awad al-Makhlaf (Yassin-Kassab and al-Shami 2016, 120–21). Another defected military intelligence officer confirmed that the regime deliberately gave radical Islamists access to weaponry: 'This is not something I heard rumours about, I actually heard the orders. These orders came down from [Military Intelligence] headquarters in Damascus' (Orton 2014).

Bassam Barabandi, who served as a diplomat in Syria's Foreign Service before defecting, explained how Assad arrived at this strategy (Barabandi and Thompson 2014a):

> His closest advisors studied the Arab Spring uprisings in Egypt, Tunisia, Libya, and Yemen to craft an approach that would protect the regime. This small group of political elites concluded that any meaningful concessions to non-violent protestors could precipitate the collapse of the regime. The advisors decided that it would enact no reforms that could weaken Assad's hold on power. Assad learned from the Libyan case that a hasty resort to large massacres, or the threat thereof, could draw intervention from NATO forces. A slower increase in violence against opponents, however, would likely go unchecked. [...]
>
> To achieve these aims, Assad first changed the narrative of the newborn Syrian revolution to one of sectarianism, not reform. He then fostered an extremist presence in Syria alongside the activists. Further, he facilitated the influx of foreign extremist fighters to threaten stability in the region. [...]
>
> The Assad regime and Iran have meticulously nurtured the rise of al-Qaeda, and then ISIS, in Syria. In his March 2011 speech addressing the protests, Assad claimed that an international terrorist conspiracy sought to topple his government. During this time, Assad released battle-hardened extremists from the infamous Sednaya prison; extremists with no association to the uprisings. These fighters would go on to lead militant groups such as ISIS and al-Qaeda affiliate Jabhat al Nusra.
>
> In conjunction with the terrorist-release policy, Assad was sure to imprison diverse, non-violent, and pro-reform activists by the thousands, many of whom are still in government prisons. These efforts, coupled with relentless barrel bombing, torture, and chemical weapons campaigns, were designed to

silence, kill, or displace civilians so that the influence of extremists would fill their absence. Assad was careful to never take any steps to attack ISIS as they grew in power and strength.

This strategy allowed Assad and his Lebanese Hezbollah, Iranian and Russian allies to bomb, gas and besiege the democratic opposition in the name of the 'war on terror', even while it tightened its grip on minorities in Syria and convinced gullible Western journalists, politicians and anti-imperialists that the opposition to Assad consisted overwhelmingly of Islamist terrorists. Moreover, he had unleashed Islamist forces which could be trusted to launch their own murderous attacks on the democratic revolution. It was a win-win situation for his regime – so long as it could give the impression of fighting against the Islamists without actually doing so – and equally propitious for ISIS. Once they had wiped out the democratic opposition, the regime and ISIS could vie with each other for control of Syria; but in the meantime they were allies who had a common enemy.

In the face of the regime's brutal assault, calls for armed resistance emerged from within the democratic opposition. These were opposed by the Local Co-ordination Committees (LCCs), who, on August 29, 2011 issued a statement:

> In an unprecedented move over the past several days, Syrians in Syria and abroad have been calling for Syrians to take up arms, or for international military intervention. This call comes [after] five and a half months of the Syrian regime's systematic abuse of the Syrian people, whereby tens of thousands of peaceful protesters have been detained and tortured, and more than 2,500 killed. The regime has given every indication that it will continue its brutal approach, while the majority of Syrians feel they are unprotected in their own homeland in the face of the regime's crimes. While we understand the motivation to take up arms or call for military intervention, we specifically reject this position as we find it unacceptable politically, nationally, and ethically. (cit. Yassin-Kassab and al-Shami 2016, 77)

Part of the rationale for the LCCs' position was that they believed that any armed opposition would not stand a chance against the Syrian army; they also suggested that taking up arms would minimise popular participation in the revolution. But, as Yassin-Kassab and al-Shami (2016, 79–80) argue,

> Abstract criticisms of the revolution's militarisation miss the point. Syria's revolutionaries didn't make a formal collective decision to pick up arms – quite the opposite; rather, a million individual decisions were made under fire … When residential areas are subjected to military attack, when neighbourhoods experience the horror of children tortured to death, when young men are ran-

domly rounded up and beaten, soon they will respond. Before moving on to media work, Ziad Homsi ... fought in Douma, in the Damascus suburbs: 'It was a matter of self-defence. Everyone defended his own home, his own alley. Brigades were formed by the residents of one neighbourhood, or by a group of men who worked together. It was a spontaneous process.' According to Assaad al-Achi, the threat of sexual violence in particular pushed people towards arms ... In this sense, the militarisation was inevitable, and once it had become an undeniable reality, most civil revolutionaries sought to adapt.

Under such circumstances, the principle of non-violence had to be rethought. As Aleppo resident Basel al-Junaidi said: 'At the start I was totally against militarisation. Now I support it. I realise the regime can't be toppled by peaceful means' (Yassin-Kassab and al-Shami 2016, 80).

Alawite[2] writer and activist Samar Yazbek had fled Syria with her daughter in July 2011 because she was being pursued by the mukhabarat after participating in peaceful demonstrations and exposing the murder and torture visited upon the protesters by the regime. But, she writes, 'I'd felt compelled to return to northern Syria, to fulfil my dream of achieving democracy and freedom in my homeland' (Yazbek 2015, 6). Her compelling accounts of her clandestine crossings into Syria make it clear that most of the fighters for democracy, including her two guides Maysara and Mohammed, had participated in the peaceful protests before joining the armed resistance, and that 'armed with very rudimentary weapons, they were facing tanks and aircraft' (Yazbek 2015, 33). In one village, the Freedom Martyr's Brigade had built a gun: 'It had been made from the remains of a government tank and put together using the most primitive tools ... "This is nothing compared with the arsenal the regime gets from Iran," Abu Waheed explained. "We will fight, we have no choice: we either die or we fight. The young men in the Freedom Martyrs are all villagers who have rallied together to protect their community. They are ordinary people"' (Yazbek 2015, 69).

The other source of fighters was the army. A defector describes what happened when his army unit raided a neighbourhood in Homs and his friend Mohammed was ordered by the officer to rape a girl, a common accompaniment to raids. At first Mohammed begs and pleads with the officer not to make him do it; then, when the officer abuses him and insists, he attacks, knocks down and beats the officer, then stops and throws down his gun. 'The officer gets up straight away and shoots Mohammed. He killed him ... He ordered another of our friends to go in and rape the girl, and he went into the room in silence, and we heard her scream, and we heard her mother and her siblings screaming, because they were all crammed into the next room. Their father was a dissident; he'd been killed two days earlier. That was the day I decided to defect and, by God, not a single day passes without me thinking of Mohammed' (Yazbek 2015, 34–35).

There were tens of thousands of defectors, mostly but not exclusively conscripts and lower-ranking soldiers:

> Very often they acted as the civilians did – they returned to their home towns, where they organised with their neighbours. These soldiers had been ordered to shoot protesters, and very often did, lest they themselves were shot by the intelligence officers at their rear. A combination of guilt, horror and fury propelled many to escape when they could, but perhaps most were killed in the attempt or hunted down in the following days. Usually they took only one weapon with them, sometimes they managed to break weapons out of stores. In every case they had to be prepared to fight to resist capture. Those who sheltered them had to face the fury too. (Yassin-Kassab and al-Shami 2016, 82)

It was this rag-tag collection of militias that came to be called the 'Free Syrian Army', but to call it an 'army' is a misnomer, since it was never centrally armed, funded or controlled, and was only bound together by 'the twin aims of destroying the regime and establishing a democratic state' (Yassin-Kassab and al-Shami 2016, 85). As they succeeded, against heavy odds, in liberating territory from Assad's army, they faced a blitzkrieg from the regime. Bombing civilian targets in rebel-held areas, especially hospitals, was a hallmark of the Assad regime's strategy. As Dr David Knott, who had worked in Aleppo reported, for Assad 'healthcare is seen as a weapon … You take out one doctor, you take out 10,000 people he or she can no longer care for' (Cooper 2016). Knott called for the international community to protect hospitals in areas such as Aleppo, by setting up humanitarian corridors and a no-bombing zone over Aleppo and Idlib provinces. 'The healthcare workers I work with are not fighters, they don't carry weapons, they're just there to help,' he said. 'What is happening to them is totally against international humanitarian law – hospitals should be protected and they are being targeted' (cit. Cooper 2016).

One of the techniques employed widely by the regime, with assistance from Lebanese Hezbollah and Iraqi Shia militias, was starvation sieges of civilian populations in rebel-held areas. 'By the spring of 2013, all the revolutionary suburbs of the western and eastern Ghouta were under siege. The Palestinian-Syrian citizen journalist Qusai Zakarya experienced the impact in Moadamiya, recalling, "I consoled parents on the deaths of their young children'" (Yassin-Kassab and al-Shami 2016, 100–101). Another area where people starved to death was the Yarmouk Palestinian refugee camp in South Damascus. When protests first broke out in other Palestinian refugee camps, Yarmouk's protests were on a smaller scale, due both to the prominence in the camp of the pro-Assad Popular Front for the Liberation of Palestine – General Command (PLFP-GC) and to a genuine desire for neutrality in the struggle for Syria's destiny. Then, on December 16, 2012, 'regime jets targeted a mosque, a school and a hospital, killing at least 40 people. The camp responded with furious protest; resistance fighters arrived from neighbouring areas the following day' (Yassin-Kassab and al-Shami 2016, 102). Immediately a partial siege was imposed by the PLFP-GC in collusion with the regime, and on July 8, 2013, the siege became total. By February 2014, more than 170 had died for lack of food and medicines. Madaya was another rebel-held area where residents were deliberately starved to death while those who tried to escape were blown up or shot (Al Jazeera 2016).

Among the most horrific of the attacks on civilians were the chemical weapons attacks in the early morning of August 21, 2013 on the Zamalka neighbourhood in Eastern Ghouta and Moadamiya neighbourhood in Western Ghouta, both in the opposition-controlled Damascus suburbs. Doctors reported that 'victims consistently showed symptoms including suffocation; constricted, irregular, and infrequent breathing; involuntary muscle spasms; nausea; frothing at the mouth; fluid coming out of noses and eyes; convulsing; dizziness; blurred vision; and red and irritated eyes, and pin-point pupils. According to an expert review of the available evidence, the symptoms exhibited by the victims are consistent with exposure to a nerve agent such as Sarin' (HRW 2013).

The large-scale nature of the attacks, involving at least a dozen surface-to-surface missiles; the fact that analysis of the remnants of the rockets used to deliver the chemicals showed them to be of types so far seen only in the possession of the Syrian regime; the large quantity of nerve agents used; the specialised procedures required to load and launch these rockets; and the fact that Assad forces had already carried out chemical attacks previously all point to the regime as the perpetrator, apart from the absurdity of suggesting that the rebels would kill themselves and their children. Further, the possibility of an accident is ruled out by the fact that the attacks took place in two places separated by about sixteen kilometres (HRW 2013). 'It was the deadliest use of chemical weapons since the Iran-Iraq war, the greatest single poisoning of civilians since Saddam Hussein's slaughter of the Kurds at Halabja. Estimates of the dead reach 1,929 – so many because people were sheltering from the artillery barrage in their basements, the worst place to be, where the gas sank and thickened. Even as spokesmen made official denials to the foreign audience, regime-associated websites were celebrating the attack' (Yassin-Kassab and al-Shami 2016, 105).

In addition to damning reports by Human Rights Watch and Amnesty, UN human rights chief Navi Pillay told the UN Security Council that by December 2011 the death toll had risen to five thousand, including civilians and soldiers executed for refusing to shoot civilians. 'The UN High Commissioner for Human Rights said the Syrian government's actions could amount to crimes against humanity, noting "alarming" developments in the besieged city of Homs', where several massacres had taken place, but action against Syria was vetoed by Russia and China (Channel 4, 2011). By August 2014, a UN study listed 191,369 dead, which Pillay said was likely to be an underestimate, and she once again denounced the paralysis of the Security Council: 'The killers, destroyers and torturers in Syria have been empowered and emboldened by the international paralysis,' she said. 'There are serious allegations that war crimes and crimes against humanity have been committed time and time again with total impunity, yet the Security Council has failed to refer the case of Syria to the International Criminal Court (ICC), where it clearly belongs' (UNHRC 2014). The reason for the failure was that the resolution to refer the situation in Syria to the ICC, which got thirteen Security Council votes in favour with no abstentions, had two votes against: China and the Russian Federation, which happen to be veto-holding members (UN 2014).

The Symbiotic Relationship between Assad and ISIS

The Assad regime continued to have a close relationship with some of the Islamist militants who had been released in 2011. One source of information about such relationships comes from the regime's defectors. Afaq Ahmed, formerly the right-hand man of General Jamil Hasan, the head of Syria's Airforce Intelligence, defected after the murder of Hamza al-Khatieb in 2011 and revealed that the mukhabarat (intelligence services) controlled several jihadi brigades which had stopped fighting the regime altogether (Weiss 2013). Nawaf Fares, a former regime loyalist who had been a security chief and ambassador, defected in July 2012. 'I was seeing all the massacres perpetrated,' he said. 'No man would be able to live with himself, seeing what I saw and knowing what I know' (Sherlock 2012).

In an interview with the *Sunday Telegraph*, Fares alleged that the regime itself had been involved in the string of suicide bombings targeting government buildings, such as the attack on an intelligence building in the al-Qazzaz suburb of Damascus in May 2012. 'I know for certain that not a single serving intelligence official was harmed during that explosion, as the whole office had been evacuated 15 minutes beforehand,' he said. 'All the victims were passers by instead. All these major explosions have been perpetrated by al-Qaeda through cooperation with the security forces' (Sherlock 2012). Fares said that he knew of a number of 'liaison officers' who were in communication with Al Qaeda, and insisted that 'al-Qaeda would not carry out activities without knowledge of the regime ... The Syrian government would like to use al-Qaeda as a bargaining chip with the West – to say: "it is either them or us"' (Sherlock 2012).

Other sources of information concerning the regime's collaboration with Al Qaeda and ISIS include captured or defected Islamist militants. After heavy fighting in the countryside of Hama, the Free Syrian Army (FSA) captured several ISIS militants, some of whom claimed to have defected after discovering the brutality of ISIS. One detainee recounted how when a Syrian regime officer and eleven others defected and drove their vehicle through Masila [north of Hama], ISIS militants received orders from their leaders to arrest them and hand them back to the regime. Another said that former ISIS leader Abu Anas al-Iraqi was 'financed directly by the regime, through Iran and Iraq. His brigade is specialized in kidnappings, car bombs, and targeted assassinations of FSA members' (Al Arabiya News 2014).

In mid-April 2013, according to pseudonymous ISIS militant Abu Ahmed, whose credentials were confirmed by his interviewers, Islamic State in Iraq's leader Abu Bakr al-Baghdadi and his deputy Haji Bakr held a series of meetings with Syrian jihadi leaders demanding that they join him under the banner of the Islamic State in Iraq and al-Sham. When members of the al-Nusra Front objected that they had already sworn allegiance to Al Qaeda leader Ayman al-Zawahiri, Baghdadi claimed that he was acting under Zawahiri's orders. Nusra Front leader Abu Muhammad al-Jolani ordered his followers not to join ISIS until Zawahiri's acquiescence had been confirmed, but the majority ignored his orders.

ISIS proceeded to seize Nusra's headquarters, ammunition caches and weapons stores, including chemical weapons that the Nusra Front had captured from the Syrian Army. The following month, Lajnat Khorasan (the Khorasan Committee, a small group of Zawahiri's envoys), travelled secretly through Syria to investigate what was happening and report back to Zawahiri. Zawahiri's response was to denounce Baghdadi's claims as lies and to try to convince Nusra members who had joined ISIS to return to the Nusra Front. Around one-third of them did so, while the rest remained with ISIS; from that time onwards, ISIS and the Nusra Front were at war with each other (Doornbos and Moussa 2016a, 2016b and 2016c). Other Salafi groups like Ahrar al-Sham and Jaish al-Islam were also eventually attacked by ISIS and pitted against it. Syrian members of Jabhat al-Nusra were the large majority when they separated organisationally from Al Qaeda and rebranded themselves as Jabhat Fatah al-Sham in August 2016 to emphasise their Syrian identity, suggesting that the majority of Nusra's foreign fighters went with ISIS (Alami 2016).

In this scenario, it appears that Assad decided to ally with ISIS, the most extreme of the Islamist groups. While secular rebels continued to be pounded unmercifully, 'We were confident that the regime would not bomb us,' an ISIS defector said. 'We always slept soundly in our bases'; meanwhile, intelligence agencies found that Jabhat al-Nusra and ISIS were both being financed by selling oil and gas from wells under their control to and through the regime (Sherlock and Spencer 2014). As Matthew M. Reed (2015) writes, 'The Syrian regime has done business with ISIS from day one, just as it did with al Qaeda's Nusra Front and other rebels who took over energy assets early in the war.' And, as a rebel fighter linked to the Muslim Brotherhood claimed, the regime 'pay[s] more than 150m Syrian lire [£1.4m] monthly to Jabhat al-Nusra to guarantee oil is kept pumping through two major oil pipelines in Banias and Latakia. Middlemen trusted by both sides are to facilitate the deal and transfer money to the organisation' (Weiss 2013).

Indeed, as a *Telegraph* article reported, Assad's regime was not simply buying oil from ISIS but running oil and gas plants in cooperation with them. One such enterprise is Russian-Syrian businessman George Haswani's company HESCO, which owns a gas plant in Taqba believed to have been operated jointly by ISIS and regime personnel. The gas plant supplies gas to Assad-controlled areas in Syria. 'Other oil and gas fields in Isil's hands are thought to be operated by personnel who remain on the payroll of the regime's oil ministry. The oil is then sold to Mr Assad, who distributes it in areas he controls at relatively low prices, helping him to win the loyalty of local people' (Telegraph 2015). A *Financial Times* investigation discovered more details of the collaboration:

> After four years of war, Ahmed thought he had finally been given a break when he landed a job at Syria's national gas company. Then he was assigned his new supervisors: the militant group, Isis ... Syrian activists and western officials have long accused the regime of making secret oil deals with Isis, which controls nearly all of Syria's petroleum-producing east. But an FT investigation shows co-operation is strongest over the gas that generates Syria's electricity ... Workers say that in agreements between Isis and the regime, the Syrian state and private gas companies pay and feed their employees and supply equipment to the facilities. The two sides divide the electricity produced from the methane heavy 'dry gas', while Isis gets the fuel products made from the plants' liquid gas. For example, employees at Tuweinan say its gas is sent to the Isis-held Aleppo thermal power plant. When facilities are working – there are frequent outages due to the instability in the area – the Tuweinan deal nets the regime 50mw of electricity each day. Isis takes 70mw.
>
> At most plants where the two sides co-operate, Isis gives its daily output of liquid petroleum or cooking gas, and condensate – used for generators – to its own members or sells it to locals ... Tuweinan is partly run by the Syrian company Hesco, whose owner, George Haswani, is under EU sanctions on suspicion of dealing with the regime and Isis. Several workers said Hesco sends Isis 15m Syrian lira (about $50,000) every month to protect its equipment, which is worth several million dollars. (Solomon and Mhidi 2015)

Apart from the Assad regime, a Russian company close to Putin has also been involved in doing business with ISIS:

> The Tuweinan gas facility, which is located roughly 60 miles southwest of the Islamic State's de facto capital of Raqqa, is the largest such facility in Syria. It was built by Russian construction company Stroytransgaz, which is owned by billionaire Gennady Timchenko, a close associate of Putin ... The Syrian government originally awarded the contract to construct the Tuweinan facility to Stroytransgaz in 2007. The construction utilized a Syrian subcontractor, Hesco, which was owned by Russian-Syrian dual national George Haswani. [...]
>
> The Islamic State has been in control of the facility since early 2014. A senior Turkish official said that after its seizure, Stroytransgaz, through its subcontractor Hesco, continued the facility's construction with the Islamic State's permission. He also claimed that Russian engineers have been working at the facility to complete the project. Syrian state-run newspaper *Tishreen* published a report appearing to corroborate this claim. In January 2014, after the fa-

cility was captured by the Islamic State, the paper cited Syrian government sources, saying that Stroytransgaz had completed 80 percent of the project and expected to hand over the facility to the regime during the second half of the year. [...]

Abu Khalid [of the Qwais al-Qarani brigade] said that Russian engineers still work at the facility, and Haswani brokered a deal with the Islamic State and the regime for mutually beneficial gas production from the facility. 'IS allowed the Russian company to send engineers and crew in return for a big share in the gas and extortion money,' he said. (Kenar and Soylu 2016)

The importance of this collaboration for ISIS is underlined by the fact that these secret deals with Assad were its most important source of funding, supplemented by taxes, charges and fines on residents, whereas foreign donors contributed very little, according to anti-ISIS group Raqqa Is Being Slaughtered Silently (Malm 2015).

Another example of collaboration is in Deir Ezzor, most of which was controlled by the FSA until 2014, when, according to an FSA commander, it was 'surrounded for several months by ISIS and the regime. The siege included no food and water. Our battalion was weakened ... The FSA numbers are big, but we don't have weapons, we don't have ammunition, we don't have anything' (Rogin 2014). Failing to obtain international assistance despite appealing to the US, the FSA was kicked out by ISIS, enabling Assad's forces to take control of most of the city, while ISIS controlled the surrounding areas. Subsequently, the regime and ISIS worked together for six months: regime engineers were sent to work on oilfields under ISIS control. 'Then on January 25th, 2015, ISIS sealed off the perimeter of the city and prevented goods from going in. On March 23rd, the regime began to restrict access to aid and control civilian mobility within the city'; this was described by civilians as a 'siege within a siege' (Galyon 2016). In April 2016, Deir Ezzor airport was still under regime control, and residents reported how the regime, along with the Syrian Arab Red Crescent, restricted access to aid and often sold aid at inflated prices (Galyon 2016).

What made this situation particularly difficult to address was that the UN classified this as solely an ISIS siege, despite reports from residents that the regime was also involved in the denial of aid and medical supplies through its control over the airport. As James Sadri of Break the Sieges Campaign pointed (2016) out, the airport was used by the regime 'several times a day for military flights to resupply its own forces, yet it is denying the UN the ability to use that airport to bring in aid for the civilian population. So the people there are essentially suffering from a double siege, with ISIS on the outside and the regime on the inside.' It was a Syrian army base overlooking the airport in this area, officially designated as besieged only by ISIS, that was struck by US coalition airstrikes in September 2016 (RT 2016b), and then reportedly overrun by ISIS but recaptured by the Syrian army almost immediately (Alalam 2016).

Aleppo is a third example of coordination between the regime and ISIS. In April 2014, as Assad's forces were attacking Aleppo while ISIS was targeting rebel forces in Deir Ezzor, the Syrian Coalition's spokesperson, Louay Safi, insisted that the connection between ISIS and Assad had 'never been so intimately interwound' than at that point: 'These advancements have not been interrupted by a single clash between regime forces and ISIS, which proves the existence of full coordination between them' (Johnson 2014). In June 2015, as regime airstrikes killed numerous rebel fighters and civilians in towns north of Aleppo, 'the Islamic State escalated a longstanding attempt to seize the area and sever the main supply route to Turkey, a lifeline for rival insurgents and the citizens living in their territory', yet there were no regime airstrikes on ISIS (Barnard 2015b).

The picture that emerges is of a marriage of convenience between the regime and ISIS, a symbiotic relationship in which ISIS gained the revenue that sustained it, Assad gained the credentials of fighting a war against terror, and both collaborated to wipe out the democratic opposition. Of course appearances demanded that there be military clashes between the two sides from time to time, albeit clashes that did not inflict major damage on either side. The most high-profile battles of this sort occurred in Palmyra. On May 20, 2015, 'residents said that by nightfall, the Islamic State had seized most of the city and was even distributing bread to some residents. Soldiers and the police could be seen fleeing, they said, prompting one cafe owner to exclaim over the phone: "Treason! It's treason"' (Barnard and Saad 2015). On March 27, 2016, Syrian government forces backed by Russian air support recaptured the city with minimal loss of life on the opposing side, since 'the bulk of the Islamic State force had withdrawn and retreated east' (Evans 2016); ISIS defectors provided documents purporting to show that ISIS had been asked by the regime to withdraw all their heavy artillery and anti-aircraft guns from Palmyra to Raqqa before the recapture (Bertrand 2016). A pro-regime website called Syrian Perspective quoted General Ali Abdullah Ayyoub, chief of the Syrian General Staff, as saying, 'the rats (ISIS men) inside were finally given the go-ahead to withdraw to Al-Sukhna, Al-Raqqa and Deir Ezzor … The Syrian high command ordered troops to stand down until the last rodent had left', leading to allegations that the whole episode had been choreographed (cit. Ismail 2016). This allegation gained credibility after the return of ISIS to Palmyra in December 2016, with residents saying that all Russian troops had pulled out and government troops had withdrawn from many areas as ISIS advanced (Barnard 2016).

Compared to the wealth of evidence that the bulk of ISIS funding came from within Syria and that most of it was from oil and gas deals with the Assad regime, there is little evidence of ISIS funding from or oil deals with other countries. Oil from Iraqi oil fields used to be smuggled to Iraqi Kurdistan, from where it was sold to Turkish and Iranian traders, but much of this was shut down on US coalition insistence (Hawramy et al. 2014). And while a small amount of oil might have been smuggled from Syria to Turkey when the oil price was high, once oil prices plunged in October 2014, it would not have been possible for ISIS to sell its poor-quality products in Turkey at a profit, nor would it make sense for Turks, who had access to high-quality oil and gas at lower prices, to buy it (Butter 2015). As for funding from the Gulf monarchies, especially Saudi Arabia, while individuals from these countries might fund ISIS, state support has gone to militant groups that are at war with ISIS; in other words, it seems safe to 'blame Assad first for ISIS' rise' (Rowell 2014). Thus the choice offered by Assad and his allies – 'it's Assad or the terrorists' – was false on two counts: (1) Assad's regime was the epitome of a terrorist state, whose atrocities were on par with those of ISIS but on a far-larger scale; (2) the regime and ISIS were in an alliance for most of the war.

Foreign Military Intervention: Assad's Allies

Foreign military intervention transformed the Syrian crisis from a civil war that might have been resolved fairly quickly into an international confrontation with no end in sight. The first foreign military intervention was by (Lebanese) Hezbollah and Iran's IRGC Quds Force. 'Hassan Nasrallah declared his organization's backing of Assad in May 2011, even before the uprising turned violent', and in September 2011, 'Lebanese media reported that several Hezbollah fighters were killed in Syria, where they were assisting the Assad regime's crackdown on protesters' (Sullivan 2014, 11). At this point Nasrallah denied that Hezbollah fighters had been sent to Syria, but not that Hezbollah and the Quds Force were training Syrian government forces from early 2011. Up until the summer of 2012, Hezbollah fighters killed in Syria were buried quietly in Lebanon, but in October 2012, when senior Hezbollah commander Ali Hussein Nassif was killed in Syria doing his 'jihadist duties', he was given a public funeral attended by large crowds. Nasrallah still denied that his organisation was fighting alongside Assad's forces, saying that Hezbollah fighters were there of their own accord; but by early 2013, when Assad's forces were on the retreat, Hezbollah entered the war openly, pouring fighters into Syria (Sullivan 2014, 12–13). Reports of Hezbollah fighters attacking Syrian villages and fighting against the rebels were greeted with outrage in Syria, where Hezbollah had been the most popular non-Syrian organisation prior to March 2011 due to its resistance to Israel; posters of Nasrallah were torn down and burned, 'as yesterday's inspirer has now become a foe and aggressor' (Hashem 2013). Even families of Hezbollah fighters who had joined the organisation to fight against Israel were unhappy about their sons and husbands fighting in Syria, and unconvinced that they were being killed there for the sake of 'jihad duty' (Hajj 2013). Its role in international conflicts from Syria to Iraq to Yemen has transformed Hezbollah into an arm of the Iranian state apparatus (Hubbard 2017).

Iranian involvement too was exposed in August 2012, when Syrian rebels captured forty-eight Quds Force members and a month later exchanged them for two thousand prisoners held by the Assad regime (Sullivan 2014, 13). In February 2013, IRGC-QF general Hassan Shateri was killed in Syria. At the funeral, to which Supreme Leader Khamenei sent a message saying that 'in the end, he drank the sweet syrup of martyrdom', IRGC-QF commander Qassem Soleimani was a prominent mourner. 'The Syrian army is useless!' Soleimani told an Iraqi politician. 'Give me one brigade of the Basij, and I could conquer the whole country!' (Filkins 2013). In an attempt to fulfil this prediction, Soleimani began to spend much more time in Damascus, coordinating strategy with leaders of the Syrian military, Hezbollah, and 'a coordinator of Iraqi shiite militias, which Suleimani mobilized and brought to the fight' (Filkins 2013). He also brought in the Basij's former deputy commander, Brigadier General Hossein Hamedani, to supervise the formation of the National Defence Forces, a paramilitary force modelled on Iran's Basij (Sullivan 2014, 14).

There is voluminous evidence of Iranian military involvement in Syria, including a video filmed by an Iranian cameraman in August 2013, which was seized when rebels overran their camp. It showed, among other things, an IRGC commander saying that for over a year he had been 'working with Syrian militias', many of whose members 'had been previously trained by us in Iran' (Naame Shaam 2014, 18). And while neither Iran nor Hezbollah employed conventional aircraft in Syria, both admitted carrying out drone strikes against Syrian rebels (NOW 2016). However, this role was not one that the Iranian regime wanted to publicise. When in February 2014 Iranian MP Seyyed Mahmoud Nabavian 'boasted during a speech that Iran had trained some 150,000 Syrian regime fighters on Iranian soil, and another 150,000 in Syria, in addition to 50,000 Hezbollah Lebanon fighters', another MP from the ruling bloc demanded that he should be prosecuted for disclosing such details, which would harm Iran's 'national interests' (Naame Shaam 2014, 79).

By 2014, the Syrian army was a spent force, weakened by defections and defeats. When Iranian general Abdullah Eskandari was killed in battle near Damascus, opposition fighters published his notebook, which included a description of the Syrian army's 'dissipation and disintegration' in Hama province; it is likely that the situation was similar in other provinces, but by this time, the army had essentially been replaced by the National Defence Forces, composed of local volunteers (Axe 2014). As IRGC fighter Sayyed Hassan Entezari revealed, it recruited Alawites to join NDF brigades of slightly more than one thousand men each, equipped with weapons from the disintegrating army and led by IRGC officers, many of whom died fighting alongside their Syrian subordinates. Although more than 24,000 militants were estimated to have died by the end of 2014, there were plenty more Alawites ready to volunteer (Axe 2014).

Iran-backed Iraqi Shia militias were also recruited to support Assad and Hezbollah, their numbers rising precipitously in 2015 (Smyth 2015). One of the first was the Abu al-Fadl al-Abbas Brigade, which in January 2013 posted a video declaring that they were in Syria to protect the Sayyida Zaynab shrine. Asaib Ahl al-Haq and Kata'ib Hezbollah were not only deployed in Syria, as were members of the Badr Organization, but were also used to recruit more 'well-trained ideological' Iraqi fighters to be sent there (Naame Shaam 2014, 34–36). In addition, the IRGC recruited Afghan and Pakistani Shi'i brigades to fight in Syria under its command (Qaidaari 2015; Dehghanpisheh 2015), and in April 2016, the regular Iranian army was dispatched to Syria in its first foreign operation since the war with Iraq (Qaidaari 2016a).

Crushing the Syrian rebels turned out to be less of a cakewalk than Soleimani had imagined. By November 2015, Iranian media were reporting

mounting Iranian deaths, including those of Basij militia member Mohsen
Fanousi and Brigadier General Hossein Hamedani, both killed in Aleppo.
The Iranian public was dismayed at the rising death toll, signifying a more
active Iranian role in the fighting than they had been given to believe; the
government sought to dissipate this sentiment by telling them that they were
fighting against ISIS militants, but this was not true (Naylor 2015, Mac-
Millan 2015). A different explanation is found in extracts from a speech by
Hamedani, published posthumously by *Mashregh News*, a website believed
to be associated with Iran's security services. In the article, Arash Karami
(2015) reports, 'Hamedani suggested that the Syrian civil war is actually
Iran's war, saying, "While there are whispers in Iran about why we are paying
the costs of Syria," it is actually the Syrians who are paying the costs of Iran's
war. Hamedani believed the war is actually against the "arrogant" countries,
a term Iranian hardliners use for the United States and other world powers.'
Karami also points out that 'the former secular army that used to punish
people for praying now has Syrian generals praying behind the leader of the
Quds Force'.

Hamedani's words shed light on how hardliners (including Soleimani)
view Iranian involvement in the Syrian war. They know very well that the
aim is not to defend Shia shrines or defeat ISIS, although this is what they
tell their people; the real aim is to export the Iranian Revolution. This interpretation was confirmed by IRGC second-in-command Hossein Salami
when he claimed that his country controlled both political and military arenas in Syria, and by IRGC commander Mohammad Ali Jafari, who linked
his troops fighting in Syria to 'the establishment of Mahdi's government
"prophesied redeemer of Islam who will rule for seven, nine, or nineteen years
(according to differing interpretations) before the Day of Judgment"', adding
that 'the persistence of the Islamic Iranian revolution needs elements that aid
the continuity of the Iranian revolution itself' (Alsalmi 2016). Hojjat al-Islam
Mehdi Taeb, the head of Khamenei's think tank Ammar Strategic Base, said
in February 2013 during a meeting with university student members of the
Basij paramilitary force that 'Syria is the 35th province of Iran and is a strategic province for us', and during a ceremony in an IRGC centre in Isfahan
in May 2014, Major General Yahya Rahim Safavi, former commander of the
IRGC and Khamenei's military advisor, described the previous forty months
of the war in Syria as a 'great strategic victory for the Islamic Republic of Iran'
(Naame Shaam 2014, 78).

These speeches lend support to the allegation by Naame Shaam, a group of Iranian, Syrian and Lebanese activists and citizen journalists, that the situation in Syria had become 'an occupation with an indigenous government in post' (of which the most famous example is probably the French Vichy regime under the Nazis), where the indigenous government was little more than a puppet, serving as an agent of the occupying force and effecting the latter's military control in the concerned state, often against the national interests of that state. Naame Shaam argues that this strategy is being implemented by the Iranian regime (i.e., by Khamenei and the IRGC-QF, which answers directly to him) rather than by the government (that is, President Rouhani and his ministers), since 'in February 2014, Iranian Foreign Minister Mohammad Javad Zarif told his American counterpart that he "did not have the authority to discuss or to negotiate on Syria," suggesting that such powers remained in the hands of Ayatollah Ali Khamenei and Gen. Qassem Soleimani' (Naame Shaam 2014, 77; 84).

How credible is this claim? There is compelling evidence that the Assad regime would have collapsed without the support of the Iranian regime and its proxies, including Hezbollah. The dominant role of the IRGC in putting down the uprising is less obvious, partly because the Iranian regime has been careful to conceal it, but evidence for that, too, has been gathered by journalists and researchers. According to regime defector Barabandi, as early as March 2011, 'the Secretary of Iran's Supreme National Security Council, Saeed Jalili, made an unannounced visit to Damascus. He came with a clear message: Do not give in to the Arab Spring in Syria ... As the tensions evolved into armed conflict, Iran immediately sent advisors, snipers, and special forces to support Bashar. To compensate for defections from his officers, Bashar padded his loyalist camp with fighters and strategic planners from Iran and Hezbollah' (Barabandi and Thompson 2014b). As the war progressed, according to Barabandi, Iran took control more firmly. Further confirmation of this claim comes from Iranian socialists Omid Ranjbar and Azadeh Shurmand (2016), who condemn Iranian imperialism in Syria and other countries.

Is the charge of Iranian control over the Assad regime compatible with the regime's accommodation with Al Qaeda and ISIS? As a nineteen-page document from the Abbottabad files recovered from Osama bin Laden's residence reveals, the relationship between the Iranian regime and Al Qaeda has been a symbiotic one, with their shared hostility to the United States overriding tensions stemming from the sectarian divide between them (Joscelyn and Roggio 2017). According to US and European intelligence, Al Qaeda had a long-standing relationship with the IRGC-QF, and many operatives, including leader of Al Qaeda in Iraq Abu Musab al-Zarqawi, fled to Iran when the US attacked Afghanistan in 2001. There, as German magazine *Cicero* reported, based on a leaked German intelligence document, Zarqawi spent months rebuilding his network under the protection of the IRGC, setting up new camps and safe houses in Zahedan, Isfahan and Tehran. When suicide bombers attacked three housing compounds in Riyadh, Saudi Arabia in May 2003, Saudi and US authorities followed the trail back to Saif al-Adel in Iran. A few days later, two restaurants, a five-star hotel, a Jewish community centre, a Jewish cemetery and other targets were blown up in Casablanca, Morocco, and again, the trail led to Saad bin Laden in Iran (Joscelyn 2007, 62; 60).

There are indications that the relationship has continued. Among others, Muhsin al-Fadhli, Al Qaeda's senior facilitator and financier in Iran, who was supposedly under 'house arrest' there but ran a group moving fighters and money through Turkey to Syria before moving to Syria himself in 2013, was reportedly killed in an airstrike in 2014; and Osama bin Laden's son-in-law Suleiman Abu Ghaith, a spokesman and recruiter for Al Qaeda, had spent at least ten years in Iran under 'house arrest' before he was arrested in Jordan in 2013 and given a life sentence in a New York court in 2014 (Karam 2014). What is interesting is that ISIS appears to have sustained this accommodation with Iran, presumably because it was convenient, despite its hostility to Shi'is. In a statement where Shi'is are referred to by the insulting epithet 'Rawafid', ISIS spokesman Abu Muhammad al-Adnani revealed that ISIS had refrained from targeting Iran in order to safeguard Al Qaeda's interests and supply lines in Iran (Roggio 2014). It is also significant that in Abu Bakr al-Baghdadi's speech urging ISIS fighters not to retreat from Mosul, he threatened Turkey and Saudi Arabia with terrorist attacks, but not Iran, suggesting that he saw Iran as an ally in Iraq and Syria, not an enemy (The Guardian 2016).

Assad's support for Sunni jihadism in Iraq after the US invasion of 2003 also suited Tehran. 'The exacerbation of sectarianism buried the prospect of a Shi'i-majority liberal-democratic government in Baghdad – a prospect that is as repulsive to Iran's Islamic Republic as it is for Syria's Baathist dictatorship. By the same token, the rise of sectarian tensions in Iraq contributed tremendously to enhancing Tehran's clout in that country by enabling the rise of a kindred Shi'i-sectarian authoritarian government in Baghdad' (Achcar 2016, 37).

This collaboration apparently extended to Syria. Mohammed Abdullah, a Syrian journalist living in Cairo, claimed that 'a number of Syrian activists analysed some of the videos posted on YouTube that display crimes committed by ISIL, and were able to track the IP addresses to Iran and Lebanon' (NCRI News 2014). Finally, the ISIS bulletin *Al-Binaa* published interviews with 'Abu Obeida', who left Al Qaeda to join ISIS in 2014; when asked how he managed to travel to Raqqa after leaving Al Qaeda, he said that 'it was an easy task as coordinators from al-Qaeda overlooked the arrangements of members entering Iran. He explained that travellers stay in "Guest Houses" until their travel arrangements to Syria are done, adding that Iranian government and security forces are aware of this. Abu Obeida stressed that … as soon as a traveller entered the "Guest House", intelligence knew of his arrival. He explained that supervisors of these homes meet with Iranian Intelligence every week and that all the houses and their phones are monitored' (al-Husseini 2016). In other words, as Karam (2014) puts it, this is a 'complicated' relationship, where the Iranian regime distrusts and monitors Al Qaeda/ISIS members to ensure that they launch no attacks in Iran, but it allows and even encourages them to launch attacks elsewhere, especially if these are against enemies of the Iranian regime.

There are three reasons why these accounts carry conviction. Firstly, while there have been devastating Al Qaeda/ISIS attacks in other countries, including those in Saudi Arabia and Turkey, whose regimes are accused of sponsoring them, there were none in Iran until June 2017, when twin attacks on the Iranian parliament and Khomeini's tomb killed at least seventeen and injured dozens. These attacks were claimed by ISIS, but there is a twist: they were carried out by Iranian Kurds, whose hatred of the state oppressing them perhaps outweighed the pragmatic reasons for ISIS's past collaboration with Iran (Hashemi 2017; Joscelyn 2017). Secondly, while hardline Islamists in Iran are comfortable with the idea that their 'jihadist duty' includes creating the conditions for Iran to rule Iraq and Syria, the bulk of fighters recruited from Iran, Iraq and Lebanon only join because they are convinced they will be fighting against *takfiri* fanatics who are destroying Shia shrines in Syria, and they would be dismayed at the thought of fighting against the Syrian people, who have respected and protected Shia shrines for centuries. The presence of Al Qaeda/ISIS in Syria is crucial to support this narrative. Thirdly, this is the strategy adopted by Assad to disarm international condemnation, and it is necessary for his allies to adopt it too.

If Iran is an occupying power in Syria, it certainly cannot be claimed that the regime in power is a secular one; indeed, the Iranian regime, as we saw in Chapter 4, is an Islamic state whose version of sharia law is similar to that of ISIS; a win for the Vichy Assad regime would thus be a win for Islamism. Secondly, it follows that 'the war in Syria should be regarded as an international conflict that warrants the application of the four Geneva Conventions and the regime-held areas of Syria should be considered occupied territory – not metaphorically but in the strict legal sense of the word. The *de facto* ruler of "Occupied Syria" is Gen. Qassem Soleimani and his colleagues in Sepah Qods and Sepah Pasdaran, who dominate the new military command structure in Syria' (Naame Shaam 2014, 88). Finally, the IRGC-QF and Hezbollah would be implicated in the war crimes and crimes against humanity committed in Syria (Naame Shaam 2015). As Palestinian Azzam Tamimi (2016) puts it, 'Both Hezbollah and its Iranian sponsor are equal partners with the Assad regime and bear responsibility for the millions who have fled their homes, the hundreds of thousands who have been killed and the many thousands who are today being starved to death.'

Despite the Iranian regime throwing all its resources and its various proxies into Syria to support Assad, the rebels continued to make gains. Soleimani was forced to visit Russia to appeal to Putin for help in July 2015 and reportedly helped to plan a Russian military intervention (Reuters 2015; Bassam and Perry 2015); according to Russian foreign minister Sergey Lavrov, 'Damascus was two to three weeks from falling' when Russia intervened (Reuters 2017a). Although Putin had already been backing Assad with weapons, ammunition and military advisors, Russian airstrikes began on September 30, 2015, targeting moderate rebels and killing almost one hundred civilians, including children, in Zaafarana, Talbiseh, Rastan, Makarmia and Ghanto in Homs Province and Latamaneh in Hama (Orton 2015a). On October 7, as Russian fighter jets blew up artillery, armoured personnel carriers and tanks belonging to Liwa Suqour al-Jabal (a US-backed brigade of the FSA) in western Aleppo, ISIS attacked a nearby Suqour al-Jabal base with explosives at the same time. Hasan Hagali, the top commander of the brigade and a former captain in the Syrian Arab Army, said that ISIS locations in the province were left untouched by the Russians (Weiss 2015c). The accusation that Russia was acting as ISIS's air force gained strength from the fact that Russian airstrikes on October 9 helped ISIS to advance into areas from which the FSA had previously kept it out:

Islamic State militants swept into villages in northwestern Syria as part of a surprise offensive against rival insurgents on Friday, activists said. The militants threatened the country's largest city, Aleppo, and dealt a blow to more moderate rebels under fire from Russian warplanes … The Islamic State extremists … seized at least five villages and a rebel-held infantry school in Aleppo province on Friday, according to Syrian activists and an online statement issued by the group. The gains were the most significant for the Islamic State in Syria in months, according to the Britain-based Syrian Observatory for Human Rights, a monitoring group. The infantry school is about 10 miles northeast of Aleppo and just a mile from a government-run industrial zone in the suburbs. Despite the Islamic State's push toward regime-controlled areas, however, the jihadists were not struck by Russian warplanes, activists said. (Cunningham 2015)

It seems fair to conclude that the 'hundreds of terrorists' whom the Russians claimed to have killed 'were the rebels who have been keeping I.S. out for years' (Orton 2015b). According to a Russian propaganda blitzkrieg, 'There is no such thing as a moderate opposition in Syria … Anyone not willing to join with Russia, Assad, Iran, and Hezbollah [i]s a "terrorist" or a covert sponsor of terrorism who'd do well to get out of Putin's way' (Weiss 2015b).

The deliberate targeting of civilians and anti-ISIS rebels became the pattern in increasingly ferocious Russian attacks. Within weeks, doctors and international observers claimed that four hospitals or more had been bombed by fighter jets in northwestern Syria. On October 20, 2015, Sarmin hospital in Idlib province was hit by two airstrikes, killing at least twelve, three of whom were believed to be medical staff. The hospital's director, Dr Mohamed Tennari, thought the hospital – situated on one of the most dangerous frontlines of the war – had been directly targeted (Chulov and Malik 2015). According to figures compiled by the organisation Physicians for Human Rights, between March 2011 and August 2015 there had been 313 attacks on medical facilities, with 679 medical staff killed. 'Syrian government forces have been responsible for more than 90% of these attacks', the organisation said, 'each of which constitutes a war crime' (Chulov and Malik 2015).

A week after the Sarmin hospital attack, at least eight hospitals had been targeted by Russian airstrikes. At a mass 'die-in' staged by medical personnel near UN headquarters in New York to protest against the targeting of hospitals by Russia and the Assad regime, the director of programmes for Physicians for Human Rights, Widney Brown, lamented, 'When you kill one doctor, it's not just the loss of that doctor, but it also impacts everyone who can't get healthcare because there's one less doctor' (Kaplan 2015).

Despite the protestors' demand that the UN enforce resolutions prohibiting the targeting of hospitals and other civilian infrastructure, the UN took no such action, and the targeting of civilians in general and medical facilities in particular continued. In late November, dozens were killed and scores wounded in Russian airstrikes, reported by local media to have used cluster bombs, on a crowded marketplace and other targets in the town of Ariha, Idlib province, where there was no presence of ISIS (Al Jazeera 2015c).

In western Aleppo Province, out of which the FSA had driven ISIS two years previously, schools were targeted by what residents identified as Russian aircraft. In Anjarah, a missile hit the building of what locals called 'the Western School'. As Mohammed al-Khatieb reported (2016b), the stairs of the building 'were drenched in blood.' According to one of the teachers, the attack had killed fifteen first-grade students as well as their teacher. 'The staff emptied the other schools in the town minutes before they too were shelled.' On January 11, Anjarah was targeted by four raids, hitting three schools and a residential neighbourhood. According to the Syrian Network for Human Rights, eighteen additional schools were targeted by Russian forces during the first three months of their intervention in Syria (al-Khatieb 2016b).

In December 2015, an Amnesty International investigation found that

> Russian air strikes in Syria have killed hundreds of civilians and caused massive destruction in residential areas, striking homes, a mosque and a busy market, as well as medical facilities ... In one of the deadliest attacks documented in the briefing three missiles were fired on a busy market in the centre of Ariha in Idleb governorate killing 49 civilians. Witnesses described how within seconds the bustling Sunday market turned to a scene of carnage ... In another suspected Russian attack, at least 46 civilians, including 32 children and 11 women who were sheltering for safety in the basement of a residential building, were killed on 15 October in al-Ghantu, Homs governorate. Video footage of the scene after the attack shows no evidence of a military presence. Weapons experts who analysed images of the attack said the nature of the destruction indicated possible use of fuel-air explosives (also known as 'vacuum bombs'), a type of weapon particularly prone to indiscriminate effects when used in the vicinity of civilians. In another attack five civilians were killed and a dozen homes were destroyed when a suspected Russian sea-launched cruise missile struck residential buildings in Darat Izza, Aleppo governorate, on 7 October. [...]
>
> The Russian authorities' reaction to an attack on Omar Bin al-Khattab mosque in central Jisr al-Shughour, Idleb governorate, on 1 October raises serious questions about the tactics they are prepared to deploy to undermine criticism of their operations. After reports and photos of the destroyed mosque

emerged, the Russian authorities responded by calling it a 'hoax', presenting a satellite image purporting to show the mosque still intact. However, the mosque shown in the image was a different one from the one destroyed in the attack. (Amnesty International 2015b).

There was a similar response when a deadly airstrike levelled a school district in Idlib province. According to a doctor at the local hospital, most of the thirty-five dead were children aged between six and fifteen, as well as female teachers; over one hundred were injured. Forty required surgery; many children had lost limbs. 'Out of 120 wounded, there were about 40 children and 30 to 40 women, and the rest were various ages, mostly parents, who went to find out what happened to their children and ended up getting hurt in follow-up airstrikes,' he said. 'They were all civilians. There were no terrorists or armed men or fighters' (Shaheen 2016b). The Russian Ministry of Defence responded by saying that 'it dispatched a drone to analyze the site of Wednesday's alleged bombing of a school in Idlib, Syria. The ministry says that the aircraft spotted no evidence of airstrikes, and accused the White Helmets [the Syrian volunteer civil defence organisation] of faking digital images of the attack' (RT 2016c).

The strategy of 'denying everything' was also evident when the family of the first Russian soldier to die in Syria was told he had hanged himself, despite the fact that 'his nose, jaw and neck had been broken, that the back of his head had been smashed in, and that he had a cut extending to his belly button' (Osborn 2015).

Putin seemed to be following his Chechnya playbook in attacking civilian targets and rebels fighting against ISIS, while sparing ISIS: 'Like Aleppo, Grozny was battered not just by conventional artillery and air power but also the TOS-1 "Buratino," able to fire salvos of 24 rockets armed with thermobaric munitions, whose devastating blasts are second only to nuclear weapons in their capacity to level city blocks and blast houses to rubble' (Galeotti 2016). An investigation conducted by Elena Milashina for *Novaya Gazeta* found that Russian special services were controlling the flow of jihadists into Syria from Dagestan, providing them with passports and establishing a 'green corridor' to allow them to migrate from Russia to Turkey and then to Syria (Weiss 2015a), thus feeding ISIS and other Islamist groups that Putin claimed to be fighting.

That claim played well with Putin's domestic audience. On October 17, there was an antiwar rally in Moscow, prior to which one woman was detained for holding up a sign with the slogan 'Putin, you murderer, stop shaming Russia' (DW 2015). However, it was a small demonstration of around

150 people, and a poll prior to it found that a large majority of Russians supported the airstrikes – partly because they projected an image of Russian power, and partly because they believed they were targeting ISIS, a significant number of whose fighters were from Russia and had carried out terrorist attacks there (Varshalomidze 2015). On the one hand, Foreign Minister Lavrov told reporters in New York, 'We don't consider Free Syrian Army a terrorist group, and believe [it] should be part of the political process' (Nichols 2015). At the same time, however, Putin's press secretary, Dmitry Peskov, justified bombing them when he claimed to doubt that they still existed, asking, 'Haven't most of them switched to [ISIS] group?' (Weiss 2015b).

The other playbook Putin appeared to be following with his 'shock and awe' campaign designed to show off Russian military might was that of George W. Bush. Syrians who had long been subjected to bombardment noticed an increase in intensity after Russia started its assault on September 30, 2015, using conventional bombs as well as vacuum or 'thermobaric' bombs which are 'highly destructive with fearful, direct physical effects' (The Conversation 2015), incendiary weapons 'designed to destroy infrastructure and inflict excruciatingly painful thermal and respiratory burns on their victims' (Solvang 2016), cluster munitions that 'have literally made Syria a minefield' (Solvang 2016), cruise missiles (Reuters 2016b), and bunker-buster bombs that leave enormous craters. A *Guardian* report on the use of the latter in Aleppo describes the reaction of Abdulkafi al-Hamdo, a teacher (Shaheen 2016a):

> When Hamdo saw the impact that one of them appeared to have had on Mashhad, he despaired. Schools, orphanages and hospitals in Aleppo that moved underground to escape the destruction around them now feel that even they are at risk. 'When I saw it I thought, my God, is it possible that there is so much destruction here and nobody wants to help us?' he said … 'I was not surprised by Russia using it,' said Hamdo. 'They're a murderous, criminal state. But I was surprised that the international community let it use those weapons. The mask fell a long time ago from Russia and the regime, but now the mask has fallen from human rights defenders, from the international community. This is hell itself.'

Citizen journalists and monitoring reports showed that Russian airstrikes added to civilian deaths, injuries and displacement (Standish 2015b). Around 90 per cent of the airstrikes, including those using cluster bombs and cruise missiles, were in areas outside the control of ISIS, and 'among the confirmed targets in the verified attacks were hospitals, mosques, schools,

markets, shelters, and residential buildings' (EA Worldview 2015). The sim-
ilarity with the Bush assault on Iraq did not end there. On March 14, 2016,
'the George W. Bush parallel was lost on very few analysts when Vladimir
Putin proudly announced that he was withdrawing a significant amount of
Russia's forces from Syria because their "mission is accomplished"' (Miller,
J. 2016), yet Russian military action in Syria was subsequently stepped up
rather than terminated.

There has been much speculation about Putin's motives for supporting the
Assad regime. Among those attributed to him, the following are most common:

1. Support for a longtime ally of Russia; the Russian intervention
    did indeed turn the tide of the war in favour of Assad, and it is
    likely that Putin's announcement of the withdrawal of troops was
    intended to send 'a signal to the Assad regime that Russian support
    is not unlimited' (Trombly 2016).
2. Projection of Russian power beyond the former Soviet Union; re-
    inforcement of Russian military bases in Syria, and becoming an
    indispensable partner in negotiating any future ceasefire or politi-
    cal solution to the war; Putin certainly succeeded in this objective,
    although this came at the cost of alienating the regime in Tehran,
    which wanted Russia to play a supporting role to its own forces, not
    the leading role (Qaidaari 2016b; Karami 2016c).
3. Embarrassing the United States (Orton 2015b); this could certainly
    be the intention behind targeting not just rebel fighters but even hu-
    manitarian NGOs and workers supported by the US, including the
    White Helmets, rescue workers who are the first responders after
    airstrikes and have saved tens of thousands of lives (Hudson 2016;
    Khaja 2016).
4. Boosting Russian arms sales by showcasing its advanced weapons
    and delivery systems; this certainly seems to have happened (Sky
    News 2016a; Luhn 2016).
5. Bringing about the disintegration of the European Union by exac-
    erbating the refugee crisis.

Evidence for this last claim comes from various sources. We saw in
Chapter 2 that Putin supports far-right Eurosceptic European parties,
which have received a boost from the flood of refugees fleeing the war in
Syria as well as the demonisation of refugees in the Russian media. The in-

tensive Russian bombing of civilians seems to suggest such a motive, since it is unlikely that Putin is as wedded to the goal of keeping Assad in power as is Assad himself. If even refugees in the relative comfort of the Netherlands say that 'the day Assad leaves Syria, [they] will return' (Scott 2015), it is hardly surprising that others, living in far-worse conditions in Turkey, also long to return to their homeland (Al Jazeera 2016b). Putin has to prevent that from happening. Hence the imperial arrogance of the Russian ultimatum to 275,000 Syrians in eastern Aleppo to abandon their homes or be pulverised by more bombing (Nechepurenko 2016).

The big success of this strategy is Britain's Brexit, which, prior to the referendum, had the support of only one world leader: Putin. 'From the tweets of the Russian Embassy to the programming of Russia Today, the Kremlin is pushing for Out,' reported Ben Judah in March 2016. 'Moscow's first weapon is the Syrian refugee ... Right now, Russian warplanes are bombing civilian areas, turning northern Syria into a refugee factory ... Look at *Russia Today*: "migrant rape" is a constant news item. Berlin says many such stories are fabricated and has ordered its counter-espionage service to investigate Russian propaganda' (Judah 2016). Indeed, the main party campaigning for Brexit, the UK Independence Party, used a poster portraying thousands of Syrian refugees in Slovenia – uncannily similar to a Nazi poster from the 1930s – with the caption 'BREAKING POINT. The EU has failed us all. We must break free of the EU and take back control over our borders' (Safdar 2016). Subsequently, Putin noted with satisfaction the impact that the issue of migration had had on European politics. 'Apparently the British people are not satisfied with the way problems are being solved in the security sphere, [and] these problems have become more acute lately with the migration processes,' he said (The BRICS Post 2016).

In the ceasefire deal signed between the US and Russia on September 10, 2016, and slated to begin on the evening of September 12 (the Eid al Adha festival), Russia succeeded in convincing the US to promise two things: to demand the rebels it supported honour the ceasefire and separate themselves from Jabhat Fatah al-Sham, and to engage in joint bombing raids on ISIS and Jabhat Fatah al-Sham should the ceasefire hold for a week. In return, Russia was to restrain the regime from bombing the rebels and demand it allow humanitarian aid into rebel-held areas, especially in Aleppo (Al Jazeera 2016c). Like an earlier truce in February, this one excluded ISIS and Jabhat Fatah al-Sham. FSA militias had reservations about the truce, pointing out that there were no sanctions specified if the regime broke it, and that Jabhat Fatah al-Sham had taken a positive step in breaking with Al Qaeda. Twenty-one other large militias, including the Sham Legion, Jaish al-Islam and Ahrar al-Sham, explicitly condemned the exclusion of Fatah al-Sham, pointing out the double standards involved in excluding it, but not foreign militias fighting alongside the regime. Nonetheless, they did not explicitly reject the truce, and it held for the first few days; children came out to play in Aleppo, and Haj Abu Ibrahim said, 'We haven't experienced this much peace since ages. There is no shelling, and I haven't heard the ambulance siren for three days. I can now sit outside my house without fear. My grandkids can play in the backyard safely' (Osman 2016).

However, the regime refused to allow trucks containing humanitarian aid to reach the besieged residents of eastern Aleppo, in what UN envoy Staffan de Mistura said was a breach of the ceasefire agreement (Wintour and Borger 2016). Almost a week later, the UN finally received permission to deliver aid to besieged areas. 'All parties, including Russia and the United States, had been notified about the cleared convoy heading to rebel-held eastern Aleppo,' a UN spokesperson said. However, just as it reached its destination in a rebel-controlled area of Aleppo, the Syrian regime declared the ceasefire over, and over half of the trucks in the convoy were attacked. The convoy had been delivering aid for 78,000 people. As Benoit Carpentier of the International Federation of Red Cross and Red Crescent Societies said, 'Life-saving aid supplies have been totally damaged and a health clinic destroyed, depriving thousands of civilians of much needed food and medical assistance' (Nebehay and Miles 2016).

> Among the dead was Omar Barakat, a father of nine who was the head of the Syrian Arab Red Crescent in the town of Orem al-Kubra, a man directly involved in securing permits for the mission – the first of its kind in the struggling eight-day truce. A total of 20 civilians and aid workers were killed, officials said. Barakat's brother Ali told Reuters that more than 20 missiles hit the area, including the one that killed his brother, who was overseeing the unloading of lorries when a bomb hit the warehouse, killing him inside his car … A rescue worker told Associated Press that missiles pounded the area for hours, even hitting his team as they searched the debris for survivors. (Chulov and Shaheen 2016b)

In the request to the government to enable the convoy to proceed, the Syrian regime had been given 'the names of the organisations involved in the convoy, the planned route and the point at which the convoy would cross the frontline. The amount and type of aid and the point of distribution were also itemised. Before the 31-lorry convoy departed in the late afternoon, the number of people travelling with it was also passed on, as were GPS coordinates of the route and destination' (Chulov and Shaheen 2016b). US officials said that there was no doubt that the convoy was destroyed in an airstrike. As Jeff Davis, a Pentagon spokesperson, stated, 'There are only three parties that fly in Syria: the coalition, the Russians and the Syrian regime. It was not the coalition. We don't fly over Aleppo. We have no reason to. We strike only Isis, and Isis is not there' (Borger and Ackerman 2016). Sergey Lavrov, the Russian foreign minister, admitted to John Kerry that the convoy had been monitored by Russian military drones (Borger and Ackerman 2016).

Amid a suspension of UN aid and allegations of a heinous war crime, spokesperson for the Russian military Igor Konashenkov gave a statement denying Russian involvement in the attack, claiming that 'all information on the whereabouts of the convoy was available only to the militants controlling these areas' (Reuters 2016c), contradicting Lavrov and voluminous evidence that Russian and Syrian officials had been informed of the precise route and coordinates of the convoy. Konashenkov said that the military had 'carefully studied the video recordings of the so-called activists from the scene and found no signs that any munitions hit the convoy,' going on to claim that 'everything shown on the video is the direct consequence of the cargo catching fire, and this began in a strange way simultaneously with militants carrying out a massive offensive in Aleppo' (Al Jazeera 2016d).

The investigative network Bellingcat carefully studied evidence available in the public domain and found that the Russian Ministry of Defence itself live-streamed surveillance drone footage tracking the convoy all the way to its destination; thus the Russians clearly knew that it had not deviated from the route and coordinates they had been given. Nor is it true, as Konashenkov claimed, that 'there are no craters, while the vehicles have their chassis intact and they have not been severely damaged, which would have been the case from an airstrike'; video footage and photographs show craters, explosions and devastating destruction, while in the audio evidence accompanying the videos, jet engines and multiple explosions can be heard. Photographs of the debris showed what Bellingcat identified as the tailfin of an OFAB 250-270 high-explosive fragmentation bomb: a type of bomb manufactured in weapons factories of the USSR and Russian Federation, and previously used extensively by both Syrian and Russian aircraft. A couple of days after the attack, the Russian Ministry of Defence changed its story and suggested that a US Predator drone was responsible, despite the fact that these bombs are not used by Predator drones (Waters and al-Khatib 2016; Higgins 2016).

The chorus from the US, UK and France in the UN Security Council accusing Russia of war crimes grew louder as incendiary and bunker-buster bombs were dropped on civilians in Aleppo in the aftermath of the aid convoy attack, destroying the water supply (Borger and Shaheen 2016) and killing 338 people, including over one hundred children, within a week, according to the World Health Organization. 'Attacking health care is both illegal and barbaric,' the executive director of WHO's health emergencies programme, Peter Salama, said in the statement. 'Blocking whole populations from access to medical care, food and water is intolerable. It is inexcusable cruelty.' UN Secretary-General Ban Ki-moon called the attacks 'war crimes' (Pascaline 2016).

Meanwhile, the Syrian state was in a terminal state of decay:

Apparently too weak to coerce and too broke to bribe those who fight under its banner, Assad has made efforts to tie his subordinates closer to his Damascus by political means instead. This April's parliamentary 'elections' further indicated the structural transformation of the regime from a centralized state to a loose hodgepodge of warlord[s]. A number of long-serving Ba'athist rubberstamp bureaucrats and local dignitaries, pillars of the regime's traditional rentier system, lost their seats in favor of upstart smugglers, militia leaders, and tribal chiefs. [...]

Over the past three years, despite foreign military aid and support, the regime under Assad has continued to atrophy at an ever increasing pace. If these trends continue, the Syrian president will soon find himself little more than a primus inter pares, a symbolic common denominator around which a loose coalition of thieves and fiefdoms can rally. Thus, with the slow decay of the once powerful state, military, and party establishment, the person of Bashar al-Assad himself has increasingly come to embody the last remaining pillar not of a state but of 'the regime' and its brutal war against its own citizens. (Schneider 2016)

Nowhere was this decay more apparent than in the Syrian Arab Army. By late 2014, Assad was already having to resort to desperate measures to conscript soldiers, round up draft evaders, and punish the growing number of deserters in order to shore up his army (Naylor 2014). By 2016, the army had largely been replaced by foreign fighters. While the recapture of Palmyra was presented as a victory for the Syrian Army, in fact, it is now clear it was an eccentric multinational force that took Palmyra. Analysis of photographs, social media posts and Iranian, Russian and even Syrian media has shown that the path was led by the Russians, with much of the 'grunt' work done by Afghan Shia and Iraqi militiamen under generals from the Iranian Revolutionary Guard ... For the first time, clear evidence emerged in Palmyra of not only Russian special forces but Russian mercenaries connected directly to President Vladimir Putin on the front lines. [One such mercenary company], known as 'Wagner', has lost members in both Ukraine and Syria – and they have been personally honoured by President Putin, despite private military contracting firms being illegal in Russia. One platoon of Wagner fighters is said to be not even Russian but Serb – adding yet another nationality to the fighters from around the world fighting on all sides of the conflict. The leader of this group, Davor Savicic, a Bosnian Serb, was nicknamed 'Elvis' and celebrated for his 'kill record' when fighting in the civil war in his own country two decades ago.[3] (Spencer 2016)

These developments add weight to the contention that Assad has been ready to reduce his country to rubble and to cede its sovereignty to foreign powers simply in order to retain his personal power. They have also changed the character of the resistance: 'Anti Assad rebels in north Aleppo are now facing a relentless assault by Russians from the air and an Iranian backed ground force comprised of various sectarian militias. This has transformed their struggle against a fascist regime into a national liberation struggle' (al-Shami 2016). Indeed, Putin's scorched-earth strategy in Syria reminds one of the US bombardment of Vietnam. Another striking parallel is with the Palestinian Nakba: Aleppo resident Abd al-Azaiz Allosh refused to leave Aleppo, explaining, 'I say this is *our* land. If we move to another place, it will be just like the Palestinians. We'll be forced into displacement, and our land will exist only in our dreams' (Al Jazeera 2016e).

Putin had successfully played the 'war against Islamic terror' card in 2001 to fend off criticism of his regime's atrocities in Chechnya, but he was less successful in 2016 because, despite the propaganda of Putinists, it was clear to human rights monitors that the US-led coalition was trying to minimise civilian deaths while the Russians were deliberately targeting civilians, with the consequence that the civilian death rate resulting from airstrikes of the latter was at least eight times that of the former. The ratio would increase if deaths resulting from the targeting of civilian infrastructure (e.g., water supply) and hospitals were added (Graham-Harrison 2016). Thus the US in particular was in a much-stronger position to condemn Russian war crimes than it had been when it was committing its own war crimes in Afghanistan.

Foreign Military Interventions: Assad's Opponents

This brings us to the military interventions of what might be called the pro-opposition forces, although their support for the opposition has been incomparably weaker than the support for Assad from the regime's allies. In August 2011, Obama and the leaders of France, Germany and Britain called for Assad to step aside because the Syrian people had rejected his regime. Although US hawks and human rights groups had been pressing for Obama to make such a statement, key US regional allies such as Turkey and Saudi Arabia had opposed such a move, hoping instead to persuade Assad to end his military assault on protesters. The statement, accompanied by sanctions, ruled out military intervention, yet it was seized upon by a beleaguered opposition:

> Until now, many Syrians have interpreted the world's response as tacit support for Assad, leaving them reluctant to turn against the government. But activists said they hoped Obama's statement would energize a movement that had begun to flag in the face of the military crackdown.
>
> 'It will encourage people that the international community is moving faster against the regime, and it will give us hope,' said Amer al-Sadeq, a Damascus-based organizer in the Syrian Revolution Coordinators Union, one of the bigger groups organizing the largely spontaneous protests.
>
> The hope is that the 'silent majority,' notably in Damascus and Aleppo, the two largest cities yet to experience large-scale protests, will declare its opposition to the regime, said another Damascus-based activist, who spoke on the condition of anonymity for security reasons. (Wilson and Warrick 2011b)

The protests did spread to Damascus and Aleppo, but these activists felt deeply betrayed when the international community did not, in fact, move against the regime, even as the crackdown intensified and Assad's forces were joined by Hezbollah, Iraqi Shia militias and the IRGC. What could Obama, in particular, have done at this stage? In April 2013, Gilbert Achcar said in an interview: 'In Syria, we see Washington's great quandary. As in Libya, it refuses to deliver weapons to the insurgency despite insistent requests (although it intervened directly in Libya, by bombing). The result is a total disproportion in weaponry and training between the regime's forces and the insurgency, even though the insurgency encompasses a much larger section of the population. The truth is that the war has dragged on much longer than it might have had the insurgency received weapons' (Achcar 2013a). It is impossible to say with certainty that the rebels would have won and that the war would have ended by 2013 had they been provided with weapons that allowed them to defend themselves against the regime's onslaught, but it is undeniable that they would have been in a much stronger position, and this would have allowed those sections of the international community that wanted to stop the war to impose a long-term ceasefire and negotiations on a political solution, thus saving hundreds of thousands of lives.

The pleas of the rebels for arms was met by two programmes. The first, the Pentagon's 'train and equip' programme, which sought to recruit non-Islamist fighters – who would undertake not to fight against Assad – for the war against ISIS, ended in dismal failure. It spent $384 million to train 180 re-cruits who, inadequately equipped and badly paid, fell apart almost as soon as they entered Syria (Gutman 2015b). Osama Abu Zeid, the FSA's legal advisor, offered the following explanation for the failure:

> We are independent and responsible toward our people to the extent that we can say no, even to the US, which sought through this program to make us fight IS only and to forget the criminal called Bashar al-Assad, who has killed more than 300,000 Syrians over the past years, displaced 10 million and is still detaining more than half a million Syrians. Although the US gave us some support, we refused its offer and confirmed that this program would fail, and it ultimately did, since it is a US project that does not meet the aspirations of the Syrians. We have a Syrian project to combat all forms of terrorism, including IS and Assad, and we accept any offer of help. IS cannot be eliminated without the FSA. We have a history of struggle against all of those who killed Syrians. Therefore, no one can question the FSA's objectives when it fights IS, because its project is purely Syrian, and it aims to protect Syrians rather than serve other agendas. (al-Khatieb 2016a)

The second response to the rebels' call for support was a CIA pro-gramme started after early reports that Assad was using chemical weapons, which also vetted recruits to ensure they were not Islamists, but did not re-quire them to undertake not to fight against Assad. The first batch of these recruits, trained in Jordan and equipped with light arms, entered Syria in September 2013 (Sanchez 2013). As it became obvious that these light arms were of little use against the heavy weapons supplied by Russia and Iran, TOW anti-tank missiles began to be supplied to the rebels in April 2014, and the supply was increased when Russia entered the war. These made a real dent in the regime's array of armoured vehicles (Crowcroft 2015). How-ever, without anti-aircraft weapons, the rebels were still unable to defend themselves and their communities from air attacks.

When chemical attacks were first reported, Obama had said that chemical warfare constituted a 'red line' which would attract retribution if it was crossed. But after the deadly Ghouta attacks occurred, Obama backed away, instead entering into a deal with Russia for Syria to sign on to the Chemical Weapons Convention, and for the Organisation for the Prohibition of Chemical Weapons to identify and dispose of Assad's chemical weapons: a deal that allowed Assad to carry on slaughtering the opposition in other ways. Indeed, the UN concluded that Assad had even continued carrying out chemical attacks after the deal (Toosi 2016). At this point, Syrians who were still hoping the US would step in to stop the carnage gave up in despair, feeling that the international community had completely abandoned them.

In his speech explaining why he backed off from military strikes to take out Assad's chemical weapons, Obama articulated that (a) action was necessary, otherwise Assad would go on using chemical weapons and so would other tyrants; (b) however, before taking military action he would prefer to have the backing of Congress (which at that point he seemed unlikely to get); (c) he would not put American boots on the ground nor pursue a prolonged air campaign, because the purpose was to send a message to Assad, not to overthrow him, ('I don't think we should remove another dictator with force'); and (d) he had a deeply held preference for peaceful solutions, which is why he wanted to give the deal with Russia a chance (The Telegraph 2013). However, the questions then arise: Why did he say that Assad should go? Why did he draw that red line?

Robert Malley, the White House advisor for the Middle East and North Africa, justified both the words and the lack of action by asking, 'is the suggestion seriously that if we harbor aspirations we cannot achieve in the foreseeable future, we should not voice them and that if we voice them, we should always act upon them? That because we can't stop human rights abuses, we shouldn't speak out against them? Because we are not willing to go to war to topple a dictator, we shouldn't support popular calls for his ouster?' With respect to the 'red line', he said, 'The United States fulfilled the stated purpose of the red line and did so without initiating military action with neither a clear endpoint nor clear international legal basis' (Miller, A. 2016). The reason given for refusing to provide secular rebels with anti-aircraft missiles was the fear that they might fall into the hands of terrorists and be used to shoot down commercial aircraft. In order to avert this outcome, the CIA was reported to be trying to engineer MANPADS (man-portable air defence systems) which can be switched off if they fall into the wrong hands, but in the meantime, hundreds of thousands were killed by aerial bombardment, and even if this experiment were successful, it would not protect rebels and civilians from Russian bombing (Groll 2016).

The reference to international law is revealing and makes sense with regard to military strikes on Assad's forces, but the fear of anti-aircraft missiles going astray is not enough to explain Obama's refusal to arm the secular rebels. All the available evidence suggests that despite being so poorly armed, these rebels fought successfully to keep the heavily armed alliance of Assad, the IRGC, Hezbollah, the Iraqi militia and the Russian forces at bay. For example, after the Russian intervention, which the FSA described as 'an occupation of Syrian territory', the regime launched offensives to regain territory in the countryside of Hama, the southern countryside of Aleppo, the northern countryside of Homs, and the Latakia mountains, but 'the FSA forces managed to preserve their regions and maintain their positions' (Hanna 2015). Some of these positions were subsequently lost, mainly due to a lack of anti-aircraft missiles.

Furthermore, as leader Abu Zeid emphasised, the FSA was equally committed to routing ISIS (al-Khatieb 2016a), and even Al Qaeda: in the city of Maarat al-Nu'man, 'FSA supporters have organized escalating protests of the town's men and women against al Qaeda, sparking such anger at the jihadist group's abuses that Nusra was forced to withdraw, at least temporarily ... Jihadists may have fared better on the battlefield because of their bigger budgets and unscrupulous tactics, FSA commanders claim, but they have failed to win the hearts and minds of liberated Syria's civilians' (Cambanis 2016). This confrontation not only makes redundant the absurd Russian demand that secular rebels separate themselves from Jabhat Fatah al-Sham, and Staffan de Mistura's equally absurd offer to escort nine hundred ex-Nusra fighters out of Aleppo in order to stop the bombing of civilians (Nebehay and Miles 2016), but also exposes the agenda behind this demand: to force secular rebels to hand over territory to Islamists. Clearly the FSA, in alliance with civilian activists, had their own ways of dealing with al-Nusra.

So why didn't Obama provide them with suitable weapons? It is hard not to agree with anti-imperialists (the genuine variety, not the fakes) that 'the U.S. refused to give the FSA the heavy armaments like anti-aircraft weaponry it needed to defend itself against Assad's aerial bombardment, fearing that such weaponry would ultimately degrade the state that the U.S.

wanted to preserve' – or in other words, allow a genuine revolution to occur (Smith 2016b). Indeed, Obama even prevented his Arab allies from supplying anti-aircraft weapons that would enable the opposition to defend their communities from slaughter and give them a chance of prevailing over Assad and his allies (Achcar 2016, 21–22).

However, this was not always his attitude towards the Arab uprisings. As Moammar Gaddafi moved to crush the uprising in Libya, Obama said that Gaddafi must leave; but he and even Hillary Clinton were at first unwilling to undertake a military intervention, especially since it was clear that enforcing a no-fly zone would not suffice to hold back Gaddafi's ground assault on the rebels. This changed when the Arab League called on the UN to enforce a no-fly zone over Libya in March 2011, and the US agreed to support a resolution drafted by Britain and France. Given Arab support for the resolution, Russia and China abstained instead of vetoing it (Wilson and Warwick 2011a). UN Security Council Resolution 1973 (2011) went beyond imposing a no-fly zone over Libya, authorising

> Member States that have notified the Secretary-General, acting nationally or through regional organizations or arrangements, and acting in cooperation with the Secretary-General, to take all necessary measures, notwithstanding paragraph 9 of resolution 1970 (2011), to protect civilians and civilian populated areas under threat of attack in the Libyan Arab Jamahiriya, including Benghazi, while excluding a foreign occupation force of any form on any part of Libyan territory, and requests the Member States concerned to inform the Secretary-General immediately of the measures they take pursuant to the authorization conferred by this paragraph which shall be immediately reported to the Security Council. (UNSC 2011)

It can be argued, against proponents of US military intervention in Syria, that military action in Libya was authorised by the Security Council, whereas there was no such authorisation in Syria. This is true. However, does this rule out providing arms and ammunition to rebels to enable them to defend themselves, their families and their communities from death and destruction? As eastern Aleppo was being pounded from the air and its inhabitants subjected to extermination, a proposal to provide rebels with weapons that would enable them to do just that was presented to Obama, 'and that's as far as it got. Neither approved nor rejected, the plan was left in a state of ambiguity ... Molham Ekaidi, deputy commander of an FSA unit in Aleppo, said in an online interview that the United States' failure to deliver advanced antiaircraft weapons to aid in the defence of Aleppo amounted to a "green light" for Moscow to lay waste to the city' (Miller and Entous 2016).

We shall return to this question later, and merely point out here the disastrous results of the US response for its credibility with Syrians. Devoid of other options, the Obama administration was forced to consider the possibility of Assad staying on during the transition, and to rely on the Russians in their peace initiatives. When peace negotiations started, there was scepticism on the ground. 'Where are these reasonable Russians that Kerry claims are starting to see the light?' asked a doctor in a hospital in Idlib, adding, 'Bashar's jets never bombed us like the Russians do. Isis never hunted us down like this.' One of the remaining residents in eastern Ghouta, Issa Khaled, confirmed: 'We've never been bombed like this' (Chulov and Shaheen 2015). When the US-Russian ceasefire deal of September 2016 was signed – agreeing, among other things, to joint US-Russian bombing of Jabhat Fatah al-Sham – 150 secular, democratic Syrians voiced the outrage felt by many more:

> Three years ago the two imperialist nations signed a reprehensible deal on chemical weapons that resolved a problem for the United States, Israel, and Russia, and even for the Assad regime, which had just murdered 1,466 of its subjects. The deal however did not resolve any of the problems facing the Syrian people. Rather it gave free rein to an extremely criminal regime that kills Syrians, destroys their villages and communities, and drives them into exile. The deal has also proved to be a priceless gift to Islamist nihilistic groups like Daesh and Jabhat an-Nusra. Three years into this contemptible deal – with the death count now at around half a million Syrians – Russians and Americans have agreed to freeze the current situation so that the two military powers can carry on their endless war against terror. The agreement remains silent on the untold number of detainees held in brutal conditions, and includes no call for lifting the blockade on besieged areas, or the withdrawal of Iran, the Hezbollah militia, or any other sectarian militia. It is also devoid of any reference to the concept of a new and democratic Syria. Nor are the warplanes of Bashar al-Assad restrained from bombing areas that will ultimately be the subject of a later agreement between Russia and the United States. (The Nation 2016)

Cooperation with Russia, and the idea that Assad might remain during a 'transition' period, was also treated with disgust by liberal commentators. As one pointed out, this would ensure it was a transition to nowhere: 'By refusing to make Assad's departure a central part of the peace plan, the West has guaranteed the negotiating process will ultimately fail and Syria will continue to burn. The man at the top has no intention of negotiating his own departure:

Assad's only objective is maintaining his family's control of Syria indefinitely, whatever the cost' (Aziz 2016). Another commentator emphasised the immorality of such an arrangement: 'The administration's fear of a slippery slope has paralyzed it, even as it slides downward and headlong into the dark unknown. If acceptance of and cooperation with a regime neck-deep in war crimes and crimes against humanity should become thinkable, then the amazingly deep extent of the fall will be painfully clear to one and all' (Hof 2014). A third commented that Assad 'has aligned himself first with the mullahs of Iran, and now with fanatically religious terrorists who are said to be too radical even for al Qaeda's taste. Meanwhile, Obama stands by, clueless as ever' (Mirengoff 2014). Nicholas Kristof (2016) wrote that 'allowing Syria's civil war and suffering to drag on unchallenged has been [Obama's] worst mistake, casting a shadow over his legacy.' Finally, after the September 2016 ceasefire collapsed in horrific carnage, Charles Lister (2016) of the Middle East Institute suggested that after working with Russia had failed to deliver a reduction in violence time after time, expecting a different result was 'the definition of insanity'.

The only alternative to the passive collusion with violent perpetrators in Syria that Obama and his advisors seemed to feel he had a legal basis for engaging in was military action against Al Qaeda and ISIS, presumably because they had declared war on the US. This was undertaken mainly in alliance with Kurdish forces, and it is worth looking at the results.

Given Obama's refusal to engage in any activity that might help in the overthrow of the Assad regime, the Kurdish Democratic Union Party (PYD), formed in 2003 by former members of the Turkish Kurdistan Workers' Party (PKK), was its only obvious ally, although it should have been evident that this alliance would be anathema to another US ally: Turkey, which regarded the PKK as a terrorist group, as did the US itself. When Abdullah Öcalan, a young Turkish Kurd, founded the Marxist-Leninist PKK in 1978, the party received support from the USSR. In 1984, it initiated its violent struggle for Kurdish independence from Turkey. Support for the PKK was continued by post-Soviet Russia, which allowed it to maintain a representative office in Moscow and run a 'cultural-educational camp' in the city of Yaroslavl to the northeast of Moscow (Reynolds 2016).

Despite clamping down on Kurdish linguistic and cultural rights in Syria, Hafez al-Assad promoted the Kurdish parties of Iraq and Turkey, including the PKK, allowing them to operate freely in Syria. However, in 1998 the Turkish government, engaged in suppressing a Kurdish insurgency in southeastern Turkey, objected strongly to Assad's support for the PKK. In order to avoid a confrontation with Turkey, the Assad regime signed the Adana Agreement, in which 'Syria labeled the PKK a terrorist organization, prohibited its activities and those of its affiliates, and agreed to block the supply of weapons, logistical materiel and money to the PKK from Syrian territory. This move forced Abdullah Öcalan out of his Syrian refuge, leading to the PKK leader's eventual capture and imprisonment. The rest of the PKK operatives left the country soon after' (Sinclair and Kajjo 2011).

In 2004, after violence erupted between Arab and Kurdish fans at a soccer match, Bashar al-Assad summoned Kurdish leaders, warning them to cease their political and cultural activities, and to stop teaching their language to children, even in private. There are a large number of Syrian Kurdish parties, and the demands they all share are linguistic – recognition of the Kurdish language and the right to teach in Kurdish – and cultural – the right to hold festivals celebrating Kurdish literature, song and dance. Many of them seek constitutional recognition of Kurds as an ethnic minority in Syria. Finally, there are some which demand not full independence but autonomy for Kurdish regions. In the run-up to the Syrian uprising, 'the Syrian regime, whose diplomatic and commercial relations with Ankara improved considerably in the era of Bashar al-Asad, has often detained PYD leaders and members in deference to its erstwhile Turkish friend' (Sinclair and Kajjo 2011), which would explain why Erdoğan's government was initially reluctant to take any action against Assad.

In the spring of 2011, as the Syrian uprising spread, twelve Kurdish parties, including the PYD, formed a coalition called the National Movement of Kurdish Political Parties. A month after an unprecedented gathering, the coalition announced its plan for resolving the Syrian crisis. 'The plan calls for an end to one-party rule, a modern, civil state that ensures the rule of law, and true equality for all citizens, among other demands. The programme is very similar to those of other opposition groups in the country. And yet, outside the Kurdish press, the National Movement's announcement was largely ignored' (Sinclair and Kajjo 2011). This failure to recognise Kurdish aspirations was evident once again when representatives of the opposition to Assad met in Istanbul in July to choose a 'National Salvation Council'. Kurdish representatives at the gathering wanted the name of the country changed from the 'Syrian Arab Republic' (which excluded non-Arab citizens) to the 'Republic of Syria'. When this request was refused by other conference delegates, 'these Kurds walked out in protest' (Sinclair and Kajjo 2011).

The failure of Arab opposition leaders to grant this most basic demand for equality highlights the lack of inclusivity in their vision for a new Syria. However, this does not mean that the PYD, which soon came to be seen as the sole representative of Kurds in Syria, was above criticism. In July 2012, Assad's forces withdrew and transferred control of most security and administrative bodies to the PYD in the Kurdish-majority areas of Afrin, Jazeera (around Qamishli) and Kobani, allowing the PYD to set up its own government in Rojava, or Western Kurdistan (Yassin-Kassab and al-Shami 2016, 73). This was almost certainly a deal brokered by Putin between two protégés, Assad and the PKK, with the PYD undertaking not to fight against Assad while Assad handed over not only power in Rojava but also weapons to the PYD and its armed wing, the People's Protection Units (YPG) (Yassin-Kassab and al-Shami 2016, 88; NRT 2015). By contrast, Mashaal Tammo, leader of the Future Movement, was one of the Kurdish leaders who walked out when other oppositionists refused to remove the term 'Arab' from the name of the Syrian state, but he also 'described the Kurds as "an inseparable part of the Syrian people", opposed negotiating with the regime and was organising anti-regime protests in Qamishli' at the time he was assassinated on October 7, 2011 (Yassin-Kassab and al-Shami 2016, 46), 'with the Bashar al-Assad regime being blamed for his murder' (Shadid 2011).

The PYD's model of democratic self-government in Rojava and its empowerment of women has gained widespread acclaim from liberals and socialists in other parts of the world (see, for example, Eiglad 2015). These are certainly achievements, but what is missing from these panegyrics is an understanding that unlike similar experiments in self-government in other parts of Syria, which are being bombed into rubble, these areas benefit from the deal between Assad and the PYD; that the solidarity the PYD received from other Kurdish groups and the FSA in the battle of Kobani against ISIS has not been reciprocated; that the PYD is only one of many Kurdish parties; and that democracy in local government is compatible with authoritarianism at a higher level. For example, the Kurdish media network *Rudaw* (2016b), linked to another party, protested:

> The canton of Kobani in Syrian Kurdistan banned the *Rudaw* Media Network from working in the region. It also banned journalists and freelancers from sending their work to *Rudaw* and warned all agencies and organizations to

cut off all contacts with the media network. The *Rudaw* Media Network has serious concerns over the Kobani Canton's decision and considers it a violation of freedom of media and expression in Syrian Kurdistan. Decisions such as this will sadden the people of Kobani, as *Rudaw* was the voice of the town in the world at the time of war and later during its liberation.

The PYD has also been accused of 'suppressing political opposition and peaceful protest, closing down independent radio stations, and assassinating, imprisoning and torturing opponents' (Yassin-Kassab and al-Shami 2016, 74). Noor Bakeer, a teacher from a village near Afrin who was working with a humanitarian organisation called Bihar, provided testimony of this:

> As a Kurd I know all about the criminal practices of the Assad regime. Even before the revolution, hundreds of Kurdish activists were arrested and too many of them died in prison. We were surrounded by corruption and our living standards were low. But nothing much happened when the regime withdrew from Afrin and the PYD took over. The terror and repression continued as the PYD imposed themselves by force. They stopped other political parties from operating and tried to rule alone ... We distributed aid in secret because the PYD banned us. They harassed us constantly, confiscating the aid, arresting our workers and accusing them of being agents for Turkey or the FSA. The real reason for this treatment is that we refused to obey their orders. (Yassin-Kassab and al-Shami 2016, 75)

Syrian-Kurdish journalist and activist Shiar Nayo commented that, despite all the hype around the PKK's and PYD's claims that they were turning into an 'anarchist' movement, 'the PKK is a highly ideological, nationalist party based on a strict military regime and blind loyalty. It still thrives on the apotheosis of the leader and the notion of one party leading state and society. It is not very different to so many leftist parties that have been riddled with these Stalinist-Leninist plagues' (Yassin-Kassab and al-Shami 2016, 218). Such testimonies are a reminder that supporting the struggle of an oppressed group like the Kurds against oppression is not the same thing as supporting a particular party (the PKK or PYD) that claims to be the sole representative of that group, and enforces its claim by means of its military dominance.[4]

The first US-led coalition airstrikes, in northern Syria on September 22, 2014, were disastrous. Aimed against not only ISIS but also the Khorasan group, al-Nusra and Ahrar al-Sham, who were at the time fighting against ISIS, they killed large numbers of men, women and children, and aroused local outrage. Monzer al-Sallal, an FSA commander, pointed out that 'because there's no coordination with the Free Army, they don't know where

Daesh is. They bomb far from the front lines where the Free Army could take advantage, and they bomb at night, when Daesh have left their positions and are sleeping in people's houses.' Across the north, civilians came out in protest against the raids: 'Towns and villages which had previously opposed ISIS condemned the intervention and in some cases raised slogans suggesting that America had joined Iran and Assad in a war on Sunnis' (Yassin-Kassab and al-Shami 2016, 141; 142). The next intervention – supporting the PYD, the Iraqi Peshmerga and the FSA as they battled from September 2014 to January 2015 to repulse an ISIS invasion of Kobani on the Turkish border – was more successful and eventually succeeded in pushing ISIS out.

This was the beginning of a more long-term cooperative arrangement between the PYD and the US-led coalition, but there were problems for the US even in terms of its limited objective of fighting against ISIS. The goal of the PYD was not to rid Syria of ISIS, but to set up an autonomous Rojava by joining up the three cantons of Afrin, Kobani and Jazeera in northern Syria (Hassan and Barabandi 2015). Realising this, in October 2015 the US had created the Syrian Democratic Forces (SDF), an alliance of the PYD with Arab tribes who were opposed to ISIS, the Syrian Arab Coalition; however, these tribes remained subordinated to the PYD.

The Liwa Thuwar al-Raqqa (Raqqa Revolutionaries), an FSA brigade, included many fighters from Raqqa and wanted to fight against ISIS there, but its leader Abu Issa complained of a shortage of resources. 'We need to have the same equipment as our enemy has,' he said, referring to the tanks and armoured vehicles ISIS had seized from the Iraqi army. 'All our weapons are spoils from the regime ... We have been fighting ISIS for almost two years. We were the first to fight them. The most important thing is we need weapons, to encourage people to come for training'; the US, however, did not lend their support (Gutman 2015a).

The Raqqa Revolutionaries subsequently joined the SDF, but Abu Issa continued to complain: 'We have seen no serious efforts to support the liberation of Raqqa. We would have been informed if any entities wanted to offer support, and liberation would have been led by Liwa Thuwar al-Raqqa. Our complement of arms right now consists of weapons seized from IS, but these weapons are not enough to liberate Raqqa and its countryside' (Drwish 2016a). The PYD was at odds with the Raqqa Revolutionaries because the latter had declared, 'Our stance vis-à-vis Russia is clear, and we will never accept Russian support here at a time when Russia is killing Syrians elsewhere' (Drwish 2016a).

Furthermore, the PYD's goal involved taking over the stretch of territory between Kobani and Afrin, inhabited by Arabs and Turkmen, and the methods used were less than ethical. On April 30, 2015, US airstrikes on the village of Bir Mahalli, about thirty-three miles south of Kobani, killed at least sixty-four people, including thirty-one children, according to the Syrian Network of Human Rights, while the Syrian Observatory for Human Rights recorded a slightly lower death toll; the former said an unknown number of the dead could still be lying beneath the rubble of their houses. The US military representative at first denied there had been any civilians in the village, claiming that the Kurdish People's Protection Units (YPG) had called in the airstrikes and had said there were none. 'A journalist from the area, who spoke by Skype to McClatchy only under the condition of anonymity for security reasons, said tensions between Kurdish and Arab populations were high. "The Kurdish forces are pressing the Arabs in the area to leave," the journalist said. He called the missile strikes "a systematic expulsion in an indirect way"' (Alhamadee 2015). This was not the only case of civilians being killed by US airstrikes called in by the YPG/SDF.

The suspicion that US airstrikes – and the threat of them – were being used for the ethnic cleansing of areas in northern Syria that the PYD wanted to claim is confirmed by an Amnesty International report that residents of villages, mainly Arabs and Turkmen but also a few Kurds, were being cleared out and not allowed to return: 'By deliberately demolishing civilian homes, in some cases razing and burning entire villages, displacing their inhabitants with no justifiable military grounds, the Autonomous Administration is abusing its authority and brazenly flouting international humanitarian law, in attacks that amount to war crimes,' said Lama Fakih, senior crisis advisor at Amnesty International. Amnesty International also reported that 'civilians said they were threatened with US-led coalition airstrikes if they failed to leave' (Amnesty International 2015a).

These examples demonstrate that minority ethnic nationalism can be as ugly as majority ethnic nationalism.[5] The participation of the US-led coalition in these war crimes should certainly be condemned. However, it appears that the US was not sufficiently gung ho about bombing civilians in non-ISIS-controlled areas for the purposes of the PYD; it needed Russian air support. The co-chair of the PYD, Asia Abdullah, welcomed the Russian airstrikes in Syria and confirmed plans to set up a Syrian Kurdistan office in Russia 'in order to intensify mutual relations with the Russian leadership'

(Spada 2015). At a meeting in Moscow on October 21, the Russians confirmed their support for the PYD, which opened a representative office there on February 10, 2016. On February 20, Bouthaina Shabaan, political and media advisor to the Assad regime, said that the Kurds were cooperating with the regime through a Russian agreement (Drwish 2016b). In an article describing the coordination between Russian airstrikes and PYD ground attacks on the FSA, and providing extensive supporting evidence for it, Michael Karadjis, who had been a supporter of the 'Rojava revolution' (2016), writes:

> Once the Russian Reich began its all-out Blitzkrieg against the Syrian revolutionary forces in Aleppo on behalf of the Assad regime – a massacre that has involved massive displacement, with tens or hundreds of thousands fleeing north towards Turkey, and the large-scale, deliberate targeting of hospitals, schools and other basic civilian infrastructure – a most unwelcome development occurred, that has led to much heated debate among supporters of the Syrian revolution.
>
> Namely, the Kurdish-based People's Protection Units (YPG), based in the Kurdish canton of Efrin on the western side of Aleppo province, launched an all-out attack on the Free Syrian Army (FSA) and other rebels in Aleppo – ie, the very forces being bombed by the Russian imperialist onslaught – attacking and conquering rebel-held, Arab-majority towns throughout the region with the direct aid of Russian bombing. [...]
>
> The PYD's Salih Muslim asks 'Do they want the Nusra Front to stay there, or for the regime to come and occupy it?' This actually combines two excuses. First, he asserts that it is OK for the YPG to seize these towns (even with the help of Russian bombing) if they are run by Nusra (me: it still wouldn't be); implying that they are mostly run by Nusra (me: they're not...), indeed, the YPG has a habit of calling whichever rebels it is fighting, or Russia is bombing, "Nusra."
>
> Second, he is claiming that it is OK for the YPG to conquer these towns while the Russians bomb them, because the YPG's intentions are good; the Russians are bombing them anyway, and Assad will try to conquer them, so better we conquer them, even against local resistance, because we are preferable to the regime.

Asked whether she saw the unification of Rojava cantons as a democratic alternative to the Assad regime, Leila al-Shami (2016) replied, 'It's not a "democratic" alternative but it's an alternative. The Self-Administration is monopolized by the PYD. Those Kurds that oppose the PYD have been silenced, imprisoned, tortured and assassinated. The PYD has now moved beyond the idea of democratic confederalism (democracy without the state) – an idea which I strongly support – towards attempts to carve out a new state through linking the cantons. This includes its expansionist turn to take over Arab majority areas under cover of Russian airstrikes.' YPG attacks on Kurdish FSA brigades were denounced in the strongest possible terms by the Kurdish Ahfad Saladin brigade, which 'called on all the rebel brigades, journalists and friends of the Syrian revolution to refrain from naming these militia forces to protect the Kurdish people' (El-Dorar al-Shamia 2016).

The perception among rebel groups that the PYD was an ally of the regime and the Russians, as well as hostility from Arabs who feared attacks and displacement at the hands of Kurdish forces, led to the postponement of the liberation of Raqqa by the PYD-led SDF; another potent factor was opposition from another US ally: Turkey (Hassan, H. 2017).

We saw that at the beginning the Erdoğan government had tried to come to an accommodation with Assad, but from early on, it allowed foreign jihadis to enter Syria via Turkey (Yazbek 2015, 49–51), while also taking in millions of refugees from Syria across the same border. Its greatest fear was that the PYD, linked to the PKK, which it regards as a terrorist group, would create a Kurdish state all along Turkey's southern border. In fact, the issue of PKK support for Rojava was reportedly one of the factors leading to the breakdown in 2015 of the peace talks between the Turkish government and the PKK that began in 2013, although the Kurdish People's Democratic Party's opposition to Erdoğan's plans for an executive presidency and government objections to the PKK imposing its own law and order regime in some southeastern provinces of Turkey also played a role (Akyol 2015).

The Turkish government, already uneasy about the US alliance with the YPG, was livid when the Russians started bombing Turkmen and Arab-inhabited border areas to allow the PYD to take them over, and shot down a Russian plane on one of these missions. This led to a complete breakdown in relations between Turkey and Russia until Erdoğan apologised in June 2016 and travelled to St Petersburg to normalise relations at a summit with Putin on August 9 (Idiz 2016). According to Fikret Bila, a veteran journalist and political commentator for the daily Hurriyet, there was a 'military trade-off' between Ankara and Moscow: 'The reconciliation allowed Turkish forces to enter Syria and to operate in the region from Jarablus to Azaz in the west, and south toward al-Bab, without any objections from Moscow. Turkey in return agreed not to help rebel forces in Aleppo' (Idiz 2016). Having cleared away this obstacle, Erdoğan sent tanks and commandos into Syria on August 24, helping Syrian rebels to clear ISIS out of the border town of

Jarablus with air support from the US. But the primary objective of 'Operation Euphrates Shield' was to force the PYD to move back east of the Euphrates where the canton of Kobani ended. Acknowledging the legitimacy of Turkish concerns, US vice president Joe Biden, at a news conference in Ankara, warned the PYD to move back east of the Euphrates (McLeary and de Luce 2016).

Turkish and FSA forces went on to clear ISIS out of Dabiq from late August, 'shattering the IS myth of an epic battle there', according to FSA commander Mahmoud Abu Hamzah, along with thirteen other nearby villages (a-Noufal et al. 2016). Following the liberation of Daqib, Operation Euphrates Shield sought to capture al-Bab, thirty kilometres south of Turkey's southern border. 'The heavily fortified city is IS's last major holding in Aleppo province, to which fighters fleeing losses in nearby Manbij and Jarablus have withdrawn in recent weeks. Al-Bab is a prize coveted not only by the FSA fighters currently battling IS in north Aleppo with the support of Turkish airstrikes and artillery, but also by the Kurdish-led SDF.' And as the SDF advanced from Afrin in the west, FSA brigades backed by Turkish airstrikes attacked them as well as Afrin itself (a-Noufal and Nelson 2016), a potentially disastrous situation, since the two forces fighting against ISIS, each with its own agenda, ended up fighting each other.

The Erdoğan government's second objective in moving into Syria was to create a safe zone for displaced Syrians and Syrian refugees. It had been arguing for this since 2012 without receiving any backing for the idea but was now able to gain tacit international support for the zone, with the US agreeing to provide air cover and, subsequently, special operations troops for the Turkish-led operations in Syria. 'The importance of this increased military cooperation between the US and Turkey goes beyond the immediate military achievements in the fight against ISIS. The presence of US troops and the promise of air cover has turned Turkey's de facto safe zone into a no-fly zone as well' (Haid 2016). Despite no official declaration of a no-fly zone, the Pentagon warned Assad that any planes threatening US forces in northern Syria would be shot down. Taking advantage of this security, around three thousand Syrian refugees returned to Jarablus from Turkey.

Thus the US-led coalition's military intervention against ISIS relied on one ally (the PYD) whose opposition to ISIS was subordinate to its goal of setting up a Kurdish state all along the Turkish border; another ally (the Turkish government) whose opposition to ISIS was subordinate to its goal of *prevent-*

ing the PYD from establishing a Kurdish state all along the Turkish border; and a third (Putin) whose opposition to ISIS, like that of his allies Assad and the IRI, was subordinate to the goal of exterminating the democratic opposition. At the same time, the coalition did not provide adequate support to the FSA, which was serious about fighting ISIS, for fear that its victory would destroy the Syrian state, which was anyway already destroyed.

However, FSA attitudes towards the SDF, which had been perceived as a front for the PYD and therefore allied with the Assad regime, shifted before the campaign to liberate Raqqa from ISIS was launched on June 6, 2017. One reason for this shift was Erdoğan's abandonment of the FSA in Aleppo after he came to an agreement with Putin, leaving the FSA with even less support. Joining the SDF, even though it was fighting against ISIS and Al Qaeda rather than against Assad, also became more attractive to the FSA when they realised that areas liberated from ISIS with support from the US-led coalition became more difficult for Assad to bomb (Hassan, H. 2017, 4–5). On the other side, Assad and his allies realised that unless they fought against ISIS instead of collaborating with it, they could lose areas liberated from ISIS by rebel groups. As the battle for Raqqa progressed, civilian casualties escalated, as ISIS used civilians as human shields by laying landmines and booby traps along exit routes and shot those trying to escape; the US-led coalition's imprecise airstrikes led to a surge of civilian casualties; and Russian-backed Syrian government forces targeted civilians in towns, villages and camps for displaced people south of Raqqa with unguided bombs and internationally banned cluster munitions (Amnesty International 2017c).

The Revolution Continues, and So Does the Repression

On February 27, 2016, an extendable two-week ceasefire agreement sponsored by the US and Russia came into effect, and almost unbelievably, there was a resurgence of the civilian protests that had started the revolution five years earlier. Mohammed al-Khatieb (2016c) reported at the time:

> At demonstrations in Aleppo and its countryside, Idlib, Daraa and the Ghouta area surrounding Damascus, protesters can be heard chanting, 'The revolution continues.' On March 4, protests were staged in 104 locations, a level of mobilization unheard of for some time now … *Al-Monitor* attended a protest organized by activists in Aleppo's Bab al-Hadeed neighborhood March 4 and saw firsthand the protesters' enthusiasm, which recalled the early days of the

revolution. Demonstrators raised the flag of the revolution as well as a large banner that read 'Long live Syria and down with Assad.'

On the sidelines of the protests, Shamel al-Ahmad, one of the organizers, told *Al-Monitor*, 'I am overjoyed … We are protesting today just like we did back in 2011, but without bullets, and the security forces are not here to repress us.' According to Ahmad, five years after the outbreak of the revolution, many Syrians have given up hope of the international community helping them achieve their demands. When asked about the reasons behind the demonstration, he said, 'We came to confirm that our revolution is ongoing, no matter what happens. We are a resilient and determined people, and we will not back down from our demands: a free Syria for all Syrians and free of Assad and terrorism.' […]

What is remarkable about the renewed demonstrations … is that the slogans from the beginning of the revolution are still being used, including 'The people want to bring down the regime' and 'Syria is ours, not Assad's.'

The ceasefire ended and so did the demonstrations, as civilians were once again pounded by airstrikes, but the 'heroism, determination and celebratory mood of these protests' (Smith 2016a), in the face of the regime's barbarism and abandonment by the international community, is truly admirable. The demonstrators had to contend not only with the visible bombardment, but also the fact that, as a UN Human Rights Council report revealed, 'massive and systematised violence – including the killing of detainees in official and makeshift detention centres – has taken place out of sight, far from the battlefield' (UNHRC 2016a). The report stated in no uncertain terms that 'detainees held by the Government were beaten to death, or died as a result of injuries sustained due to torture. Others perished as a result of inhuman living conditions. The Government has committed the crimes against humanity of extermination, murder, rape or other forms of sexual violence, torture, imprisonment, enforced disappearance and other inhuman acts' (UNHRC 2016a).

In Saydnaya prison, described as a 'human slaughterhouse', around 13,000 political prisoners were hanged between 2011 and 2015, in addition to the thousands who died as result of starvation and torture (Amnesty International 2017b). The Nakba-style expulsion of the original inhabitants of rebel-held neighbourhoods also continued. In August 2016, the last remaining residents of the Darayya suburb of Damascus, who had survived the massacre four years previously and a siege and airstrikes ever since, were forced to leave. As Martin Chulov and Kareem Shaheen (2016a) reported, in the years since the massacre in 2012, the area had been governed by a civilian council. The council's authority had been respected by the local fighters, who were part of a

Western-backed coalition called the Southern Front. 'We never had behead-
ings or criminality against civilians or extremism,' said Abu Samer, a spokesman for the local fighters. 'Darayya was always a thorn in Assad's side, and
now they will have the rubble of all the buildings they destroyed.' Apart from
a small aid shipment in May 2016, the area had received no supplies since the
2012 massacre, and after the aid workers left, the town was bombed again by
Syrian helicopters, destroying the last remaining hospital. It was this incident
that forced the local rebel groups to surrender to Assad. 'The civilians were
starving. We surrendered for them, to keep them alive,' said Abu Samer. But,
as a spokesperson for the Southern Front put it, 'The only surrender today is
the ongoing surrender of the international community to the regime's incessant
campaign of war crimes. It is their inaction that sponsors this ethnic cleansing
today' (Chulov and Shaheen 2016a).

A week later, residents of the suburb of Moadamiya, similarly besieged
and bombed, were expelled. According to the director of programmes for
Physicians for Human Rights, Widney Brown (2016),

> The Syrian government gave the people of Moadamiya two choices: either
> surrender or starve … Nothing about this evacuation is voluntary, and noth-
> ing about this evacuation is legal. Under international law, both forced evac-
> uations and besiegement, in which Moadamiya's thousands of civilians are
> being deprived of vital food and medicine, are war crimes and crimes against
> humanity … The people of Moadamiya, along with the nearly one million
> other Syrians under siege across the country, are living under conditions of
> total deprivation that have claimed countless lives and led to extreme suf-
> fering. … It's a deliberate strategy of the Syrian government: to slaughter its
> own people by bombing their homes, attacking hospitals, and starving them
> to death. The failure of the UN Security Council to prevent yet another
> atrocity is inexcusable.

Far from preventing such atrocities, UN agencies were guilty of complicity in the Assad regime's war crimes and crimes against humanity when
they oversaw such expulsions, after having colluded in the starvation sieges
that led to them. A report by The Syria Campaign (2016a), written with the
contribution of UN workers, found that the UN had 'provided the Syrian
government with an effective veto over aid deliveries to areas outside of government control, enabling its use of sieges as a weapon of war … In August
2015, the government directed over 99% of UN aid from Damascus to its
territories. In 2015, less than 1% of people in besieged areas received UN
food assistance each month.' It gets worse. The UN awarded tens of millions

of dollars to people closely associated with Assad, including charities set up by his wife, Asma al-Assad, and cousin, Rami al-Makhlouf, who was linked to several pro-regime militias. It also awarded contracts worth hundreds of millions of dollars to companies linked to the regime. According to Reinoud Leenders, an expert in war studies at King's College London, UN agencies had paid 'lucrative procurement contracts to Syrian regime cronies who are known to bankroll the very repression and brutality that caused much of the country's humanitarian needs' (Hopkins and Neals 2016). Signatories to the report from The Syria Campaign on UN complicity in starvation sieges recommended that 'the UN immediately define a set of public conditions under which the UN humanitarian agencies could continue to cooperate with the Syrian government and still maintain impartiality, independence and neutrality. If these conditions are not met, the UN should suspend cooperation with the Syrian government' (The Syria Campaign 2016a).

Top officials in the UN Office for the Coordination of Humanitarian Affairs (OCHA) not only collaborated with the regime as it starved civilians to death but also covered up what was happening, allowing the Assad regime to edit its reports so as to remove references to 'sieged' or 'besieged' areas – such as Madaya, in which twenty-three people starved to death – and to the 'barrel bombs' dropped on civilian areas (Bradley 2016; Gutman 2016a, 2016b).

The UN Human Rights Council, however, under both previous high commissioner Navi Pillay and her successor Zeid Ra'ad al-Hussein, played an exemplary role, calling for ICC investigations into war crimes and crimes against humanity being perpetrated in Syria. On October 21, 2016, it launched a special inquiry into war crimes in Aleppo as well as the use of starvation and air strikes there. Stephanie Nebehay (2016) outlined Zeid's statement:

[Zeid] said that the siege and bombing [in Aleppo] constituted 'crimes of historic proportions' that have caused heavy civilian casualties amounting to war crimes. Zeid did not name Russia or the Syrian air force, whose jets have attacked the rebel-held districts of Aleppo for weeks, but his reference was clear. 'Armed opposition groups continue to fire mortars and other projectiles into civilian neighborhoods of western Aleppo, but indiscriminate air strikes across the eastern part of the city by government forces and their allies are responsible for the overwhelming majority of civilian casualties,' he said in a speech to a special session of the U.N. Human Rights Council. Such violations constituted war crimes and if there was intent to commit them as part of a widespread or systematic attack against civilians, they would amount to crimes against humanity, he said.

Instead of depending solely on the regime to distribute aid, in rebel areas the UN could have depended on the local councils which, as al-Shami (2016) describes, 'ensure the governance of each area and have kept providing services to the local population in the absence of the state'; Aleppo alone had over a hundred civil society organisations, including twenty-eight free media groups, women's organisations, emergency and relief organisations, and educational organisations, such as Kesh Malek, which provided 'non-ideological education for children, often in people's basements,' to ensure school continued under bombardment.' For al-Shami (2016), the difference from regime-controlled areas was stark: 'Under Assad's totalitarian state, independent civil society was non-existent and no independent media sources existed. But in Free Aleppo democracy is being practiced as the people themselves self-organize and run their communities.' Indeed, such councils could constitute the local government institutions in a secular, democratic Syria, provided they were able to get their concerns addressed by regime defectors in exile working on a new constitution in the High Negotiations Commission (HNC), in which most sections of the opposition, including the Kurdish National Council, are members (Al Jazeera 2016f; HNC 2016). Equal rights for women and minorities would have to be high on the agenda, including a just and inclusive settlement of Kurdish demands; the economic inequality and deprivation suffered by large sections of the population before the revolution would also need to be addressed (Daher 2016).

Between November and December 2016, numerous chlorine gas attacks by the Assad regime, combined with indiscriminate bombing by Russian forces and a ground assault by the Lebanese Hezbollah and IRGC-QF, succeeded in dislodging the opposition from eastern Aleppo and taking it over (HRW 2017a; Gordon 2017). Syrian and Russian forces continued to target other rebel-held areas with starvation sieges, bombardment and forced displacement even as Putin's government claimed to be organising peace negotiations (Reuters 2017a, 2017b; Al Jazeera 2017a, 2017b, 2017c; Associated Press 2017; BBC News 2018). As Amnesty International (2017d) has noted, so-called 'reconciliation' agreements, arrived at by horrific sieges and intensive bombing of civilian populations so that they have no choice but to leave or die, constitute crimes against humanity, and any reconstruction efforts by the international community must ensure that the displaced can return in safety and dignity. The Assad regime's strategy, on the contrary, is to consolidate its political and economic power, replacing evacuees from the opposition with docile upper-class residents and rewarding foreign allies, especially Iran and Russia (Daher and Osseiran 2017).

In April 2017, a banned chemical weapons attack by the Assad regime in Khan Sheikhoun in Idlib province, where evacuees from Aleppo and elsewhere had been settled, killed at least seventy-two people, including many children, and injured hundreds, just days after the Trump administration's UN ambassador, Nikki Haley, had said that getting rid of Assad was not a priority and Secretary of State Tillerson repeated Russia's mantra that the Syrian people should decide who ruled them (without explaining how they could do that while the opposition and its supporters were being exterminated or forced into exile). A UN report as well as a subsequent report by a Joint Investigative Mechanism of the UN Organisation for the Prohibition of Chemical Weapons confirmed that this chemical attack, like more than two dozen others, was by Syrian government forces (Nebehay 2017; Campos 2017).

Shortly afterwards, the hospital treating victims was also bombed. Trump blamed Obama for not acting on his 'red line' in 2013 (although he himself had tweeted 'DO NOT ATTACK SYRIA' at the time) (Dearden 2017b; Chulov and Shaheen 2017; Borger 2017) and ordered Tomahawk missile strikes on the airfield from which it was suspected the attacks were launched, after ensuring that Russian and Syrian armed forces were informed and evacuated (Rosenfeld 2017). In July 2017, in a move long sought by Putin, Trump ended the CIA programme to arm and train moderate rebels, eliciting applause from Russia and consternation from the rebels, who were not even informed beforehand (Jaffe and Entous 2017; O'Connor 2017; Perry and al-Khalidi 2017).

In spite of all these setbacks, 169 Syrian civil society organisations which had continued their activities wrote to UN Special Envoy Staffan de Mistura in August 2017, reminding him that 'Syrian civil society's priority is to achieve an inclusive transition to a free and democratic Syria,' adding, 'We expect all parties in Geneva – including you – to work for this purpose' at the peace negotiations (SNHR 2017). And in Homs Central Prison, five hundred of the more than ten thousand political prisoners held by the Assad regime staged a hunger strike to call attention to their plight (Alliance of Middle-East Socialists 2017b).

Pseudo-anti-imperialists Support the Counterrevolution

It is no surprise that the far right in Europe has been very supportive of Assad. Yassin-Kassab and al-Shami (2016) outline the connections: 'British

National Party leader Nick Griffin visited Damascus in support of the regime in June 2013. The European Solidarity Front, with strong fascist connections, has been prominent in anti-intervention demonstrations, and has sent various extremist delegations to Damascus. The Greek fascists of the Black Lily organisation – a member of the European Solidarity Front – have gone so far as to fight in Syria along Assadist forces' (Yassin-Kassab and al-Shami 2016, 219). In France's increasingly powerful extreme right, Leela Jacinto (2015) argues, 'the romance with Assad … never faded. A day after the [Paris] attacks, right-wing French weekly *Valeurs Actuelles* featured an exclusive interview with Assad that was chilling both for the sycophantic questions and the hubris of the replies'. In the US, former Ku Klux Klan leader David Duke described Assad, who has become an idol for white supremacists including the neo-Nazis demonstrating at Charlottesville, as 'an amazing leader' and 'a modern day hero' (Elba 2017). However, support for Assad also comes from self-professed socialists. What can explain this?

The only plausible explanation I can think of for why Syria and Libya are so often listed alongside Iraq in order to demonstrate the disastrous consequences of 'regime change' is orientalism. Why is this tendency orientalist? Because it fails to distinguish between Iraq, where regime change was carried out by an external power, and Libya and Syria, where the *people* wanted the downfall of the regime. Indeed, the term *al-nizam*, in the slogan *al-shaab yureed isqat al-nizam* (the people want the downfall of the regime), means something more than simply the head of state. It means the whole system: one-party rule, an all-powerful president, a police state, rampant imprisonment, torture, rape and murder of dissidents, and so on.

People in liberal democracies take it for granted that they have a right to form a political opposition – that they are free to campaign against the party in power without being jailed, tortured or killed. But apparently Libyans and Syrians are too backward even to want these rights and freedoms; hence, US imperialism must have been responsible for the uprisings. What is that if not orientalism? Articles that equate Libya and Syria with Iraq basically assume that non-Western peoples have no agency of their own, and that they can only be victims or puppets of the West.

The intervention of David North and Alex Lantier on the World Socialist Web Site (2013) also echoes the anti-Muslim bigotry that has become the hallmark of the neo-fascist right. By characterising the entire Syrian opposition to Assad as 'Islamist', it ignores non-Muslim dissidents and blurs the distinction between four distinct categories of Muslims who oppose him. The first category designates Muslim believers who are secular and progressive. The second is composed of Muslim fundamentalists ('Salafis') who, despite their beliefs, want to live in a secular state. Like the majority of Deobandis who supported a secular state in India rather than opting for the Islamic state of Pakistan, many opponents of Assad are conservative Muslims who want a secular state in Syria, hence the ubiquitous chant of the revolution, 'One, one, one, the Syrian people are one!' (Kahf 2011). There are problems with all religious fundamentalisms – they promote patriarchy, authoritarianism and illogical thinking – but ideological opposition to these traits is possible in a secular and democratic state. The third category is composed of political Islamists who want to establish an Islamic state through elections. These are potentially dangerous, because they inevitably undermine democratic rights and freedoms if they do come to power, so they have to be opposed both ideologically and politically. The fourth category consists of political Islamists who want to establish an Islamic state through violence. They should be put behind bars if possible, and it may be necessary to oppose them militarily to protect the civilians whom they routinely blow up.

As Thomas Pierret (2016) observes, Salafis in Syria span the spectrum from quietists who want a secular state to violent jihadis. Individuals may cross over from one category to another, and there has indeed been a drift towards religiosity among Syrians as the international community has failed to protect them from massacres. Secular fighters have joined Islamist militias in order to get access to weapons. But to conflate Al Qaeda and ISIS with all Syrian Muslims who oppose Assad – not to mention non-Muslims who also oppose Assad – is equivalent to conflating terrorist Timothy McVeigh with all Americans who oppose US government policies (Prescott 2010). Combating Islamists ideologically and politically is precisely what democracy activists like Razan Zaitouneh were doing when she and her associates were forcibly disappeared by an Islamist militia, probably Jaish al-Islam (Yassin-Kassab and al-Shami 2016, 125). The complexity of the situation is underlined by the fact that this very group, Jaish al-Islam, was one of the forty-nine armed factions expressing their solidarity with France, along with civil society activists, after the ISIS terrorist attacks in Paris in November 2015 (Yahoo News 2015), and these armed groups have also been fighting against ISIS militarily. Of course, after all their talk about Islamists in the opposition, North and

Lantier are silent on Assad's promotion of ISIS, and his ceding of Syria's sovereignty to the Islamic state of Iran.

Finally, it is an irony that people who see themselves as socialists fail to note the class dimension of the uprising. Janine di Giovanni provides a vivid description of the Damascus elite who support Assad: '[In June 2012,] for several weeks running, I watched the fevered hedonism of the Thursday afternoon pool parties at the Dama Rose Hotel ... By lunchtime, women were rushing to hairdressers; the roads leading out of the city ... were clogged with luxury cars ... Restaurants such as Narenj, which ... served traditional Arabic food to the elite, were still packed' (di Giovanni 2016, 8). By contrast, in 2007 a third of Syrians were living beneath the poverty line, with nearly another third only slightly above this level. Swiss-Syrian socialist activist and scholar Joseph Daher (2016) writes that 'even the regime-controlled Syrian General Federation of Trade Unions deplored in 2009 that "the rich have become richer and the poor poorer ... (and) low income earners who make up 80 percent of the Syrian population are looking for additional work to support themselves"'. He continues, 'We must not forget that the popular revolution in Syria began as a result of social economic injustices and widespread poverty, in addition to political issues.' Without a doubt, on this issue, The World Socialist Web Site sides with the bourgeoisie against the working class.

Apart from vilifying the uprising, pseudo-anti-imperialists need to whitewash Assad, for example by reproducing the regime version of the Darayya massacre of August 2012. As Robert Fisk wrote at the time, after he accompanied Syrian Army soldiers into town, 'The men and women to whom we could talk ... told a story quite different from the popular version that has gone round the world: theirs was a tale of hostage-taking by the Free Syrian Army and desperate negotiations between the armed opponents of the regime and the Syrian army, before Bashar al-Assad's government decided to storm into the town and seize it back from rebel control' (cit. di Giovanni 2016, 78–79). Recalling the scorn and derision with which we viewed the reports of 'embedded' journalists in Iraq, I can't help asking: What did Fisk expect people to say in the hearing of Assad's soldiers?

People who spoke to di Giovanni, who went in with a local woman, contradicted Fisk's account. A mechanic who searched for his father for three days and eventually found him dead 'was grief-stricken ... "Can you tell me why they would kill an old man?" he asked, bent over crying. "An old man? He can't fight any more"' (di Giovanni 2016, 75). Others 'remembered "intense shelling from helicopters with mounted machine-guns", "mortars from a government military airport near the Mezzeh neighbourhood", and "snipers in buildings" north of the city. They spoke of soldiers moving from house to house, of informers pointing out where the activists lived; they spoke of bodies lying in the street; of groups of civilians hiding underground only to be found, lined up and summarily executed' (di Giovanni 2016, 75). She heard of more than three hundred people being killed, including women and children.

Another example is Seymour Hersh's December 2013 article in the *London Review of Books* which suggests that al-Nusra might be responsible for the sarin attack in Ghouta. Chemical weapons expert Dan Kaszeta commented,

> Mr. Hersh does not address the physical evidence ... Assad's regime has now admitted to a chemical weapons research, development, and production infrastructure which has now been inspected and inventoried by OPCW [Organisation for the Prohibition of Chemical Weapons] inspectors. ... There are many ways to make sarin, and it appears to me that the way the regime went about it correlates very closely with the physical evidence reported by the original UN/OPCW inspection team. (Kaszeta 2013)

Moreover, as we saw above, the quantity of sarin required for the attacks and the rockets used to deliver them are also physical evidence pointing to the regime as the perpetrator. Seymour Hersh also gave an interview for *RT* in 2016 in which, as Louis Proyect (2016) pointed out, he 'refer[red] darkly to American support for "moderate" rebel groups aligned with the dreaded Sharm al-Sharma that actually was in favor of Sharia law and expelling all Christians and Alawites from Syria'. There is no such group, of course. This is sloppy journalism at best, but why does Hersh engage in it? After citing numerous interactions and a history of correspondence between Hersh and Assad, Clay Claiborne (2013b) concludes, 'So we can see that Seymour Hersh has enjoyed a long relationship with Bashar al-Assad ... Seymour M. Hersh wants Assad to win.'

It is sad that two journalists – Hersh and Fisk – who in their glory days uncovered massacres in Vietnam and Iraq respectively, should end their careers by covering up massacres in Syria. John Pilger, likewise, ends his career ignominiously by characterising those, including the many children, blown to bits in Aleppo by regime and Russian bombs as 'fanatics, who commit terrible atrocities, such as beheading people' (Pilger 2016). Patrick Cockburn (2017) misrepresents an Amnesty report of atrocities by Islamists in Aleppo and Idlib governorates, in order to pretend that 'groups linked to

Al Qaida had a monopoly on the supply of news from East Aleppo' city, and downplays the massacres carried out by Assad and his allies. Max Blumenthal (2016) chose to attack the civil defence group, the White Helmets – hundreds of whom have been killed while rescuing tens of thousands of civilians after bombing raids, and for reporting on airstrikes – as 'anything but impartial' because 'behind the lofty rhetoric about solidarity and the images of heroic rescuers rushing in to save lives is an agenda that aligns closely with the forces from Riyadh to Washington clamoring for regime change'. For him, apparently, the millions of Syrians clamouring for regime change don't count, and the White Helmets should allow more children to die under the rubble, and hide the dead and wounded from the public, rather than accept humanitarian assistance from the West.

Whitewashing Assad also involves covering up his role as godfather of ISIS, which began, as we have seen, with his divide-and-rule strategies and his release of large numbers of Islamist prisoners who would become key ISIS figures, and continued in his long and complex cooperation with ISIS throughout the war. Yet, after Putin and his sidekicks spread the story that the Obama administration was supporting ISIS (Weiss 2015a), it was repeated by pseudo-anti-imperialists (see Introduction). Those who propagate this story are either as gullible as those who believed that Saddam Hussein was allied to Al Qaeda, or they are doing it for the same reason that the Saddam story was propagated – to justify war.

Of course, backing the killers is easier and safer than supporting those who are being killed. Janine di Giovanni had her Syrian visa revoked and was warned that if she returned she would end up in a Syrian jail. Samar Yazbek dodged airstrikes along with her interviewees. And Marie Colvin and Rémi Ochlik, along with Syrian citizen journalists, were killed in targeted attacks. Colvin and Ochlik had been in Baba Amr reporting on the regime's siege of the opposition-held areas of Homs, in which hundreds lost their lives.

> Jean-Pierre Perrin, senior foreign correspondent at the French daily *Libéra-tion*, said he had been with Colvin and other journalists at a makeshift press centre in Homs and had left with her several days ago after being warned that the army was preparing an offensive and that journalists could be targeted. Colvin waited, decided the offensive against the press centre had not happened and returned to Homs. Perrin told *Libération* the press centre, which had a generator and a patchy internet connection, was the only means of telling the world what was happening. 'If the press centre were destroyed, there would be no more information out of Homs.'

He said the army recommended 'killing any journalist that stepped on Syrian soil'. Journalists had been aware of this, and of reports of intercepted communications between Syrian officers that recommended killing all journalists between the Lebanon border and Homs, and making out they had been killed in combat between terrorist groups ... In the deadliest time for the media since the uprising began, at least three citizen journalists have also been killed in recent days, in an apparent attempt by the regime to prevent news emerging from Homs. The three had played prominent roles in chronicling the army's assault on Homs (Chulov and Chrisafis 2012)

Labour Party MP Jo Cox not only called for refugees to be welcomed to Britain, but also listened to what Syrians were saying about the conflict in their country, understood that it was completely different from the Iraq war (which she had opposed passionately), campaigned for the protection of civilians from bombing and starvation sieges, and supported the White Helmets, nominating them for the Nobel Peace Prize (The Syria Campaign 2016b; McVeigh 2016). Cox was brutally murdered by white supremacist neo-Nazi Thomas Mair in June 2016.

The West-centrism and anti-Muslim bigotry of pseudo-anti-imperialists feeds the racism of the far right: 'It was the left which spread the idea that Syrian revolutionaries were "all al-Qaida" before the right applied the slur to Syrian refugees' (Yassin-Kassab 2016). Pseudo-anti-imperialism has also had a devastating impact on the antiwar movement. It is notable that, as Ashley Smith (2016b) writes, 'everyone on the left supported the Tunisian and Egyptian revolutions of early 2011 because these countries were considered U.S. allies. But the [Stalinist] campists opposed pro-democracy uprisings in Libya and Syria, even though these revolts were driven by the same economic and political grievances – and clearly inspired by the revolts in Tunisia and Egypt'. In the US and Britain, the Stop the War Coalition, the Campaign for Nuclear Disarmament, the Workers' World Party and others organised a 'Hands Off Libya' campaign to oppose Western intervention in Libya – quite an irony, because although the US had certainly been extremely hostile to Gaddafi prior to the 2003 deal with him, after that the US had been deeply involved with his regime, while Western European powers had been involved ever since the UN sanctions on Libya had been lifted in 1999 (Chorin 2012, 2–4). There was increasing privatisation of the economy, which had suffered greatly due to sanctions; the oil industry was largely turned over to Western and Russian corporations; and arms from the UK, France, Italy, Russia and China poured in (Chorin 2012, 98–101; 139).

It is true that in the early years after the 1969 coup in which Gaddafi seized power, he spent Libya's oil wealth on infrastructure, public health, education and housing, creating a welfare state that immensely improved the living standards of the majority of Libya's population (Chorin 2012, 36). However, after an attempted assassination by one of his associates in 1975, he built up a police state centred on himself, much like the Assads' state in Syria. Human rights violations were routine, one of the worst being the Abu Salim prison massacre of around 1,200 (mainly political) prisoners in 1996 (HRW 2006). At the same time, Gaddafi continued his support for various anti-imperialist insurgent groups like the Sandinistas and IRA. His relationship with Black Africans can be gauged from his 2008 agreement with Berlusconi to take back migrants intercepted at sea, and from his demand that the EU pay him €5 billion a year to stop African migrants and refugees from attempting to reach Europe, because, in his words, 'we don't know what will happen, what will be the reaction of the white and Christian Europeans faced with this influx of starving and ignorant Africans' (BBC News 2010). From 2002 onwards, the CIA and MI6 even assisted the Gaddafi regime to kidnap, imprison and torture Libyan dissidents (Cobain 2017).

In the context of desperate pleas for help from the people of Benghazi as well as a bloodthirsty speech by Gaddafi on February 22, 2011 – a speech 'whose tone and vocabulary (in particular the description of his opponents as rodents and insects) were reminiscent of the 1930s', and in which he 'evoked as precedents that he intended to imitate, among others, the 1989 massacre in Tiananmen and the 2004 one in Falluja ... the 2008-9 Israeli onslaught on Gaza ... [and] Spanish dictator Francisco Franco's attack on Madrid' (Achcar and Wearing 2011) – some socialists and antiwar activists, such as Gilbert Achcar, decided not to oppose a NATO-enforced no-fly zone. Justifying this position, Achcar said, 'In opposing the no-fly zone from day one, you are rejecting a request made by the insurgents themselves, and you hence behave as if you regard the fate of Benghazi's population as totally secondary to your sacrosanct anti-imperialism.'[6] He pointed out that even Russia and China did not oppose it, suggesting that they did not want to take responsibility for an impending massacre that they knew Gaddafi had the means and the intent to carry out (Achcar and Wearing 2011).

However, a section of the antiwar left campaigned against the NATO intervention simply because it was a NATO intervention, just as Pavlov's dogs reacted as if they were being fed when they heard a bell ring, regardless of whether any food was actually being served ... Nothing else mattered except that NATO chose to act; what Libyans said, did, thought, and organized was simply not a factor for them. These anti-imperialists airbrushed the Libyans out of their own revolution. ... Libyan sovereignty emerged from the revolution intact despite NATO's involvement. This would not be the case if NATO was directly or indirectly in charge of Libya or set up some sort of neocolonial regime. The bottom line is that the bulk of the Western left could not bring itself to wholeheartedly support a democratic revolution that co-opted foreign intervention for its own ends. The revolution landed safe and sound at a qualitatively more democratic destination precisely because control of the revolution *never left Libyan hands* ... The Western left ought to join the revolutionary masses of the Arab and North African world in *celebrating* this historic victory, not isolate ourselves from them by mourning (or slandering) it. (Pham Binh 2012)

Subsequently, as Libya descended into chaos, with a predominantly secular elected parliament being driven from Tripoli to Tobruk by Islamist militias who set up their own Libya Dawn government in the capital, there were recriminations from right to left about the negative consequences of the overthrow of Gaddafi. Western powers were afraid that ISIS would exploit the power vacuum, as indeed it did, and the EU in particular was desperate at the loss of its bulwark against migrants and refugees from sub-Saharan Africa. On the left, there were legitimate criticisms of racist attacks by rebel forces on Black Africans, who, as Achcar explained, were seen as enemies because 'a significant proportion of Gaddafi's troops were composed of mercenaries recruited from poor African countries, like Chad, Sudan, Niger, and Mali. This old and well-known fact was compounded by the forced recruitment of African migrants to fight with Gaddafi's troops when the uprising started, with such forced recruits often cruelly deployed on the front line' (Achcar and Wearing 2011). Achcar emphasised, however, that the leadership of the National Transitional Council firmly opposed such acts. Moreover, racism against non-Arabs, both Black and Amazigh (Berber), had been fostered by Gaddafi's Libyan Arab Jamahiriya, which discriminated against Black Libyans and treated sub-Saharan Africans attempting to cross over to Europe via Libya with the utmost brutality (Solieman 2011; Claiborne 2015); in 2000, dozens of sub-Saharan Africans were lynched in Zawiya (Chorin 2012, 57).

The chaos in Libya is certainly disheartening, but it is exactly what might be expected after a totalitarian regime is overthrown. There would be defected regime elements, who had experience running the country but might carry over authoritarian attitudes; religious extremists, who were able to organise under the cover of mainstream religious institutions; and social and political activists with progressive politics but little experience in running anything, because they had been so totally crushed by the regime. In April 2016, the Government of National Accord, put together by the UN and headed by one of the elected representatives, Fayez al-Sarraj, succeeded in taking control of the banks and National Oil Corporation (NOC), but it was not accepted by either of the other governments; governance and the economy continued to suffer catastrophic disruption (Middle East Eye 2016a). However, a coordinated fight against ISIS, with US air support, did succeed in more or less dislodging it, and General Khalifa Haftar, affiliated to the eastern government in Tobruk, seized and handed over control of four key oil terminals to the NOC – thereby enabling oil exports, essential to the economy, to be ramped up (Middle East Eye 2016b). In July 2017, after a meeting in Paris, Sarraj and Haftar agreed to call a ceasefire and hold elections in early 2018 (Wintour and Stephen 2017). While this state of affairs is hardly satisfactory for the people of Libya, it is arguably better than what happened in Iran, where a peaceful democratic revolution was followed by a violent Islamist counterrevolution. It is undeniably better than the simultaneous events in Syria.

The relevance of referring to Libya is that, as political analyst Marwan Bishara (2016) pointed out, Obama's failure to provide sufficient support to the secular opposition fighting ISIS in Syria or to help protect civilians from daily barrel-bombings – despite the fact that 'as the US and others held back, the situation deteriorated dangerously, the death toll rose and the prospects for a decent outcome dimmed' – was partly a result of the lesson he said he had learned from the Libyan debacle. The protests against the Libyan intervention, and the chorus of recrimination afterwards, convinced Obama that helping to overthrow a dictator was a bad idea; better to allow him to slaughter half a million people, displace half the population, and destroy the country.

Continuing on the same trajectory, antiwar groups in the US, Canada and Britain invited Mother Superior Agnes Mariam de la Croix – an Assad regime propagandist who covered up the massacre in East Ghouta and was complicit in the murder of French journalist Gilles Jacquier – for speaking tours, while Nobel Peace laureate Mairead Maguire – after heading a delegation to Syria invited by the Mussalaha Reconciliation Movement under the leadership of Mother Agnes – propagated her support of the regime (Claiborne 2013a). In an open letter to the British Stop the War Coalition, which had invited

Mother Agnes to speak alongside Labour Party MPs Diane Abbott and Jeremy Corbyn and journalists Owen Jones and Jeremy Scahill, a group of genuine antiwar activists wrote:

> According to Father Paolo Dall'Oglio, a Jesuit priest exiled by the Assad regime for speaking out against its suppression of peaceful protests and currently a prisoner of … ISIS, Mother Agnes "has been consistent in … spreading the lies of the regime, and promoting it through the power of her religious persona. She knows how to cover up the brutality of the regime". Moreover, Syrian Christians for Peace have denounced Mother Agnès for claiming there had never been a single peaceful demonstration in Syria. They also accused her of failing to disburse any of the money she raised in the name of their beleaguered community' (Pulsemedia 2013).

In response to the protests, Jones and Scahill refused to share a platform with her, and she was forced to withdraw. Later, in the midst of the Russian bombing of Syria, a spokesman for Jeremy Corbyn implied that the civilian casualties resulting were no greater than those from US-led coalition bombing, whereas the rate was actually eight times higher (Graham-Harrison 2016). Most egregiously, Corbyn and his colleagues attacked the unarmed Free Syrian Police, who provided security to civilians in liberated areas, and supported the Astana 'peace process', which is designed to perpetuate the power of Assad and Iranian and Russian imperialism in Syria (Hamad 2017).

Protesting against Stop the War Coalition's refusal 'to acknowledge the agency of the oppressed Syrian people struggling against a fascist regime or to support their struggle in any form', British Syrian anarchist Leila al-Shami urged, 'As for the anti-war left, if they are to have any relevance or moral compass, they must oppose all those who are bombing Syrians, including the Assad regime and its imperial backers, Russia and Iran. Most of all, they must listen to the voices of Syrians instead of sticking to their patronizing and unprincipled stance of inviting "experts" of dubious credentials speak on their behalf' (al-Shami 2015). The two themes mentioned by al-Shami are repeated by other critics of antiwar activists supporting the counterrevolution in Syria: On the one hand, they highlight ignorance about Syria and the denial of agency to Syrians, to the extent that 'most people on the left know absolutely nothing about Syria. They know nothing of its history, political economy, or contemporary circumstances, and they don't see us' (Saleh et al. 2016). On the other, they point to 'selective anti-imperialism' (Boothroyd 2015) that supports 'Russian imperialism and Iranian mini-imperialism in the Middle East' (Palestinian

Reflections 2014), and which, by supporting some imperialisms against others, actually perpetuates imperialism as such (Ayoub 2016).

This situation is echoed in the United States. Supporters of the US Hands Off Syria Coalition 'dismiss criticism of the Syrian regime and Russia by talking about a U.S. media bias that "demonizes Assad" and builds support for "regime change"' (Fanning and Bean 2016). Speaking out against the group, Roy Fanning and Brian Bean (2016) observe: 'Opponents of American wars have a well-founded and necessary distrust of the media. But it is naïve to not have a similar distrust of the Russian-funded *RT.com* or the Syrian state *SANA* media.' They note that one of the member groups of the US Hands Off Syria coalition, the US Peace Council, is the US section of the World Peace Council (WPC), set up in 1949 by the Stalin regime. However,

> as other socialists and opponents of war recognized at the time, the WPC's parroting of Stalinist foreign policy left the council in the position of defending Russian 'peace-loving' tanks when they moved in to crush workers' uprisings in Hungary in 1956 and Czechoslovakia in 1968, among other rebellions in the USSR's Eastern European empire. The WPC also supported the Russian invasion of Afghanistan starting in 1979 ... This 'peace-loving' invasion left over a million dead, hundreds of thousands disabled, huge numbers made refugees and the countryside littered with mines. (Fanning and Bean 2016)

The involvement of Stalinists and the use of former Comintern networks explain how these warmongers in antiwar clothing pop up all over the world. But neo-Stalinism does not require its proponents to pretend to be Marxists; recruits can come from outside this circle too, including from the US Green Party. A critic, Stanley Heller, who suggests that the Green Party platform should include support for the Syrian uprising and denounce any deal that gives Assad, Russia and Iran a free hand to crush it, wrote a piece titled 'A Challenge to the Green Party on Syria' (2016):

> This should fit in perfectly with your principles, but I admit it may be a hard sell. It conflicts with the reigning Conspiracist worldview on the Left that everything is the fault of the U.S. including Syria. On the face of it Russia and Iran (and plenty of other countries outside the NATO orbit) are grasping capitalist powers on the make, but in the Conspiracist worldview they're all just poor victims of imperialism and if they appear to stomp on their own citizens or some other nation it's really a U.S. plot.
>
> Jill Stein's pick for vice president Ajamu Baraka certainly sees Syria that way. He thinks Syrians voted for Assad to continue running the country after shooting down peaceful demonstrations and torturing to death thousands of

prisoners. Continued opposition supposedly is the fault of the U.S., Saudis and Turkey. ... He even says ISIS is a creation of the West that went a little sour. [...]

Jill Stein's position is only somewhat better. In Moscow ... she said 'US pursuit of regime change in Libya, Iraq, and Syria created the chaos that promotes power grabs by extremist militias.' So there was no popular uprising. It was all a U.S. plot against Assad. I heard her speak in [Connecticut] in February and she said more or less the same thing, lumping Syria in with Iraq and Afghanistan as being just another U.S. inspired disaster, no mention of Assad's torture-to-death prisons, no anger over the 1,400 killed by sarin gas, no outrage about what the Russians and Iranians were doing, no demands that the sieges end.

In Moscow, after dinner with Putin, Stein commented, 'Putin did appear to respond in his formal remarks to the call for greater dialogue and collaboration made by myself and three other political figures on the foreign policy panel earlier that day' (Stein 2016). Donald Trump agreed with Baraka and Stein on Obama's responsibility for ISIS and the necessity to collaborate with Putin. This brings us, as Joe Gill (2016) puts it, to 'the peculiar, almost unconscious and habitual liking for [Putin's] interventions in the Arab world and outplaying of the Western powers. This apparent preference seems an odd fit for antiwar socialists since he has a consistent habit of dropping bombs on innocent and poor civilians who happen to be Muslims, which, were it done so consistently by any Western leader, would be seen as a form of genocide.' Gill continues, in a way that circles back to the arguments in Chapters 1 and 2, 'Marx opposed despotism and the great power chauvinism of Tsarist Russia. Putin is a modern tsar with designs on the Near East and wants to push the West out. This is what Lenin called inter-imperialist rivalry.'

In other words, what we are looking at here is neither antiwar nor anti-imperialist; it is the support for some imperialisms against others, and for wars fought by those preferred imperialists, which, as Joey Ayoub (2016) points out, perpetuates imperialism. It also involves support for some Islamists against others. In Yemen, Islamist Saudi Arabia (an ally of the US) is rightly condemned for its airstrikes against civilians, but neither the mainstream media nor the neo-Stalinist left criticises or even mentions the other side – namely, former dictator Ali Abdullah Saleh, against whom the 2011 popular uprising occurred, who was allied with the Shia Islamist Ansarollah (Houthis) supported by the Islamic state of Iran (ShahidSaless 2015) until the Houthis killed him in December 2017, after he announced his intention of making peace with the Saudis (Wintour 2017). The Saleh-Houthi alliance thus embodied an alliance of authoritarian and Islamist counter-revolutionary forces. Both sides were responsible for the war and both were committing war crimes (Lackner 2016; UNHRC 2016b; Amnesty International 2017a); criticising only one side signals support for the other. Syria is another conflict where pseudo-anti-imperialists support the occupation of the country by the Islamic state of Iran.

In this way, attitudes towards the Syrian uprising epitomise the dangerous convergence of neo-fascists and neo-Stalinists: 'Recently, an event in Rome that displayed images of those tortured and killed by Assad was attacked by fascists. Just days before, it had also been attacked in a local communist newspaper for promoting "imperialism."' (Saleh et al. 2016). Orientalism – the inability to 'see' Syrians, to acknowledge their agency, their ownership of their own country and their own revolution – is one reason for this convergence; support for Iranian and Russian imperialism, and their wars of conquest, is another.

Solidarity with the Syrian Revolution

Fortunately, there are sections of the left – some of whom have been quoted above – who see and denounce this convergence, and admire the courage, resilience, creativity, solidarity and love that inspired and sustain the revolution. Palestinian activist and journalist Budour Hassan (2016) describes how the Syrian revolution transformed her, teaching her the lesson of her life:

> It was delivered with love, by the women and men dancing and singing in the streets, challenging the iron fist with creativity, refusing to give up while being chased by security forces, turning funeral processions into exuberant marches for freedom, rethinking ways to subvert regime censorship; introducing mass politics amidst unspeakable terror; and chanting for unity despite sectarian incitement; and chanting the name of Palestine in numerous protests and carrying the Palestinian flag without needing a superstar Egyptian blogger to ask them to do so.
>
> It was a gradual learning process in which I had to grapple with my own prejudices of how a revolution should 'look like,' and how we should react to a movement against a purportedly pro-Palestinian regime. I desperately tried to overlook the ugly face beneath the mask of resistance worn by Hezbollah, but the revolution tore that mask apart. And that was not the only mask torn apart, many more followed. And now the real faces of self-styled freedom fighters and salon leftists were exposed; the long-crushed Syrian voices emerged.

Hassan's article was followed by a solidarity statement with the Syrian revolution by hundreds of Palestinian activists, distancing themselves from supporters who tried to undermine the legitimacy of the Syrian struggle (Collective Signatories 2016). Among the most eloquent denunciations of Assad and his allies were those by Lebanese Shia cleric Sheikh Subhi al-Tufayli, who compared the bombardment of Aleppo to Karbala, mourned by Shia Muslims as a catastrophe; Iranian diplomat Mir Mahmoud Mousavi, who warned that the Iranian assault on the Syrian opposition would only lead to hatred and violence; and Lebanese Shia academic and political analyst Hareth Sleiman, who wrote, 'Shame on the monsters Putin, Khamenei, Assad and mercenaries from all corners of the world, those who dance with glee to the crime, and those who gloat in the face of the blood of children and tears of women' (El-Bar 2016). And as we saw, a student at Amir Kabir University in Tehran who condemned Iran's role in the 'horrible genocide in Syria' was greeted with enthusiastic applause by the audience (Alliance of Middle-East Socialists 2016). Solidarity with the democratic revolution in Syria may be muted, but it does exist.

8. What Can We Do?

What do Vladimir Putin, Ali Khamenei, Bashar al-Assad, Abu Bakr al-Baghdadi, Benjamin Netanyahu and Donald Trump have in common? Despite their superficial differences, these are all political leaders who have contempt for human rights and have waged war against democracy. This consensus came clearly into view during Trump's presidential campaign and in the reactions to his victory. At a conference in Germany in October 2016, white supremacists from Europe and the US, including the KKK, stated that Trump's campaign represented a win for their movement (Liebelson 2016). During the campaign, Iran's *Press TV* repeated Trump's rants against 'crooked Hillary' and the American media as if they were fact (Press TV 2016b). Netanyahu called Trump 'a true friend of Israel'; Israel's education secretary said that 'Trump's victory eradicated the idea of a Palestinian state' (Akbar 2016); Assad called him a 'natural ally' (The Telegraph 2016).

They are not the only ones to show a reinvigorated contempt for democracy and human rights. A wave of far-right politics has swept the world since the 1990s. What is most alarming is that it has swept along with it a section of the anti-imperialist left, which now joins hands with the right in opposing democratic revolutions. Unless this situation changes, the threat of fascist and totalitarian regimes, which inflict mass incarceration, torture, rape and murder upon their own people as well as other peoples, looms over much of the world. How are we to counter this threat? I want to suggest five ways in which we might begin: (1) pursuing the truth and telling the truth; (2) bringing morality and humanity back into politics; (3) fighting for democracy; (4) bringing internationalism centre stage; and (5) pushing for global institutions to promote human rights and democracy.

Pursuing the Truth and Telling the Truth

In many countries, investigative journalists who try to uncover the truth, such as Anna Politkovskaya, are killed, media are heavily censored, and free access to the internet is blocked; in such circumstances, it is understandable if people give up the struggle to find out what is really happening because it takes too much effort and may be too dangerous. But the situation in the West, according to journalist Peter Pomerantsev (2016b), is far more insidious:

> As his army blatantly annexed Crimea, Vladimir Putin went on TV and, with a smirk, told the world there were no Russian soldiers in Ukraine. He wasn't lying so much as saying the truth doesn't matter. And when Donald Trump makes up facts on a whim, claims that he saw thousands of Muslims in New Jersey cheering the Twin Towers coming down, or that the Mexican government purposefully sends 'bad' immigrants to the US, when fact-checking agencies rate 78% of his statements untrue but he still becomes a US Presidential candidate – then it appears that facts no longer matter much in the land of the free. When the Brexit campaign announces 'Let's give our NHS the £350 million the EU takes every week' and, on winning the referendum, the claim is shrugged off as a 'mistake' by one Brexit leader while another explains it as 'an aspiration', then it's clear we are living in a 'post-fact' or 'post-truth' world. Not merely a world where politicians and media lie – they have always lied – but one where they don't care whether they tell the truth or not.

This 'don't care' attitude to the truth was on display on Trump's first full day in office, when he and his press secretary lied about the size of the crowd at his inauguration and denied his previous attacks on intelligence agencies – both easily checkable facts – while his aide Kellyanne Conway defended these 'alternative facts' (Baumann and Calderone 2017; Swaine 2017). The cavalier attitude of these politicians is matched by an equal disregard for the truth on the part of other politicians, journalists and ordinary citizens, who not only swallow lies without any scrutiny but repeat and propagate them too. What is most disturbing is that this is also happening on the left. Thus we have Pilger propagating Putin's lies; Fisk and Hersh repeating Assad's propaganda; the British Labour Party leadership massively underestimating deaths from Russian bombing in Syria while websites like *Counterpunch*, *Alternet* and *Jacobin* publish articles that do the same; in addition to countless people spreading such falsehoods on social media despite being under no threat of arrest, incarceration, torture or death if they were to try to find out the truth.

So why do they do it? Part of the reason, Pomerantsev (2016b) suggests, might be technology. 'Instead of ushering a new era of truth-telling, the information age allows lies to spread in what techies call "digital wildfires",' he argues. 'By the time a fact-checker has caught a lie, thousands more have been created, and the sheer volume of "disinformation cascades" make unreality unstoppable. All that matters is that the lie is clickable, and what determines that is how it feeds into people's existing prejudices.' But why do those particular lies feed into people's existing prejudices? One reason – which would also explain why, as a study from Northeastern University showed, people less trusting of mainstream media are more likely to fall for disinformation (Pomerantsev 2016b) – is that social and economic insecurity feeds a retreat into nostalgia and fantasy. Pomerantsev continues,

> 'The twenty-first century is not characterized by the search for new-ness' wrote the late Russian-American philologist Svetlana Boym, 'but by the proliferation of nostalgias ...' ... Thus Putin's internet-troll armies sell dreams of a restored Russian Empire and Soviet Union; Trump tweets to 'Make America Great Again'; Brexiteers yearn for a lost England on Facebook; while ISIS's viral snuff movies glorify a mythic Caliphate. 'Restorative nostalgia', argued Boym, strives to rebuild the lost homeland with 'paranoiac determination', thinks of itself as 'truth and tradition', obsesses over grand symbols and 'relinquish[es] critical thinking for emotional bonding ... In extreme cases it can create a phantom homeland, for the sake of which one is ready to die or kill. Unreflective nostalgia can breed monsters'. (Pomerantsev 2016b)

Zeid Ra'ad al-Hussein (2016) has a similar explanation in his speech criticising Trump and the European right for seeking to restore a mythical, ethnically pure past. It is easy to understand why the far right buys into these patent lies, and likewise sections of the white working class of declining imperialist powers, who are nostalgic for the privileges of empire. However, explaining why anyone on the left subscribes to such falsehoods is not so easy. Take, for example, the myth that Obama founded ISIS, which, like the myth that Obama was not born in the US, was peddled by Trump. People like self-professed socialist Glen Ford (2016) of *Black Agenda Report*, who might be uncomfortable with the patent racism of the latter claim, are quite happy to agree that Obama created ISIS. This is presumably because, as Stanford professor Michael McFaul testifies, 'Trump's line that Obama founded ISIS echoes exactly a myth propagated by Russian state-controlled media and bloggers ... For years, I have seen posts nearly every day from Russian bloggers suggesting that President Obama founded and continues to fund ISIS. It seems to be one of their standard talking points ... Last night, after I posted and refuted what Trump said in Russian, dozens of Russians jumped in to say that Trump was right, and I was wrong' (cit. Nuzzi 2016).

Another example: When US intelligence analysts determined that Russia had intervened to help Trump win the 2016 election, Russian officials denied the charge, while Trump said, 'I don't believe they interfered' and alleged that the intelligence agencies 'are the same people that said Saddam Hussein has weapons of mass destruction' (Walcott 2016). This is such a complex web of lies that it takes an effort to disentangle it. First, even if we discount the intelligence agencies, the evidence that Russian state-owned media and social media were trying to get Trump elected is there for all to see (see Chapter 2). Second, the intelligence agencies did not unanimously say that Saddam Hussein had weapons of mass destruction. CIA agent Valerie Plame 'had been involved in finding intelligence that showed Iraq had no active nuclear weapons programme', while her husband Joe Wilson 'wrote an article for *The New York Times* ... rubbishing the Bush-Blair claims that Saddam Hussein had bought uranium from Niger. The Bush administration hit out at them by leaking Plame's identity as a CIA operative, thus ending her career, with Bush retorting that she was 'fair game' (Iley 2011).[1] Even the document provided by the intelligence agencies said that they lacked 'specific information' on 'many key aspects' concerning Saddam's WMD programme and cast doubt on Donald Rumsfeld's allegation that there was an operational link between Saddam and Al Qaeda (Leopold 2015); as the Chilcot Inquiry concluded, this was not a sufficient basis for waging war on Iraq. It was the governments of the US and Britain which fabricated lies to justify the war, contradicting weapons inspectors who also denied that there was evidence of an ongoing WMD programme in Iraq (Thielmann 2013).

Thus Trump repeats the lies of one president – Putin – who falsely claims that Russia was not supporting Trump in the 2016 US elections and that he is helping Assad to fight terrorists in Syria – while also repeating the lies of another president – George W. Bush – claiming that intelligence reports all said that Saddam Hussein had weapons of mass destruction. Given the death and destruction that such lies seek to conceal and perpetuate – almost two million Iraqis and Syrians dead, tens of millions displaced, and both countries devastated – it is imperative to expose them for what they are. One should ask the same questions as in any criminal investigation. Is there consistency between the various stories an actor puts out, or do they chop and change (for example, was MH17 shot down by a Ukrainian plane, or was it shot down by a ground-to-air missile from Ukrainian territory)? Does their story conform with evidence from reliable witnesses (for example, does the Bush administration's story about Saddam's WMD conform with reports by weapons inspectors who have reliable information as a result of their inspections)?[2] Does visual and forensic evidence contradict their story (for example, the denial of concentration camps in Bosnia in the 1990s)? Do those who are accused of a crime have a motive for committing it?

It is worth looking at a diversity of sources, and not just those that confirm what one already believes, that is to say, one's existing prejudices. *Al Jazeera* is anti-Assad, *Al-Monitor* pro-Assad; but once aware of their biases, one can obtain useful information from both. And for those who are familiar with the Israeli propaganda machine (see Levy 2015), it will not take long to identify the themes that dominate Assadist propaganda, which is so similar that if you substitute 'Syria' for 'Israel' and 'the rebels' for 'the Palestinians', the justifications for mass slaughter are identical (Zunes 2016). The main thing is to keep one's critical faculties awake instead of swallowing fake news in a zombified stupor. At the same time, orientalist prejudices, like the idea that only people in the West have agency or desire democratic rights and freedoms, should be examined and discarded.

Bringing Morality and Humanity Back into Politics

Morality requires standing up for the truth, but it also requires something more: taking sides. One of Janine di Giovanni's headquotes in her book on Syria (2016) is Howard Zinn's simple but profound observation in *A People's History of the United States*: 'In such a world of conflict, a world of victims and executioners, it is the job of thinking people … not to be on the side of the executioners.' Nothing sums up the moral degradation of pseudo-anti-imperialists more than their propensity to take the side of the executioners: Milošević, Karadžić and Mladić in Bosnia; Putin in Russia, Ukraine and Syria; Khomeini and Khamenei in Iran, Iraq and Syria; and Assad in Syria. Even where they do not actively take the side of the executioners, they do so passively by opposing any sympathy or help for the victims. Sympathy requires an effort to listen to what the victims are experiencing and saying; instead pseudo-anti-imperialists vilify the people in death camps, the political prisoners undergoing torture, rape and execution, and the men, women and children suffering continuous bombardment and poison gas attacks. They oppose not only the military aid that would help the victims defend themselves, but even the humanitarian aid that would help them to stay alive and the communication equipment that would help them make the world outside aware of their plight. In effect, even if pseudo-anti-imperialists make some token criticism of the executioners, they still assist them to carry on raping, torturing and killing their victims.

Double standards are another symptom of moral degradation: condemning US support for brutal dictators but condoning Russian support for brutal dictators; condemning US military intervention in other countries but condoning Russian military intervention in other countries; and so on. Much of this follows from Stalinist support for Russian imperialism during the Cold War, carried forward by neo-Stalinism into a post–Cold War generation. Double standards underlie the 'We will oppose only our own imperialism' stance of some Western anti-imperialist and antiwar groups. Of course, opposing the imperialism of one's own country is absolutely necessary, but silence about other imperialisms constitutes passive support for them and a refusal to extend solidarity to their victims.

The lack of sympathy among pseudo-anti-imperialists towards innocent victims of other imperialisms and the brutal regimes they back puts a question mark over their sincerity when they express sympathy for the victims of Western imperialism and the brutal regimes *they* back. How can anyone who feels anguish when Palestinian children are targeted and killed in Gaza not feel anguish when Syrian children are targeted and killed in Aleppo? Such double standards expose the hypocrisy of those who claim to support the Palestinian cause but – like the IRI, Hezbollah, and their supporters – pursue a very different agenda. Unlike them, the Palestinian children in Gaza who protested in solidarity with Aleppo spontaneously identify with the victims (Ma'an News Agency 2016). Unless compassion, kindness, humanity, imagination, sympathy and love are brought back into politics, unless you take the side of the victims and not the executioners, it becomes a completely cynical exercise and you miss the inspiring stories of heroism and altruism that are to be found even in the darkest of times.

Fighting for Democracy

On the issue of democracy, liberal democrats are to the left of many people who call themselves socialists. This is partly a consequence of Stalinism, which represented a complete negation of democracy but also propagated the idea – shared by right-wingers with socialists who are fond of the term 'bourgeois democracy' – that democracy is organically linked to capitalism. Nothing could be further from the truth. It is true that during the bourgeois revolutions[3] against precapitalist ruling elites or imperial powers, the bourgeoisie needed the support of the popular masses, who put their democratic slogans and demands – like *liberté, égalité, fraternité* (freedom, equality, solidarity) – on the agenda. But, as we see from Albert Soboul's (1977) history of the paradigmatic French revolution, once the bourgeoisie is ensconced in power, it often turns on its erstwhile allies and crushes their democratic revolution. Thus we might say that while a nation-state may be necessary for the development of capitalism (Hobsbawm 1990, 28–30), democracy is not. Democracy is only a result of unremitting struggle by working people demanding the rights to life; to freedom from arbitrary arrest, detention, and cruel, inhuman or degrading treatment; to freedom of expression, association and peaceful assembly; to equality before the law and equal protection by the law; and to participation in government either directly or through freely chosen representatives. And, even where these rights are won, they can be lost again if a totalitarian or fascist state comes to power.

In other words, bourgeois counterrevolutions almost inevitably follow bourgeois-democratic revolutions, making it necessary for the popular masses to keep fighting for even the limited form of democracy that is compatible with capitalism. And they do. It is a myth that freedom, equality and friendship are exclusively Western values; people around the world have fought for them throughout history. In all the countries examined in this book, they have fought desperately for these values, sometimes against unimaginable odds. The struggle for a democratic revolution may go on for decades under various types of authoritarian capitalist states.

For liberal democrats, the need to engage in this fight is self-evident. Socialists, however, have taken ambivalent stands. Rosa Luxemburg was one of the few who defended it explicitly. In 'Reform or Revolution' (1900), she wrote,

> If democracy has become superfluous or annoying to the bourgeoisie, it is on the contrary necessary and indispensable to the working class. It is necessary to the working class because it creates the political forms (autonomous administration, electoral rights, etc.) which will serve the proletariat as fulcrums in its task of transforming bourgeois society. Democracy is indispensable to the working class because only through the exercise of its democratic rights, in the struggle for democracy, can the proletariat become aware of its class interests and its historic task.

With admirable consistency, she continued to argue for a democratic revolution in Russia and against the imposition of authoritarian rule after the Bolshevik revolution: 'Freedom only for the supporters of the government, only for the members of one party – however numerous they may be – is no freedom at all. Freedom is always and exclusively freedom for the one who thinks differently … Without general elections, without unrestricted freedom of press and assembly, without a free struggle of opinion, life dies out in every public institution, becomes a mere semblance of life, in which only the bureaucracy remains as the active element' (Luxemburg 1918). To give up the struggle for these democratic rights and freedoms to be incorporated in the state is to abandon a crucial element of working class struggle; as Nicos Poulantzas (1978, 132) argued, 'Class contradictions are the very stuff of the State: they are present in its material framework and pattern its organization; while the State's policy is the result of their functioning within the state.'

Luxemburg's intuition that communism is incompatible with a one-party authoritarian state was ignored by Lenin and Trotsky, and buried by Stalin, who, on the contrary, presided over a regime which *identified* communism as the rule of a one-party totalitarian state. This conception was conveyed around the world by the Comintern, which imposed Stalin's policies on its members. Most disastrous, perhaps, was the 'third periodism' imposed on the Communist Party of Germany, which, at a time when galloping inflation and unemployment was turning millions of voters towards the Nazi Party, was told to attack the 'social fascist' Social Democratic Party instead of forming a united front with it against the Nazis. This helped to create a split in what was then the most powerful labour movement in the world and allowed Hitler to come to power in 1933 (Bois 2015).

Another source of the contempt for democracy displayed by many left groups and parties is the notion that a socialist or communist revolution is made not by the working class – which would need to prepare for it by exercising their democratic rights, as Luxemburg explains – but by a party that claims to speak and act for it. As Martin Grainger (a pen name of Christopher Pallis) observed in his pamphlet on 'Revolutionary Organization' in 1961, 'The Labour Party, Communist Party and the various Trotskyite and Leninist sects all extol the virtues of professional politicians or revolutionaries. All practise a rigid division within their own organizations of leaders and led. All fundamentally believe that socialism will be instituted from above and through their own particular agency. Each of them sees socialism as nothing more than the conquest of political power, and the transformation, by decree, of economic institutions' (cit. Goodway 2006, 300).

Despite the catastrophic consequences, Stalinists, and even sections of the non-Stalinist left, have never acknowledged the importance of fighting for democracy, nor of defending it when it already exists. We see this failure in the 1979 Iranian Revolution, where 'none of the Marxist organisations believed in any type of political democracy' (Behrooz 1999, 159), thus allowing some of them to collude in the establishment of an Islamist theocracy. We see it in their willingness to allow eastern Aleppo's experiment in democracy (al-Shami 2016; Chouikrat 2016), similar in so many ways to the Paris Commune, to be drowned in blood by Assad's totalitarian regime backed by Iranian Islamism and Russian imperialism (The New Arab 2016; Sky News 2016b), in a massacre reminiscent of the massacre of the Communards, with pseudo-anti-imperialists cheering on the counterrevolution (Smith 2016c).

The failure of sections of the left to support democratic revolutions and defend democracy where it has been established is all the more dangerous at a time when rising unemployment, insecurity, poverty and inequality has led to widespread disillusionment with the existing order. Liberal democrats may be sincere in their defence of democracy and, to this extent, should be seen as an essential part of the struggle against the extreme right (white supremacist, Islamist or other), but their commitment to capitalism makes them incapable of explaining why workers are losing jobs and getting poorer. Here the role of revolutionary socialists who have a critique of capitalism is indispensable. However, they can play this role if and only if they support all struggles to establish or defend democracy, understanding that socialism and communism are not the negation of democracy but, rather, the extension of democracy to areas – such as production – from which it is excluded under capitalism. If the emancipation of the working classes is to be achieved by the working classes themselves, the democratic revolution cannot be skipped.

Bringing Internationalism Centre Stage

Despite her valuable contribution on the importance of democracy for socialists, Luxemburg failed to realise that even the proletariat of an imperialist country may share the racist ideology of imperialism. This led her to oppose the right to national liberation of the Russian colonies, despite the fact that she was strongly opposed to tsarist imperialism. Partly because she was expecting a Europewide socialist revolution in the near future, she saw only the danger of reactionary forces coming to power in these countries, but not the even greater danger of reactionary forces staging a counterrevolution in Russia; and since she was murdered by the proto-fascist Freicorps in 1919, she did not live to revise her views, which, however, do have valuable suggestions for safeguarding the rights of ethnoreligious minorities.

By contrast, Ukrainian Marxist Roman Rosdolsky, who in the 1920s had been the chief theoretician of the Communist Party of Western Ukraine, had the benefit of hindsight in 1948 when 'he was reinterpreting a particularly devilish theoretical issue, the national question, whose horrifying *actualité* had just been demonstrated by Hitler's infamous policy towards Jews and other *"Untermenschen"* as well as by Stalin's less well known, and only somewhat less deadly, policies towards non-Russian nationalities in the Soviet Union' (Himka 1986, 8). Among Rosdolsky's conclusions was the observation that 'just as the working class cannot be socialist or revolutionary *a priori, neither is it internationalist a priori* ... Far from being "by nature without national prejudice,"[4] the proletariat of every land must first acquire *through arduous effort* the internationalist attitude that its general, historical interests demand from it' (Rosdolsky 1986, 182–83, emphasis in original).

At the time Rosdolsky was writing, the hard work of acquiring an 'internationalist attitude' included the need for workers in imperialist countries to support freedom struggles in the colonies. Today, when independence has led to industrialisation in many former colonies as well as to labour migration from them to former imperialist countries, internationalism must include principled opposition not only to racism and xenophobia against migrant workers, but also a theoretical separation of globalisation (freedom of movement of commodities, money, capital and labour across international borders) from neoliberalism (privatisation of public utilities and public services, attacks on social security and welfare, financial deregulation, pro-corporate clauses in trade agreements, and assaults on workers' rights and environmental protections), and opposition only to the latter (Hensman 2011, 41–43). Protectionism is justified when an industrialising country is trying to protect its infant industries from competition that would destroy them before they are able to stand on their own feet; there are also isolated cases – like apartheid South Africa and occupied Palestine – where workers of a country themselves may request that other countries refuse to import their products, because such imports support racism and occupation in their own countries. In all other cases, opposition to freedom of movement of commodities and labour across international borders is wrong, because the message it sends is that the workers of other countries, who produce the commodities that are being imported or who come to your country in search of employment, *are your enemies*. If the imported products are cheaper because workers in these countries are deprived of labour rights, there are various ways to help them to gain those rights, as I have argued elsewhere (Hensman 2011, 320–36). But solidarity with workers of other countries is not a luxury or something separate and distinct from working-class interests: it is an intrinsic element of working-class interests.

Lenin and the Bolsheviks broke with the Second International because its nationalist social-democratic parties backed their own bourgeoisies in World War I, but Stalin reinstated nationalism in the Third International with his doctrine of 'socialism in one country'; thus, there is a tradition of nationalism among both social democrats and Stalinists. This explains the overt and covert support for Brexit from sections of the left in Britain, whose arguments echoed sentiments from 1971 when 'national sovereignty' was defended from the left (see Nairn 1973, 11), despite the racism and xenophobia driving the Brexit campaign. Similarly, opposition by Bernie Sanders to free trade deals on the grounds that they resulted in US workers losing jobs to workers in Vietnam, China and Latin America (OnTheIssues 2016) dovetailed with Trump's xenophobic campaign to put America first.

These sections of the left failed to counter the economic nationalism of Farage and Trump by failing to tell workers: 'The workers of Poland, Mexico, China or any other country are *not* your enemies, they are your class brothers and sisters; neoliberal capitalism is your real enemy, but you will never succeed in defeating neoliberalism, much less capitalism, unless you join together with the workers of other countries.' They allowed workers to think that keeping out imports and workers from other countries would restore jobs and raise wages in their own, reinforcing the right-wing illusion that national capitalism can solve the problems of unemployment and poverty. The exact opposite is the case. Capitalism is inherently global, and it has become even more so over the past half-century; unless the opposition to it is equally global, capitalism will always win. Globalising the opposition even to neoliberalism, in the first place, requires organising across national borders, which is facilitated by freedom of movement across those borders. Closing borders, as the far right wants to do, only sabotages the struggle against neoliberalism.

By contrast, the transnational Democracy in Europe Movement 2025 (DiEM25) offers a 'Progressive Agenda for Europe'. It rejects both 'Euro-reformism', which cannot counter neoliberalism nor democratise the EU, as well as 'Lexit', which willy-nilly strengthens the racist and xenophobic right.[5] Instead, as former Greek finance minister Yanis Varoufakis (2016) writes it

> proposes a pan-European movement of civil and governmental disobedience with which to bring on a surge of democratic opposition to the way European elites do business at the local, national and EU levels ... The Left's traditional internationalism is a key ingredient of DiEM25, along with other constituent democratic traditions from a variety of political projects (including progressive liberalism, feminist and ecological movements, the 'pirate' parties etc.)
>
> [...] [O]ne may cheekily ask: 'Why stop at the EU level? As internationalists, why don't you campaign for worldwide democracy?' Our answer is that we do campaign for democracy everywhere and from an internationalist point of view ... But, given that history has, for better or for worse, delivered a borderless EU, with common policies on the environment and a variety of other realms, the (by definition internationalist) Left must defend this absence of borders, the existing EU commons of climate change policy, even the Erasmus program that gives young Europeans the opportunity to mingle in a borderless educational system. Turning against these splendid artefacts of an otherwise regressive EU is not consistent with what the Left ought to be about.

Organising against neoliberalism requires freedom of association, a basic democratic right. Supporting – or failing to oppose – totalitarian regimes like the Assad regime, which crush all democratic rights and kill or drive out all opponents, ultimately results in weakening the global opposition to neoliberalism; unless we support democracy in other countries, we will face the right-wing backlash in our own. A moving expression of solidarity with democratic revolutions everywhere is found in a letter from Razan Zaitouneh in 2011, when she received the Anna Politkovskaya award on the fifth anniversary of Politkovskaya's murder:

> Dear Anna Politkovskaya,
>
> I am well aware that this honor, which bears your name, is not merely awarded to me personally but rather to the sons and daughters of Syria, and the 3,000 whose blood was spilled over the past 7 months by the same criminal exclusionary mentality that spilled your own blood.

I am aware that your passion for truth and the defense of human dignity, for which you gave your life, is but a link in a chain that stretches across the world, through individuals and entire peoples, all of whom believe in everyone's right to live free of oppression, humiliation, and subjugation.

Nonetheless, bestowing this honor on me personally out of all other Syrians assumes another dimension, as it comes on the fifth anniversary of your death. It means a lot to me to receive an award in your name, Anna, as a Russian citizen – even as the Russian government continues to support the Syrian regime, which has been committing crimes against humanity for several months now; crimes that have been documented by international human rights organizations.

This vividly exemplifies that what we share in humanity transcends languages, nationalities, and borders, just as tyranny and corruption share the same essence although they differ in details.

For this very reason I believe the battle for freedom, being fought by Syrians for months now, would bring comfort to your soul: because each step forward towards peace and justice in any part of the world benefits all humanity [...]

Just as we are proud, dear Anna, that you found loyal friends who kept your name alive to remind us of who you were, and what you sacrificed for the sake of truth and human rights, I wish I could recite the names of all our martyrs, one by one. [...]

And so, Anna Politkovskaya, we continue. We continue in your memory, and in the memory of all the other symbols of truth and freedom in the world, until freedom, justice, and democracy prevail in our Syria and the entire world. (Zaitouneh 2011)

Pushing for Global Institutions to Promote Human Rights and Democracy

What are the ideas, and the global institutions organised to uphold them, that have been involved in the various struggles for democracy described above, and what is their record?

One key concept is that of sovereignty, believed to derive from the Peace of Westphalia at the end of the Thirty Years' War in 1648, which 'is said to have consecrated the principle of sovereign equality of states, which has been at the core of international law ever since' (Beaulac 2004). A closer look at the two treaties that constitute the Peace of Westphalia shows, however, that they

do not at all support the traditional position that the *Peace of Westphalia* constitutes a paradigm shift whereby the political entities involved gained exclusive power over their territories. The two main purposes of the agreements related to the practice of religion and the settlement of territories, not to the creation of distinct separate polities independent from any higher authority. ... 1648 cannot legitimately be deemed a turning point in the development of the present state system. Rather, the outcome of the congress constituted nothing more than a step further – even, arguably, a relatively modest one – in the gradual shift from the ideal of a universal overlordship to the idea of distinct separate political entities enjoying full autonomy over their territories. (Beaulac 2004)

If it is true, as Beaulac (2004) argues, that 'Westphalia constitutes a myth, an aetiological myth, or origin myth', it is equally true that this myth 'has represented, as well as indeed created, a new reality, a mythical reality, about the present international state system'. It is important to remember that this myth dates from the seventeenth century, a time when the people of a state were subjects rather than citizens; to apply it unchanged to the twenty-first century is anachronistic. For this reason, there have been attempts to formulate a notion of 'democratic sovereignty'.

The Charter of the United Nations, which was signed and came into force in 1945, includes notions of both state sovereignty and democratic sovereignty, the rights of states as well as the fundamental rights and freedoms of individuals. Thus its preamble begins, 'We the peoples of the United Nations determined ... to reaffirm faith in fundamental human rights, in the dignity and worth of the human person, in the equal rights of men and women and of nations large and small.' According to Article 1,

the Purposes of the United Nations are:

1. To maintain international peace and security, and to that end: to take effective collective measures for the prevention and removal of threats to the peace, and for the suppression of acts of aggression or other breaches of the peace, and to bring about by peaceful means, and in conformity with the principles of justice and international law, adjustment or settlement of international disputes or situations which might lead to a breach of the peace;
2. To develop friendly relations among nations based on respect for the principle of equal rights and self-determination of peoples, and to take other appropriate measures to strengthen universal peace;
3. To achieve international co-operation in solving international problems of an economic, social, cultural, or humanitarian character, and in promoting and encouraging respect for human rights and for fundamental freedoms for all without distinction as to race, sex, language, or religion; and
4. To be a centre for harmonizing the actions of nations in the attainment of these common ends. (UN n.d.a)

Article 2.4. says, 'All Members shall refrain in their international relations from the threat or use of force against the territorial integrity or political independence of any state, or in any other manner inconsistent with the Purposes of the United Nations' (UN n.d.a). This makes sense, and if implemented consistently would have prevented many of the conflicts examined in the foregoing chapters. It certainly would have prevented the US/UK invasion and occupation of Iraq in 2003, which is easily identified as unlawful under Article 2.4. A careful critique of the arguments used to justify the Russian annexation of Crimea shows that it, too, is unlawful under Article 2.4., as it amounts to the use of force against the territorial integrity of another state, namely Ukraine (Balouziyeh 2014); the same could be said of the Russian incursion into eastern Ukraine.

The military intervention of Iranian, Lebanese Hezbollah, Iraqi and Russian forces in Syria is a more complicated case because it can be argued that it occurred at the request of the existing head of state who, unlike Yanukovych, had not abandoned his post. But is it lawful for a head of state to surrender the country's sovereignty to foreign powers in return for retaining a formal role? It can be argued that these interventions were 'inconsistent with the Purposes of the United Nations', and specifically with the requirement 'to achieve international co-operation ... in promoting and encouraging respect for human rights and for fundamental freedoms for all', and also that they compromised the territorial integrity and political independence of Syria. This would make the Syrian struggle for national liberation lawful in terms of the UN Charter's support for 'the self-determination of peoples'. If none of these forces, nor the Turkish, nor the US-led coalition forces had intervened, and the Syrian people's sovereignty had been respected, it is entirely possible that they would have had greater success in solving their internal problems, including dealing with the Islamists unleashed by Assad. Even after the humanitarian catastrophe created by these multiple interventions, respecting 'the territorial integrity and political independence' of Syria would require the cessation of all foreign military action and withdrawal of all foreign forces from the country.

The abject failure of the UN to prevent or halt these conflicts, or even to provide humanitarian aid to the civilian populations being subjected to military assault, needs to be explained. We will return to this issue after examining two other strands of international law.

The Universal Declaration of Human Rights (UDHR), signed by the General Assembly of the UN on December 10, 1948, is generally seen as the founding document of international human rights law. 'It represents the universal recognition that basic rights and fundamental freedoms are inherent to all human beings, inalienable and equally applicable to everyone, and that every one of us is born free and equal in dignity and rights. Whatever our nationality, place of residence, gender, national or ethnic origin, colour, religion, language, or any other status, the international community on December 10 1948 made a commitment to upholding dignity and justice for all of us' (UN n.d.b). Its commitment to securing for all human beings the democratic rights and freedoms outlined above, as well as its explanation of the right to freedom of conscience and belief, the right to form or join trade unions, and the right to social security and welfare, affirm that 'everyone is entitled to a social and international order in which the rights and freedoms set forth in this Declaration can be fully realized' (UN n.d.c).

It is often assumed that the UDHR represents a Western notion of human rights and democracy, but this is far from the truth. Eleanor Roosevelt chaired the drafting committee, but there were important contributions from others, including many from the Third World: Ricardo Alfaro of Panama (who proposed the idea and wrote the first draft), René Cassin of France, Hansa Mehta of India (who insisted on the wording 'all human beings are equal in dignity and rights' rather than 'all men'), Charles Malik of Lebanon, Begum Shaista Ikramullah of Pakistan, Charles Romulo of the Philippines, Wahid Rafaat of Egypt, Hernán Santa Cruz of Chile, and representatives from the Soviet Union, Yugoslavia, China, Australia, Canada and the UK. Fifty countries voted for the Declaration, none voted against, and Saudi Arabia, South Africa and the Soviet bloc abstained (Sehgal 2014).

The UN Commission on Human Rights (replaced in 2006 by the UN Human Rights Council) had already been established in 1946, periodically compiling human rights reports on member states and investigating complaints. Its procedures involved the participation of human rights defenders and activists from the various countries. The International Covenant on Civil and Political Rights and the International Covenant on Economic, Social and Cultural Rights developed most of the rights enshrined in the UDHR and entered into force in 1976. Together with the UDHR, they comprise the International Bill of Human Rights. In addition, numerous other human rights conventions, declarations and resolutions have been adopted by the UN, covering issues ranging from racial discrimination, torture and enforced disappearances to the rights of women, children, migrants, minorities, people with disabilities, and indigenous people. Together they comprise a large and growing corpus of international law protecting human and democratic rights.

This means that any member state, or any citizen of a member state, is authorised by international law to provide people in other countries with assistance in their struggles for human rights and democracy in the form of funding, literature, education and training, whereas the despots (and their followers) who complain that this constitutes support for regime change have no basis in international law for their pursuit of unbridled power. Indeed, wherever such despots are in power, regime change by the people of the country itself is a democratic right supported by international law. The governments of Russia and China routinely ignore this enormous body of international human rights law when they speak and act as if state sovereignty is the only right protected by international law (and in the case of Russia, even this right has been violated).

A third strand of international law emerges from the codification of the laws of war after the mid-nineteenth century, in the Geneva Convention of 1864 and the Hague Conventions of 1899 and 1907. What came to be known as 'international humanitarian law' dealt with issues like the protection of civilians and their property, and the prohibition of the abuse of prisoners; at first violations were seen as illegal rather than criminal, yet soon these came to be regarded as war crimes. After World War II, Nazi war criminals were tried in Nuremberg by the International Military Tribunal, for which the groundwork was laid by the four major victorious powers (France, the UK, the US and the USSR), each of which also supplied a judge and prosecution team when the trials began on November 20, 1945. The charges included crimes against peace, war crimes, and a new category – crimes against humanity – to take account of the extermination of millions of European Jews. 'But the Nuremberg Charter seemed to indicate that crimes against humanity could only be committed in time of war, not a critical obstacle to the Nazi prosecutions but a troubling precedent for the future protection of human rights' (Schabas 2000, 10).

Dissatisfied with this approach, others, including Raphael Lemkin, worked on the Convention on the Prevention and Punishment of the Crime of Genocide, which was adopted by the UN General Assembly on December 9, 1948. The General Assembly confirmed 'that genocide, whether committed in time of peace or in time of war, is a crime under international law which they undertake to prevent and to punish', and defined it as 'acts committed with intent to destroy, in whole or in part, a national, ethnical, racial or religious group, as such'. As William Schabas explains: 'By defining an international crime, and spelling out obligations upon States parties in terms of prosecution and extradition, the Convention falls under the rubric of international criminal law' (Schabas 2000, 5).

The Genocide Convention breaks with the concept of state sovereignty, legally justifying even military intervention if there is no other way to prevent or halt genocide. It certainly justifies arming victims to defend themselves from genocide. The UN Security Council resolution of 1991 – which placed an embargo on the delivery of weapons and military equipment to Yugoslavia and thereby prevented Bosnian Muslims from defending themselves against the genocidal assault of far better armed Serb nationalists – did the exact opposite. In Bosnia, the Security Council violated the Genocide Convention by facilitating genocide rather than preventing it.

On the same day that the General Assembly adopted the Genocide Convention, it also passed a resolution calling on the International Law Commission, a body of experts named by the UN General Assembly and charged with the codification and progressive development of international law, to prepare the statute of an international court to investigate, prosecute and try individuals – not states – accused of committing the most serious crimes of concern to the international community, namely war crimes, crimes against humanity, genocide and aggression. The prosecutorial policy was to focus on those bearing the greatest responsibility for the crimes, including those highest up in the chain of command.[6] 'The International Law Commission made considerable progress on its draft code and actually submitted a proposal in 1954. Then, the General Assembly suspended the mandates, ostensibly pending the sensitive task of defining the crime of aggression. In fact, political tensions associated with the Cold War had made progress on the war crimes agenda virtually impossible' (Schabas 2001, 9), and serious work on an international criminal court was resumed only in 1989. In 1994, the commission submitted a draft statute focused on procedural and organisational matters, and two years later adopted the final draft of its 'Code of Crimes Against the Peace and Security of Mankind'. These two drafts played a seminal role in the preparation of the Statute of the International Criminal Court, which was also influenced by the rulings of two ad hoc tribunals set up by the UN to deal with the genocides in Bosnia and Rwanda.

But the Tribunals did more than simply set legal precedent to guide the drafters. They also provided a reassuring model of what an international criminal court might look like. This was particularly important in debates concerning the role of the prosecutor. The integrity, neutrality and good judgment of Richard Goldstone and his successor, Louise Arbour, answered those who warned of the dangers of a reckless and irresponsible 'Dr Strangelove prosecutor'. (Schabas 2001, 12–13)

In 1995, the General Assembly convened a 'Preparatory Committee' (PrepCom), inviting Member states, NGOs and various international organisations to study the International Law Commission draft and propose amendments. This resulted in the active participation of a large number of groups around the world, and significant contributions from them. One of the most significant was that of a diverse range of women's groups:

> Women's rights activists throughout the world – of every political stripe, faith, sexual orientation, nationality, and ethnicity – mobilized at each step of the International Criminal Court (ICC) process. They have worked to create an independent court to afford women greater protection from violations of human rights and humanitarian law.
>
> Women's rights activists participated in every major United Nations preparatory meeting on the ICC. They worked to ensure that the range of abuses that happen to women was accurately reflected in the list of crimes over which the ICC would have jurisdiction. They worked to ensure that the rules and procedures governing how the court functions would be responsive to gender-specific crimes.
>
> Activists held in-country workshops to educate other women and policy makers about the benefits of ICC adoption and ratification. They lobbied their home country officials to sign and then ratify the Rome Statute, which outlined the establishment and structure of the ICC. [...]
>
> Thanks to women around the world, violence and persecution of women will be treated as the serious criminal and humanitarian law violations that they are. The ICC offers a dramatic and long-awaited improvement in how international crimes against women are treated and greatly increases the possibility for redress. (HRW 2002)

The enthusiastic participation of NGOs and activists in the PrepCom marked a departure from much of the work of the UN. Together with the 'like-minded caucus', comprising sixty members of the 160 participating state parties attending the Diplomatic Conference of Plenipotentiaries on the Establishment of an International Criminal Court convened on June 15, 1998 in Rome, they put forward a conception of the ICC which was, 'by and large, in conflict with the conception of the court held by the permanent members of the Security Council. The principles of the like-minded were: an inherent jurisdiction of the Court over the "core crimes" of genocide, crimes against humanity and war crimes (and, perhaps, aggression); elimination of a Security Council veto on prosecutions; an independent prosecutor with the power to initiate proceedings *proprio motu*; and the prohibition of reservations to the statute' (Schabas 2001, 15–16).

The final text of the Rome Statute of the ICC was a compromise, adopted on July 17, 1998 by a vote of 120 to 7, with 21 countries abstaining. Iraq, Israel, Libya, China, Qatar, Yemen and the United States voted against, but the Clinton administration eventually signed it on December 31, 2000. The crime of aggression was almost left out, due to lack of agreement on its definition. It was the non-aligned countries as well as the German and Japanese delegations who insisted that aggression remain within the jurisdiction of the Court, and they pursued a compromise according to which aggression would be included as a generic crime, pending the definition of its elements at a later date (Schabas 2001, 26–27). This amendment was enacted at a conference in Kampala on June 11, 2010; it would come into force after thirty states had ratified it (which was achieved in 2016), and a decision to do so was taken after January 1, 2017 by a two-thirds majority of member states (Coalition for the International Criminal Court n.d.).

The definition of genocide closely followed the definition in the Genocide Convention, but the decision to limit the definition to acts intended to destroy 'national, ethnical, racial or religious groups' was contested, with suggestions that, for example, social and political groups should be included. However, the final decision was to retain the narrower definition. One drawback is that equally heinous crimes may not attract similar international condemnation. For example, we commonly refer to the 'Cambodian genocide', and the scale of killings, incarceration, torture and cruelty perpetrated against the victims makes this appear logical. Yet the majority of victims were from the same Khmer ethnic group as the perpetrators and were targeted not because of their ethnicity, but because they belonged to certain social groups (urban dwellers, intellectuals, etc.), or were politically opposed to the Khmer Rouge. This issue has not been resolved (Schabas 2000, 118–19).

The Cambodian atrocities would fall clearly under the definition of 'crimes against humanity' as defined in the Rome Statute, but there is dissatisfaction with this solution because crimes against humanity, although more serious than war crimes, are commonly seen as being less serious than genocide. However, 'it now seems broadly accepted that genocide inheres within the broader concept of crimes against humanity' (Schabas 2000, 11), and this provides a better way to look at it: that genocide is one particular crime against humanity, and there are others which are no less heinous. Logically, this requires the UN General Assembly to adopt a Convention on the Prevention and Punishment of Crimes Against Humanity modelled on the Genocide Convention, using the same definition of crimes against humanity as the Rome Statute. This would provide legal justification for military intervention to prevent crimes against humanity like the slaughter in Aleppo; indeed, there is already strong moral justification for providing the victims with adequate means to defend themselves. The definition of sovereignty in the UN Charter does not allow a state to exterminate a section of its own people; still less does it allow foreign military forces like the Iranian IRGC, Lebanese Hezbollah and Russian military to exterminate hundreds of thousands and displace tens of millions. Such a convention would be better than the rather nebulous and ill-defined 'Responsibility to Protect' (ICRtoP n.d.).

One reason for Clinton's reservations about the ICC was that although the UN Security Council could refer cases to it, it remained independent of the UN, and the prosecutor could proceed with prosecutions based on referrals by member states or on the prosecutor's own initiative, whereas the US wanted an ICC that was controlled by the UN Security Council, where the US had a veto (Krohnke 2011). For this reason, and fear that it could be used against Americans, the Bush administration effectively unsigned the treaty and attempted to sabotage it, passing the American Service-Members' Protection Act, which cut off US funding for the ICC, and signing bilateral immunity agreements with other countries guaranteeing mutual immunity from ICC prosecution, under threat of sanctions if they refused. The Obama administration's relationship with the ICC was more positive, but ASPA was not repealed (Lambert 2014).

Russia had similar concerns and therefore signed but did not ratify the Rome Statute (Kaye 2012). In November 2016, Putin, like Bush, unsigned the treaty after ICC prosecutor Fatou Bensouda issued a report on the status of her ongoing investigation into Russia's annexation of Crimea and involvement in eastern Ukraine. The case had been referred to the ICC by Ukraine, which had signed but not ratified the Rome Statute; however, it accepted ICC jurisdiction in 2013. The ICC's preliminary list of alleged crimes included 'harassment of the Crimean Tatar population; the killing and abduction of at least 10 people in Crimea; the ill-treatment of individuals who had been detained or abducted in Crimea ... the detention of opponents of Russian assimilation of Crimea; killings as a result of armed hostilities in Eastern Ukraine; destruction of civilian objects in Eastern Ukraine; the capture, detention, ill-treatment, torture, and disappearance of people in Eastern Ukraine; and, finally, sexual and gender-based crimes in Eastern Ukraine'. It was in response to this report, as well as an ongoing investigation of crimes committed by Russians in Georgia in 2008, that Putin issued his decree withdrawing Russia from the ICC (Newcity 2016).

The ICC's independence from the UN Security Council, which these states object to, is seen as the strongest point of the ICC by other states, some of which objected strongly to Article 16, allowing the Security Council to pass a resolution deferring an investigation or prosecution for twelve months. If we see the ICC as part of a world judiciary, its independence would certainly be a requirement from a democratic point of view. There has been a great deal of criticism of the ICC because it has prosecuted mainly Africans; but this is because African countries participated vigorously in its creation and constituted the largest number of states (thirty-four) that signed and ratified the Rome Statute. It seems unfair and it *is* unfair, but this is a consequence of the limited jurisdiction of the ICC. Its jurisdiction should be wider, covering the nationals and territories not just of members but of all states. Even if in practice it might be impossible to bring to trial nationals of states that do not accept its jurisdiction, it should at least have the power to investigate their crimes and indict them. This change, as well as more states signing and ratifying the Rome Treaty, would make the ICC more effective.

This brings us to the question of why the UN, despite having such an impressive array of human rights laws and principles at its disposal, backed sanctions against Iraq that killed hundreds of thousands of children, facilitated the Bosnian genocide, has done nothing to prevent or punish genocidal assaults on Palestinians by the Israeli state, and has done nothing to halt the carnage in Syria or even to provide humanitarian aid to almost a million civilians subjected to starvation sieges by the state and its allies.

Article 2.1 of the UN Charter states that 'the Organization is based on the principle of the sovereign equality of all its members.' In the General Assembly, therefore, which can be seen as akin to a parliament, all members are equal. However, Article 23.1 says, 'The Security Council shall consist of fifteen Members of the United Nations. The Republic of China, France, the Union of Soviet Socialist Republics, the United Kingdom of Great Britain and Northern Ireland, and the United States of America shall be perma-nent members of the Security Council. The General Assembly shall elect ten other Members of the United Nations to be non-permanent members of the Security Council.' This introduces an element of inequality. But it gets worse. Article 27 says,

1. Each member of the Security Council shall have one vote.
2. Decisions of the Security Council on procedural matters shall be made by an affirmative vote of nine members.
3. Decisions of the Security Council on all other matters shall be made by an affirmative vote of nine members *including the concurring votes of the permanent members*; provided that, in decisions under Chapter VI, and under paragraph 3 of Article 52, a party to a dispute shall abstain from voting. (emphasis added)

It is the veto power of the permanent members of the Security Council that most radically undermines the democratic character of the UN and its ability to carry out its mandate. It means that the permanent members and their protégés (like Israel in the case of the US and Syria in the case of Rus-sia) can commit the most horrific crimes and get away with them because not even a condemnation of them can be passed in the Security Council without being vetoed. And if they are not member states of the ICC, their nationals cannot be prosecuted by the ICC unless they happen to commit their crimes, and get caught, on the territory of a member state. Without that veto power, even if they continued to remain permanent members, the other members could take a decision without them. With it, one member state can block the functioning of the entire UN. So long as permanent members retain their veto power, there can be no equality, democracy or justice in the UN. If the UN is to accomplish the purposes for which it was formed, the veto powers of permanent members of the UN Security Council must be abolished.

◆

At a time when rising unemployment, insecurity, poverty and inequality are leaving many people disillusioned with mainstream liberalism, it is import-ant for the left to offer a clear alternative that supports *all* national liberation struggles and democratic revolutions. Neo-Stalinists who actively support

Russian imperialism and the far-right despots it sponsors offer no serious alternative, nor do those who fail to oppose Russian imperialism and the despots it sponsors because, in the name of a distorted anti-imperialism, they lose sight of what real democracy and internationalism look like. Thus, we have on one side the menacing growth of the far right, and on the other a disastrously divided band of liberals and socialists. Unless the measures outlined above are taken, the threat of fascist and totalitarian regimes, which inflict mass incarceration, torture, rape and murder upon their own people as well as other peoples, looms over much of the world.

Acknowledgements

I would like to thank Jairus Banaji for suggesting that I write this book in the first place, and for providing encouragement and moral support while I was working on it. I am grateful to Sughosh Mazmundar and Shaku and Murad Banaji for helping me to get some of the books and articles I needed for it, and to Ashley Smith, Savi Hensman and Ammar Al-Ghabban for helpful suggestions on the text. Finally, my thanks to the Haymarket team, and especially to Nisha Bolsey, Miri Davidson and Rachel Cohen, for their help and support. If the book makes any contribution towards mobilising solidarity for the struggles described in it, that will be thanks to their inputs.

Notes

Introduction

1. For which 'Daesh' is the Arabic acronym. Al-Sham or Greater Syria, along with Iraq, is believed by ISIS to be the heart of their caliphate.
2. I am a proponent of non-violent struggle, have never participated in anything else, and believe that in most circumstances it is more effective and more conducive to democracy in the long term. However, I do recognise that there are situations in which non-violent resistance cannot succeed against overwhelming violent oppression. In such circumstances, I believe that armed opposition is better than allowing violent oppression to continue without effective resistance.
3. Articles supporting Assad and his Hezbollah, Iranian, Iraqi Shia and Russian allies are ubiquitous, and it would be both tedious and nauseating to quote them all. What is disturbing is that sites like *Counterpunch* publish articles supporting the Russian bombing of Syria and spouting rhetoric about 'bombing the hell out of the jihadis' and 'killing these jokers until every last one of them is dead' (Whitney 2015), regardless of the fact that hospitals are being bombed and helpless civilians including children are being killed (Al Jazeera 2015b).
4. Lemkin was a Polish Jew, most of whose relatives were wiped out by the Nazis.
5. Ceylon was an unusual case where Trotskyists outnumbered Stalinists in the Lanka Sama Samaj Party (LSSP) and expelled the latter rather than the other way around (see Hensman 2009, which also gives an account of the degeneration of the left). My parents were never members of any party, but they had friends and acquaintances in the LSSP. This could partly explain why I grew up with books by Trotsky on the bookshelves and took it for granted that the Moscow trials and crushing of the Hungarian uprising of 1956 were evidence of condemnable totalitarianism, rather than anything to do with socialism.

1 The Politics of Anti-imperialism

1. I prefer 'national liberation' to 'national self-determination', which, as Luxemburg points out, begs the question of who constitutes the 'self' of a nation divided by class and other divisions.
2. According to Marx, increases in the productivity of labour under capitalism are

reflected not just in a larger *mass* of machinery and raw materials being put into motion by the same number or a smaller number of workers, but also in a rising ratio of the *value* of means of production (constant capital) to the value of the wages (variable capital) of the workers required to put it into motion (the 'organic composition of capital'). Since surplus value, and therefore profit, is created only by living labour, there is a tendency for the rate of profit – the amount of profit gained from a given amount of capital – to fall (Marx 1981 [1894], Chapters 2 and 13).

3.   There have been what I feel are valid criticisms of Snyder's book, for example of the arbitrary restriction of the time period it covers, which should have gone further back; the restriction of the geographical area it covers to those affected by both Soviet and Nazi occupation, rather than a larger area affected by mass killings; the artificial distinction between intentional killings and large-scale deaths resulting from deliberate subjection of people to conditions inimical to life, and exclusion of the latter from the death toll, resulting in its underestima- tion; and the downplaying of the scale of mass killings by equally vicious third parties (i.e., neither Soviet nor Nazi) (Muehlenkamp 2010; Sémelin 2013). There are also moderate neo-Stalinists (who refuse to admit that Stalin carried out a counterrevolution although they might concede that he made 'mistakes' or committed atrocities), who take issue with Snyder for equating mass killings by Stalin with those by Hitler (e.g., Lazare 2014); and hardcore neo-Stalinists, who simultaneously insist that 'Stalin did not "kill" people at all', while holding that Bolsheviks like Bukharin and Trotsky, not to mention others who were executed, were traitors who deserved to die (e.g., Furr 2015).

4.   A friend who was in the Communist Party of India (CPI) and working for Novosty and the Russian news agency TASS at that time says that there was opposition not only in the CPI but also by his Russian boss to the Soviet inva- sion of Afghanistan, but that it was not heeded.

5.   The demoralisation resulting from the collapse of the Soviet Union and Yugoslavia spread far beyond the ranks of the official Stalinists (the Communist and Maoist parties); for many on the left, the USSR had been an instance of 'actually existing socialism', and they felt homeless without it. Even Trotskyists – apart from 'state capitalists' like Tony Cliff, who saw it as a vindication of their theory – were affect- ed when the 'degenerated workers' state' disintegrated. The unconscious nostalgia of these people makes them particularly vulnerable to neo-Stalinist pseudo-anti-im- perialism. This is why it is so important for socialists to recognise the Soviet Union for what it really became under Stalin (cf. Filtzer 1987, 270–71).

6.   At least Putin, unlike most Stalinists, is honest enough to admit that endorsing Stalin entails rejecting Lenin. Both Stalin and Putin are embodiments of the Great Russian chauvinism that Lenin opposed so vehemently.

7.   In my book on *Workers, Unions and Global Capitalism* (2011), I have explored what struggles by workers and unions against global capitalism in the twen- ty-first century might involve.

8.   We will come back to the issue of Putin's right-wing links and politics in Chapter 2.

2 Russia and Ukraine

1. The Cheka, and after 1922 the GPU.
2. Although the apartment bombings might not have been the work of Chechen separatists, there were other gruesome terrorist attacks that were. Nothing can justify such attacks on civilians, including children, and they only help to delegitimise the forces carrying them out. Nor am I arguing for the breakup of the Russian Federation: countries may come together voluntarily in a federation that is mutually beneficial. Problems arose in the Russian Federation, as in the case of the Yugoslav Federation after Tito's death, because there was an attempt to impose the domination of one ethnoreligious group over all others.
3. I believe 'anti-Muslim bigotry' is a more accurate term for what is commonly referred to as 'Islamophobia'.
4. Alexei Gasparov, a democratic socialist who opposed the Russian intervention in Ukraine, was released in October 2016 after serving a three-and-a-half-year sentence (Gerasimenko 2016).
5. As chancellor, Schröder signed a gas pipeline deal with Russia in September 2005, and once he left office he accepted a top job in the consortium building the pipeline (BBC News 2005a).

3 Bosnia and Kosovo

1. I have discussed the grave dangers involved in defining 'nations' in ethnic terms, thus linking ethnicity with territory, elsewhere (Hensman 2015).
2. The overwhelming majority of Bosnian Muslims were secular and called themselves 'Bosniaks' to avoid being assigned a religious identity.
3. In his preface to the 1996 edition of this book, Sells writes: 'The story told here is not one I wish to believe or to tell. My mother's family is Serbian American, and I know personally that Serbs have suffered in the Bosnian war – some of my Serb relatives in Bosnia and Krajina (the Serb-inhabited area of Croatia) have been killed, some are missing, and others are living in refugee camps. However, the evidence in Bosnia leads to conclusions that are as unavoidable as they are unpalatable. Genocide has occurred' (Sells 1998, xxi).
4. I strongly support Lily Lynch's suggestion that such stories should be collected. There were plenty of 'Sinhalese Schindlers' in Sri Lanka – indeed, my own family was saved by them on one occasion – and I too felt it important to collect their stories as a contribution to reconciliation.

4 Iran

1. Not a single foreign government condemned the massacre. US president Jimmy Carter, who had earlier put pressure on the shah to democratise, failed to condemn it, while the Chinese press accused the demonstrators of being 'financed

and organized from abroad' (Halliday 1979, 295).

2.   The Iranian Communist Party was formed in 1920 and active throughout the 1920s, but it was crushed by Reza Shah Pahlavi in the 1930s. Those who survived joined forces with the remnants of the Marxist Group of Fifty-Three to form the Tudeh Party in 1941. Despite establishing a strong base among the working class and young modern intelligentsia, it was crushed again after the 1953 coup (Behrooz 1999, xi–xiv). Its Moscow orientation led it to support oil concessions to the Soviet Union in northern Iran in 1944, in opposition to Mossadegh, who was trying to end all foreign control of the oil industry (Behrooz 1999, 5–6).

3.   Hekmat went on to join forces with the Kurdish Komala to form the Communist Party of Iran in 1981, but then broke with the latter due to its Kurdish nationalism and formed the Worker-Communist Party of Iran (WPI) in 1983. His biography by close comrade Hamid Taghvaie (n.d.) conveys the story of a communist engaged in crafting a genuinely advanced theory and principled practice, especially in his emphasis on women's equality, but he seems to have subscribed to Lenin's vanguardist, substitutionist theory of the party.

4.   The Zionist intention of dismembering Iraq could also explain the US neoconservative fixation on invading Iraq (see Chapter 1).

5.   Bernard Kramer (1990) offers an accessible explanation of the ways in which Khomeini's Shia fundamentalism differs radically from traditional Twelver Shiism. While it has become fairly common in the West to distinguish between Salafism and more progressive interpretations of Sunni Islam, the parallel distinction between fundamentalist Shia Islamism and more progressive interpretations of Shia Islam is rarely made. This is unfortunate, since the fundamentalist interpretations of Sunni and Shia Islam are much closer to each other than either is to progressive interpretations of the respective sects, and the latter are much closer to each other than to the fundamentalist interpretations of their respective sects.

6.   The entire episode has been uploaded at www.youtube.com/watch?v=Uab_q5Afu7s.

7.   Fascist minds think alike, apparently. The Bharatiya Janata Party in India launched an almost identical programme after it came to power in 2014, except that Islamist ideology and organisations were replaced by Hindutva ones. Of course, it faced stiff resistance.

5 Iraq

1.   Sassoon's account is based on millions of pages of government documents and audiotape recordings of leadership meetings captured by the United States in 2003.

2.   I don't pretend to be objective on this issue, having been one of the millions of people around the world who marched and marched, in the hope that the war could be averted, and watched with rage and despair as the bombs were dropped regardless. However, as I am now engaged in a critique of knee-jerk

anti-Americanism, I am looking again at my opposition to the 2003 Iraq war to assess whether it was justified. I think it was.

3.   Like many cases in India and Sri Lanka, this demonstrates that the political leadership of an oppressed ethnic group can also become oppressive to local minorities when fighting to establish control over territory claimed as belonging to their ethnic group.

6 Syria: The Assad Regime

1.   I use 'terrorism' here to mean the use or threat of violence against civilians in the pursuit of a political objective.

7 The Syrian Uprising

1.   Yassin-Kassab and al-Shami base their account of the Syrian uprising on conversations and interviews with myriad Syrians who participated in it, conducted over several years.

2.   I dislike labelling people in this communal fashion and do so only to make it clear that there were Alawites fervently on the side of the revolution. It was not a Sunni revolt.

3.   Here we come full circle from our starting point: the same fighters on the same side in Bosnia, Ukraine and Syria.

4.   I can't help thinking of the LTTE (Liberation Tigers of Tamil Eelam), which similarly claimed to be the sole representative of an oppressed group – the Tamils of Sri Lanka – and enforced this claim by wiping out both civilian opposition and militant rivals. The LTTE too attracted socialists and had a large number of women fighters, but any women who challenged the leadership were ruthlessly killed.

5.   It is unquestionable that the Tamils of Sri Lanka have suffered horrific oppression, yet I have always opposed Tamil nationalism, and I later joined with other Tamils to make a critique of the LTTE's totalitarian vision of national self-determination. I have tried to explore the complexities of this position theoretically in Hensman 2015, and fictionally in my novel *Playing Lions and Tigers*.

6.   This was also my position.

8 What Can We Do?

1.   The political thriller entitled 'Fair Game', starring Naomi Watts as Valerie Plame and Sean Penn as Joe Wilson, follows the real events closely.

2.   Doctors Without Borders has roundly condemned US airstrikes on a hospital in Kunduz and Saudi airstrikes on hospitals in Yemen, so they can be treated as reliable witnesses when they say that Russian and Syrian government airstrikes

have deliberately targeted hospitals in Syrian rebel-held territory. Other human rights organizations like Amnesty International and Human Rights Watch are relatively reliable, especially when they confirm each other. On the other hand, we know that Bush, Blair, Trump, Assad and Putin have lied; they are not reliable witnesses.

3.   I use this term to mean any revolution in which a capitalist class comes to power, even if it is not a 'bourgeoisie' in the strict sense.

4.   This references a quotation from Engels in 1845.

5.   A spike in racist attacks was recorded after the Brexit referendum.

6.   A useful introduction to the ICC can be found at www.icc-cpi.int/iccdocs/pids/publications/uicceng.pdf. The text of the Rome Statute can be found at www.icc-cpi.int/nr/rdonlyres/ea9aeff7-5752-4f84-be94-0a655eb30e16/0/rome_statute_english.pdf.

References

Abdo, Geneive, 2009. 'The Rise of the Iranian dictatorship', *Foreign Policy*, 7 October. http://foreignpolicy.com/2009/10/07/the-rise-of-the-iranian-dictatorship/.

Abdul-Ahad, Ghaith, 2005. 'Outside Iraq but deep in the fight', *The Washington Post*, 8 June. www.washingtonpost.com/wp-dyn/content/article/2005/06/07 /AR2005060702026.html.

Abrahamian, Ervand, 2010. 'I am not a speck of dirt, I am a retired teacher', in *The People Reloaded: The Green Movement and the Struggle for Iran's Future*, eds Nader Hashemi and Danny Postel, New York: Melville House, pp. 60–70.

Achcar, Gilbert, 2013a. 'Syria's bloody civil war: an interview with Gilbert Achcar', *Znet*, 27 April. https://zcomm.org/znetarticle/syrias-bloody-civil-war-an-interview -with-gilbert-achcar-by-gilbert-achcar/.

———, 2013b. *The People Want: A Radical Exploration of the Arab Uprising*. London: Saqi Books.

———, 2016. *Morbid Symptoms: Relapse in the Arab Uprising*. London: Saqi Books.

Achcar, Gilbert and David Wearing, 2011. 'After Gaddafi', *New Left Project*, 4 September. www.newleftproject.org/index.php/site/article_comments/after_gaddafi.

Adams, Gordon and Richard Sokolsky, 2015. 'The GOP Plan to Bring Back a Unipolar World', *Foreign Policy*, 30 December. http://foreignpolicy.com/2015/12/30 /rubio-bush-republican-presidential-politics/.

Afary, Janet, 2009. *Sexual Politics in Modern Iran*, Cambridge and New York: Cambridge University Press.

Afary, Janet and Kevin Anderson, 2004. 'Revisiting Foucault and the Iranian revolution', *New Politics*, 10(1), Summer. http://newpol.org/content/revisiting -foucault-and-iranian-revolution.

Ajiri, Denise Hassanzade, 2016. 'Zibakalam on Iranian elections: "We had to choose between bad and worse"', *The Guardian*, 26 February. www.theguardian.com /world/iran-blog/2016/feb/26/iran-zibakalam-grand-reformists-coalistion -includes-intelligence-ministers.

Akbar, Jay, 2016. 'Trump invites Netanyahu to the US "at the first possible opportunity" just hours after the Israeli PM called the president-elect a "true friend"', *MailOnline*, 9 November. www.dailymail.co.uk/news/article-3919902

/Israel-minister-says-Palestinian-state-Trump-win.html.

Aktar, Cengiz, 2015. 'Turning into Kosovo?' *Today's Zaman*, 23 December. www.todayszaman.com/columnist/cengi-z-aktar/turning-into-kosovo _407735.html.

Akyol, Mustafa, 2015. 'Who killed Turkey-PKK peace process?' *Al-Monitor*, 4 August. www.al-monitor.com/pulse/originals/2015/08/turkey-syria-iraq-pkk -peace-process-who-killed-kurds.html.

Alalam, 2016. 'Syrian army troops repel ISIS offensive on military air base in Deir Ezzor', 21 September. http://en.alalam.ir/news/1864136.

Alami, Mona, 2015. 'Is a new approach needed in the war on IS in Iraq?' *Al-Monitor*, 29 December. www.al-monitor.com/pulse/originals/2015/12/iraq-isis -military-measures.html.

———, 2016. 'Jabhat al-Nusra's rebranding is more than a simple name-change', *Al-Monitor*, 5 August. www.al-monitor.com/pulse/originals/2016/08/jabhat -al-nusra-sever-al-qaeda-focus-local-syria.html.

Al Arabiya News, 2014. 'Al-Qaeda detainees reveal ties with Assad', 20 January. http://english.alarabiya.net/en/News/middle-east/2014/01/21/Al-Qaeda -detainees-reveal-ties-with-Assad.html.

Alavi, Nasrin, 2010. 'This magic green bracelet', in *The People Reloaded: The Green Movement and the Struggle for Iran's Future*, eds Nader Hashemi and Danny Postel, New York: Melville House, pp. 209–15.

Al-'Azm, Sadiq Jalal, interviewed by Zuhour Mahmoud, 2013. 'The Syrian revolution and the role of the intellectual', *Al-Jumhuriya*, 27 April. www.aljumhuriya .net/en/en/the-role-of-the-intellectual/interview-with-dr-sadiq.

Alexander, Joshua, 2016. 'Two articles by Mirsaid Sultan-Galiev, 1919', *Anti-imperialism.org*, 8 August. https://antiimperialism.wordpress .com/2016/08/08/two-articles-by-mirsaid-sultan-galiev-1919/.

Alfoneh, Ali, 2007. 'How intertwined are the Revolutionary Guards in Iran's economy?' *American Enterprise Institute*, 22 October. www.aei.org/publication /how-intertwined-are-the-revolutionary-guards-in-irans-economy/.

Alfoneh, Ali, 2008. 'The Revolutionary Guards' role in Iranian politics', *Middle East Quarterly*, 15(4), Fall, pp. 3–14. www.meforum.org/1979/the-revolutionary -guards-role-in-iranian-politics.

Alhamadee, Mousab, 2015. 'Another Syrian group charges that U.S. airstrikes killed civilians', *McClatchy*, 6 May. www.mcclatchydc.com/news/nation-world/world /article24784177.html.

Al Husseini, Huda, 2016. 'Al-Qaeda leaders fight Iran in Syria…and Iran welcomes them!' *Asharq al-Awsat*, 2 June. https://eng-archive.aawsat.com/huda-al -husseini/opinion/al-qaeda-leaders-fight-iran-syriaand-iran-welcomes.

Alizadeh, Hamid, 2016. 'Heavy blows to hardliners opens new era in Iranian politics', *Marxist.com*, 5 March. www.marxist.com/iran-elections-heavy-blows-to -hardliners-opens-new-era-in-iranian-politics.htm.

al-Jaffal, Omar, 2016. 'Iraq's technocrat ministers under threat', *Al-Monitor*, 25 Sep-

tember. www.al-monitor.com/pulse/originals/2016/09/technocrat
-independent-ministers-iraq-reform-militias.html.

Al Jazeera, 2015a. 'Russia vetoes UN genocide resolution on Srebenica', 9 July.
www.aljazeera.com/news/2015/07/russia-vetoes-genocide-resolution
-srebrenica-150708150057291.html.

———, 2015b. 'Hundreds killed by Russian airstrikes in Syria', 29 October.
www.aljazeera.com/news/2015/10/hundreds-killed-russian-air-strikes
-syria-151029130146883.html.

———, 2015c. 'Russia blamed for deadly air strike in Syria's Idlib', 30 November.
www.aljazeera.com/news/2015/11/20-killed-russian-air-strike-syrian-market
-151129082103978.html.

———, 2016a. '"Cowardly weapon" of starvation claims lives of Syrians cut off from
the world', 8 January. http://america.aljazeera.com/articles/2016/1/8/23-die
-of-starvation-in-syrian-town-madaya.html.

———, 2016b. 'Syria's war refugees return home for Eid celebrations', 4 July.
www.youtube.com/watch?v=jqEhZxuCNxU.

———, 2016c. 'Syria's civil war: US and Russia clinch ceasefire deal', 11 September.
www.aljazeera.com/news/2016/09/syria-civil-war-russia-clinch-syria
-deal-160910031517683.html.

———, 2016d. 'Russia and Syria deny striking UN aid convoy in Aleppo', 21 September. www.aljazeera.com/news/2016/09/suspends-syria-aid-convoy
-bombed-160920080213025.html.

———, 2016e. 'Syria war: Aleppo ceasefire extended by Russia', report by Mohammed Adow, 19 October. www.youtube.com/watch?v=9GDP9SstBu4.

———, 2016f. 'Syrian opposition coordinator: "US policy is weak"', 29 September.
www.aljazeera.com/programmes/talktojazeera/2016/09/syrian-opposition
-coordinator-policy-weak-160929150413519.html.

———, 2016g. 'Battle for Mosul: Turkish-trained Nineveh guards on the ground',
report by Jamal Elhayyal, 3 November. www.youtube.com/watch?v
=AJCf3xGnKEM.

———, 2017a. 'Fighting intensifies in Syria's Deraa', 17 February. www.aljazeera.com
/news/2017/02/russia-targets-rebel-held-areas-syria-deraa-170216185755749
.html.

———, 2017b. Syria's war: dozens killed in Idlib airstrikes', www.aljazeera.com
/video/news/2017/03/syrias-war-dozens-killed-idlib-air-strikes
-170316060500481.html.

———, 2017c. 'Syria rebels agree to leave Homs' besieged al-Waer', 13 March. www
.aljazeera.com/news/2017/03/syria-rebels-agree-leave-homs-beseiged-al-waer
-170313134154656.html.

al-Khatieb, Mohammed, 2016a. 'FSA adviser: IS cannot be eliminated without us',
Al-Monitor, 15 January. www.al-monitor.com/pulse/originals/2016/01
/free-syrian-army-leader-regime-russia.html.

———, 2016b. 'Russian air-raid hits Syrian schools', *Al-Monitor*, 4 February. www.

al-monitor.com/pulse/originals/2016/02/syria-aleppo-anjarah-school-russia
-regime-bombing.html.

———, 2016c. 'How Syrian cease-fire has reignited spark of the revolution',
Al-Monitor, 9 March. www.al-monitor.com/pulse/originals/2016/03/syria
-ceasefire-aleppo-peaceful-protests.html.

Alliance of Middle-East Socialists, 2016. 'Iranian university student questions Iran's
role in Syria genocide'. www.allianceofmesocialists.org/iranian-university
-student-questions-irans-role-syria-genocide/.

———, 2017a. 'Statement by Iranian activists opposed to Iran's intervention in
Syria,' 1 January. www.allianceofmesocialists.org/statement-iranian-activists
-opposed-irans-intervention-syria/.

———, 2017b. 'Statement from detainees in Homs Central Prison', 17 October.
www.allianceofmesocialists.org/statement-detainees-homs-central-prison/.

al-Marashi, Ibrahim, 2016. 'How Iraq recaptured Ramadi and why it matters', *Al
Jazeera*, 3 January. www.aljazeera.com/indepth/opinion/2016/01/iraq
-recaptured-ramadi-matters-160103061219164.html.

Alnasrawi, Abbas, 2002. 'Long-term consequences of war and sanctions', in *Iraq's
Economic Predicament*, ed. Kamil A. Mahdi, Reading: Ithaca Press, pp. 343–48.

al-Salhy, Suadad and Cathy Otten, 2014. 'Uncertainty as Iraq election results revealed', *Al Jazeera*, 26 May. www.aljazeera.com/news/middleeast/2014/05
/uncertainty-as-iraq-election-results-revealed-201452611145311548.html.

Alsalmi, Adil, 2016. 'IRGC commander: We control both political and military
arenas in Syria', *Asharq al-Awsat*, 11 February. http://english.aawsat.com
/2016/02/article55347477/irgc-commander-we-control-both-political-and
-military-arenas-in-syria.

al-Shami, Leila, 2015. 'Stop the War and the authoritarian left', *Leila's blog*, 2 December. https://leilashami.wordpress.com/2015/12/02/stop-the-war-and-the
-authoritarian-left/.

———, 2016. 'The assault on Aleppo', 25 February. https://leilashami.wordpress
.com/2016/02/25/the-assault-on-aleppo/#more-368.

Aman, Fatemeh, 2014. 'Iran's Headscarf Politics', Middle East Institute, 3 November.
www.mei.edu/content/article/irans-headscarf-politics.

Amnesty International, 2012. 'Syria: 30 years on, Hama survivors recount the horror', 28 February. www.amnesty.org/en/latest/news/2012/02/syria-years
-hama-survivors-recount-horror/.

———, 2015a. 'Syria: US ally's razing of villages amounts to war crimes', 13 October. www.amnesty.org/en/press-releases/2015/10/syria-us-allys-razing-of
-villages-amounts-to-war-crimes/.

———, 2015b. 'Syria: Russia's shameful failure to acknowledge civilian killings', 23
December. www.amnesty.org/en/latest/news/2015/12/syria-russias-shameful
-failure-to-acknowledge-civilian-killings/.

———, 2016a. 'Iran's hypocrisy exposed as scores of juvenile offenders condemned
to gallows', 26 January. www.amnesty.org/en/latest/news/2016/01/irans

-hypocrisy-exposed-as-scores-of-juvenile-offenders-condemned-to-gallows/.

———, 2016b. 'Banished and dispossessed: Forced displacement and deliberate destruction in Northern Iraq', 15 January. www.amnestyusa.org/research /reports/banished-and-dispossessed-forced-displacement-and-deliberate -destruction-in-northern-iraq.

———, 2017a. 'Yemen 2016/2017'. www.amnesty.org/en/countries/middle-east -and-north-africa/yemen/report-yemen/.

———, 2017b. 'Syria: secret campaign of mass hangings and extermination at Saydnaya Prison', 7 February. www.amnesty.org/en/latest/news/2017/02/syria -investigation-uncovers-governments-secret-campaign-of-mass-hangings -and-extermination-at-saydnaya-prison/.

———, 2017c. 'Syria: "Deadly labyrinth" traps civilians trying to flee Raqqa battle against Islamic State', 24 August. www.amnesty.org/en/latest/news/2017/08 /syria-deadly-labyrinth-traps-civilians-trying-to-flee-raqqa/.

———, 2017d. 'Syria: "Surrender or starve" strategy displacing thousands amounts to crimes against humanity', 13 November. www.amnesty.org/en/latest/news /2017/11/syria-surrender-or-starve-strategy-displacing-thousands-amounts -to-crimes-against-humanity/.

Anarchist Writers, 2008. 'What was the Kronstadt rebellion?', 11 December. http://anarchism.pageabode.com/afaq/append42.html.

Anderson, Jack, 1986. 'Iranians protest treatment of holy man', *Santa Cruz Sentinel*, 6 May.

A-Noufal, Waleed Khaled, Mohammad Abdulssattar Ibrahim and Maria Nelson, 2016. 'Apocalypse delayed: Turkish-backed rebels strike symbolic blow to IS in north Aleppo', *Syria Direct*, 16 October. http://syriadirect.org/news/apocalypse -delayed-turkish-backed-rebels-strike-symbolic-blow-to-is-in-north-aleppo/.

A-Noufal, Waleed Khaled and Maria Nelson, 2016. 'Kurdish-led coalition inches closer to Al-Bab, prompting swift Turkish response', *Syria Direct*, 20 October. http://syriadirect.org/news/kurdish-led-coalition-inches-closer-to-contested -al-bab-prompting-swift-turkish-response/.

Ansari, Ali, 2010. 'Urban myths revisited: The 2009 presidential election', in *The People Reloaded: The Green Movement and the Struggle for Iran's Future*, ed. Nader Hashemi and Danny Postel, New York: Melville House, pp. 345–51.

Arango, Tim and Michael Gordon, 2017. 'Iraqi Prime Minister Arrives in Mosul to Declare Victory Over ISIS', *The New York Times*, 9 July. www.nytimes .com/2017/07/09/world/middleeast/mosul-isis-liberated.html?_r=0.

Arendt, Hannah, 1968. *The Origins of Totalitarianism*. New York: Harcourt.

Aron, Leon, 2011. 'Everything You Think You Know About the Collapse of the Soviet Union Is Wrong', *Foreign Policy*, 20 June. http://foreignpolicy.com /2011/06/20/everything-you-think-you-know-about-the-collapse-of-the -soviet-union-is-wrong/.

Asharq al-Awsat, 2005. 'UN Hariri murder report unravels Abu Adas mystery', 22 October. https://eng-archive.aawsat.com/theaawsat/news-middle-east

/un-hariri-murder-report-unravels-abu-adas-mystery.

Associated Press, 2016a. 'Vladimir Putin accuses Lenin of placing a "time bomb" under Russia', *The Guardian*, 25 January. www.theguardian.com/world/2016 /jan/25/vladmir-putin-accuses-lenin-of-placing-a-time-bomb-under-russia.

———, 2017. 'Death toll from airstrikes on market in Syria climbs to 61', *Business Insider*, 14 November. http://uk.businessinsider.com/ap-death-toll-from -airstrikes-on-market-in-syria-climbs-to-61-2017-11?IR=T.

Axe, David, 2014. 'Iran transformed Syria's army into a militia that will help Assad survive another year', *Reuters*, 17 December. http://blogs.reuters.com/great -debate/2014/12/16/iran-transformed-syrias-army-into-a-militia-that-will -help-assad-survive-another-year/.

Ayoub, Joey, 2016. 'The left's hollow anti-imperialism over Syria', *Middle East Eye*, 30 August. www.middleeasteye.net/columns/left-s-hollow-anti-imperialism -over-syria-1081590395.

Aziz, Omer, 2016. 'Dear Obama, Assad is the problem', *Foreign Policy*, 26 January. http://foreignpolicy.com/2016/01/26/dear-obama-assad-is-the-problem/.

Bagchi, Amiya Kumar, 1972. *Private Investment in India, 1900–1939*, Cambridge: Cambridge University Press.

Bailey, Sydney D., 1955. 'Stalin's Falsification of History: The Case of the Brest-Litovsk Treaty', *Russian Review*, 14(1), January, pp. 24–35.

Balouziyeh, John, 2014. 'Russia's Annexation of Crimea: An Analysis under the Principles of Jus ad Bellum', *LexisNexis*, 14 April. www.lexisnexis.com /legalnewsroom/international-law/b/international-law-blog/archive/2014 /04/14/russia-s-annexation-of-crimea-an-analysis-under-the-principles-of -jus-ad-bellum.aspx.

Barabandi, Bassam, and Tyler Jess Thompson, 2014a. 'Inside Assad's playbook: Time and terror', *MENA Source*, 23 July. www.atlanticcouncil.org/blogs/menasource /inside-assad-s-playbook-time-and-terror.

———, 2014b. 'A Friend of My Father: Iran's Manipulation of Bashar al-Assad', *MENA Source*, 28 August. www.atlanticcouncil.org/blogs/menasource /a-friend-of-my-father-iran-s-manipulation-of-bashar-al-assad.

Baran, Paul A. and Paul M. Sweezy, 1966. *Monopoly Capital: An Essay on the American Economic and Social Order*, Harmondsworth: Penguin.

Barnard, Anne, 2015a. 'Iraqi Campaign to Drive ISIS from Tikrit Reveals Tensions With US', *The New York Times*, 3 March. www.nytimes.com/2015/03/04 /world/middleeast/iraq-drive-against-isis-reveals-tensions-with-us.html?_r=0.

———, 2015b. 'Assad's Forces May Be Aiding New ISIS Surge', *New York Times*, 2 June. www.nytimes.com/2015/06/03/world/middleeast/new-battles -aleppo-syria-insurgents-isis.html?_r=0.

———, 2016. 'ISIS Close to Recapturing Palmyra From Syrian Forces', *New York Times*, 10 December. www.nytimes.com/2016/12/10/world/middleeast /isis-palmyra-syria.html?_r=0.

Barnard, Anne and Hwaida Saad, 2015. 'ISIS Fighters Seize Control of Syrian City of

Palmyra, and Ancient Ruins', *The New York Times*, 20 May. www.nytimes.com
/2015/05/21/world/middleeast/syria-isis-fighters-enter-ancient-city-of
-palmyra.html?_r=0.

Barratt Brown, Michael, 1972. *Essays on Imperialism*, Nottingham: Bertrand Russell
Peace Foundation.

Barry, Ellen, 2011. 'Rally Defying Putin's Party Draws Tens of Thousands', *The New
York Times*, 10 December. www.nytimes.com/2011/12/11/world/europe
/thousands-protest-in-moscow-russia-in-defiance-of-putin.html.

Bashiriyeh, Hossein, interviewed by Danny Postel, 2010. 'Counter-revolution and
revolt in Iran', in *The People Reloaded: The Green Movement and the Struggle
for Iran's Future*, eds Nader Hashemi and Danny Postel, New York: Melville
House, pp. 82–105.

Bassam, Leila and Tom Perry, 2015. 'How Iranian general plotted out Syrian assault
in Moscow', *Reuters*, 6 October. www.reuters.com/article/us-mideast-crisis
-syria-soleimani-insigh-idUSKCN0S02BV20151006.

Batou, Jean, 2015, 'Putin, the War in Ukraine, and the Far Right', *New Politics*, Summer. http://newpol.org/content/putin-war-ukraine-%E2%80%A8and
-far-right.

Bauer, Otto, 1913. 'The explanation of imperialism', *Neuer Zeit*, 24.

Baumann, Nick and Michael Calderone, 2017. 'Trump And His Press Secretary
Flagrantly Lied On Their First Full Day In Office. That Matters', *The Huffington
Post*, 22 January. www.huffingtonpost.in/entry/trump-lies-crowd-size
_us_5884104ae4b0e3a735699697.

Bayat, Asef, 1987. *Workers and Revolution in Iran*, London: Zed Books.

———, 2010. *Life as Politics: How Ordinary People Change the Middle East*, Stanford: Stanford University Press.

BBC News, 2003. 'Flashback: 1991 Gulf War', 20 March. http://news.bbc.co.uk/1
/hi/world/middle_east/2754103.stm.

———, 2005a. 'Schroeder attacked over gas post', 10 December. http://news.bbc
.co.uk/2/hi/europe/4515914.stm.

———, 2005b. 'Killing of Iraq Kurds "genocide"', 23 December. http://news.bbc
.co.uk/1/hi/world/europe/4555000.stm.

———, 2010. 'Gaddafi wants EU cash to stop African migrants', 31 August.
www.bbc.com/news/world-europe-11139345.

———, 2016. 'IS conflict: Falluja detainees "tortured by Shia militias"', 6 June.
www.bbc.co.uk/news/world-middle-east-36458954.

———, 2018. 'Eastern Ghouta Syria: The neighbourhoods below the bombs',
2 March. http://www.bbc.com/news/world-middle-east-43154146.

BBC World Service, 2016. 'The Polygon people', 18 December. www.bbc.co.uk
/programmes/p04km496.

Beauchamp, Zack, 2017. 'The WikiLeaks-Russia connection started way before the
2016 election', *Vox*, 6 January. www.vox.com/world/2017/1/6/14179240
/wikileaks-russia-ties.

Beaulac, Stéphane, 2004. 'The Westphalian model in defining international law: Challenging the myth', *Australian Journal of Legal History*, 9. www.austlii.edu .au/au/journals/AJLH/2004/9.html.

Beaumont, Peter, 2007a. 'How the good land turned bad: Part one', *The Guardian*, 18 March. www.theguardian.com/world/2007/mar/18/iraq.peterbeaumont.

———, 2007b. 'How the good land turned bad: Part two', *The Guardian*, 18 March. www.theguardian.com/world/2007/mar/18/iraq.peterbeaumont1.

———, 2016. 'US abstention allows UN to demand end to Israeli sttlements', *The Guardian*, 23 December. www.theguardian.com/world/2016/dec/23/us -abstention-allows-un-to-demand-end-to-israeli-settlements.

Behrooz, Maziar, 1999. *Rebels With a Cause: The Failure of the Left in Iran*, London: I. B. Tauris.

———, 2005. 'Responses to terror: reflections on Iran's prison system during the Montazeri years (1985–1988)'. http://iranian.com/Behrooz/2005/May /Prison/index.html.

Beinart, Peter, 2014. 'Vladimir Putin, Russian Neocon', *The Atlantic*, 24 March. www.theatlantic.com/international/archive/2014/03/vladimir-putin -russian-neocon/284602/.

Bennetts, Marc, 2015. 'The Kremlin's Holy Warrior', *Foreign Policy*, 24 November. http://foreignpolicy.com/2015/11/24/the-kremlins-holy-warrior-chaplin -putin-russia-turkey-syria/.

Benraad, Myriam, 2011. 'Iraq's tribal "Sahwa": Its rise and fall', *Middle East Policy Council*, XVIII(1), spring. www.mepc.org/journal/middle-east-policy -archives/iraqs-tribal-sahwa-its-rise-and-fall.

Berger, J. M., 2016. 'How white nationalists learned to love Donald Trump', *Politico*, 25 October. www.politico.com/magazine/story/2016/10/donald-trump-2016 -white-nationalists-alt-right-214388.

Berman, Ilan, 2013. 'Why Russia Is Growing More Xenophobic', *The Atlantic*, 22 October. www.theatlantic.com/international/archive/2013/10/why-russia -is-growing-more-xenophobic/280766/.

Bertrand, Natasha, 2016. 'The Assad regime reportedly struck an ominous deal with ISIS to take back a strategic city', *Business Insider*, 3 May. www.businessinsider .in/The-Assad-regime-reportedly-struck-an-ominous-deal-with-ISIS-to-take -back-a-strategic-city/articleshow/52083812.cms.

Bettelheim, Charles, 1976. *Class Struggles in the USSR*, New York: Monthly Review Press. www.marx2mao.com/Other/CSSUi.76i.html.

Bishara, Marwan, 2016. 'Arabs in the eye of history', *Al Jazeera*, 19 January. www .aljazeera.com/indepth/opinion/2016/01/arabs-eye-history -160119093305885.html.

Blackie, Duncan, 1995. 'The left and the Balkan war', *International Socialism*, winter. www.marxists.org/history/etol/newspape/isj2/1995/isj2-069/blackie.htm.

Blanc, Eric, 2016. 'Anti-imperial Marxism: Borderland socialists and the evolution of Bolshevism on national liberation', *International Socialist Review*, 100, http://isreview.org/issue/100/anti-imperial-marxism.

Blank, Stephen, 1990. 'Stalin's first victim: The trial of Sultangaliev', *Russian History/ Histoire Russe*, 17(2), summer, pp. 155–78.

Blumenthal, Max, 2016. 'Inside the Shadowy PR Firm That's Lobbying for Regime Change in Syria', *Alternet*, 3 October. www.alternet.org/world/inside-shadowy -pr-firm-thats-driving-western-opinion-towards-regime-change-syria.

BMJ, 2008. 'Fifty years of violent war deaths from Vietnam to Bosnia: analysis of data from the world health survey program', 26 June. www.bmj.com /content/336/7659/1482.full#REF16.

Bois, Marcel, 2015. 'Hitler Wasn't Inevitable', *Jacobin*, 25 November. www.jacobinmag .com/2015/11/nuremberg-trials-hitler-goebbels-himmler-german-communist -social-democrats/.

Boot, Max, 2017. 'WikiLeaks Has Joined the Trump Administration', *Foreign Policy*, 8 March. http://foreignpolicy.com/2017/03/08/wikileaks-has-joined-the- trump-administration/.

Boothroyd, Mark, 2015. 'The Syrian revolution and the crisis of the antiwar move- ment', *rs21*, 10 September. https://rs21.org.uk/2015/09/10/the-syrian -revolution-and-the-crisis-of-the-anti-war-movement/.

Borger, Julian, 2015. 'Bosnia's bitter, flawed peace deal, 20 years on', *The Guardian*, 10 November. www.theguardian.com/global/2015/nov/10/bosnia-bitter-flawed -peace-deal-dayton-agreement-20-years-on.

———, 2016. 'Trump's plan to seize Iraq's oil: "It's not stealing, we're reimbursing ourselves"', *The Guardian*, 21 September. www.theguardian.com/us-news /2016/sep/21/donald-trump-iraq-war-oil-strategy-seizure-isis.

———, 2017. 'Donald Trump's response to Syria gas attack: blame Obama', *The Guardian*, 5 April. www.theguardian.com/world/2017/apr/04/syria-gas-attack -trump-us-foreign-policy.

Borger, Julian and Spencer Ackerman, 2016. 'Russian planes dropped bombs that destroyed UN aid convoy, US officials say', *The Guardian*, 21 September. www .theguardian.com/world/2016/sep/20/un-aid-convoy-attack-syria-us-russia.

Borger, Julian and Kareem Shaheen, 2016. 'Russia accused of war crimes in Syria at UN Security Council session', *The Guardian*, 26 September. www.theguardian .com/world/2016/sep/25/russia-accused-war-crimes-syria-un-security -council-aleppo.

Bosnia Today, 2016a. 'Islamic State threatens Muslim leader in Osve', 4 January. www.bosniatoday.ba/12249-2/.

Boutilier, Cody, 2014. 'Racism Runs Deep in Russia', *National Review*, 1 February. www .nationalreview.com/article/370083/racism-runs-deep-russia-cody-boutilier.

Bradley, Jane, 2016. 'UN Accused of Allowing Assad Regime to Censor Syria Aid Plan', *Buzzfeed*, 22 January. www.buzzfeed.com/janebradley/un-accused-of -allowing-assad-regime-to-censor-syria-aid-plan#.siBw2ZPo3X.

Brandt, Conrad, 1966 [1958]. *Stalin's Failure in China 1924–1927*, New York: The Norton Library.

Brecher, Jeremy, 2003. 'Solidarity and Student Protests in Iran', *Foreign Policy in Focus*, 1 July. http://fpif.org/solidarity_and_student_protests_in_iran/.

Bridges, Tyler, 2009. 'Now, Ahmadinejad's corner: Chavez, Swaziland and Hamas', *McClatchy*, 17 June. www.mcclatchydc.com/news/nation-world/world /article24542614.html.

Brinded, Lianna, 2016. 'Chilcot: "UK joined the Iraq war before peaceful options were exhausted" and "on flawed intelligence"', *Business Insider*, 16 July. http://uk.businessinsider.com/chilcot-report-iraq-inquiry-executive-summary -statement-key-points-iraq-war-tony-blair-2016-7.

Bruce, James, 2016. 'The growing power of Iran's "international brigade"', *Middle East Online*, 31 October. www.middle-east-online.com/english/?id=79565.

Bunting, Madeleine, 2003. 'Bombs and biscuits', *The Guardian*, 31 March. www.theguardian.com/media/2003/mar/31/Iraqandthemedia.comment.

Butter, David, 2015. 'Does Turkey really get its oil from Islamic State?' *BBC News*, 1 December. www.bbc.com/news/world-europe-34973181.

Bykov, Dmitri, 2016. 'Russia was in charge of its own fate in 1991', *DW*, 20 August. www.dw.com/en/russia-was-in-charge-of-its-own-fate-in-1991/a-19489707.

Cafiero, Giorgio. 2017. 'What's next for GCC-Iraq ties after Sadr's UAE visit?' *Al-Monitor*, 15 August. www.al-monitor.com/pulse/originals/2017/08/saudi -arabia-iran-iraq-sadr-visit-gcc-abu-dhabi.html.

Cain, P. J., and A. G. Hopkins, 2002. *British Imperialism 1688–2000*. Harlow: Pearson Education.

Cambanis, Thanassis, 2016. 'The Syrian Revolution Against Al Qaeda', *Foreign Policy*, 29 March. http://foreignpolicy.com/2016/03/29/the-syrian-revolution -against-al-qaeda-jabhat-al-nusra-fsa/.

Campbell, David, 2002. 'Atrocity, memory, photography: imaging the concentration camps of Bosnia – the case of ITN versus *Living Marxism*, Part 2', *Journal of Human Rights*, 1(2), June, pp. 143–72. www.politicalbeauty.de/trnopolje /Bosnische_Konzentrationslager_files/atrocities_campbell_2.pdf.

Campbell, Scott and Chris Kitching, 2016. 'Malaysia Airlines Flight MH17: Footage shows Russian-made missile that downed plane being trucked into eastern Ukraine', *Mirror*, 28 September. www.mirror.co.uk/news/world-news/mh17 -missile-downed-jet-fired-8931364.

Campos, Rodrigo, 2017. 'Syrian government to blame for April sarin attack: UN', *Reuters*, 27 October. www.reuters.com/article/us-mideast-crisis-syria-un /syrian-government-to-blame-for-april-sarin-attack-u-n-report -idUSKBN1CV3GP?il=0.

Capaccio, Tony, 2014. 'Sale of 4,000 US missiles to Iraq said to be readied', *Bloomberg*, 2 July. www.bloomberg.com/news/articles/2014-07-01/sale-of-4 -000-u-s-missiles-to-iraq-said-to-be-readied.

Carr, E. H., 1966. *The Bolshevik Revolution 1917–1923*, vol. 1. Harmondsworth: Penguin.

———, 1970. *Socialism in One Country 1924–1926*, vol. 2. Harmondsworth:

Penguin.

Chalabi, Fadhil, 2002. 'The oil capacity of post-war Iraq: Present situation and future prospects', in *Iraq's Economic Predicament*, ed. Kamil A. Mahdi, Reading: Ithaca Press, pp. 141–68.

Channel 4, 2011. 'Syria death toll "over 5,000"', 13 December. www.channel4.com /news/syria-death-toll-over-5000.

Chediac Joyce, 2004 [1991]. 'Remember the 1991 Gulf War: The Massacre of Withdrawing Soldiers on "The Highway of Death"', *Global Research*, 8 July. www .globalresearch.ca/remember-the-1991-gulf-war-the-massacre-of-withdrawing -soldiers-on-the-highway-of-death/767.

Chomsky, Noam, 1972/1973. 'The Pentagon Papers and U.S. Imperialism in South East Asia', *The Spokesman*, winter. http://chomsky.info/1972____/#11.

Chorin, Ethan, 2012. *Exit the Colonel: The Hidden History of the Libyan Revolution*, New York: Public Affairs.

Chossudovsky, Michel, 1996. 'NATO and US Government War Crimes in Yugoslavia', *Global Research*, www.globalresearch.ca/articles/CHO202G.html.

———, 2014. 'The U.S. Has Installed a Neo-Nazi Government in Ukraine', *Global Research*, 6 March. www.globalresearch.ca/the-u-s-has-installed-a-neo-nazi -government-in-ukraine/5371554.

Chouikrat, Thilleli, 2016. 'Governing over rubble: Aleppo's exiled opposition council leader speaks', *The New Arab*, 9 December. www.alaraby.co.uk/english/indepth /2016/12/9/mayor-of-rubble-aleppos-exiled-opposition-council-leader -speaks?utm_source=twitter&utm_medium=sf.

Chulov, Martin, 2010. 'Iran brokers behind-the-scenes deal for pro-Tehran government in Iraq', *The Guardian*, 17 October. www.theguardian.com/world/2010 /oct/17/iraq-government-iran-tehran-deal.

———, 2014a. 'Rafik Hariri assassination: trial of Hezbollah suspects begins', 16 January. www.theguardian.com/world/2014/jan/16/rafik-hariri-assassination -trial-hezbollah-suspects.

———, 2014b. 'Isis: the inside story', *The Guardian*, 11 December. www.theguardian .com/world/2014/dec/11/-sp-isis-the-inside-story.

———, 2016. 'Shia leaders in two countries struggle for control over Iraqi state', *The Guardian*, 15 April. www.theguardian.com/world/2016/apr/15/shia-leaders -iraq-iran-ayatollah-ali-sistani.

Chulov, Martin and Angelique Chrisafis, 2012. 'Marie Colvin's killing piles pressure on Assad as civilian death toll rises', *The Guardian*, 22 February. www.theguardian .com/world/2012/feb/22/sunday-times-marie-colvin-killed-syria.

Chulov, Martin and Shiv Malik, 2015. 'Four Syrian hospitals bombed since Russian airstrikes began, doctors say', *The Guardian*, 22 October. www.theguardian.com /world/2015/oct/22/three-syrian-hospitals-bombed-since-russian-airstrikes -began-doctors-say.

Chulov, Martin and Kareem Shaheen, 2015. 'Russia's airstrikes on Syria appear futile with little progress on ground', *The Guardian*, 21 December. www.theguardian

.com/world/2015/dec/21/russias-airstrikes-on-syria-struggle-to-spur
-progress-on-the-ground.

———, 2016a. 'Syria: evacuation of rebels and families from Darayya under way',
The Guardian, 26 August. www.theguardian.com/world/2016/aug/26/syria
-evacuation-of-rebels-and-families-from-darayya-under-way.

———, 2016b. 'Syria aid convoy attack: "the bombardment was continuous"', *The
Guardian*, 21 September. www.theguardian.com/world/2016/sep/20/the
-bombardment-was-continuous-the-rescue-teams-werent-even-able-to-work.

———, 2017. 'Syria chemical weapons attack rises to 70 as Russian narrative is
dismissed', *The Guardian*, 5 April. www.theguardian.com/world/2017/apr/04
/syria-chemical-attack-idlib-province.

Claiborne, Clay, 2013a. 'Nobel Peace Laureate Mairead Maguire's Syria connection',
16 June. http://claysbeach.blogspot.in/2013/06/mairead-maguires-syria
-connection.html.

———, 2013b. 'Whose Seymour Hersh?' 9 December. http://claysbeach.blogspot
.in/2013/12/whose-seymour-hersh.html.

———, 2015. 'How Libya's Muammar Qaddafi handled African refugees and migrants', 21 September. http://claysbeach.blogspot.in/2015/09/how-libyas
-mummar-qaddafi-handled.html.

Cliff, Tony, 1974 [1955]. *State Capitalism in Russia*, London: Bookmarks Publications. www.marxists.org/archive/cliff/works/1955/statecap/index.htm.

Coalition for the International Criminal Court, n.d. 'Delivering on the promise of a
fair, effective and independent Court: The crime of aggression'. http://iccnow
.org/?mod=aggression.

Coates, Ta-Nehisi, 2014. 'Grappling With Holodomor', *The Atlantic*, 3 January.
www.theatlantic.com/international/archive/2014/01/grappling-with-holodomor
/282816/.

Cobain, Ian, 2017. 'How Britain did Gaddafi's dirty work', *The Guardian*, 9 November.
www.theguardian.com/news/2017/nov/09/how-britain-did-gaddafis-dirty
-work-libya.

Cockburn, Patrick, 2014. 'Iraq descends into anarchy: Shia militias abducting and
killing Sunni civilians in revenge for Isis attacks', *Independent*, 14 October.
www.independent.co.uk/news/world/middle-east/shia-militias-abducting-and
-killing-sunni-civilians-in-revenge-for-isis-attacks-9792838.html.

———, 2015. *The Rise of Islamic State*, London: Verso.

———, 2017. 'Who supplies the news?' *London Review of Books*, 2 February.
www.lrb.co.uk/v39/n03/patrick-cockburn/who-supplies-the-news.

Cohen, Nick, 2014. 'Russia Today: why western cynics lap up Putin's TV poison',
The Guardian, 8 November. www.theguardian.com/commentisfree/2014/nov
/08/russia-today-western-cynics-lap-up-putins-tv-poison.

Cole, Juan, 2014. 'Top 10 mistakes of former Iraq PM Nouri al-Maliki (that ruined
his country)', *Informed Comment*, 15 August. www.juancole.com/2014/08
/mistakes-maliki-country.html.

Collective Signatories, 2016. 'Solidarity statement – on the allies we're not proud of: A Palestinian response to troubling discourse on Syria', Europe Solidaire Sans Frontières, 13 October. www.europe-solidaire.org/spip.php?article39221.

Collyns, Sam, 2010. 'Iraq's militia leaders reveal why they turned on al-Qaeda', BBC News, 29 September. www.bbc.co.uk/news/world-middle-east-11417211

Colvin, Marie, 1998. 'The massacre at Prekaz', The Sunday Times, 15 March. www.bosnia.org.uk/news/news_body.cfm?newsid=2842.

Comisso, Ellen T., 1980. 'Yugoslavia in the 1970s: Self-management and bargaining', Journal of Comparative Economics, 4(2), pp. 192–208.

Connell, Tula, 2016. 'Women make historic gains in new Iraq labor law', Solidarity Center AFL-CIO, 23 March. www.solidaritycenter.org/women-make-historic-gains-in-new-iraq-labor-law/.

Conrad, Peter, 2005. 'Call it what you like – this is hell', The Guardian, 20 February. www.theguardian.com/world/2005/feb/20/iraq.middleeast.

Cooke, Miriam, 2012. 'Inside dissident Syria', Al Jazeera, 15 October. www.aljazeera.com/indepth/opinion/2012/10/20121010784881623.html.

Cooke, Shamus, 2014. 'How ISIS finally became Obama's enemy', Counterpunch, 11 August. www.counterpunch.org/2014/08/11/how-isis-finally-became-obamas-enemy/.

Cooper, Charlie, 2016. 'David Nott interview: War surgeon reveals how healthcare workers are being "systematically" targeted in Syria', Independent, 25 January. www.independent.co.uk/news/world/middle-east/david-nott-interview-war-surgeon-reveals-how-healthcare-workers-are-being-targeted-in-syria-a6831646.html.

Corasaniti, Nick, 2016. 'Donald Trump Calls Obama "Founder of ISIS" and Says It Honors Him', The New York Times, 10 August. www.nytimes.com/2016/08/11/us/politics/trump-rally.html.

Cordesman, Anthony H., 2001. 'Saudi Arabia and Iran', Centre for Strategic and International Studies, June. http://csis.org/files/media/csis/pubs/saudi_iran.pdf.

Council on Foreign Relations, 2011. 'UN Resolutions on the Mideast and North Africa', 21 September. www.cfr.org/backgrounder/un-resolutions-mideast-and-north-africa.

Cowell, Alan, 1997. 'Berlin Court Says Top Iran Leaders Ordered Killings', The New York Times, 11 April. www.nytimes.com/1997/04/11/world/berlin-court-says-top-iran-leaders-ordered-killings.html?pagewanted=all.

Craine, Naomi, 2015. 'Putin glorifies despotic czars as examples of Russian pride', The Militant, 79(15), 27 April. www.themilitant.com/2015/7915/791550.html.

Croucher, Shane, 2014. 'Berlin Wall 25th anniversary: How Mikhail Gorbachev prevented a massacre in East Germany', IB Times, 5 November. www.ibtimes.co.uk/berlin-wall-25th-anniversary-how-mikhail-gorbachev-prevented-massacre-east-germany-1473132.

Crowcroft, Orlando, 2015. 'Syrian sniper: US TOW missiles transform CIA-backed Syria rebels into ace marksmen in the fight against Assad', International Business Times, 30 October. www.ibtimes.co.uk/syrian-sniper-us-tow-missiles-transform

-cia-backed-syria-rebels-into-ace-marksmen-fight-against-1526468.

Cunningham, Eric, 2015. 'Islamic State advances over wide swaths of Aleppo, activists report', *The Washington Post*, 9 October. www.washingtonpost.com /world/islamic-state-advances-over-wide-swathes-of-aleppo-activists-report /2015/10/09/4ed462d2-6de9-11e5-91eb-27ad15c2b723_story.html.

Cushman, Thomas, ed., 2005. *A Matter of Principle: Humanitarian Arguments for War in Iraq*. Berkeley: University of California Press.

Dabashi, Hamid, 2010. 'Iran's Green Movement as a Civil Rights Movement', in *The People Reloaded: The Green Movement and the Struggle for Iran's Future*, eds Nader Hashemi and Danny Postel, New York: Melville House, pp. 22–25.

Daher, Joseph, 2016. 'Federalism might be an Option, but Inclusiveness is a Must', *Syria Untold*, 19 July. www.syriauntold.com/en/2016/07/federalism-might -be-an-option-but-inclusiveness-is-a-must/.

Daher, Joseph and Hashem Osseiran, 2017. 'The Likely Winners in the Race to Rebuild Syria', *Syria Deeply*, 13 September. www.newsdeeply.com/syria /community/2017/09/13/the-likely-winners-in-the-race-to-rebuild-syria.

Dalima, Bella, 2014. 'President Rajapaksa receives Peace and Democracy Award from Bolivia', *News1st*, 17 June. http://newsfirst.lk/english/2014/06/president -receives-peace-democracy-award-bolivia/40374.

Davidzon, Vladislav, 2016. 'Kiev Begins Weeklong Memorial To Mark 75 Years Since Babi Yar Massacre', *Tablet*, 28 September. www.tabletmag.com/scroll /214769/kiev-begins-weeklong-memorial-to-mark-75-years-since-babi-yar -massacre.

Davydov, Yuriy, 2000. 'Should Russia Join NATO?' Nato Office of Information and Press: Moscow. www.nato.int/acad/fellow/98-00/davydov.pdf.

Day, Aaron, 2014. 'The 25 most shocking anti-gay stories from Russia so far', *Pink News*, 7 February. www.pinknews.co.uk/2014/02/07/the-25-most-shocking -anti-gay-stories-from-russia-so-far/.

Day, Richard B., 1973. *Leon Trotsky and the Politics of Economic Isolation*, Cambridge: Cambridge University Press.

Dearden, Lizzie, 2017a. 'Iran's Supreme Leader claims gender equality is "Zionist plot" aiming to corrupt role of women in society', *Independent*, 21 March. www.independent.co.uk/news/world/middle-east/iran-supreme-leader -ayatollah-khamenei-gender-equality-women-zionist-plot-society-role -islamic-a7641041.html.

———, 2017b. 'Idlib chemical weapons attack: Hospitals treating patients for "toxic gas" exposure bombed in Syria', *Independent*, 4 April. www.independent.co.uk /news/world/middle-east/syrian-civil-war-chemical-weapons-attack-idlib -hospital-bombed-khan-sheikhoun-gas-sarin-chlorine-a7665816.html.

Dehghan, Saeed Kamali, 2016. 'Iran executed all adult men in one village for drug offences, official reveals', *The Guardian*, 26 February. www.theguardian.com /world/2016/feb/26/all-adult-males-in-one-iranian-village-executed-for -drug-offences-official-says.

Dehghanpisheh, Babak, 2015. 'Iran recruits Pakistani Shi'ites for combat in Syria', *Reuters*, 10 December. www.reuters.com/article/us-mideast-crisis-syria-pakistan-iran-idUSKBN0TT22S20151210.

De Luce, Dan and Henry Johnson, 2016. 'Can the US Control Iran's Militias in the Fight for Fallujah?' *Foreign Policy*, 9 June. http://foreignpolicy.com/2016/06/09/can-the-u-s-control-irans-militias-in-the-fight-for-fallujah-shiite-iraq-isis/.

di Giovanni, Janine, 2016. *The Morning They Came for Us: Dispatches from Syria*, London and New York: Bloomsbury.

Dolgov, Anna, 2014. 'Russia's Igor Strelkov: I Am Responsible for War in Eastern Ukraine', *The Moscow Times*, 21 November. www.themoscowtimes.com/news/article/russia-s-igor-strelkov-claims-responsibility-for-unleashing-war-in-ukraine/511584.html.

———, 2015. 'Putin defends Ribbentrop-Molotov Pact in press conference with Merkel', *The Moscow Times*, 11 May. www.themoscowtimes.com/news/article/putin-defends-ribbentrop-molotov-pact-in-press-conference-with-merkel/520513.html.

Doornbos, Harald and Jenan Moussa, 2016a. 'Present at the Creation', *Foreign Policy*, 16 August. https://foreignpolicy.com/2016/08/16/present-at-the-creation/.

———, 2016b. 'How the Islamic State Seized a Chemical Weapons Stockpile', *Foreign Policy*, 17 August. https://foreignpolicy.com/2016/08/17/how-the-islamic-state-seized-a-chemical-weapons-stockpile/.

———, 2016c. 'The Greatest Divorce in the Jihadi World', *Foreign Policy*, 18 August. http://foreignpolicy.com/2016/08/18/the-greatest-divorce-in-the-jihadi-world/.

DPA, 2016. 'Iraqi premier vows hard line after attacks on Sunni mosques', 19 January. https://aboutcroatia.net/news/world/iraqi-premier-vows-hard-line-after-attacks-sunni-mosques-7002.

Dreyfuss, Bob, 2008. 'Is Iran winning the Iraq war?' *The Nation*, 21 February. www.thenation.com/article/iran-winning-iraq-war/.

Drum, Kevin, 2015. 'Obama's Economic Performance is Even Better Than it Looks', *Mother Jones*, 28 December. www.motherjones.com/kevin-drum/2015/12/obamas-economic-performance-even-better-it-looks.

Drwish, Sardar Mlla, 2016a. 'Raqqa brigade continues to raise flag of Syrian revolution', *Al-Monitor*, 18 March. www.al-monitor.com/pulse/originals/2016/03/syria-raqqa-revolutionaries-brigade-liberation-isis.html.

———, 2016b. 'Why Syria's Kurds are cooperating with Russia', *Al-Monitor*, 22 June. www.al-monitor.com/pulse/originals/2016/06/syria-kurds-accusation-cooperation-regime-russia.html.

Dudin, Vitali and Denis Pilach, 2015. '"Alternative development policy for Ukraine" – Report of Kiev conference 7th Nov 2015', Europe Solidaire Sans Frontieres, 7 November. www.europe-solidaire.org/spip.php?article36473.

Dunayevskaya, Raya. 1941. 'The Union of Socialist Soviet Republics is a capitalist society', *Internal Discussion Bulletin of the Workers' Party*, March. www.marxists

.org/archive/dunayevskaya/works/1941/ussr-capitalist.htm.

Dunn, Brian J., 2009. 'The First Gulf War: Iran and Iraq at War in the 1980s', *The Dignified Rant*, 3 June. http://thedignifiedrant.blogspot.in/2009/06/first-gulf -war-iran-and-iraq-at-war-in.html.

Durdan, Tyler, 2015. 'Something Strange is Taking Place in the Middle of the Atlantic Ocean', *Zero Hedge*, 16 December. www.zerohedge.com/news/2015-12-16 /something-strange-taking-place-middle-atlantic-ocean.

DW, 2015. 'Moscow activists rally against Russian airstrikes in Syria', 18 October. www.dw.com/en/moscow-activists-rally-against-russian-airstrikes-in-syria /a-18789209.

EA Worldview, 2015. 'Syria Report: Russia's Attacks on Civilians, Including Cruise Missiles and Cluster Bombs', 22 November. http://eaworldview.com/2015/11 /syria-report-russias-attacks-on-civilians-including-cruise-missiles-and-cluster -bombs/.

———, 2016. 'Iran daily: Revolutionary Guards Turn Against Nuclear Deal and Government', 6 April. http://eaworldview.com/2016/04/iran-daily -revolutionary-guards-turn-against-nuclear-deal-and-government/.

Ebadi, Shirin, 2003. 'Shirin Ebadi – Biographical', Nobelprize.org, www.nobelprize.org /nobel_prizes/peace/laureates/2003/ebadi-bio.html.

———, 2016. 'Tricked Into Cheating and Sentenced to Death', *The New York Times*, 3 March. www.nytimes.com/2016/03/06/opinion/sunday /tricked-into-cheating-and-sentenced-to-death.html.

Economic and Political Weekly, 1979. 'Iran: Suppressing national minorities', 14(36), 8 September, p. 1540.

———, 1992. 'Bosnia: Western double-talk', 27(42), 17 October, p. 2274.

———, 1993. 'Bosnia: Behind-the-scene players', 28(37), 11 September, p. 1898.

———, 1994. 'Bosnia: Prolonging the conflict', 29(18), 30 April., p. 1042.

Egan, Matt, 2015. 'Obama economy is "amazing," says hedge fund billionaire', *CNN Money*, 9 October. http://money.cnn.com/2015/10/09/investing/hedge -fund-billionaire-defends-obama-chanos/.

Eiglad, Eirik, 2015. 'Statement From the Academic Delegation to Rojava', *New Compass*, 15 January. http://new-compass.net/articles/statement-academic -delegation-rojava.

Elba, Mariam, 2017. 'Why white nationalists love Bashar al-Assad', *The Intercept*, 8 September. https://theintercept.com/2017/09/08/syria-why-white -nationalists-love-bashar-al-assad-charlottesville/.

El-Bar, Karim, 2016. '"Wait until the harvest": Leading figures in Iran, Lebanon, warn of Aleppo fallout', *Middle East Eye*, 20 December. www.middleeasteye. net/news/wait-until-harvest-leading-figures-iran-lebanon-warn-aleppo -fallout-26695263.

Elder, Miriam, 2010. 'Two dead as far-right football fans riot in Moscow', *The Guardian*, 13 December. www.theguardian.com/world/2010/dec/13/two-dead -football-racist-riot-moscow.

———, 2011. 'Mikhail Gorbachev lambasts Vladimir Putin's "sham" democracy', *The Guardian*, 21 February. www.theguardian.com/world/2011/feb/21 /gorbachev-birthday-putin-democracy-russia.

El-Dorar al-Shamia, 2016. 'Kurdish faction of FSA condemns YPG attacks', 17 February. http://en.eldorar.com/node/1500.

El-Shenawi, Eman, 2016. 'Read the damning documents revealing Iran's Al Qaeda links to 9/11', *Al Arabiya*, 19 March. http://english.alarabiya.net/en /perspective/features/2016/03/19/Damning-documents-reveal-9-11-links -between-Iran-and-al-Qaeda.html.

Encyclopædia Britannica, n.d. 'Chechnya'. www.britannica.com/place/Chechnya.

———, 2015. 'Aryan'. www.britannica.com/topic/Aryan.

Engineer, Asghar Ali, 1981. 'Iran: Revolution going awry?', *Economic and Political Weekly*, 16 (25–26), 20 June, pp. 1091–1093.

Erdbrink, Thomas, 2017. 'Rouhani Wins Re-election in Iran by a Wide Margin', *The New York Times*, 20 May. www.nytimes.com/2017/05/20/world/middleeast /iran-election-hassan-rouhani.html.

EU observer, 2013. 'Ukraine pulls the plug on EU treaty', 21 November. https://euobserver.com/foreign/122190.

Euronews, 2013. 'Ukrainian president asks for laws to be passed to facilitate EU association agreement', 3 September. www.euronews.com/2013/09/03 /ukranian-president-asks-for-laws-to-be-passed-to-facilitate-eu-association-/.

Evans, Dominic, 2016. 'Islamic State driven out of Syria's ancient Palmyra city', *Reuters*, 27 March. www.reuters.com/article/us-mideast-crisis-syria-palmyra -idUSKCN0WT04R.

Fadel, Leila and Karen DeYoung, 2010. 'Ayad Allawi's bloc wins most seats in Iraqi parliamentary elections', *The Washington Post*, 27 March. www.washingtonpost .com/wp-dyn/content/article/2010/03/26/AR2010032602196.html.

Faghihi, Rohollah, 2016a. 'Iranians gear up for parliamentary elections', *Al-Monitor*, 16 February. www.al-monitor.com/pulse/originals/2016/02/iran-conservatives -consensus-haddad-adel-larijani.html.

———, 2016b. 'Hardliners move to keep Iranian voters at home', *Al-Monitor*, 25 February. www.al-monitor.com/pulse/originals/2016/02/iran-hardliners -discourage-voter-turnout-parliamentary-vote.html.

———, 2016c. 'Trump's unlikely Iranian fans', *Al-Monitor*, 5 April. www.al-monitor .com/pulse/originals/2016/04/trump-shariatmadari-iranian-republican -hardliners.html.

Falk, Richard, 2000. 'Kosovo revisited', *The Nation*, 22 March. www.thenation.com /article/kosovo-revisited/.

Fanning, Rory and Brian Bean, 2016. 'Opposing war means opposing dictatorship', *SocialistWorker.org*, 24 October. https://socialistworker.org/2016/10/24 /opposing-war-means-opposing-dictators.

Farria, Dewaine, 2012. 'Racism in Russia and the Caucasus', *World Policy Blog*, 13 January. www.worldpolicy.org/blog/2012/01/13/racism-russia-and-caucasus.

Filkins, Dexter, 2013. 'The shadow commander', *The New Yorker*, 30 September.
www.newyorker.com/magazine/2013/09/30/the-shadow-commander.

Filtzer, Don, 1987. *Soviet Workers and Stalinist Industrialisation*, London: Pluto Press.

Fisk, Robert, 2001. *Pity the Nation: Lebanon at War*, Oxford: Oxford University
Press.

———, 2003a. 'Wailing children, the wounded, the dead: victims of the day cluster
bombs rained on Babylon', *Independent*, 3 April.

———, 2003b. 'Is there some element in the US military that wants to take out
journalists?', *Independent*, 9 April.

———, 2015. 'Rafiq Hariri tribunal: Was the former Lebanon PM's assassination
the work of Syria's President Assad?', *Independent*, 13 May. www.independent
.co.uk/news/world/middle-east/rafiq-hariri-tribunal-was-the-former-lebanon
-pms-assassination-the-work-of-syrias-president-assad-10245381.html.

Fitzgerald, Nora and Vladimir Ruvinsky, 2015. 'The Fear of Being Gay in Russia',
Politico, 22 March. www.politico.com/magazine/story/2015/03/russia-putin
-lgbt-violence-116202.

Ford, Glen, 2016. 'Yes, Obama and Clinton created ISIS – too bad Trump can't
explain how it happened', *Global Research*, 19 August. www.globalresearch.ca
/yes-obama-and-clinton-created-isis-too-bad-trump-cant-explain-how-it
-happened/5541695.

France 24, 2012. 'Assad "the butcher" must go, says France's Fabius', 16 August.
www.france24.com/en/20120816-france-syria-assad-butcher-must-go-says
-foreign-minister-laurent-fabius.

Freeman, Colin, 2010. 'Why Ayad Allawi is Iraq's greatest political survivor', *The
Telegraph*, 19 September. www.telegraph.co.uk/news/worldnews/middleeast
/iraq/8011173/Why-Ayad-Allawi-is-Iraqs-greatest-political-survivor.html.

———, 2014, 'Iraq calls publicly for America to bomb Isis terrorists', *The Telegraph*,
18 June. www.telegraph.co.uk/news/worldnews/middleeast/iraq/10910368
/Iraq-calls-publicly-for-America-to-bomb-Isis-terrorists.html.

Friedman, Thomas L., 2015. 'Obama Makes His Case on Iran Nuclear Deal', *The
New York Times*, 14 July. www.nytimes.com/2015/07/15/opinion
/thomas-friedman-obama-makes-his-case-on-iran-nuclear-deal.html?_r=0.

Frontline, n.d. 'NATO's 1999 war against Serbia over Kosovo: Interviews with three
KLA soldiers'. www.pbs.org/wgbh/pages/frontline/shows/kosovo/interviews
/kla.html.

Fuentes, Carlos. 1963. 'The Argument of Latin America: Words for the North
Americans', *Monthly Review*, 14(9), January, pp. 487–504.

Fuller, Liz, 2015. 'The unstoppable rise of Ramzan Kadyrov', *Radio Free Europe Radio
Liberty*, 19 January. www.rferl.org/a/profile-ramzan-kadyrov-chechnya-russia
-putin/26802368.html.

Furr, Grover, 2015. 'Remarks on interview of Professor Stephen Cohen on
RT.COM on November 1, 2015'. https://msuweb.montclair.edu/~furrg
/research/furr_cohen_rt11012015.html.

Galeotti, Mark, 2016. 'Putin is Playing by Grozny Rules in Aleppo', *Foreign Policy*, 29
    September. http://foreignpolicy.com/2016/09/29/putin-is-playing-by
    -chechen-rules-in-aleppo-syria-russia/.

Galyon, Shiyam, 2016. 'Besieged, Twice-over: Acitivists Push for Food Drops in
    Deir Ezzor', *Warscapes*, 19 April. http://warscapes.com/opinion/besieged
    -twice-over-activists-push-food-drops-deir-ezzor.

Gambill, Gary C., 2001. 'Is Syria losing control of Lebanon?' *Middle East Quarterly*,
    spring, 8(2), pp. 41–49. www.meforum.org/28/is-syria-losing-control-of-lebanon.

Garnsey, Monica, 2006. 'Death of a teenager', *The Guardian*, 27 July. www.theguardian
    .com/media/2006/jul/27/iran.broadcasting.

Gatehouse, Gabriel, 2016. 'The Russians who fear a war with the West', *BBC News*,
    25 October. www.bbc.com/news/world-europe-37766688.

Gazdar, Haris and Athar Hussain, 2002. 'Crisis and Response: A Study of the Im-
    pact of Economic Sanctions in Iraq', in *Iraq's Economic Predicament*, ed. Kamil
    A. Mahdi, Reading: Ithaca Press, pp. 31–83.

Geist, Dan, 2011. '"A Darker Horizon": The Assassination of Shapour Bakhtiar', *PBS
    Frontline Tehran Bureau*, 6 August. www.pbs.org/wgbh/pages/frontline
    /tehranbureau/2011/08/a-darker-horizon-the-assassination-of-shapour
    -bakhtiar.html.

Gellman, Barton, 1991. 'Allied air war struck broadly in Iraq', *The Washington Post*,
    23 June. www.washingtonpost.com/archive/politics/1991/06/23/allied
    -air-war-struck-broadly-in-iraq/e469877b-b1c1-44a9-bfe7-084da4e38e41/.

George, Alan, 2003. *Syria: Neither Bread Nor Freedom*. London: Zed.

Gerasimenko, Olesya, 2016. 'Alexei Gasparov: What politics?' *The Russian Reader*, 1
    November. https://therussianreader.com/tag/bolotnaya-square-case/.

GFBV (Gesellschaft Für Bedrohte Völker), 2012. 'Memorial ceremony in Berlin for
    8372 victims of Srebrenica: human rights campaigners recall how genocide claimed
    the lives of 150,000 Bosnians', 7 October. www.gfbv.de/en/news/memorial
    -ceremony-in-berlin-for-8372-victims-of-srebrenica-human-rights-campaigners
    -recall-how-genocide-claimed-the-lives-of-150000-bosnians-5586-1/.

Gheissari, Ali and Vali Nasr, 2009. *Democracy in Iran: History and the Quest for
    Liberty*, Oxford: Oxford University Press.

GICJ (Geneva International Centre for Justice), 2013. 'Urgent appeal on the massa-
    cre of Iraqi demonstrators at Al-Hawija', April. www.gicj.org/un-special
    -procedures-appeals/iraq/245-gicj-urgent-appeal-on-the-massacre-of-iraqi
    -demonstrators-in-hawija.

Gill, Joe, 2016. 'Still fighting the last war: Syria and the Western peace movement',
    Middle East Eye, 28 October. www.middleeasteye.net/essays/still-fighting-last
    -war-syria-and-western-peace-movement-2070686647.

Gilligan, Emma, 2010. *Terror in Chechnya: Russia and the Tragedy of Civilians in
    War*, Princeton: Princeton University Press.

Goble, Paul, 2014. 'Kazan Tatars see no future for themselves in Putin's Russia', *The
    Interpreter*, 24 March. www.interpretermag.com/kazan-tatars-see-no-future

-for-themselves-in-putins-russia/.

Goldman, Emma, 1923. *My Disillusionment in Russia*. www.marxists.org/reference
/archive/goldman/works/1920s/disillusionment/ch27.htm.

Goodenough, Patrick, 2014. 'Kurdish gov't, "alone" in fight against ISIS, appeals for
airstrikes and urgent aid', *CNS News*, 7 August. http://cnsnews.com/news
/article/patrick-goodenough/kurdish-gov-t-alone-fight-against-isis-appeals
-airstrikes-and-urgent.

Goodway, David, 2006. *Anarchist Seeds Beneath the Snow: Left-Libertarian Thought
and British Writers from William Morris to Colin Ward*, Liverpool: Liverpool
University Press.

Gordon, Michael, 2017. 'Report Rebuts Russia's Claim of Restraint in Syrian Bombing Campaign', *The New York Times*, 12 February. www.nytimes.com/2017
/02/12/us/politics/russia-syria-aleppo-bombing-campaign-restraint.html.

Gordon, Michael R. and Wesley S. Morgan, 2012. 'The General's Gambit', *Foreign
Policy*, 1 October. http://foreignpolicy.com/2012/10/01/the-generals-gambit/.

Goya, Abbas, 2012. 'War and peace in Iran', *Economic and Political Weekly*, 47(9), 3
March, pp. 13–17.

Graham-Brown, Sarah, 2002. 'Humanitarian needs and international assistance in
Iraq aafter the Gulf War', in *Iraq's Economic Predicament*, ed. Kamil A. Mahdi,
Reading: Ithaca Press, pp. 267–88.

Graham-Harrison, Emma, 2016. 'Reality check: are US-led airstrikes on Syrians as
bad as Russia's?', *The Guardian*, 12 October. www.theguardian.com/world
/reality-check/2016/oct/12/reality-check-are-us-led-airstrikes-on-syrians
-as-bad-as-russias.

Gray, Rosie, 2017. 'Bill Browder's Testimony to the Senate Judiciary Committee', *The
Atlantic*, 25 July. www.theatlantic.com/politics/archive/2017/07/bill
-browders-testimony-to-the-senate-judiciary-committee/534864/.

Gregory, Paul, 2009. 'Did Stalin poison Lenin?', 15 June. http://paulgregorysblog
.blogspot.in/2009/06/did-stalin-poison-lenin.html.

Grey, Stephen, Tom Bergin, Sevgil Musaieva and Roman Anin, 2014. 'Special report:
Putin's allies channeled billions to Ukraine oligarch', *Reuters*, 26 November.
www.reuters.com/article/russia-capitalism-gas-special-report-pix
-idUSL3N0TF4QD20141126.

Groll, Elias, 2016. 'The U.S. wants to design safer anti-aircraft missiles for Syria's
rebels', *Foreign Policy*, 20 April. http://foreignpolicy.com/2016/04/20/the-u-s
-wants-to-design-safer-anti-aircraft-missiles-for-syrias-rebels/.

Gutman, Roy, 1992. 'Death camps: Survivors tell of captivity, mass slaughter in
Bosnia', *American Journalism Review*, June.

———, 2015a. 'New allies in northern Syria don't seem to share U.S. goals', *Mc-
Clatchy*, 27 October. www.mcclatchydc.com/news/nation-world/world
/article41559747.html.

———, 2015b. 'What really happened to the US train-and-equip programme in
Syria?' *McClatchy*, 21 December. www.mcclatchydc.com/news/nation-world

/world/article50919765.html.

———, 2016a. 'The UN Knew for Months That Madaya Was Starving', *Foreign Policy*, 15 January. http://foreignpolicy.com/2016/01/15/u-n-knew-for-months-madaya-was-starving-syria-assad/.

———, 2016b. 'How the UN Let Assad Edit the Truth of Syria's War', *Foreign Policy*, 27 January. http://foreignpolicy.com/2016/01/27/syria-madaya-starvation-united-nations-humanitarian-response-plan-assad-edited/.

Guzina, Dejan, 2004. 'Why Yugoslavia failed', *Federations*, 4(1), pp. 18–20. www.forumfed.org/libdocs/Federations/V5N1SEen-yu-Guzina.pdf.

Habibi, 2016. 'Jeremy Corbyn and Khomeinist Iran,' Harry's Place, 1 November. http://hurryupharry.org/2016/09/01/jeremy-corbyn-and-khomeinist-iran/.

Hafezi, Parisa and Babak Dehghanpisheh, 2017. 'Iranians demanding change deliver emphatic victory for Rouhani', *HuffPost*, 20 May. www.huffingtonpost.com/entry/iran-presidential-elections-rouhani-change_us_59202f3fe4b03b485cb1e4af.

Haid, Haid, 2016. 'Turkey's de facto safe zone in northern Syria', *NOW*, 27 September. https://now.mmedia.me/lb/en/commentaryanalysis/567385-turkeys-de-facto-safe-zone-in-northern-syria.

Hajj, Elie, 2013. 'Lebanon's Shiites Begin to Question Hezbollah', *Al-Monitor*, 12 April. www.al-monitor.com/pulse/originals/2013/04/hezbollah-lebanon-fighters-syria-questions.html.

Halliday, Fred, 1979. *Iran: Dictatorship and Development*, Harmondsworth: Penguin Books.

Hamad, Sam, 2017. 'Comrade Corbyn supports Russian imperialism in Syria', *TheNewArab*, 15 December. www.alaraby.co.uk/english/comment/2017/12/15/comrade-corbyn-supports-russian-imperialism-in-syria.

Hammer, Joshua, 2008. 'Getting Away With Murder?', *The Atlantic*, December. www.theatlantic.com/magazine/archive/2008/12/getting-away-with-murder/307149/.

Hanchett, Ian, 2015. 'Trump on Putin controlling Syria: "OK, fine," him fighting ISIS "wonderful thing," "very little downside"', *Breitbart*, 29 September. www.breitbart.com/video/2015/09/29/trump-on-putin-controlling-syria-okay-fine-him-fighting-isis-wonderful-thing-very-little-downside/.

Hands Off the People of Iran, 2007. 'Iran Controversy at Stop the War Coalition AGM', 17 October. www.labournet.net/other/0710/hopi1.html.

Hanna, Asaad, 2015. 'Despite Russian airstrikes, FSA continues to confront regime', *Al-Monitor*, 20 November. www.al-monitor.com/pulse/originals/2015/11/free-syrian-army-tow-missiles-regime-russia-air-cover.html.

Hanna, Jason, Ben Brumfield and Christiane Amanpour, 2015. 'Srebrenica ceremony: Crowd chases Serbian PM as more victims buried', *CNN*, 17 July. http://edition.cnn.com/2015/07/11/europe/bosnia-srebrenica-massacre-commemoration/.

Hansen, Lene, 2006. *Security as Practice: Discourse Analysis and the Bosnian War*, Abingdon and New York: Routledge.

Harding, Luke, 2014. 'We should beware Russia's links with Europe's right', *The Guardian*, 8 December. www.theguardian.com/commentisfree/2014/dec/08/russia-europe-right-putin-front-national-eu.

Harfoush, Mohammed, 2013. 'Hezbollah, Part 1: Origins and Challenges', *Al-Monitor*, 11 July. www.al-monitor.com/pulse/originals/2013/02/hezbollah-beginnings-challenges.html.

Harlan, Chico, 2015. 'How plunging oil prices have created a volatile new force in the global economy', *The Guardian*, 21 July. www.theguardian.com/business/2015/jul/21/falling-oil-prices-fracking-us-iran-saudi-arabia-opec.

Hartmann, Florence and Ed Vulliamy, 2015. 'How Britain and the US decided to abandon Srebrenica to its fate', *The Guardian*, 4 July. www.theguardian.com/world/2015/jul/04/how-britain-and-us-abandoned-srebrenica-massacre-1995.

Harvey, David, 2003. *The New Imperialism*, Oxford: Oxford University Press.

Hashem, Ali, 2013. 'SNC cites Hezbollah Role in Syria', *Al-Monitor*, 19 February. www.al-monitor.com/pulse/originals/2013/02/hezbollah-in-syria.html.

———, 2015. 'The many names of Abu Bakr al-Baghdadi', *Al-Monitor*, 23 March. www.al-monitor.com/pulse/originals/2015/03/isis-baghdadi-islamic-state-caliph-many-names-al-qaeda.html.

Hashemi, Nader, 2017. 'Surely some mistake. Why did ISIS attack Iran?' *Newsweek*, 15 June. www.newsweek.com/surely-some-mistake-why-did-isis-attack-iran-625253.

Hassan, Budour, 2016. 'How the Syrian revolution has transformed me', 19 May. https://budourhassan.wordpress.com/2016/05/19/how-the-syrian-revolution-has-transformed-me/.

Hassan, Hassan, 2017. 'The Battle for Raqqa and the Challenges after Liberation', *CTC Sentinel*, 10(6), June/July, pp. 1–10. https://ctc.usma.edu/v2/wp-content/uploads/2017/07/CTC-Sentinel_Vol10Iss6-4.pdf.

Hassan, Hassan and Bassam Barabandi, 2015. 'Kurds Can't Be Syria's Saviors', *Foreign Policy*, 18 November. http://foreignpolicy.com/2015/11/18/kurds-cant-be-syrias-saviors/.

Hassan, Omar, 2017. 'The origins of the criminal Assad dynasty', *Marxist Left Review*, 13, summer. http://marxistleftreview.org/index.php/no-13-summer-2017/141-the-origins-of-the-criminal-assad-dynasty.

Haugbolle, Sune, 2010. *War and Memory in Lebanon*, Cambridge: Cambridge University Press.

Hawramy, Fazel, Shalaw Mohammed and Luke Harding, 2014. 'Inside Islamic State's oil empire: how captured oilfields fuel Isis insurgency', *The Guardian*, 19 November. www.theguardian.com/world/2014/nov/19/-sp-islamic-state-oil-empire-iraq-isis.

Hedges, Chris, 1998. 'Albanians Bury 24 Villagers Slain by Serbs', *The New York Times*, 4 March. www.nytimes.com/1998/03/04/world/albanians-bury-24-villagers-slain-by-the-serbs.html.

Hekmat, Mansoor, 1987. 'Left Nationalism and Working Class Communism'.

www.m-hekmat.com/en/2530en.html.

———, 2000. 'June 20, 1981: One of the Greatest Crimes of the 20th Century', *Radio International*, www.m-hekmat.com/en/1910en.html.

———, 2001. 'The obvious lessons of Berlin'. http://m-hekmat.com/en/1700en.html.

Heller, Stanley, 2016. 'A challenge to the Green Party on Syria', *Economic Uprising*, 4 August. http://economicuprising.com/?p=1832#more-1832.

Hensman, Rohini, 2009. 'The role of socialists in the civil war in Sri Lanka', *Platypus Review* 13, July. http://platypus1917.org/2009/07/01/the-role-of-socialists-in-the-civil-war-in-sri-lanka/.

———, 2011. *Workers, Unions, and Global Capitalism: Lessons from India*, New York: Columbia University Press.

———, 2015. 'Post-war Sri Lanka: Exploring the path not taken', *Dialectical Anthropology*, 39, pp. 273–93.

Herman, Edward S., 2005. 'The Politics of the Srebrenica Massacre', *Global Research*, 7 July. www.globalresearch.ca/the-politics-of-the-srebrenica-massacre/660.

Higgins, Eliot, 2016. 'Confirmed: Russian Bomb Remains Recovered from Syrian Red Crescent Aid Convoy Attack', *Bellingcat*, 22 September. www.bellingcat.com/news/mena/2016/09/22/russian-bomb-remains-recovered-syrian-red-crescent-aid-convoy-attack/.

Hilferding, Rudolf, 1981 [1910]. *Finance Capital: A Study of the Latest Phase of Capitalist Development*, trans. Morris Watnick and Sam Gordon, London: Routledge and Kegan Paul.

Hilterman, Joost, 2016. 'Chemical wonders', *London Review of Books*, 38(3), 4 February. www.lrb.co.uk/v38/n03/joost-hiltermann/chemical-wonders.

Himka, John-Paul, 1986. 'Introduction', in Roman Rosdolsky, *Engels and the 'Nonhistoric' Peoples: The National Question in the Revolution of 1848*, Glasgow: Critique Books, pp. 1–13.

Hinnebusch, Raymond, 2001. *Syria: Revolution from Above*, London and New York: Routledge.

Hiro, Dilip, 1985. *Iran Under the Ayatollahs*, London: Routledge and Kegan Paul.

History Commons, n.d. 'Neoconservative Think Tank Influence on US policies: Project for the New American Century'. www.historycommons.org/timeline.jsp?timeline=neoconinfluence&neoconinfluence_neoconservative_think_tanks=neoconinfluence_pnac.

Hitchens, Christopher, 1999. 'Srebrenica Revisited', *The Nation*, 1 April. www.thenation.com/article/srebrenica-revisited/.

HNC (High Negotiations Commission), 2016. 'Executive Framework for a Political Solution Based on the Geneva Communiqué (2012)', September. http://english.riadhijab.com/userfiles/HNC%20Executive%20Summary%20-%20English.pdf.

Hoare, Marko Attila, 2003. 'Nothing is Left', *Bosnia Report*, 36, October–December. www.bosnia.org.uk/bosrep/report_format.cfm?articleid=1041&reportid=162.

Hobson, J. A., 1902. *Imperialism: A Study*, New York: James Pott & Company.

Hobsbawm, E. J., 1990. *Nations and Nationalism Since 1780: Programme, Myth, Reality*, Cambridge: Cambridge University Press.

Hodge, Nathan, 2017. 'Russia's Putin praises Trump in wide-ranging year-end press conference', *The Wall Street Journal*, 14 December. www.marketwatch.com /story/russias-putin-praises-trump-in-wide-ranging-year-end-press-conference -2017-12-14.

Hof, Frederic C., 2014. 'Should the West Work With Assad?', *Atlantic Council*, 10 July. www.atlanticcouncil.org/blogs/menasource/syria-should-the-west -work-with-assad.

Hoff, Brad, 2015a. 'A Marine in Syria', *Medium*, 27 April. https://medium.com /news-politics/a-marine-in-syria-d06ff67c203c.

———, 2015b. 'ISIS leader Omar al-Shishani Fought Under US Umbrella as Late as 2013', *Levant Report*, 18 September. http://levantreport.com/2015/09/18 /isis-leader-omar-al-shishani-fought-under-u-s-umbrella-as-late-as-2013/.

Hoodfar, Homa, 1999. *The Women's Movement in Iran: Women at the Crossroads of Secularization and Islamization*, Grabels: Women Living Under Muslim Laws.

Hopkins, Nick and Emma Neals, 2016. 'UN pays tens of millions to Assad regime under Syria aid programme', *The Guardian*, 29 August. www.theguardian.com /world/2016/aug/29/un-pays-tens-of-millions-to-assad-regime-syria-aid -programme-contracts.

Hosler, Karen, and Mark Matthews, 1995. 'Senate votes to lift Bosnia arms embargo', *The Baltimore Sun*, 27 July. http://articles.baltimoresun.com/1995-07-27 /news/1995208099_1_arms-embargo-bosnia-peacekeepers.

Hubbard, Ben, 2017. 'Iran Out to Remake Middle East with Arab Enforcer: Hezbollah', *The New York Times*, 27 August. www.nytimes.com/2017/08/27 /world/middleeast/hezbollah-iran-syria-israel-lebanon.html?utm_source =Sailthru&utm_medium=email&utm_campaign=EBB%2008.28.2017 &utm_term=Editorial%20-%20Early%20Bird%20Brief&_r=1.

Hudson, John, 2016. 'Russia Bombs Offices of American NGO in Syria, Says Group', *Foreign Policy*, 11 January. https://foreignpolicy.com/2016/01/11 /russia-bombs-offices-of-american-ngo-in-syria-says-group/.

Hukanović, Rezak, 1996. 'The evil at Omarska', *The New Republic*, 12 February, 24–29.

Human Rights Council, 2009a. 'Human Rights Council Adopts Resolution on Assistance to Sri Lanka in the Promotion and Protection of Human Rights', 27 May. www.ohchr.org/EN/NewsEvents/Pages/DisplayNews.aspx ?NewsID=9105&LangID=E.

———, 2009b. 'Council Concludes Special Session After Adopting Resolution on Assistance to Sri Lanka in Promotion and Protection of Human Rights', 27 May. https://reliefweb.int/report/sri-lanka/council-concludes-special -session-after-adopting-resolution-assistance-sri-lanka.

HRW (Human Rights Watch), 1990. *Human Rights in Iraq*, New Haven: Yale University Press. www.hrw.org/sites/default/files/reports/Iraq90N.pdf.

———, 1991. 'Needless deaths in the Gulf War'. http://pantheon.hrw.org/reports /1991/gulfwar/.

———, 1993. 'Genocide in Iraq: The Anfal Campaign Against the Kurds'. www.hrw.org/reports/1993/iraqanfal/.

———, 2002. 'International Justice for Women: The ICC Marks a New Era', 1 July. www.hrw.org/legacy/campaigns/icc/icc-women.htm.

———, 2006. 'Libya: June 1996 Killings at Abu Salim prison', 27 June. www.hrw.org/news/2006/06/27/libya-june-1996-killings-abu-salim-prison.

———, 2007. 'No room to breathe: State repression of human rights activism in Syria', 16 October. www.hrw.org/report/2007/10/16/no-room-breathe /state-repression-human-rights-activism-syria.

———, 2013. 'Attacks on Ghouta: Analysis of alleged use of chemical weapons in Syria', 10 September. www.hrw.org/report/2013/09/10/attacks-ghouta /analysis-alleged-use-chemical-weapons-syria.

———, 2014a. '"No one is safe": The Abuse of Women in Iraq's Criminal Justice System', 6 February. www.hrw.org/report/2014/02/06/no-one-safe /abuse-women-iraqs-criminal-justice-system.

———, 2014b. 'Iraq: Don't Legalize Marriage for 9-year-olds', 11 March. www.hrw.org/news/2014/03/11/iraq-dont-legalize-marriage-9-year-olds.

———, 2015. 'Iraqi Kurdistan: Arabs Displaced, Cordoned off, Detained', 25 February. www.hrw.org/news/2015/02/25/iraqi-kurdistan-arabs-displaced -cordoned-detained.

———, 2016a. 'Iraq: Possible War Crimes by Shia militia', 31 January. www.hrw.org/news/2016/01/31/iraq-possible-war-crimes-shia-militia.

———, 2016b. 'Iraq: Fallujah Abuses Test Control of Militias', 9 June. www.hrw.org/news/2016/06/09/iraq-fallujah-abuses-test-control-militias.

———, 2017a. 'Syria: Cordinated Chemical Attacks on Aleppo', 13 February. www.hrw.org/news/2017/02/13/syria-coordinated-chemical-attacks-aleppo.

———, 2017b. 'Iraq: Civilian Casualties Mount in West Mosul: Coalition, Iraqi Forces Taking Inadequate Precautions', 6 June. www.hrw.org/news/2017/06 /06/iraq-civilian-casualties-mount-west-mosul.

Humphreys, R. Stephen, 1999. *Between Memory and Desire: The Middle East in a Troubled Age*, Berkeley and Los Angeles: University of California Press.

Hunter, Shireen T., 2014. *Iran Divided: The Historical Roots of Iranian Debates on Identity, Culture, and Governance in the Twenty-First Century*, Lanham, MD.: Rowman and Littlefield.

Hussein, Sadam, 2009 [1971]. 'Women: One Half of our Society', in his *Social and Foreign Affairs in Iraq*, trans. Khalid Kishtainy, Abingdon: Routledge.

ICC (International Criminal Court), 1998. 'Rome Statute of the International Criminal Court'. https://www.icc-cpi.int/nr/rdonlyres/ea9aeff7-5752-4f84 -be94-0a655eb30e16/0/rome_statute_english.pdf.

———, n.d. 'Understanding the International Criminal Court'. www.icc-cpi.int /iccdocs/pids/publications/uicceng.pdf.

———, 2010. 'Adoption of amendments on the crime of aggression', 11 June. https://asp.icc-cpi.int/iccdocs/asp_docs/RC2010/AMENDMENTS/CN.651.2010-ENG-CoA.pdf.

Iconic Photos, 2009. 'Trnopolje, Bosnia, 1992'. https://iconicphotos.wordpress.com/2009/05/26/trnopolje-bosnia-1992/.

ICRtoP (International Coalition for the Responsibility to Protect), n.d. 'An introduction to the Responsibility to Protect'. www.responsibilitytoprotect.org/index.php/about-rtop.

Idiz, Semih, 2016. 'What's behind Ankara's "deafening silence" on Aleppo?', Al-Monitor, 4 October. www.al-monitor.com/pulse/originals/2016/10/turkey-syria-ankara-deafening-silence-over-aleppo.html.

IHRI (International Campaign for Human Rights in Iran), 2011. 'A Brief History of "House Arrests" and Detentions in "Safe Houses": What Will Be the Fate of Disappeared Leaders?', 6 March. www.iranhumanrights.org/2011/03/history-of-house-arrests/.

———, 2015a. 'The Emergence of Vigilante Groups', 23 February. www.iranhumanrights.org/2015/02/womenreport-the-emergence-of-vigilante-groups/.

———, 2015b. 'Highest Ranked Woman in Iran's Government to Sue Extremist Publication', 31 December. www.iranhumanrights.org/2015/12/shahindokht-mowlaverdi/.

———, 2016. 'Hardliners Handpick Candidates to Block Moderates and Rig Elections', 9 February. www.iranhumanrights.org/2016/02/elections/.

Iley, Chrissy, 2011. 'Valerie Plame Wilson: the housewife CIA spy who was "fair game" for Bush', The Telegraph, 15 February. www.telegraph.co.uk/culture/film/8318075/Valerie-Plame-Wilson-the-housewife-CIA-spy-who-was-fair-game-for-Bush.html.

Institute for the Study of War, 2010. 'Fact sheet: Ibrahim al-Jaafari'. www.understandingwar.org/reference/fact-sheet-ibrahim-al-jaafari.

International Committee for Crimea, n.d. 'Ethnic composition of Crimea'. www.iccrimea.org/population.html.

International Crisis Group, 2013. 'Make or Break: Iraq's Sunnis and the State', Middle East Report 144, 14 August. www.crisisgroup.org/middle-east-north-africa/gulf-and-arabian-peninsula/iraq/make-or-break-iraq-s-sunnis-and-state.

Ioffe, Julia, 2017. 'The Secret Correspondence Between Donald Trump Jr. and WikiLeaks', 13 November. www.theatlantic.com/politics/archive/2017/11/the-secret-correspondence-between-donald-trump-jr-and-wikileaks/545738/.

Iran Constitution. www.servat.unibe.ch/icl/ir00000_.html.

Iran Human Rights Review, 2014. 'Sexual torture of women political prisoners in the Islamic Republic of Iran', January. www.ihrr.org/ihrr_article/violence-en_sexual-torture-of-women-political-prisoners-in-the-islamic-republic-of-iran/.

Iraqi LGBT, 2006. 'Sistani removes "death to gays" fatwa', 12 May. http://iraqilgbtuk.blogspot.co.uk/2006/05/sistani-removes-death-to-gays-fatwa.html.

Iraqi Spring, 2013. 'From Samarra', 15 March. www.flickr.com/photos/92086970
@N02/8559634860/.

Ireland, Doug, 2006. 'Iran Exports Anti-Gay Pogrom to Iraq', *In These Times*, 31
May. http://inthesetimes.com/article/2659.

Ismail, Nehad, 2016. 'Palmyra: A Choreographed Liberation', *The What & The Why*,
31 March. www.thewhatandthewhy.com/palmyra-a-choreographed-liberation/.

Issa, Ali, 2015. *Against All Odds: Voices of Popular Struggle in Iraq*, Washington, DC:
Tadween Publishing.

Jabar, Faleh A., 1992. 'Why the Uprisings Failed', *Middle East Report*, 176(22), May/
June. www.merip.org/mer/mer176/why-uprisings-failed.

Jacinto, Leela, 2015. 'Sympathy for the Syrian Devil', *Foreign Policy*, 24 November.
http://foreignpolicy.com/2015/11/24/sympathy-for-the-syrian-devil
-france-hollande-russia-putin/.

Jaffe, Greg and Adam Entous, 2017. 'Trump ends covert CIA program to arm
anti-Assad rebels in Syria, a move sought by Moscow', *The Washington Post*, 19
July. www.washingtonpost.com/world/national-security/trump-ends-covert
-cia-program-to-arm-anti-assad-rebels-in-syria-a-move-sought-by-moscow
/2017/07/19/b6821a62-6beb-11e7-96ab-5f38140b38cc_story.html.

James, C. L. R. 1986. 'Fully and absolutely assured', in C. L. R. James, Raya
Dunayevskaya and Grace Lee, *State Capitalism and World Revolution*, Chicago:
Charles H. Kerr Publishing Company, vii–x.

Jawad, Saad N. and Sawsan I. al-Assaf, 2013. 'Iraq today: The failure of re-shaping a
society on sectarian and quota lines', *LSE blogs*. http://blogs.lse.ac.uk/ideas
/2013/06/iraq-today-the-failure-of-re-shaping-a-state-on-sectarian-and
-quota-lines/.

Johnson, Bridget, 2014. 'Assad and ISIS More "Intimately Interwound" Than Ever',
PJ Media, 11 July. https://pjmedia.com/blog/assad-and-isis-more-intimately
-interwound-than-ever/.

Johnson, Chalmers, 2006. *Nemesis: The Last Days of the American Republic*, New
York: Metropolitan Books.

———, 2008. 'Going Bankrupt: Why the debt crisis is now the greatest threat to
the American republic', *TomDispatch*, 22 January. www.tomdispatch.com
/post/174884.

Johnson, Jenna, 2015. 'Donald Trump on waterboarding: "If it doesn't work, they
deserve it anyway"', *The Washington Post*, 23 November. www.washingtonpost
.com/news/post-politics/wp/2015/11/23/donald-trump-on-waterboarding
-if-it-doesnt-work-they-deserve-it-anyway/.

Joscelyn, Thomas, 2007. *Iran's Proxy War Against America*, Claremont: The Claremont Institute. www.aina.org/reports/ipwaa.pdf.

———, 2017. 'Here's How Al Qaeda Protected Iran – Until Now', *The Daily Beast*,
7 June. www.thedailybeast.com/heres-how-al-qaeda-protected-iranuntil-now.

Joscelyn, Thomas and Bill Roggio, 2017. 'Analysis: CIA releases massive trove of
Osama bin Laden's files', *Long War Journal*, 1 November. www.longwarjournal

.org/archives/2017/11/analysis-cia-releases-massive-trove-of-osama-bin
-ladens-files.php?utm_source=Sailthru&utm_medium=email&utm
_campaign=New%20Campaign&utm_term=%2ASituation%20Report.

Judah, Ben, 2016. 'Those who call for Brexit are handing European power to the
Kremlin', 9 March. www.independent.co.uk/voices/those-who-call-for-brexit
-are-handing-european-power-to-the-kremlin-a6921386.html.

Judicial Watch, 2015. www.judicialwatch.org/wp-content/uploads/2015/05
/Pg.-291-Pgs.-287-293-JW-v-DOD-and-State-14-812-DOD-Release-2015
-04-10-final-version11.pdf.

Kadhim, Abbas, 2017. 'A Major Crack in Iraqi Shia Politics', *Huffington Post*, 26 July.
www.huffingtonpost.com/entry/a-major-crack-in-iraqi-shia-politics_us
_59766ab6e4b01cf1c4bb72bd.

Kadivar, Cyrus, 2002. 'Trading human rights', *The Iranian*, November 26.
http://bahai-library.com/newspapers/2002/021126-3.html.

Kadivar, Mohsen, interviewed by *Rooz Online*, 2010. 'The Key Features of the Green
Movement', in *The People Reloaded: The Green Movement and the Struggle for
Iran's Future*, eds. Nader Hashemi and Danny Postel, New York: Melville
House, pp. 109–19.

Kahf, Mohja, 2011. 'One, one, one, the Syrian people are one', *The Guardian*, 28 May.
www.theguardian.com/commentisfree/2011/may/28/syrian-alawites-protests.

Kamm, Oliver, 2015. 'Genocide at Srebrenica: We must unmask the new deniers',
The Jewish Chronicle, 28 May. www.thejc.com/comment-and-debate/columnists
/136926/genocide-srebrenica-we-must-unmask-new-deniers.

Kaplan, Michael, 2015. 'Syrian and Russian Airstrikes Target Hospitals: Medical
Relief Organizations Stage Mass "Die-In" Demonstration Blocks From UN',
International Business Times, 29 October. www.ibtimes.com/syrian-russian
-airstrikes-target-hospitals-medical-relief-organizations-stage-mass-2162510.

Karadjis, Michael, 2014. 'Shameless Cooke Knifes Syrian people's resistance to As-
sad/ISIS fascism', 13 August. https://mkaradjis.wordpress.com/2014/08/13
/shameless-cooke-knifes-syrian-peoples-resistance-to-assadisis-fascism/.

———, 2015. 'Conspiracy theories that "the US fuelled the rise of ISIS": Why they
are a back-handed attack on the Syrian uprising', 8 June. https://mkaradjis
.wordpress.com/2015/06/08/conspiracy-theories-that-the-us-fuelled-the-rise
-of-isis-why-they-are-a-back-handed-attack-on-the-syrian-uprising/.

———, 2016. 'The Kurdish PYD's alliance with Russia against Free Aleppo: Evidence and analysis of a disaster', 28 February. https://mkaradjis.wordpress
.com/2016/02/28/the-kurdish-pyds-alliance-with-russia-against-free-aleppo
-evidence-and-analysis-of-a-disaster/.

Karam, Joyce, 2014. 'Iran's relationship with al-Qaeda: It's complicated', *Al Arabiya*,
25 September. http://english.alarabiya.net/en/views/news/middle-east
/2014/09/25/Iran-s-relationship-with-al-Qaeda-It-s-complicated.html.

Karami, Arash, 2015. 'Will Iran pursue high-cost strategy in Syria?' *Al-Monitor*, 18
November. www.al-monitor.com/pulse/originals/2015/11/iran-killed-syria

-hamedani-civil-war.html.

———, 2016a. 'Rouhani calls for more Iranian women to "lean in" to politics', *Al-Monitor*, 8 February. www.al-monitor.com/pulse/originals/2016/02/iran -rouhani-women-vote-parliament-elections.html.

———, 2016b. 'Iran MP: We've created artificial red lines on free speech', *Al-Monitor*, 16 February. www.al-monitor.com/pulse/originals/2016/02/iran-elections -motahhari-aref-parliament-reformist.html.

———, 2016c. 'Iranian foreign ministry: Russian use of air base has ended', *Al-Monitor*, 22 August. http://www.al-monitor.com/pulse/originals/2016/08 /hamadan-airbase-iran-russia-syria-ghassemi-dehghan.html.

Karsh, Efraim, 2002. *The Iran-Iraq War: 1980-1988*, Oxford: Osprey.

Kaszeta, Dan, 2013. 'Why Seymour Hersh has it wrong this time', *NOW*, 27 October. https://now.mmedia.me/lb/en/commentaryanalysis/524969-524969-why -seymour-hersh-has-it-wrong-this-time.

Kaye, David, 2012. 'Some thoughts on Russia and the International Criminal Court', *Councilandcourt.org*, November. http://councilandcourt.org/files/2012/11 /Russia-and-ICC.pdf.

Keaten, Jamey and Bradley Klapper, 2016. 'Russia lodges formal complaint with UN over criticism of Trump', *Toronto Star*, 7 October. www.thestar.com/news /world/2016/10/07/russia-lodges-formal-complaint-with-un-over-criticism -of-trump.html.

Keating, Fiona, 2017. 'Russian city sees domestic violence incidents double after Putin decrminalises beatings', *International Business Times*, 11 February. www.ibtimes.co.uk/russian-city-sees-domestic-violence-incidents-double -after-putin-decriminalises-physical-abuse-1606038.

Kenar, Ceren and Ragip Soylu, 2016. 'Why Are Russian Engineers Working at an Islamic State-Controlled Gas Plant in Syria?', *Foreign Policy*, 9 February. https://foreignpolicy.com/2016/02/09/why-are-russian-engineers-working -at-an-islamic-state-controlled-gas-plant-in-syria/.

Khaja, Nagieb, 2016. 'A day in the life of Aleppo's White helmets', *Al Jazeera*, 15 August. www.aljazeera.com/indepth/features/2016/08/day-life-aleppo-white -helmets-160814213655658.html.

Kim, Lucian, 2014. 'Should Putin fear the man who "pulled the trigger of war" in Ukraine?', *Reuters*, 25 November. http://blogs.reuters.com/great-debate /2014/11/25/should-putin-fear-the-man-who-pulled-the-trigger-of-war -in-ukraine/.

Kimball, Spencer, 2014. 'Putin's power play jeopardizes Eurasian Union plans', *DW*, 15 March. www.dw.com/en/putins-power-play-jeopardizes-eurasian-union -plans/a-17493164.

King, David, 1997. *The Commissar Vanishes: The Falsification of Photographs and Art in Stalin's Russia*, New York: Metropolitan Books.

Kinstler, Linda, 2015. 'ISIL didn't target "the West"', *Politico*, 21 November. www.politico.eu/article/isil-didnt-target-the-west-islamist-extremists-france/.

Knight, Amy, 2012. 'Finally, we know about the Moscow bombings', *The New York Review of Books*, 22 November. www.nybooks.com/articles/2012/11/22/finally-we-know-about-moscow-bombings/.

Kohlmann, Evan, 1999. 'A Bitter Harvest: The Soviet Intervention in Afghanistan and its Effects on Afghan Political Movements'. http://wayback.archive.org/web/20070614165958/http://law.upenn.edu/~ekohlman/afghanistan.pdf.

Kolata, Gina, 2012. 'Lenin's Stroke: Doctor has a Theory (and a Suspect)', *The New York Times*, 7 May. www.nytimes.com/2012/05/08/health/research/lenins-death-remains-a-mystery-for-doctors.html.

Kornbluh, Peter, 2003. *The Pinochet File: A Declassified Dossier on Atrocity and Accountability*, New York: The New Press.

Kovalev, Sergei, 2000. 'Putin's war', *The New York Review of Books*, 10 February. www.nybooks.com/articles/2000/02/10/putins-war/.

Kowalewski, Zbigniew, 1989. 'For the independence of Soviet Ukraine', *International Marxist Review*, autumn. Reproduced by Louis Proyect, 2014. 'Lenin's party, Great Russian chauvinism and the betrayal of Ukrainian national aspirations', 20 April. https://louisproyect.org/2014/04/20/lenins-party-great-russian-chauvinism-and-the-betrayal-of-ukrainian-national-aspirations/.

Kramer, Bernard, 1990. 'Shiite Islam and Islamic Fundamentalism', *Sandbox*, http://martinkramer.org/sandbox/reader/archives/shiite-islam-and-islamic-fundamentalism/.

Kreisler, Harry, 1997. 'Conversation with Roy Gutman', Institute of International Studies, UC Berkeley, 10 April. http://globetrotter.berkeley.edu/conversations/Gutman/gutman-con6.html.

Krieger, Heike, ed., 2001. *The Kosovo Conflict and International Law: An Analytical Documentation 1974–1999*, Cambridge: Cambridge University Press.

Kristof, Nicholas, 2016. 'Obama's worst mistake', *The New York Times*, 11 August. www.nytimes.com/2016/08/11/opinion/obamas-worst-mistake.html.

Krohnke, Duane W., 2011. 'The International Criminal Court and the Clinton administration', 11 May. https://dwkcommentaries.com/2011/05/11/the-international-criminal-court-and-the-clinton-administration/.

Lackner, Helen, 2016. 'Yemen's "peaceful" transition from autocracy: Could it have succeeded?', International Institute for Democracy and Electoral Assistance. www.idea.int/sites/default/files/publications/yemens-peaceful-transition-from-autocracy.pdf.

Lalpychak, Chrystyna, 1991. 'INDEPENDENCE: Over 90% vote yes in referendum; Kravchuk elected president of Ukraine', *The Ukrainian Weekly*, 8 December. www.ukrweekly.com/old/archive/1991/499101.shtml.

Lambert, Caitlin, 2014. 'The evolving US policy towards the ICC', International Justice Project, 6 March. www.internationaljusticeproject.com/the-evolving-us-policy-towards-the-icc/.

Lando, Barry, 2007. 'How George H.W. Bush helped Saddam Hussein prevent an Iraqi uprising', *Alternet*, 29 March. www.alternet.org/story/49864/how

_george_h.w._bush_helped_saddam_hussein_prevent_an_iraqi_uprising.

Lasseter, Tom, 2005. 'Iran gaining influence, power in Iraq through militia', *McClatchy*, 12 December. www.mcclatchydc.com/latest-news/article24452749.html.

Lavasani, Masoud, 2015. 'How one Iranian TV show is breaking censorship boundaries', *Al-Monitor*, 17 December. www.al-monitor.com/pulse/originals/2015/12/iran-shahrzad-tv-series-private-sector-irib-censorship.html.

Lazare, Daniel, 2014. 'Timothy Snyder's Lies', *Jacobin*, September. www.jacobinmag.com/2014/09/timothy-snyders-lies/.

Lemkin, Raphael, 1953. 'Soviet Genocide in the Ukraine'. www.uccla.ca/SOVIET_GENOCIDE_IN_THE_UKRAINE.pdf.

Lenin, V. I., 1917. 'Imperialism, the Highest Stage of Capitalism'. https://www.marxists.org/archive/lenin/works/1916/imp-hsc/.

———, 1920. 'Draft Theses on National and Colonial Questions'. https://www.marxists.org/archive/lenin/works/1920/jun/05.htm.

———, 1922. 'The question of nationalities or "autonomisation"'. https://www.marxists.org/archive/lenin/works/1922/dec/testamnt/autonomy.htm.

———, 1922–1923. 'Letter to the Congress'. www.marxists.org/archive/lenin/works/1922/dec/testamnt/congress.htm.

Leopold, Jason, 2015. 'The CIA Just Declassified the Document That Supposedly Justified the Iraq Invasion', *Vice News*, 19 March. https://news.vice.com/article/the-cia-just-declassified-the-document-that-supposedly-justified-the-iraq-invasion.

Lepeska, David, 2016. 'Kiev's new revolution: young Ukrainians spur cultural revival amid the conflict', *The Guardian*, 31 August. www.theguardian.com/cities/2016/aug/31/kiev-new-revolution-young-ukrainians-cultural-revival-amid-conflict.

Leviev, Ruslan, 2015. 'Three Graves: Russian Investigation Team Uncovers Spetsnaz Brigade in Ukraine', *Bellingcat*, 22 May. www.bellingcat.com/news/uk-and-europe/2015/05/22/three-graves/?_ga=1.166273980.340944329.1475161711.

Levy, Gideon, 2015. 'Israeli Propaganda Isn't Fooling Anyone – Except Israelis', *Haaretz*, 4 June. www.haaretz.com/opinion/.premium-1.659480.

Lewin, Moshe, 1968. *Lenin's Last Struggle*, trans. A. M. Sheridan Smith, New York: Pantheon Books.

Liebelson, Dana, 2016. 'Even if Trump loses, white nationalists say they've won', *The Huffington Post*, 3 November. www.huffingtonpost.in/entry/donald-trump-white-nationalists_us_581a103be4b0a76e174c51bb.

Lister, Charles, 2016. 'Obama's Syria Strategy is the Definition of Insanity', Foreign Policy, 21 September. https://foreignpolicy.com/2016/09/21/obamas-syria-strategy-is-the-definition-of-insanity/.

Little, Alan, 2000. 'Moral combat: NATO at war', *Panorama*, BBC, 12 March. http://news.bbc.co.uk/hi/english/static/events/panorama/transcripts/transcript_12_03_00.txt.

Lokshina, Tanya, 2009. 'Natalia Estemirova, champion of ordinary Chechens', *Open*

Democracy, 1 September. www.opendemocracy.net/article/email/natalia
-estemirova-champion-of-ordinary-chechens.

———, 2016. 'Why Anna Politkovskaya still inspires', *CNN*, 6 October.
http://edition.cnn.com/2016/10/06/opinions/anna-politkovskaya-killing
-anniversary-lokshina/.

Lordkipanidze, Boris and Tatiana Traktina, 2016. 'Can Russia ban abortion?', *Pravda.
ru*, 3 October. www.pravdareport.com/society/stories/03-10-2016/135772
-russia_abortion-0/.

Losh, Jack, 2016. 'Is Russia killing off Eastern Ukraine's warlords?', *Foreign Policy*, 25
October. http://foreignpolicy.com/2016/10/25/who-is-killing-eastern
-ukraines-warlords-motorola-russia-putin/.

Loshak, Andrei and Svetlana Reiter, 2011. 'Decency, hope, friendship: the real story
from Moscow's race riots', *Open Democracy*, 10 January. www.opendemocracy
.net/od-russia/andrei-loshak-svetlana-reiter/decency-hope-friendship-real
-story-from-moscows-race-riots.

Lozovsky, Ilya, 2015. 'The Spirit of Lviv', *Foreign Policy*, 16 September.
http://foreignpolicy.com/2015/09/16/the-spirit-of-lviv-ukraine-corruption/.

———, 2016. 'Why Ukraine's Desperate Struggle Gives Me Hope', *Foreign Policy*,
21 September. http://foreignpolicy.com/2016/09/21/why-ukraines-desperate
-struggle-gives-me-hope/.

Luhn, Alec, 2016. 'Russia's campaign in Syria leads to arms sale windfall', *The Guardian*, 29 March. www.theguardian.com/world/2016/mar/29/russias-campaign
-in-syria-leads-to-arms-sale-windfall.

———, 2017. 'Alexei Navalny: Russian opposition leader found guilty of embezzlement', *The Guardian*, 8 February. www.theguardian.com/world/2017/feb/08
/alexei-navalny-russian-opposition-leader-found-guilty-embezzlement.

Luxemburg, Rosa, 1900. *Reform or Revolution*, Chapter 8. https://www.marxists
.org/archive/luxemburg/1900/reform-revolution/ch08.htm.

———, 1918. *The Russian Revolution*, Chapter 6. www.marxists.org/archive
/luxemburg/1918/russian-revolution/ch06.htm.

———, 1972 [1921]. 'The Accumulation of Capital: An Anti-Critique', in Kenneth
Tarbuck, ed., *Imperialism and the Accumulation of Capital*, London: Allen Lane,
pp. 45–150.

———, 2003 [1913]. *The Accumulation of Capital*, trans. Agnes Schwarzschild,
London: Routledge.

Lynch, Lily, 2015. 'Forgetting Resistance in the Balkans', *Balkanist*, 1 April.
http://balkanist.net/forgetting-resistance-in-the-balkans/.

Lyon, James, 2015. 'Is war about to break out in the Balkans?' *Foreign Policy*, 26 October. http://foreignpolicy.com/2015/10/26/war-break-out-balkans
-bosnia-republika-srpska-dayton/.

Ma'an News Agency, 2016. 'Tens of Palestinian children in Gaza protest in solidarity
with Aleppo', 14 December. www.maannews.com/Content.aspx?id=774430.

Macleod, Hugh and Annasofie Flamand, 2011a. 'Assad's regime of torture', *Al Jazeera*,

15 May. www.aljazeera.com/indepth/features/2011/05
/2011515113431187136.html.

———, 2011b. 'Tortured and killed: Hamza al-Khateeb, age 13', *Al Jazeera*, 31 May.
www.aljazeera.com/indepth/features/2011/05/201153185927813389.html.

MacMillan, Arthur, 2015. 'As Iranian deaths in Syria rise, debate opens at home',
Yahoo News, 27 October. http://news.yahoo.com/iranian-deaths-syria-rise
-debate-opens-home-142527091.html.

Madi, Mohamed, 2014. 'Haider al-Abadi: A new era for Iraq?', *BBC News*, 9 September. www.bbc.co.uk/news/world-middle-east-28748366.

Mainville, Michael, 2006. 'Death in Russia: The Silencing of Anna Politkovskaya',
Spiegel Online, 13 October. www.spiegel.de/international/death-in-russia
-the-silencing-of-anna-politkovskaya-a-442392.html.

Malik, Hamdi, 2017. 'What's behind controversial Iraqi cleric's visit to Saudi Arabia?', *Al-Monitor*, 11 August. www.al-monitor.com/pulse/originals/2017/08
/muqtada-sadr-saudi-iraq-iran.html.

Malik, Kenan, 2015. 'Kneejerk finger-pointing after Paris attacks', *Al Jazeera*, 15
November. www.aljazeera.com/indepth/opinion/2015/11/knee-jerk-finger
-pointing-paris-attacks-151114130014452.html.

Malm, Sara, 2015. 'How ISIS is funded by black-market oil trading, illegal drugs and
internet cafes', *Mail Online*, 22 February. www.dailymail.co.uk/news
/article-2964028/oil-drugs-internet-ISIS-funded.html.

Mamouri, Ali, 2015. 'Is Iraq's Dawa Party on verge of division?', *Al-Monitor*, 28 October. http://www.al-monitor.com/pulse/originals/2015/10/iraq-dawa-party
-division-maliki-abadi.html.

———, 2016a. 'Why Shiites are divided over Iranian role in Iraq', *Al-Monitor*, 12
May. www.al-monitor.com/pulse/originals/2016/05/sadrist-stances-iraqi
-shiites-opposing-iranian-policy.html.

———, 2016b. 'Iraqi ministers fall like dominoes as Maliki's bloc targets Abadi',
Al-Monitor, 29 September. www.al-monitor.com/pulse/originals/2016/09
/maliki-abadi-barzani-iraq-is-pmu-iran-us.html.

Marshall, Josh, 2016a. 'Trump and Putin. Yes, It's Really a Thing', *TPM*, 23 July.
http://talkingpointsmemo.com/edblog/trump-putin-yes-it-s-really-a-thing.

———, 2016b. 'Trump Rolls Out Anti-Semitic Closing Ad', *TPM*, 5 November.
http://talkingpointsmemo.com/edblog/trump-rolls-out-anti-semitic-closing-ad.

Marx, Karl, 1976 [1867]. *Capital*, vol. 1, trans. Ben Fowkes, Harmondsworth:
Penguin.

———, 1981 [1894]. *Capital*, vol. 3, trans. David Fernbach, Harmondsworth:
Penguin.

Masi, Alessandria, 2014. 'MH17 crash: Full transcript of alleged phone intercepts
between Russian intelligence officers', *International Business Times*, 17 July.
www.ibtimes.com/mh17-crash-full-transcript-alleged-phone-intercepts
-between-russian-intelligence-1631992.

Mattick, Paul, 1978. 'Introduction to "Anti-Bolshevik Communism"', London: The

Merlin Press. www.marxists.org/archive/mattick-paul/1978/introduction.htm.

———, 1981. *Economic Crisis and Crisis Theory*, London: The Merlin Press.

McFadden, Cynthia, William Arkin and Tracy Connor, 2017. 'President Obama Commutes Chelsea Manning's Sentence', *NBC News*, 17 January. www.nbcnews.com/news/us-news/president-obama-commutes-chelsea-manning-s-sentence-n708046.

McKinsey Global Institute, 2016. *The Power of Parity: Advancing Women's Equality in the United States*, April. www.mckinsey.com/global-themes/employment-and-growth/the-power-of-parity-advancing-womens-equality-in-the-united-states.

McLeary, Paul, 2015. 'Winning Hearts and Minds in Ramadi', *Foreign Policy*, 28 December. https://foreignpolicy.com/2015/12/28/winning-hearts-and-minds-in-ramadi/.

McLeary, Paul and Dan de Luce, 2016. 'Turkey is Finally Bombing Syria, But It's Not Hitting Who the US Wants', *Foreign Policy*, 24 August. https://foreignpolicy.com/2016/08/24/turkey-is-finally-bombing-syria-but-its-not-hitting-who-the-u-s-wants/.

McVeigh, Tracy, 2016. 'Jo Cox to share peace prize with Syrian group she championed', *The Guardian*, 12 November. www.theguardian.com/uk-news/2016/nov/12/jo-cox-white-helmets-peace-prize-coventry.

Mearsheimer, John, and Stephen Walt, 2007. *The Israel Lobby and U.S. Foreign Policy*, New York: Farrar, Straus & Giroux.

Melman, Seymour, 2001. *After Capitalism: From Managerialism to Workplace Democracy*, New York: Knopf.

———, 2008. *War Inc. AmeriQuests*, 5(2). http://ejournals.library.vanderbilt.edu/ojs/index.php/ameriquests/issue/view/7.

Meyer, Henry, 2017. 'Putin has a really big Trojan horse in Germany', 2 May. www.bloomberg.com/news/articles/2017-05-02/putin-s-trojan-horse-for-merkel-is-packed-with-russian-tv-fans.

Middle East Eye, 2016a. 'Rival faction challenges Libya's UN-backed government in Tripoli', 15 October. www.middleeasteye.net/news/rival-faction-challenges-libyas-un-backed-government-tripoli-754810947.

———, 2016b. 'US pounds Sirte as Libyan forces advance against IS', 18 October. www.middleeasteye.net/news/us-air-strikes-pound-libyas-sirte-pro-government-forces-advance-against-803588091.

Middle East Monitor, 2014. 'Outgoing Iraqi prime minister insists to seek third term', 5 July. www.middleeastmonitor.com/20140705-outgoing-iraqi-prime-minister-insists-to-seek-third-term/.

Milani, Abbas and Michael McFaul, 2015. 'What the Iran-Deal Debate is Like in Iran', *The Atlantic*, 11 August. www.theatlantic.com/international/archive/2015/08/iran-deal-politics-rouhani-khamenei/400985/.

Miller, Aaron David, 2016. 'A Defense of Obama's Middle East "Balancing Act"', *Foreign Policy*, 15 August. http://foreignpolicy.com/2016/08/15/a-defense-of-obamas-middle-east-balancing-act-syria-russia-iran-nsc/.

Miller, Greg, and Alan Entous, 2016. 'Plans to send heavier weapons to CIA-backed rebels in Syria stall amid White House scepticism', *The Washington Post*, 23 October. www.washingtonpost.com/world/national-security/plans-to-send -heavier-weapons-to-cia-backed-rebels-in-syria-stall-amid-white-house -skepticism/2016/10/23/f166ddac-96ee-11e6-bb29-bf2701dbe0a3_story.html.

Miller, James, 2016. 'Putin's attack helicopters are winning the war for Assad', *Foreign Policy*, 30 March. http://foreignpolicy.com/2016/03/30/putins-attack -helicopters-and-mercenaries-are-winning-the-war-for-assad/.

Milne, Seamus, 2015. 'Now the truth emerges: how the US fuelled the rise of Isis in Syria and Iraq', *The Guardian*, 3 June. www.theguardian.com/commentisfree /2015/jun/03/us-isis-syria-iraq.

Mirengoff, Paul, 2014. 'The ISIS-Assad alliance', *Powerline*, 15 July. www.powerlineblog .com/archives/2014/07/the-isis-assad-alliance.php.

Mir-Hosseini, Ziba, 2010. '"Multiplied, not humiliated": Broken taboos in post-election Iran', in *The People Reloaded: The Green Movement and the Struggle for Iran's Future*, eds Nader Hashemi and Danny Postel, New York: Melville House, pp. 140–47.

Moaveni, Azadeh, 2009. 'Iran's Opposition Awaits Leadership', *The Washington Post*, 26 July. www.washingtonpost.com/wp-dyn/content/article/2009/07/24 /AR2009072402083.html.

———, 2016. 'Once I Saw Light in Iran. Now It's Mostly Shadows', *The New York Times*, 29 February. www.nytimes.com/2016/03/01/opinion/once-i-saw-light -in-iran-now-its-mostly-shadows.html.

Mobayed, Yasmeen, 2013. 'An introduction to Syria, its history and its present revolutionary struggles', *Qawem*, 23 August. https://muqawameh.wordpress.com /2014/08/23/an-introduction-to-syria-its-history-and-its-present-revolutionary -struggles/.

Momen, Moojen, 1985. *An Introduction to Shi'i Islam: The History and Doctrines of Twelver Shi'ism*, Oxford: George Ronald.

Monbiot, George, 2001. 'America's pipe dream', *The Guardian*, 23 October. www.theguardian.com/world/2001/oct/23/afghanistan.terrorism11.

Monteleone, Davide, 2016. '25 Years After Independence, A Country at a Crossroads', *National Geographic*, 9 September. www.nationalgeographic.com /photography/proof/2016/09/tajikistan-independence-soviet-union-russia -davide-monteleone/.

Mouri, Leila, 2012. 'Compulsory Hijab in Iran: There Is No Room for Appeasement', *Huffington Post*, 24 July. www.huffingtonpost.com/entry/compulsory -hijab-in-iran-_b_1698338.html?section=india.

Mousavi, Mir Hossein, 2010. 'The Green Movement Charter', in *The People Reloaded: The Green Movement and the Struggle for Iran's Future*, eds Nader Hashemi and Danny Postel, New York: Melville House, pp. 332–44.

Muehlenkamp, Roberto, 2010. 'A critique of Timothy Sneider's *Bloodlands*', *Holocaust Controversies*, 8 December. http://holocaustcontroversies.blogspot.

in/2010/12/critique-of-timothy-snyders-bloodlands.html.

Muhsin, Abdullah and Alan Johnson, 2006. *Hadi Never Died: Hadi Saleh and the Iraqi Trade Unions*, London: Trades Union Congress.

Musings on Iraq, 2015. 'Badr Organization A view into Iraq's violent past and present', 20 January. http://musingsoniraq.blogspot.in/2015/01/badr -organization-view-into-iraqs.html.

Mustafa, Seema, 2015. 'And now it is confirmed, the Islamic State is a US creation', *The Citizen*, 14 November. http://www.thecitizen.in/index.php /OldNewsPage/?Id=4778.

Naame Shaam, 2014. *Iran in Syria: From an Ally of the Regime to an Occupying Force*, September. www.naameshaam.org/wp-content/uploads/2014/10/report _iran_in_syria_201411.pdf.

———, 2015. *Silent Sectarian Cleansing: Iranian Role in Mass Demolitions and Population Transfers in Syria*, May. www.naameshaam.org/wp-content/uploads /2015/05/Silent_Ethnic_Cleansing_in_Syria_NaameShaamReport _ENGLISH_May20151.pdf.

Naimark, Norman, 2010. *Stalin's Genocides*, Princeton: Princeton University Press.

Nairn, Tom, 1973. *The Left Against Europe?*, Harmondsworth: Penguin Books.

Namazie, Maryam, 2015. 'On Jeremy Corbyn and Islamism: You can't be progressive some of the time', 24 September. http://maryamnamazie.com/jeremy-corbyn/.

Nandy, Amrita and Rohini Hensman, 2015. 'The Work Women Do', *The Indian Express*, 7 November. http://indianexpress.com/article/opinion/columns /the-work-women-do/.

Naser, Mustafa, 2016. 'Why did Iraq's Shiite National Alliance choose new leader?', *Al-Monitor*, 18 September. www.al-monitor.com/pulse/originals/2016/09 /iraq-shiite-national-alliance-ammar-al-hakim.html.

Natali, Denise, 2016. 'Don't underestimate Iraqi nationalism', *Al-Monitor*, 20 January. www.al-monitor.com/pulse/originals/2016/01/underestimate-iraq -nationalism.html.

Naylor, Hugh, 2014. 'Desperate for soldiers, Assad's government imposes harsh recruitment measures', *The Washington Post*, 28 December. www.washingtonpost .com/world/middle_east/desperate-for-soldiers-assads-government-imposes -harsh-recruitment-measures/2014/12/28/62f99194-6d1d-4bd6-a862-b3ab- 46c6b33b_story.html.

———, 2015. 'Iranian media is revealing that scores of the country's fighters are dying in Syria', *The Washington Post*, 27 November. www.washingtonpost.com /world/iranian-media-is-revealing-that-scores-of-the-countrys-fighters-are -dying-in-syria/2015/11/27/294deb02-8ca0-11e5-934c-a369c80822c2_story .html.

NCRI News, 2014. 'Iranian regime uses ISIL to preserve Syria interests: analysts', 18 April. www.ncr-iran.org/en/news/terrorism-fundamentalism/16365.

Nebehay, Stephanie, 2016. 'U.N. says to pursue perpatrators of war crimes in Aleppo', *Reuters*, 21 October. www.reuters.com/article/us-mideast-crisis-syria

-warcrimes-idUSKCN12L0VX?il=0.

Nebehay, Stephanie and Tom Miles, 2016. 'UN suspends aid convoys in Syria after hit, ICRC warns on impact', *Reuters*, 20 September. www.reuters.com/article /us-mideast-crisis-syria-aid-idUSKCN11Q0W1.

Nechepurenko, Ivan, 2016. 'Assault on Aleppo Will Halt for 8 Hours, Russia Says', *The New York Times*, 17 October. www.nytimes.com/2016/10/18/world /middleeast/aleppo-syria-russia-ceasefire.html?_r=0.

Nemtsov, Boris, 2014. 'Boris Nemtsov: "This is Vladimir Putin's war"', *Kyiv Post*, 27 February. www.kyivpost.com/article/opinion/op-ed/why-does-putin-wage -war-on-ukraine-362884.html.

Newcity, Michael, 2016. 'Why Russia withdraws from the International Criminal Court', Russia Direct, 24 November. www.russia-direct.org/opinion/why -russia-withdraws-international-criminal-court.

Niv, Kobi, 2013. 'Israel's "White supremacists"', *Haaretz*, 26 August. www.haaretz .com/opinion/.premium-1.543542.

Nolan, Anna, 2015. 'Ending the refugee crisis starts with ending the Syria crisis', The Syria Campaign, 7 September. https://diary.thesyriacampaign.org/ending-the -refugee-crisis-starts-with-ending-the-syria-crisis/.

Norouzi, Ebrahim, 2009. 'Mossadegh, Islam and Ayatollahs: The story behind the fall of democracy, rise of fundamentalism in Iran', *The Mossadegh Project*, 24 November. www.mohammadmossadegh.com/biography/islam/.

North, David and Alex Lantier, 2013. 'The International Socialist Organization and the imperialist onslaught against Syria', *WSWS*, 11 May. www.wsws.org/en /articles/2013/05/11/isos-m11.html .

NotGeorgeSabra, 2013. 'Every Friday: New Slogans of the People's Revolution', 18 October. https://notgeorgesabra.wordpress.com/2013/10/18/every-friday -new-slogans-of-the-peoples-revolution/.

———, 2015. 'Egyptian Thuwar Blasts @stwuk's Syria Hypocrisy, Pseudo-Intellectu-al @JohnWRees Flips'. http://notgeorgesabra.tumblr.com/post/114685533623 /egyptian-thuwar-blasts-stwuks-syria-hypocrisy.

NOW, 2016. 'Iran admits conducting drone strikes in Syria', 26 September. https:// now.mmedia.me/lb/en/NewsReports/567378-iran-admits-conducting-drone -strikes-in-syria.

N.P. and Erasmus, 2015. 'Religious diplomacy in Iraq: In Shia Muslims' holiest site, a new openness to other faiths', *The Economist*, 5 December. www.economist. com/blogs/erasmus/2015/12/religious-diplomacy-iraq.

NRT, 2015. 'Assad admits sending weapons to Kurdish forces'. www.nrttv.com/EN /Details.aspx?Jimare=4358.

Nuzzi, Olivia, 2016. 'Donald Trump's ISIS-Obama Comments First Came From the Russians and Crazy People', *The Daily Beast*, 12 August. www.thedailybeast .com/articles/2016/08/12/donald-trump-s-isis-obama-comments-first-came -from-the-russians-and-crazy-people.html.

O'Connor, Tom, 2017. 'Russian senator praises Trump for backing Kremlin in Syria

by cutting ties to 'moderate' rebels', *Newsweek*, 20 July. www.newsweek.com
/us-cut-support-moderate-syria-rebels-improve-russia-ties-moscow-639762.

Olszański, Tadeusz A., 2014. 'A strong vote for reform: Ukraine after the parliamentary elections', *Osrodek Studiow Wschodnich*, 29 October. www.osw.waw.pl
/en/publikacje/analyses/2014-10-29/a-strong-vote-reform-ukraine-after
-parliamentary-elections.

OnTheIssues, 2016. 'Bernie Sanders on Free Trade'. www.ontheissues.org/2016
/Bernie_Sanders_Free_Trade.htm.

Orton, Kyle, 2014. 'The Assad Regime's Collusion with ISIS', 24 March. https://
kyleorton1991.wordpress.com/2014/03/24/assessing-the-evidence-of
-collusion-between-the-assad-regime-and-the-wahhabi-jihadists-part-1/.

———, 2015a. 'Russia's War For Assad', 30 September. https://kyleorton1991
.wordpress.com/2015/09/30/russias-war-for-assad/.

———, 2015b. 'Russia Teams Up With Islamic State Against Syrian rebels', 11
October. https://kyleorton1991.wordpress.com/2015/10/11/russia-teams
-up-with-islamic-state-against-syrias-rebels/.

Osborn, Andrew, 2015. 'Parents of first Russian to die in Syria demand repeat
autopsy', *Haaretz*, 28 October. www.haaretz.com/world-news/1.682760.

Osman, Tamer, 2016. 'How are Aleppo's residents dealing with the truce?',
Al-Monitor, 16 September. www.al-monitor.com/pulse/originals/2016/09
/syria-ceasefire-people-aleppo-factions-reservations.html.

OWFI (Organization of Women's Freedom in Iraq), International Gay and Lesbian
Human Rights Commission and MADRE, 2014. 'When coming out is a death
sentence: Persecution of LGBT Iraqis'. www.outrightinternational.org/sites
/default/files/ComingOutDeathSentence_Iraq_0.pdf.

Palestinian Reflections, 2014. 'The anti-imperialism of fools', 26 August. https://
palestinianreflections.wordpress.com/2014/08/26/the-anti-imperial-
ism-of-fools/.

Panah, Hamid Yazdan, 2015. 'Iran's Repression Targets Kurds, Other Minorities',
Iran Focus, 23 February. www.iranfocus.com/en/index.php?option=com
_content&view=article&id=30068:iran-s-repression-targets-kurds-other
-minorities&catid=50&Itemid=137.

———, 2016. 'Iran's Forgotten Prisoners', *The Huffington Post*, 11 February. www
.huffingtonpost.com/entry/irans-forgotten-prisoners_b_9208950.html?
section=india.

Parry, Robert, 2015. 'When Israel/Neocons Favoured Iran', *Consortium News*, 28 July.
https://consortiumnews.com/2015/07/28/when-israelneocons-favored-iran/.

Pascaline, Mary, 2016. 'Syria conflict: Aleppo airstrikes kill over 338 people, including 100 kids, WHO says', *International Business Times*, 1 October. www.ibtimes
.com/syria-conflict-aleppo-airstrikes-kill-over-338-people-including-100-kids
-who-says-2424904.

Pecquet, Julian, 2014. 'US shuns tribal leaders who claim to have infiltrated IS',
Al-Monitor, 29 August. www.al-monitor.com/pulse/originals/2014/08

/us-shun-iraq-tribal-leaders-sunni-isis-spies.html.

———, 2015. 'US threatens to bypass Baghdad, arm Sunnis against IS', *Al-Monitor*, 1 December. www.al-monitor.com/pulse/originals/2015/12/us-threat-bypass -baghdad-arm-sunnis-fight-isis.html.

Perry, Tom and Suleiman Al-Khalidi, 2017. 'Syria rebels blindsided by U.S. move, say jihadists to benefit', *Reuters*, 20 July. www.reuters.com/article/us-mideast -crisis-syria-usa-idUSKBN1A52AE.

Peter, Laurence, 2013. 'Magnitsky trial: Russia accused of "travesty" over dead lawyer', *BBC News*, 11 March. www.bbc.com/news/world-europe-21682470.

Petras, James, 2009. 'Separatism and empire building in the twenty-first century', *Journal of Contemporary Asia*, 39(1), February, pp. 116–126.

———. 2017. 'Twenty Truths about Marine Le Pen', *Dissident Voice*, 1 May. http://dissidentvoice.org/2017/05/twenty-truths-about-marine-le-pen/.

Pham Binh, 2012. 'Libya and Syria: When anti-imperialism goes wrong'. www.thenorthstar.info/?p=1097.

Physicians for Human Rights, 2016. 'PHR calls forced evacuation of Syrian suburb a war crime', 2 September. http://physiciansforhumanrights.org/press/ press-releases/phr-calls-forced-evacuation-of-syrian-suburb-a-war-crime.html.

Pierret, Thomas, 2016. 'Salafis at war in Syria: Logics of fragmentation and realign-ment', in Francesco Cavatorta and Fabio Merone, eds, *Salafism After the Arab Awakening: Contending With People's Power*, London: Hurst.

Pifer, Steven, 2014. 'Ukraine's Parliamentary Election: What Happened? What's Next?', *Up Front*, Brookings Institute, 27 October. www.brookings.edu/blogs /up-front/posts/2014/10/27-ukraine-parliamentary-election-pifer.

Pilger, John, 2014. 'In Ukraine, the US is dragging us towards war with Russia', *The Guardian*, 13 May. www.theguardian.com/commentisfree/2014/may/13 /ukraine-us-war-russia-john-pilger.

———, 2016. 'Inside the invisible government: John Pilger on war, propaganda, Clinton and Trump', *New Matilda*, 28 October. https://newmatilda .com/2016/10/28/inside-the-invisible-government-john-pilger-on-war -propaganda-clinton-and-trump/.

Pironti, Alexandra Di Stefano, 2014. 'Iranian repression of Kurds behind rise of militant PJAK', *Rudaw*, 23 January. http://rudaw.net/english/middleeast /iran/23012014.

Piskunov, Egor, n.d. 'Prominent Russians: Mikhail Gorbachev', *RT Russiapedia*. http://russiapedia.rt.com/prominent-russians/leaders/mikhail-gorbachev/.

Pomerantsev, Peter, 2016a. 'Murder in Mayfair', *London Review of Books*, 38(7), 31 March, pp. 3–6. www.lrb.co.uk/v38/n07/peter-pomerantsev/murder-in -mayfair.

———, 2016b. 'Why we're post-fact', *Granta*, 20 July. https://granta.com/why-were -post-fact/.

Pomfret, John, 1994. 'In Bosnia, Zhirinovsky vows to support Serbs', *Washington Post*, 1 February. https://news.google.com/newspapers?nid=1314&dat

=19940201&id=Z11WAAAAIBAJ&sjid=9_ADAAAAIBAJ&p-
g=5548,19884&hl=en.

Pooya, Fariborz, 2009. 'Misinformation campaign of the Islamic regime of Iran, Press TV and George Galloway', *MaryamNamazie blog*, 3 July. http://maryamnamazie.blogspot.in/2009/07/misinformation-campaign-of-islamic.html.

Popular Resistance, 2014a. 'Despite Propaganda: Americans Oppose Interventions in Iraq', 22 June. www.popularresistance.org/despite-propaganda-americans-oppose-u-s-intervention-in-iraq/.

Postel, Danny, 2006. *Reading Legitimation Crisis in Tehran: Iran and the Future of Liberalism*, Chicago: Prickly Paradigm Press.

Potarskaya, Nina interviewed by Jean Batou, 2014. 'Ukraine: Resisting nationalist polarization and Russian invasion', *New Politics*, 29 September. http://newpol.org/content/ukraine-resisting-nationalist-polarization-and-russian-invasion.

Poulantzas, Nicos, 1978. *State, Power, Socialism*, trans. Patrick Camiller, London: New Left Books.

Prescott, Bruce, 2010. 'An Accurate Look at Timothy McVeigh's Beliefs', *EthicsDaily.com*, 26 January. www.ethicsdaily.com/an-accurate-look-at-timothy-mcveighs-beliefs-cms-15532.

Press TV, 2016a. 'US-led air-raids destroying Iraqi infrastructure', 16 January. Available at https://www.youtube.com/watch?v=DuPj0l8RW28.

———, 2016b. 'Clinton is part of global elite dominating Americans: Trump', 14 October. http://presstv.ir/Detail/2016/10/14/489048/Donald-Trump-Hillary-Clinton-global-elite.

Price, Wayne. 2005. 'The US Deserves to Lose in Iraq – But Should We "Support the Iraqi Resistance"?', The Anarchist Library. http://theanarchistlibrary.org/library/wayne-price-the-u-s-deserves-to-lose-in-iraq-but-should-we-support-the-iraqi-resistance.

Prothero, Mitchell, 2015. '"Star pupil": Pied piper of ISIS recruits was trained by U.S.', *The Seattle Times*, 15 September. www.seattletimes.com/nation-world/the-us-trained-pied-piper-of-chechen-recruits-to-the-islamic-state-group/.

Proyect, Louis, 2016. 'No, Seymour Hersh, the shish kebab does not favor Sharia law', *Louis Proyect: The Unrepentant Marxist*, 25 April. https://louisproyect.org/2016/04/25/no-seymour-hersh-the-shish-kebab-does-not-favor-sharia-law/.

Pulse Media, 2013. 'Open letter to the Stop the War Coalition', 20 November. https://pulsemedia.org/2013/11/20/open-letter-to-the-stop-the-war-coalition/.

Putin, Vladimir, 2005. 'Annual address to the Federal Assembly of the Russian Federation', 25 April. http://archive.kremlin.ru/eng/speeches/2005/04/25/2031_type70029type82912_87086.shtml.

Qaidaari, Abbas, 2015. 'Has Syria been a military success for Iran?', *Al-Monitor*, 11 November. www.al-monitor.com/pulse/tr/contents/articles/originals/2015/11/iran-syria-army.html.

———, 2016a. 'Who sent Iranian Green Berets to Syria?', *Al-Monitor*, 28 April.

www.al-monitor.com/pulse/originals/2016/04/iran-army-brigade-65-green
-berets-syria-deployment.html.

———, 2016b. 'Why Iran still doesn't trust Russia on Syria', *Al-Monitor*, 15 June.
www.al-monitor.com/pulse/originals/2016/06/iran-russia-syria-defense
-ministers-tehran-meeting.html.

Rafizadeh, Majid, 2013. 'In Syria, Follow the Money to Find the Roots of the Revolt', *The Daily Beast*, 8 April. www.thedailybeast.com/articles/2013/04/08
/in-syria-follow-the-money-to-find-the-roots-of-the-revolt.html.

———, 2014. 'The Islamic state of Iran and gender discrimination', *Frontpage*, 23
February. www.frontpagemag.com/fpm/219504/islamic-state-iran-and
-gender-discrimination-dr-majid-rafizadeh.

———, 2016. 'New evidence: Iran's role in 9/11', *Frontpage*, 25 March.
www.frontpagemag.com/fpm/262273/new-evidence-irans-role-911-dr
-majid-rafizadeh.

Rahnema, Ali and Farhad Nomani, 1990. *The Secular Miracle: Religion, Politics and
Economic Policy in Iran*, London and New Jersey: Zed Books.

Ranjbar, Omid and Azadeh Shurmand, 2016. 'Challenging intellectuals who justify
Iranian imperialism; Searching for socialist solidarity', *Alliance of Middle-East
Socialists*, 23 August. www.allianceofmesocialists.org/challenging-intellectuals
-justify-iranian-imperialism-searching-socialist-solidarity/.

Reed, Matthew, 2015. 'Revealed: Assad Buys Oil From ISIS', *The Daily Beast*, 10
December. www.thedailybeast.com/articles/2015/12/10/isis-is-the-con-ed
-of-syria.html.

Reeves, Phil, 1998. 'Russia's racist skinheads terrorise foreigners', *Independent*, 8 May.
www.independent.co.uk/news/russias-racist-skinheads-terrorise
-foreigners-1160477.html.

Reich, Wilhelm, 1946. *The Mass Psychology of Fascism*, trans. Theodore Wolfe, New
York: Orgone Institute Press.

Reuter, Christoph, 2015. 'Islamic State files show structure of Islamist terror group',
Spiegel Online, 18 April. www.spiegel.de/international/world/islamic-state
-files-show-structure-of-islamist-terror-group-a-1029274.html#js-article
-comments-box-pager.

Reuters, 2015. 'Iran Quds chief visited Russia despite UN travel ban: Iran official', 7
August. www.reuters.com/article/us-russia-iran-soleimani
-idUSKCN0QC1KM20150807.

———, 2016a. 'Islamic State committing genocide against Yazidis: UN', 16 June.
www.reuters.com/article/us-mideast-crisis-syria-yazidi-idUSKCN0Z20WR.

———, 2016b. 'Russian cruise missiles target Syria', 19 August. www.reuters.com
/article/us-mideast-crisis-syria-aleppo/russian-cruise-missiles-target-syria
-idUSKCN10U1EE.

———, 2016c. 'Moscow says Russian and Syrian planes did not strike Aleppo aid
convoy', 20 September. www.reuters.com/article/us-mideast-crisis-syria-russia
-convoy-idUSKCN11Q1HE?mod=related&channelName=worldNews.

———, 2017a. 'Damascus was 2–3 weeks from falling when Russia intervened: Lavrov', 17 January. www.reuters.com/article/us-russia-lavrov-syria-damascus-idUSKBN15111N?il=0.

———, 2017b. 'Air strikes hit Syria's rebel-held Idlib, around 30 dead: residents, monitor', 7 February. www.reuters.com/article/us-mideast-crisis-syria-idlib-idUSKBN15M0Y9?feedType=RSS.

———, 2017c. 'Leader of Germany's far-right party meets Putin allies in Moscow', 21 February. www.reuters.com/article/us-germany-election-afd/leader-of-germanys-far-right-party-meets-putin-allies-in-moscow-idUSKBN16012C.

Reynolds, Michael A., 2016. 'Vladimir Putin, Godfather of Kurdistan?', *The National Interest*, 1 March. http://nationalinterest.org/feature/vladimir-putin-godfather-kurdistan-15358.

Ricchiardi, Sherry, 1993. 'Exposing genocide…For what?', *American Journalism Review*, June. http://ajrarchive.org/Article.asp?id=1516.

Rich, Roland, 1993. 'The recognition of states: The collapse of Yugoslavia and the Soviet Union', *European Journal of International Law*, 4(1), pp. 36–65. www.ejil.org/pdfs/4/1/1207.pdf.

Robin, Benedict, 2016. 'Translation and analysis: Madaniyoun launch statement – 2nd July', 24 July. https://benedictrobin.wordpress.com/2016/07/24/translation-analysis-madaniyoun-launch-statement-2nd-july/.

Roche, Cody, 2017. 'The Trotskyist León Sedov Brigade in the Syrian revolution', *Medium*, 5 December. https://medium.com/@badly_xeroxed/the-trotskyist-le%C3%B3n-sedov-brigade-in-the-syrian-revolution-bf6ebf5ae851.

Rodinson, Maxime, 2004. 'Sultan Galiev – a forgotten precursor. Socialism and the national question'. www.europe-solidaire.org/spip.php?article3638.

Roggio, Bill, 2014. '"Iran owes al Qaeda invaluably," ISIS spokesman says', *The Long War Journal*, 12 May. www.longwarjournal.org/archives/2014/05/iran_owes_al_qaeda_invaluably.php.

Rogin, Josh, 2014. 'US Ignored Warnings Before ISIS Takeover of a Key City', *The Daily Beast*, 10 July. www.thedailybeast.com/articles/2014/07/10/u-s-ignored-warnings-before-isis-takeover-of-a-key-city.html.

Rosdolsky, Roman, 1986. *Engels and the "Nonhistoric" Peoples: The National Question in the Revolution of 1848*, trans. John-Paul Himka, Glasgow: Critique Books.

Rosen, Nir, 2007. 'What Bremer got wrong in Iraq', *The Washington Post*, 16 May. www.washingtonpost.com/wp-dyn/content/article/2007/05/15/AR2007051501322.html.

Rosenfeld, Everett, 2017. 'Trump launches attack on Syria with 59 Tomahawk missiles', *CNBC*, 7 April. www.cnbc.com/2017/04/06/us-military-has-launched-more-50-than-missiles-aimed-at-syria-nbc-news.html.

Roth, Andrew, Brian Murphy and Thomas Gibbons-Neff, 2015. 'Dutch report: Buk missile downed MH17 in Ukraine', *Washington Post*, 13 October. www.washingtonpost.com/news/worldviews/wp/2015/10/13/a-dutch-report-will-say-what-downed-mh17-it-wont-blame-the-russians/?_ga=1.255814094

.790230886.1480488190&utm_term=.37c1d51b155c.

Rowell, Alex, 2014. 'Blame Assad first for ISIS' rise', *NOW*, 17 June. https://now
.mmedia.me/lb/en/commentaryanalysis/551852-blame-assad-first-for-isis-rise.

Royce, Knut, 1990. 'Middle East crisis: Secret offer – Iraq sent pullout deal to US',
Newsday, 29 August. www.scribd.com/doc/38969813/MIDDLE-EAST
-CRISIS-Secret-Offer-Iraq-Sent-Pullout-Deal-to-U-S-ALL-EDITIONS.

RT, 2014a. 'Russian MPs seek to sue Gorbachev over USSR collapse', 10 April.
www.rt.com/politics/gorbachev-ussr-collapse-lawsuit-568/.

———, 2014b. '"Don't bomb Iraq and Syria!", Stop the War protests at Downing
Street', 25 September. www.rt.com/uk/190532-uk-isis-iraq-cameron/.

———, 2016a. '"Grandma's WWII stories still send shivers down my spine"', 22
June. www.rt.com/news/347829-russia-june22-wwii-heroes/.

———, 2016b. 'US-led coalition aircraft strike Syrian army positions, kill 62 soldiers – military', 17 September. www.rt.com/news/359678-us-strikes
-syrian-army/.

———, 2016c. 'School in Syria's Idlib province not hit by airstrike, drone photos
show – Russian MoD', 27 October. www.rt.com/news/364454-russia-idlib
-school-comment/.

Rudaw, 2016a. 'Iraq's grand Ayatollah discourages sectarian violence in Diyala', 16
January. http://rudaw.net/english/middleeast/iraq/15012016.

———, 2016b. 'Rudaw expresses regret over ban by Kobani authorities in Syria', 25
February. http://rudaw.net/english/kurdistan/250220161.

Ruiz-Marrero, Carmelo, 2014. 'The October Surprise Was Real', *Counterpunch*, 11
July. www.counterpunch.org/2014/07/11/the-october-surprise-was-real/.

Russian Socialist Movement, 2016. 'The left face of the Putin regime', *International
Viewpoint*, 22 August. www.internationalviewpoint.org/spip.php?article4666.

Ryzhkov, Vladimir, 2014. 'Russia's treatment of Crimean Tatars echoes mistakes
made by Soviets', *The Guardian*, 25 November. www.theguardian.com/world
/2014/nov/25/-sp-russia-crimean-tatars-soviet-ukraine.

Saadoun, Mustafa, 2015. 'Iraq's Popular Mobilization Units warn against "renewed
occupation" by US', *Al-Monitor*, 30 December. www.al-monitor.com/pulse
/originals/2015/12/iraq-us-forces-presence-isis-pmu-threats.html.

———, 2016a. 'It's official: Sunnis joining Iraq's Popular Mobilization Units',
Al-Monitor, 14 January. www.al-monitor.com/pulse/originals/2016/01
/iraq-sunnis-join-shiite-popular-mobilization-forces.html.

———, 2016b. 'Iraqis divided over Soleimani's role in their country', *Al-Monitor*, 20
May. www.al-monitor.com/pulse/originals/2016/05/iraq-iran-commander
-soleimani-role-flags.html.

———. 2017. 'If Iran has its way, Abadi won't see a second term in Iraq', *Al-Monitor*,
21 July. www.al-monitor.com/pulse/originals/2017/07/iran-iraq-prime
-minister-abadi-khamenei-pmu-shiite-militias.html.

Sadri, James, interviewed by Syria Deeply, 2016. 'Breaking the silence around sieges',
Mesopotamische Gesellscaft, 17 January. www.mesop.de/west-kurdistan

-syria-mesop-syria-interview-breaking-the-silence-around-sieges/.

Safdar, Anealla, 2016. 'Brexit: UKIP's "unethical" anti-immigration poster', *Al Jazeera*, 28 June. www.aljazeera.com/indepth/features/2016/06/brexit-anti-immigration-ukip-poster-raises-questions-160621112722799.html.

Sahimi, Muhammad, 2009. 'The Bloody Red Summer of 1988', PBS Frontline, Tehran Bureau, 25 August. www.pbs.org/wgbh/pages/frontline/tehranbureau/2009/08/the-bloody-red-summer-of-1988.html.

———, 2011. 'The Chain Murders: Killing Intellectuals and Dissidents, 1988–1998', PBS Frontline, Tehran Bureau, 5 January. www.pbs.org/wgbh/pages/frontline/tehranbureau/2011/01/the-chain-murders-killing-dissidents-and-intellectuals-1988-1998.html.

Sakr, Rita, 2013. *'Anticipating' the 2011 Arab Uprisings: Revolutionary Literatures and Political Geographies*, Basingstoke and New York: Palgrave Macmillan.

Saleh, Ibrahim, 2016. 'Baghdad Locals Still Fear Being Kidnapped By Militias or Police', *Niqash*, 28 April. www.niqash.org/en/articles/security/5235/.

Saleh, Yassin al-Haj, Murtaza Hussein and Marwan Hisham, 2016. 'Syria's "Voice of Conscience" has a message for the West', *The Intercept*, 26 October. https://theintercept.com/2016/10/26/syria-yassin-al-haj-saleh-interview/.

Salemi, Ladan, 2010. 'The eleven-pronged assault of the illegitimate government on universities in Iran', *Gozaar*, 15 September. www.gozaar.org/english/articles-en/The-Eleven-Pronged-Assault-of-the-Illegitimate-Government-on-Uni.html.

Salih, Mohammed A., 2014. 'After taking Sinjar, IS draws Iraqi Kurds into full-scale war', *Al-Monitor*, 7 August. www.al-monitor.com/pulse/originals/2014/08/iraq-kurdistan-yazidis-peshmerga-isis-islamic-state.html.

Salih, Mohammed A., 2015. 'With the Islamic State gone from Sinjar, Kurdish groups battle for control', *Al-Monitor*, 10 December. www.al-monitor.com/pulse/originals/2015/12/iraq-kurdistan-sinjar-liberated-isis-hegemony.html.

Samaha, Nour, 2016. 'Iraq's "Good Sunni"', *Foreign Policy*, 16 November. http://foreignpolicy.com/2016/11/16/iraqs-good-sunni/.

Sanchez, Raf, 2013. 'First Syria rebels armed and trained by CIA "on way to battlefield"', *The Telegraph*, 3 September. www.telegraph.co.uk/news/worldnews/middleeast/syria/10283758/First-Syria-rebels-armed-and-trained-by-CIA-on-way-to-battlefield.html.

Sarkohi, Faraj, 2012. 'Writers in Iran: Fighting a Losing Battle', *Quantara.de*. https://en.qantara.de/content/writers-in-iran-fighting-a-losing-battle

Sarotte, Mary Elise, 2014. 'Putin's view of power was formed watching East Germany collapse', *The Guardian*, 1 October. www.theguardian.com/commentisfree/2014/oct/01/putin-power-east-germany-russia-kgb-dresden.

Sassoon, Joseph, 2012. *Saddam Hussein's Ba'th Party: Inside an Authoritarian Regime*, Cambridge: Cambridge University Press.

Sattar, Omar, 2016. 'Party squabbles have Iraqi PM by the coattails', *Al-Monitor*, 8 February. www.al-monitor.com/pulse/originals/2016/02/iraq-abadi-reforms-cabinet-reshuffle-disappoints-protests.html.

———, 2017. 'Iraqi Islamist MPs' proposal would allow child marriages', *Al-Monitor*, 16 November. www.al-monitor.com/pulse/originals/2017/11/iraq-personal-status-law-child-marriage.html.

Schabas, William, 2000. *Genocide in International Law*, Cambridge: Cambridge University Press.

———, 2001. *An Introduction to the International Criminal Court*, Cambridge: Cambridge University Press.

Schlesinger, Stephen C. and Stephen Kinzer, 2005 [1982]. *Bitter Fruit: The Story of the American Coup in Guatemala*, Harvard: Harvard University Press.

Schneider, Tobias, 2016. 'The decay of the Syrian regime is much worse than you think', *War on the Rocks*, 31 August. http://warontherocks.com/2016/08/the-decay-of-the-syrian-regime-is-much-worse-than-you-think/.

Schuman, Michael, 2012. 'Why Vladimir Putin Needs Higher Oil Prices', *Time*, 5 July. http://business.time.com/2012/07/05/why-vladimir-putin-needs-higher-oil-prices/.

Sciolino, Eliane, 2003. 'Daughter of The Revolution Fights the Veil', *The New York Times*, 2 April. www.nytimes.com/2003/04/02/international/middleeast/02IRAN.html.

Scott, Alev, 2015. 'The day Assad leaves Syria, I will return', *Politico*, 25 November. www.politico.eu/article/the-day-assad-leaves-syria-i-will-return-refugees-migrants/.

Scott, Mark, 2017. 'US Far-Right Activists Promote Hacking Attack Against Macron', *The New York Times*, 6 May. www.nytimes.com/2017/05/06/world/europe/emmanuel-macron-hack-french-election-marine-le-pen.html?_r=0.

Secor, Laura, 2016. 'War of words: A woman's battle to end stoning and juvenile execution in Iran', *The New Yorker*, 4 January. www.newyorker.com/magazine/2016/01/04/war-of-words-annals-of-activism-laura-secor.

Seddon, Max, 2014. 'Documents show how Russia's troll army hit America', *BuzzFeed News*, 3 June. www.buzzfeed.com/maxseddon/documents-show-how-russias-troll-army-hit-america?utm_term=.vwJ4qvW86j#.kxwAXknQ8K.

Sehgal, Gita, 2014. 'Who wrote the Universal Declaration of Human Rights?', *OpenDemocracy*, 10 December. www.opendemocracy.net/5050/gita-sahgal/who-wrote-universal-declaration-of-human-rights.

Sells, Michael, 1998. *The Bridge Betrayed: Religion and Genocide in Bosnia*, Berkeley: University of California Press.

Sémelin, Jacques, 2013. 'Timothy Snyder and his Critics', *Books and Ideas*, 14 February. www.booksandideas.net/Timothy-Snyder-and-his-Critics.html.

Serge, Victor, 1927a. 'The Outcome of an Experience of Class Collaboration'. www.marxists.org/archive/serge/1927/china/letter4.html.

———, 1927b. 'The Strength of the Agrarian Revolution: The Red Spears'. www.marxists.org/archive/serge/1927/china/letter3.html.

———, 2012. *Memoirs of a Revolutionary*, trans. Peter Sedgewick with George Paizis, New York: New York Review of Books.

Serie, Jack, 2016. 'Obama casualty numbers a fraction of those recorded by the Bureau', *The Bureau of Investigative Journalism*, 1 July. www.thebureauinvestigates.com/2016/07/01/obama-drone-casualty-numbers-fraction-recorded-bureau/.

Shadid, Anthony, 2011. 'Killing of opposition leader in Syria provokes Kurds', *The New York Times*, 8 October. www.nytimes.com/2011/10/09/world/middleeast/killing-of-opposition-leader-in-syria-provokes-kurds.html.

Shahak, Israel, 1994. *Jewish History, Jewish Religion: The Weight of Three Thousand Years*, London: Pluto Press.

Shaheen, Kareem, 2016a. '"Hell itself: Aleppo reels from alleged use of bunker-buster bombs', *The Guardian*, 26 September. www.theguardian.com/world/2016/sep/26/hell-itself-aleppo-reels-from-alleged-use-of-bunker-buster-bombs.

———, 2016b. 'Russia or Syria was behind deadly Idlib school attack, says US', *The Guardian*, 27 October. www.theguardian.com/world/2016/oct/27/airstrike-on-syrian-village-kills-26-people-reports-say.

ShahidSaless, Shahir, 2015. 'Does Iran really control Yemen?', *Al Monitor*, 12 February. www.al-monitor.com/pulse/originals/2015/02/iran-yemen-houthis-axis-of-resistance.html.

Shandra, Alya, 2015. 'Right Sector, Putin take same view on gay rights', *Kyiv Post*, 11 June. www.kyivpost.com/opinion/op-ed/right-sector-putin-take-same-view-on-gay-rights-390857.html.

Shear, Michael and Jennifer Steinhauer, 2017. 'Trump to Seek $54 Billion Increase in Military Spending', *The New York Times*, 27 February. www.nytimes.com/2017/02/27/us/politics/trump-budget-military.html?_r=0.

Shear, Michael and Maggie Haberman, 2017. 'Trump Defends Initial Remarks on Charlottesville; Again Blames "Both Sides"', *The New York Times*, 15 August. www.nytimes.com/2017/08/15/us/politics/trump-press-conference-charlottesville.html?mcubz=3&_r=0.

Shekhovtsov, Anton, 2014a. 'European right-wing extremists and other pro-Russian activists "observed" the Crimean "referendum"', *Searchlight*, 23 March. www.searchlightmagazine.com/news/featured-news/european-right-wing-extremists-and-other-pro-russian-activists-observed-the-crimean-referendum.

———, 2014b. 'The Kremlin's marriage of convenience with the European far right', *OpenDemocracy*, 28 April. www.opendemocracy.net/od-russia/anton-shekhovtsov/kremlin%E2%80%99s-marriage-of-convenience-with-european-far-right.

Sherlock, Ruth, 2012. 'Exclusive interview: why I defected from Bashar al-Assad's regime, by former diplomat Nawaf Fares', *The Telgraph*, 14 July. www.telegraph.co.uk/news/worldnews/middleeast/syria/9400537/Exclusive-interview-why-I-defected-from-Bashar-al-Assads-regime-by-former-diplomat-Nawaf-Fares.html.

Sherlock, Ruth and Richard Spencer, 2014. 'Syria's Assad accused of boosting al-Qaeda with secret oil deals', *The Telegraph*, 20 January. www.telegraph.co.uk/news/worldnews/middleeast/syria/10585391/Syrias-Assad-accused-of-boosting-al-Qaeda-with-secret-oil-deals.html.

Siddiqi, Ahmad, 2004. 'Khatami and the search for reform in Iran', *Stanford Journal of International Relations*. https://web.stanford.edu/group/sjir/6.1.04_siddiqi.html.

Siegel, Jacob, 2015. 'The ISIS conspiracy that ate the web', *The Daily Beast*, 6 June. www.thedailybeast.com/articles/2015/06/06/the-isis-conspiracy-that-ate-the -web.html.

Silber, Laura and Allan Little, 1997. *Yugoslavia: Death of a Nation*, Harmondsworth: Penguin.

Sinclair, Christian and Sirwan Kajjo, 2011. 'The evolution of Kurdish politics in Syria', *Middle East Research and Information Project*, 31 August. www.merip.org /mero/mero083111#_19_.

Sinelschikova, Yekaterina, 2016. 'Anna Politkovskaya murder: 10 years later, still no clear answers', *Russia Beyond the Headlines*, 8 October. http://rbth.com/politics _and_society/2016/10/08/anna-politkovskaya-murder-10-years-later-still-no -clear-answers_636919.

Sky News, 2016a. 'Russia shows off military might at Syria base', 20 January. https:// uk.news.yahoo.com/russia-shows-off-military-might-syria-133002148.html.

———, 2016b. '"Meltdown of humanity" in Aleppo as Assad troops close in', 13 December. http://news.sky.com/story/aleppo-rebels-told-to-surrender-or-die- as-assad-troops-near-victory-10694126.

Slackman, Michael, 2009. 'Hard-Line Force Extends Grip Over a Splintered Iran', *The New York Times*, 20 July. www.nytimes.com/2009/07/21/world /middleeast/21guards.html.

Smith, Ashley, 2016a. 'Syria's revolutionaries return to the streets', *SocialistWorker.org*, 10 March. https://socialistworker.org/2016/03/10/syrias-revolutionaries -return-to-streets.

———, 2016b. 'Anti-imperialism and the Syrian revolution', *SocialistWorker.org*, 25 August. https://socialistworker.org/2016/08/25/anti-imperialism-and-the -syrian-revolution.

———, 2016c. 'The counterrevolution crushed Aleppo', *SocialistWorker.org*, 13 December. https://socialistworker.org/2016/12/13/the-counterrevolution -crushes-aleppo.

Smith, Jeremy, 1999. *The Bolsheviks and the National Question, 1917–1923*, New York: St. Martin's Press.

———, 2004. 'Nationalities Policies, Soviet', *Encyclopedia of Russian History*. www.encyclopedia.com/doc/1G2-3404100888.html.

Smyth, Gareth, 2013. 'Iran's Khatami strikes back', *The Guardian*, 19 September. www.theguardian.com/world/iran-blog/2013/sep/20/iran-khatami-revenge -rouhani-victory.

Smyth, Philip, 2015. 'Iran-backed Iraqi militias are pouring into Syria', *Business Insider*, 2 October. www.businessinsider.com/iran-backed-iraqi-militias-are -pouring-into-syria-2015-10?IR=T.

SNHR (Syrian Network for Human Rights), 2017. 'Syrian Civil Society Call for Credible Syrian-led Political Process for Syria', 4 August. http://sn4hr.org

/blog/2017/08/04/45034/.

Snyder, Timothy, 2010. *Bloodlands: Europe Between Hitler and Stalin*, London: Vintage.

———, 2014. 'The Battle in Ukraine Means Everything', *New Republic*, 12 May. https://newrepublic.com/article/117692/fascism-returns-ukraine.

Soboul, Albert, 1977. *A Short History of the French Revolution*, trans. Geoffrey Symcox, Berkeley: University of California Press.

Socialist Worker, 2013. 'Solidarity with the Syrian Revolution', 1 May. http://socialistworker.org/2013/05/01/solidarity-with-the-revolution.

Socor, Vladimir, 2014. 'Ukraine's Presidential Election Reveals Unexpected Trends', *Eurasia Daily Monitor*, 11(101), 30 May. https://jamestown.org/program/ukraines-presidential-election-reveals-unexpected-trends/.

Solieman, Ishra, 2011. 'Denied existence: Libyan-Berbers under Gaddafi and Hope for the Current revolution', *Muftah*, 24 March. http://muftah.org/denied-existence-libyan-berbers-under-gaddafi-and-hope-for-the-current-revolution/#.V63GP6IY4bY.

Solomon, Erica and Ahmed Mhidi, 2015. 'Isis Inc: Syria's mafia-style gas deals with jihadis', *Financial Times*, 15 October. www.ft.com/cms/s/2/92f4e036-6b69-11e5-aca9-d87542bf8673.html#axzz3yRNy5UVH.

Solvang, Ole, 2016. 'Russian Cluster Munitions Have Literally Made Syria a Minefield', *The Moscow Times*, 12 October. https://themoscowtimes.com/articles/russian-cluster-munitions-have-literally-made-syria-a-minefield-53518.

Sotiropoulos, Evagelos, 2016. 'Russia's Holy Power Play', *The Huffington Post*, 26 January. www.huffingtonpost.com/evagelos-sotiropoulos/russias-holy-power-play_b_9071654.html.

Southern Poverty Law Centre, n.d. 'Pamela Geller', *Extremist Files*. www.splcenter.org/fighting-hate/extremist-files/individual/pamela-geller.

Spada, Andrea, 2015. 'PYD leader supports Russian airstrikes in Syria', *Islam Media Analysis*, 21 October. www.islamedianalysis.info/pyd-leader-supports-russian-airstrikes-in-syria/.

Spencer, Richard, 2016. 'Where are the Syrians in Assad's Syrian Arab army?' *The Telegraph*, 9 April. www.telegraph.co.uk/news/2016/04/09/where-are-the-syrians-in-assads-syrian-arab-army/?ref=yfp.

Srebrenica Genocide Blog, 2010. 'Gen Sir Michael Rose testifies against Radovan Karadžić, Serbs responsible for Markhale', 7 October. http://srebrenica-genocide.blogspot.in/2010/10/gen-sir-michael-rose-testifies-against.html.

Stalin, J. V., 1927. 'Talk with Students at Sun Yat-sen University', *On the Opposition*, Peking: Foreign Languages Press. www.marx2mao.com/Stalin/SYSU27.html.

Standish, Reid, 2015a. 'Putin's Eurasian Dream is Over Before it Began', *Foreign Policy*, 6 January. http://foreignpolicy.com/2015/01/06/putins-eurasian-dream-is-over-before-it-began/.

———, 2015b. 'Meet the Man Showing the World What Airstrikes are Doing to Syria', *Foreign Policy*, 21 December. https://foreignpolicy.com/2015/12/21

/meet-the-man-showing-the-world-what-airstrikes-are-doing-to-syria/.

Stauber, John and Sheldon Rampton, 1995. *Toxic Sludge is Good for You: Lies, Damn Lies and the PR Industry*, Monroe, Maine: Common Courage Press. www.prwatch.org/books/tsigfy10.html.

Stecklow, Steve, Babak Dehghanpisheh and Yeganeh Torbati, 2013. 'Khamenei controls massive financial empire built on property seizures', *Reuters*, 11 November. www.reuters.com/investigates/iran/#article/part1.

Steele, Jonathan, 2003. 'Museum's treasures left to the mercy of looters', *The Guardian*, 14 April. www.theguardian.com/world/2003/apr/14/internationaleducationnews.arts.

Steele, Jonathan and Mikhail Gorbachev, 2011. 'Mikhail Gorbachev: I should have abandoned the Communist Party earlier', *The Guardian*, 16 August. www.theguardian.com/world/2011/aug/16/gorbachev-guardian-interview.

Stein, Jill, 2016. 'In Moscow, Stein Called for Foreign Policy of Principled Collaboration', Jill Stein for President. www.jill2016.com/stein_in_russia_calls_for_principled_collaboration.

Stella, Francesca and Nadya Nartova, 2016. 'Sexual citizenship, nationalism and biopolitics in Putin's Russia', in *Sexuality, Citizenship and Belonging: Trans-National and Intersectional Perspectives*, eds Francesca Stella, Yvette Taylor, Tracey Reynolds and Antoine Rogers, New York and Abingdon: Routledge.

Stephenson, David, 2016. 'Russia, Ukraine or CIA? BBC documentary tries to expose the truth about MH17', *Express*. www.express.co.uk/news/world/663787/Ukrainian-fighter-jet-shot-Russian-crash-MH17-BBC-documentary.

Stevenson, Seth, 2001. 'Pipe Dreams', *Slate*, 6 December. www.slate.com/articles/arts/tangled_web/2001/12/pipe_dreams.single.html.

Stiglitz, Joseph, 2000. 'The Insider', *The New Republic*, 17 April. https://newrepublic.com/article/61082/the-insider.

StopFake, 2015. 'Russia's Top 200 Lies', 1 December. www.stopfake.org/en/russia-s-top-200-lies-international-edition/.

———, 2016. 'Fake: Lavrov Lies about Russia's Budapest Memorandum Obligation to Ukraine', 27 January. www.stopfake.org/en/fake-lavrov-lies-about-russia-s-budapest-memorandum-obligation-to-ukraine/.

Stubbs, Jack, 2016. 'Russia's Stepanova – "No accident" if something happens to me', *Reuters*, 15 August. https://uk.sports.yahoo.com/news/russias-stepanova-no-accident-something-happens-192422226--spt.html.

Subtelny, Orest, 2000. *Ukraine: A History*, Toronto: University of Toronto Press.

Sudetic, Chuck, 1991. 'Serbs Refuse to Negotiate in Croatia', *The New York Times*, 5 August. www.nytimes.com/1991/08/05/world/serbs-refuse-to-negotiate-in-croatia.html.

Sullivan, Marisa, 2014. 'Hezbollah in Syria', *Middle East Security Report* 19, April. www.understandingwar.org/sites/default/files/Hezbollah_Sullivan_FINAL.pdf.

Susskind, Yifat, 2007. 'Promising Democracy, Imposing Theocracy: Gender-Based Violence and the US War on Iraq', *Madre*, March 19. www.madre.org/press

-publications/human-rights-report/promising-democracy-imposing-theocracy
-gender-based-violence.

Swaine, Jon, 2017. 'Donald Trump's team defends "alternative facts" after widespread
protests', *The Guardian*, 23 January. www.theguardian.com/us-news/2017
/jan/22/donald-trump-kellyanne-conway-inauguration-alternative-facts.

Sweeney, John, 2000. 'Revealed: Russia's worst war crime in Chechnya', *The Guardian*, 5 March. www.theguardian.com/world/2000/mar/05/russia.chechnya.

Swidey, Neil, 2016. 'Where did ISIS come from? The story starts here', *The Boston
Globe*, 10 March. www.bostonglobe.com/magazine/2016/03/10/where-did-isis
-come-from-the-story-starts-here/eOHwJQgnZPNj8SE91Vw5hK/story.html.

Taghvaie, Hamid, n.d. 'Who was Mansoor Hekmat?' www.m-hekmat.com/biographyEn
.html.

Taher, Ali, 2016. 'Accusations fly as Basra cafes hit by string of bombings', *Al-Monitor*,
31 August. www.al-monitor.com/pulse/originals/2016/08/islamisation
-basra-shiite-militias-civil-life.html.

Tamimi, Azzam, 2016. 'Madaya: A huge concentration camp where Hezbollah
starves people to death', *Middle East Eye*, 7 January. www.middleeasteye.net/
columns/madaya-huge-concentration-camp-where-hezbollah-starves-people
-death-786110749.

Tanner, Marcus, 2000. 'Cartoon retells forgotten plight of Gorazde', *Independent*, 21
October. www.independent.co.uk/news/world/europe/cartoon-retells
-forgotten-plight-of-gorazde-635065.html.

Tatchell, Peter, 2009a. 'Support the Iranian people, oppose Tehran's clerical fascism',
Red Pepper, February. www.redpepper.org.uk/support-the-iranian-people
-oppose/.

———, 2009b. 'Far Left collusion with the Islamofascism of Iran's clerical tyranny'.
www.petertatchell.net/international/iran/islamo-fascism.htm.

The BRICS Post, 2016. 'BRICS react cautiously to Brexit', 24 June. http://
thebricspost.com/brics-reacts-cautiously-to-brexit/#.V_8vockY4ba.

The Conversation, 2016. 'Vacuum bombs in Syria: the latest chapter in a long history of atrocity from the skies', 17 August. https://theconversation.com
/vacuum-bombs-in-syria-the-latest-chapter-in-a-long-history-of-atrocity
-from-the-skies-63733.

The Economic Times, 2015. 'Bashar al-Assad must go as soon as possible: Francois
Hollande', 25 November. http://economictimes.indiatimes.com/news
/international/world-news/bashar-al-assad-must-go-as-soon-as-possible
-francois-hollande/articleshow/49914398.cms.

The Economist, 2015. 'Boris Nemtsov's parting shot', 13 May. www.economist
.com/news/europe/21651130-posthumously-completed-report-details
-russias-involvement-war-ukraine-boris-nemtsovs.

The Guardian, 2012. 'Hundreds detained after Moscow anti-Putin protest', 5 March.
www.theguardian.com/world/blog/2012/mar/05/russian-election-reaction
-putin-live.

———, 2014. 'Nigel Farage: I admire Vladimir Putin', 31 March. www.theguardian. com/politics/2014/mar/31/farage-i-admire-putin.

———, 2016. 'Isis leader Abu Bakr al-Baghdadi urges fight to death in Iraq, audio claims', 3 November. www.theguardian.com/world/2016/nov/03/isis-leader -abu-bakr-al-baghdadi-issues-first-message-since-mosul-offensive.

The Nation, 2016. 'Syrian Writers, Artists and Journalists Speak Out Against US and Russian Policy', 21 September. www.thenation.com/article/syrian-writers -artists-and-journalists-speak-out-against-us-and-russian-policy/.

The New Arab, 2016. '"Bloodbath" in Aleppo as Syrian regime advance', 30 September. www.alaraby.co.uk/english/news/2016/9/30/bloodbath-in-aleppo-as -syrian-regime-advance

The Soufan Group, 2015. 'Assad's atrocities continue', 18 August. http:// soufangroup.com/tsg-intelbrief-assads-atrocities-continue/.

The Syria Campaign, 2015. Syria: The facts and figures', 23 September. https://diary.thesyriacampaign.org/whats-happening-to-civilians-in-syria /?akid=258.109184.UJu7Wh&rd=1&t=5.

———, 2016a. 'Taking Sides: The United Nations' Loss of Impartiality, Independence and Neutrality in Syria'. http://takingsides.thesyriacampaign.org /wp-content/uploads/2016/06/taking-sides.pdf.

———, 2016b. '8 Reasons Why Syrians Will Never Forget Jo Cox', 21 June. https://diary.thesyriacampaign.org/8-reasons-why-syrians-will-never-forget -jo-cox/.

The Telegraph, 2013. 'Barack Obama's speech on Syria in full', 11 September. www. telegraph.co.uk/news/worldnews/barackobama/10300943/Barack-Obamas -speech-on-Syria-in-full.html.

———, 2015. 'REVEALED: The oil middleman between the Syrian regime and ISIS', 7 March. www.businessinsider.com/revealed-the-oil-middleman -between-the-syrian-regime-and-isis-2015-3?IR=T.

———, 2016. 'Bashar al-Assad says Donald Trump a "natural ally" for Syria alongside Russia and Iran', 15 November. www.telegraph.co.uk/news/2016/11/15 /bashar-al-assad-says-donald-trump-a-natural-ally-for-syria-along/.

Thompson, Elizabeth F., 2013. Justice Interrupted: The Struggle for Constitutional Government in the Middle East, Cambridge, MA: Harvard University Press.

Timberg, Craig, 2016. 'Russian propaganda effort helped spread "fake news" during election, experts say', The Washington Post, 24 November. www.washingtonpost .com/business/economy/russian-propaganda-effort-helped-spread-fake-news -during-election-experts-say/2016/11/24/793903b6-8a40-4ca9-b712 -716af66098fe_story.html?hpid=hp_hp-top-table-main_propaganda -8pm%3Ahomepage%2Fstory.

Timmerman, Kenneth R., 2003. 'Invitation to September 11', Insight, 22 December. www.kentimmerman.com/2003_12_22-beirut.htm.

Thielmann, Greg, 2013. 'The Cost of Ignoring UN Inspectors: An Unnecessary War with Iraq', Arms Control Now, 5 March. https://armscontrolnow.org/2013/03

/05/the-cost-of-ignoring-un-inspectors-an-unnecessary-war-with-iraq/.

Thoburn, Hannah, 2016. 'For Putin, for Stalin', *Foreign Policy*, 25 January. http://
foreignpolicy.com/2016/01/25/for-putin-for-stalin-russia-propaganda/.

Tibon, Amir and Tal Shalev, 2015. 'Scenes from a marriage: The worst relationship
between a US president and an Israeli prime minister ever – as autopsied by
the people closest to them', *The Huffington Post*. http://highline.huffingtonpost
.com/articles/en/bibi-obama/.

Toosi, Nahal, 2016. 'Assad again used chemical weapons: UN report', *Politico*, 25
August. www.politico.eu/article/un-report-assad-again-used-chemical
-weapons-defying-obama/.

Traboulsi, Fawwaz, interviewed by Mohammed al Attar, 2013. 'Syrian revolutionaries owe nobody an apology', April. www.boell.de/sites/default/files/assets
/boell.de/images/download_de/democracy/2013-04-Fawwaz-Traboulsi
-Interview-engl.pdf.

Trombly, Daniel, 2016. 'Analysis: What Russia's Military Withdrawal From Syria
Means for Fight Against ISIS, Assad Regime', *USNI News*, 15 March. https://
news.usni.org/2016/03/15/analysis-what-russias-military-withdrawal-from
-syria-means-for-fight-against-isis-assad-regime.

Trotsky, Leon, 1923. *Voina i Revolyutsiya*, vol. 1, Moscow: Gosudarstvennoe Izda-
tel'stvo.

Tugendhat, Christopher, 1973. *The Multinationals*, Harmondsworth: Penguin Books.

Uehling, Greta Lynn, n.d. 'The Crimean Tatars', International Committee for
Crimea. www.iccrimea.org/scholarly/krimtatars.html.

Umland, Andreas, 2008. 'Who is Alexander Dugin?', *Open Democracy*, 26 September. www.opendemocracy.net/article/russia-theme/who-is-alexander-dugin.

UN, n.d.a. 'Charter of the United Nations'. www.un.org/en/charter-united-nations/.

———, n.d.b. 'The Foundation of International Human Rights Law'. www.un.org
/en/sections/universal-declaration/foundation-international-human-rights-law
/index.html.

———, n.d.c. 'Universal Declaration of Human Rights'. www.un.org/en/universal
-declaration-human-rights/.

———, 2014. 'Referral of Syria to the International Criminal Court Fails as Negative Votes Prevent Security Council from Adopting Draft Resolution', 22 May.
www.un.org/press/en/2014/sc11407.doc.htm.

———, 2015. 'Report of the Special Rapporteur on the situation of human rights
in the Islamic Republic of Iran'. www.un.org/ga/search/view_doc.asp
?symbol=A/70/411.

UNHRC (UN Human Rights Council), 2014. 'Pillay castigates "paralysis" on Syria
as new UN study indicates over 191,000 people killed', 22 August. www.ohchr
.org/EN/NewsEvents/Pages/DisplayNews.aspx?NewsID=14959&.

———, 2016a. 'Out of Sight, Out of Mind: Deaths in Detention in the Syrian Arab
Republic', 3 February. www.ohchr.org/Documents/HRBodies/HRCouncil
/CoISyria/A-HRC-31-CRP1_en.pdf.

———. 2016b. 'Situation of human rights in Yemen', 4 August. http://reliefweb.int
/sites/reliefweb.int/files/resources/G1617238.pdf.

UNSC (UN Security Council), 2005. 'Syria's withdrawal from Lebanon "Historic
day" for Middle East, Special Envoy Terje Roed-Larsen tells Security Council',
29 April. www.un.org/press/en/2005/sc8372.doc.htm.

———, 2011. 'Resolution 1973 (2011)'. www.nato.int/nato_static_fl2014/assets
/pdf/pdf_2011_03/20110927_110311-UNSCR-1973.pdf.

US Labor Against the War, 2015. 'New Iraqi Labor Law offers more protection than
US law', 25 October. http://uslaboragainstwar.org/Article/74419/new-iraqi
-labor-law-offers-more-protection-than-us-law.

van Herpen, Marcel H., 2015. *Putin's Wars: The Rise of Russia's New Imperialism*,
Lanham and London: Rowman and Littlefield.

Varshalomidze, Tamila, 2015. 'Moscow rally against Russia's Syria strikes falls short',
Al Jazeera, 18 October. www.aljazeera.com/news/2015/10/moscow-rally
-russia-syria-air-strikes-151017170228299.html.

Varoufakis, Yanis, 2016. 'Europe's Left after Brexit', 8 September. https://
yanisvaroufakis.eu/2016/09/08/europes-left-after-brexit/.

Vasovic, Alexandar, and Maria Kiselyova, 2014. 'Russian forces seize two Ukrainian
bases in Crimea', Reuters, 20 March. www.reuters.com/article/2014/03/20
/us-ukraine-crisis-idUSBREA2I0TR20140320.

Vice News, 2016. 'Iraq halts assault against Islamic State-held Fallujah to "protect
civilians"', 1 June. https://news.vice.com/article/iraq-halts-assault-against
-islamic-state-held-fallujah-to-protect-civilians-trapped-inside.

Vulliamy, Ed, 2017. 'Ratko Mladić will die in jail. But go to Bosnia: you'll see that he
won', *The Guardian*, 22 November. www.theguardian.com/commentisfree
/2017/nov/22/ratko-mladic-bosnia-camps-mass-murder-torture-rape-serbian.

Walcott, John, 2016. 'Russia intervened to help Trump win election – intelligence
officials', *Reuters*, 11 December. http://uk.reuters.com/article/uk-usa-election
-cyber-russia-idUKKBN13Z05D.

Walker, Shaun, 2015. 'Vladimir Putin calls Donald Trump a "very colourful and tal-
ented man"', *The Guardian*, 17 December. www.theguardian.com/world/2015
/dec/17/vladimir-putin-donald-trump-very-bright-talented-man-russia-us
-presidential-race.

———, 2016. 'The murder that killed free media in Russia', *The Guardian*, 5 October. www.theguardian.com/world/2016/oct/05/ten-years-putin-press-kremlin
-grip-russia-media-tightens.

———, 2017a. 'Putin approves legal change that decriminalizes some domestic
violence', *The Guardian*, 7 February. www.theguardian.com/world/2017/feb/07
/putin-approves-change-to-law-decriminalising-domestic-violence.

———, 2017b. 'Russia's "irrefutable evidence" of US help for Isis appears to be video
game still', *The Guardian*, 14 November. www.theguardian.com/world/2017
/nov/14/russia-us-isis-syria-video-game-still.

Wang, Nanfu, 2016. 'I want you to understand the sense of fear that Chinese people

feel every day', *The Guardian*, 22 January. www.theguardian.com/commentisfree
/2016/jan/22/i-want-you-to-understand-the-sense-of-fear-that-chinese
-people-feel-every-day?CMP=fb_cif.

Warren, Marcus, 2001.'50 bodies point to Chechnya war crime', *The Telegraph*, 6
March. www.telegraph.co.uk/news/worldnews/europe/russia/1325228
/50-bodies-point-to-Chechnya-war-crime.html.

Waters, Nick and Hadi Al-Khatib, 2016.'Analysis of Syrian Red Crescent aid convoy attack', *Bellingcat*, 21 September. www.bellingcat.com/news/mena/2016
/09/21/aleppo-un-aid-analysis/.

Weir, Fred, 2015.'Curbing the kleptocrats: Kiev chips away at its pervasive corruption', *The Christian Science Monitor*, 16 April. www.csmonitor.com/World
/Europe/2015/0416/Curbing-the-kleptocrats-Kiev-chips-away-at-its
-pervasive-corruption.

Weisburd, Andrew, Clint Watts and J. M. Berger, 2016.'Trolling for Trump: How
Russia is trying to destroy our democracy', *War on the Rocks*, 6 November.
http://warontherocks.com/2016/11/trolling-for-trump-how-russia-is-trying
-to-destroy-our-democracy/.

Weiss, Michael, 2013.'Assad's no enemy of al-Qaeda', *NOW*, 31 July. https://now
.mmedia.me/lb/en/commentaryanalysis/assads-no-enemy-of-al-qaeda.

———, 2015a.'Russia's Double Game with Islamic Terror', *The Daily Beast*, 23
August. www.thedailybeast.com/articles/2015/08/23/russia-s-playing-a
-double-game-with-islamic-terror0.html.

———, 2015b.'Russia's Propaganda Blitzkrieg', *The Daily Beast*, 4 October. www
.thedailybeast.com/articles/2015/10/04/russia-s-propaganda-blitzkrieg.html.

———, 2015c.'Russia's Giving ISIS an Air Force', *The Daily Beast*, 8 October. www
.thedailybeast.com/articles/2015/10/08/russia-s-giving-isis-an-air-force.html.

Whitney, Mike, 2015.'Kerry's Debacle in Vienna', *Counterpunch*, 3 November.
www.counterpunch.org/2015/11/03/kerrys-debacle-in-vienna/.

Wintour, Patrick and Chris Stephen, 2017.'Libyan rival leaders agree to a ceasefire
after Macron-hosted talks', *The Guardian*, 25 July. www.theguardian.com/world
/2017/jul/25/france-raises-hopes-of-deal-between-libyan-rival-factions.

Wilson, Scott and Joby Warrick, 2011a.'Obama's shift towards military action in
Libya', *The Washington Post*, 19 March. www.washingtonpost.com/politics
/obamas_shift_toward_military_action_in_libya/2011/03/18/ABiClIs_story
.html?nav=emailpage.

———, 2011b.'Assad must go, Obama says', *The Washington Post*, 18 August.
www.washingtonpost.com/politics/assad-must-go-obama-says/2011/08/18
/gIQAelheOJ_story.html.

Wintour, Patrick, 2017.'Yemen Houthi rebels kill former president Ali Abdullah
Saleh', *The Guardian*, 4 December. www.theguardian.com/world/2017
/dec/04/former-yemen-president-saleh-killed-in-fresh-fighting.

Wintour, Patrick and Julian Borger, 2016.'Syrian regime is blocking aid from entering
eastern Aleppo, claims UN', *The Guardian*, 13 September. www.theguardian

.com/world/2016/sep/13/syrian-regime-is-blocking-aid-from-entering-eastern
-aleppo-claims-un.

Wong, Edward, and John F. Burns, 2005. 'Iraq Rift Grows After Discovery of Prison',
The New York Times, 17 November. www.nytimes.com/2005/11/17/world
/middleeast/iraqi-rift-grows-afterdiscovery-of-prison.html.

Wornan, Julie, 2005. 'The Politics of the Srebrenica Massacre by Edward S. Herman',
ZNet, 18 July. https://zcomm.org/znetarticle/the-politics-of-the-srebrenica
-massacre-by-edward-s-herman-by-julie-wornan/.

Yahoo News, 2015. 'Syria rebels, activists denounce IS attack on Paris', 15 November. http://news.yahoo.com/syria-rebels-activists-denounce-attack
-paris-231706004.html.

Yaphe, Judith S., 2012. 'Maliki's maneuvering in Iraq', *Foreign Policy*, 6 June.
http://foreignpolicy.com/2012/06/06/malikis-manuevering-in-iraq/.

Yassin-Kassab, Robin, 2016. 'Inland American conspiracies', *Qunfuz*, 9 August.
https://qunfuz.com/2016/08/09/inland-american-conspiracies/.

Yassin-Kassab, Robin and Leila al-Shami, 2016. *Burning Country: Syrians in Revolution and War*, London: Pluto Press.

Yazbek, Samar, 2015. *The Crossing: My Journey to the Shattered Heart of Syria*, trans.
Nashwa Gowanlock and Ruth Ahmedzai Kemp, London: Rider.

Yinon, Oded, 1982. 'A Strategy for Israel in the Nineteen Eighties', Association of
Arab-American University Graduates, Inc., Belmont, MA.

Zaitouneh, Razan, 2011. 'Syrians Want Freedom', *Huffington Post*, 7 October. www
.huffingtonpost.co.uk/razan-zaitouneh/syrians-want-freedom_b_998118.html.

Zeid Ra'ad al-Hussein, 2016. 'Zeid warns against populists and demagogues in
Europe and U.S.' *YouTube*, 6 September. www.youtube.com/watch?v
=2FgipIiN4nQ.

Zenko, Micah, 2016. 'Who Is to Blame For the Doomed Iraqi Uprisings of 1991?',
The National Interest, 7 March, http://nationalinterest.org/blog/the-buzz
/behind-the-doomed-iraqi-uprisings-1991-15425.

Zetkin, Clara, 1923. 'Fascism', *Labour Monthly*, August, pp. 69–78. www.marxists
.org/archive/zetkin/1923/08/fascism.htm.

Zipper, Ricardo Israel, 1989. *Politics and Ideology in Allende's Chile*, Arizona: Arizona
State University Press.

Zuesse, Eric, 2015. 'Crimea: Was It Seized by Russia, or Did Russia Block Its Seizure By The US?', *Countercurrents*, 21 February. www.countercurrents.org
/zuesse210215.htm.

Zunes, Stephen, 2016. 'From Gaza to Aleppo: A Handy Guide for Defending War
Crimes', *In These Times*, 7 October. http://inthesetimes.com/article/19519
/from-gaza-to-aleppo-a-handy-guide-for-defending-war-crimes.

Zuvela, Maja, 2016. 'Postcard stunt sees Bosnia peace envoy threatened with death',
Reuters, 15 January. https://uk.reuters.com/article/uk-bosnia-envoy-threats
/postcard-stunt-sees-bosnia-envoy-threatened-with-death
-idUKKCN0UT1XZ.

Index

al-Abadi, Haidar: 184, 186, 187, 188, 189, 192, 193

Achcar, Gilbert: 4, 210, 230, 243, 247, 270, 271

Afghanistan: 37–38, 39, 43, 44, 45, 227, 230, 242, 274, 275, 306 n.4

Afrin: 251, 252, 253, 254, 255, 257

Ahmadinejad, Mahmoud: 140–141, 143, 144, 146, 148, 180

Albanians (Kosovar): 96, 97, 98–99, 110–113, 114

Aleppo: 195, 196, 198, 206, 213, 216, 217, 222, 224, 228, 232–233, 234, 235, 236, 238, 239–241, 242, 243, 246, 247–248, 255, 256, 257, 258, 261, 262, 263, 277, 284, 287, 299

Allende, Salvador: 27

Al Qaeda: 2, 5, 17, 149, 168, 172, 173–175, 178, 179–180, 205, 214, 220, 221, 229–231, 239, 246, 249, 258, 265, 282

Al-Shami, Leila: 197, 198, 201, 202, 209, 211, 213–214, 215–216, 217–219, 242, 251, 252, 253, 255–256, 262, 263–264, 273, 287, 309 n.1

Amini, Asieh: 136–137

Anglo-Iranian Oil Company: 26

Ansar-e Hezbollah: 124, 138, 140, 147

anti-Semitism: 9, 49, 52, 89

Arab Socialist Party (ASP): 195–196

Àrbenz, Jacobo: 27

Arendt, Hannah: 37

Asaib Ahl al-Haq (League of the Righteous): 177, 187, 188, 227

al-Assad, Bashar: 3, 4, 5–6, 10, 12, 47, 51, 82, 84–85, 172, 180, 181, 182, 189, 200–207, 210–269, 272–277, 279, 280, 283, 287, 290, 305 n.3, 310 n.2

   bombing of hospitals: 217, 218, 233, 260, 263

   chemical weapons, use of: 215, 218–219, 245, 248, 262, 263, 267

   relationship with Al Qaeda and ISIS: 214–215, 219–225, 230, 268

al-Assad, Hafez: 163, 195–200

Assange, Julian: 13

austerity: 45, 97, 162

authoritaranism: 9, 13, 34, 39, 47, 48, 49, 50, 51, 52, 54, 62, 71, 75, 81, 83, 95, 139, 147, 195, 201, 209, 230, 251, 265, 272, 276, 285, 286,

al-'Azm, Sadiq Jalal: 13, 210

Baath Party: 151, 153–155, 157, 160, 167–168, 170, 171, 172, 173–175, 182, 195, 196–197, 202, 207, 230

Badr Organisation (Corps): 171–172, 177, 179, 180, 187, 188, 227

al-Baghdadi, Abu Bakr: 173, 174, 220, 230, 279

Baha'i: 130

Bakhtiar, Shapour: 121–122, 129
Barabandi, Bassam: 214–215, 229
Baraka, Ajamu: 274–275
Basij Force: 124, 133, 138, 140,
    142–143, 158, 159, 226, 228
Batou, Jean: 8–9
Bauer, Otto: 22
Bayramova, Fausziya: 72
Bazargan Mehdi: 122, 124, 126, 157
Begin, Menachem: 125
Behrooz, Maziar: 121, 128, 287
Bettelheim, Charles: 34, 35
bigotry: 18, 49, 50, 70, 98, 107, 117,
    264, 269, 307 n.3
Bishara, Marwan: 272
Blumenthal, Max: 268
Bolsheviks: 29, 54, 58, 61, 289, 306 n.3
Bosnia: 95, 96, 97, 100–109, 111, 112,
    114–117, 169, 242, 283, 296, 300,
    307 n.2, n.3, 309 n.3
Brecher, Jeremy: 147
Bremer, Paul: 170–171, 174, 176, 192
Brexit: 82, 238, 280, 281, 289, 310 n.5
Bush, George H. W.: 104, 107,
    163–167, 168
Bush, George W.: 43–44, 47, 69, 144,
    147, 168, 172, 175, 190, 236, 237,
    282, 283, 299, 310 n.2

Campaign for Nuclear Disarmament
    (CND): 148, 269
capital: 21–26, 28, 29, 40, 41–43, 47,
    48–50, 58, 60, 120, 165, 196, 274,
    285, 287, 288, 289, 305–306 n.2,
    306 n.5, n.7, 310 n.3
  finance: 21, 26, 41
  oligarchic: 45, 48, 274
  state: 32–34, 45, 47, 48, 54, 62, 63,
    121
  theocratic: 124, 130, 133, 139, 141,

    142–143, 144, 175, 181, 192
Carter, Jimmy: 124, 307 n.1
Central Intelligence Agency (CIA): 26,
    27, 149, 244, 245
Chávez, Hugo: 148
Chechnya: 4, 66–72, 73, 74–75, 76,
    235, 242
chemical warfare
  in Iraq: 161
  in Syria: 214, 218–219, 221, 244,
    245, 248, 262, 263, 267, 284
Chemical Weapons Convention: 245
Chilcot Report: 43, 168, 282
Chile: 27, 294
China: 13, 14, 21, 25, 26, 34, 42, 50,
    134, 159, 219, 247, 269, 270, 289,
    294, 295, 298, 301, 307–308 n.1
Chinese Communist Party: 38
Chossudovsky, Michel: 10, 16, 113
Christoslavism: 79, 98, 117
Chubarov, Refat: 9, 10
Cliff, Tony: 32–34, 306 n.5
Clinton, Bill: 104, 106–107, 115, 116,
    166, 298, 299
Clinton, Hillary: 83, 247
Cockburn, Patrick: 2, 172, 183–184, 267
Code Pink: 185
Cold War: 13, 15, 26–40, 44, 46,
    51–52, 63, 284, 296
Colvin, Marie: 111, 268–269
Committee for the Defence of Dem-
    ocratic Freedoms and Human
    Rights in Syria (CDF): 199
communism, communist(s): 30–31, 37,
    38, 45, 53, 54, 55, 56, 58, 63, 95,
    98, 127, 134, 151–153, 155, 167,
    170, 171, 196, 201, 276, 286–287,
    306 n.5
Communist International (Comintern,
    Third International): 30–31, 61,

63, 274, 286
Communist Party of Iran: 308 n.3
Communist Party of Western Ukraine:
    288
concentration camps: 100–101, 104,
    107, 114, 115, 283
Cooke, Shamus: 5, 11
Corbyn, Jeremy: 148, 273
counterrevolution: 15, 33, 63, 64, 76,
    77, 86, 119, 126, 127, 132, 134,
    147, 148, 263, 272, 273, 276, 285,
    287, 288, 306 n.3
Cox, Jo: 269
Crimea: 6, 7, 8, 9–10, 52, 72, 76, 81, 84,
    86, 87, 92, 280, 293, 299–300
Crimean Tatars: 9–10, 35–36
crimes against humanity: 5, 13, 14, 51,
    69, 70, 108, 109, 168, 217–219,
    232, 241, 249, 259–262, 291,
    295–299, 301
Croatia: 95, 96, 97, 98, 99–100, 101,
    102, 104, 106, 109, 113, 114, 115,
    117, 307 n.3
Cuba: 9, 14, 27
Cushman, Thomas: 168, 169
Czechoslovakia: 8, 34, 35, 37, 64, 96, 274

Daher, Joseph: 262, 263, 266
Darayya: 259–260, 266–267
Dawa Party: 156, 157, 167, 171, 172,
    184, 186
Dayton Accord: 106, 108, 109
de Mistura, Staffan: 239, 246, 263
democracy: 14–15, 21, 30–31, 48,
    50–51, 264, 269, 271, 272, 279,
    283, 284–287, 290–291, 292,
    294–295, 300–302, 305 n.2
  in Europe: 285, 290
  in Guatemala: 26
  in Iran: 26, 119–121, 122, 123, 128,
    139, 144, 146–147, 148, 149,
  in Iraq: 151–152, 170, 171, 174, 176,
    189–194, 230
  in the Soviet Union/Russia: 39–40,
    45, 47, 54, 61, 64–65, 66, 67, 69,
    76, 82, 84
  in Syria: 3, 5, 12, 195–197, 199, 200,
    201, 206, 209–212, 215–217,
    224, 248, 251, 255, 258, 262,
    263, 265, 277
  in Ukraine: 7, 86–92
  in the US: 43
  in Yugoslavia: 95–96, 104, 108
Democratic League of Kosovo: 110
Democracy in Europe Movement 2025
    (DiEM25): 290
di Giovanni, Janine: 266, 268, 283
Dudayev, Dzhokhar: 66
Dugin, Alexander: 77, 82, 84
Dunayevskaya, Raya: 32
Dzemilev, Mustafa: 9, 10

Ebadi, Shirin: 137, 138
Edelmann, Marek: 104
Electrical Utility Workers' Union
    (Iraq): 194
Erdoğan, Recep Tayyip: 85, 250,
    256–258
Estemirova, Natalya: 74–75
European Union (EU): 7, 14, 40, 50,
    51, 72, 82, 88, 106–107, 147, 222,
    237–238, 270–271, 290

Falk, Richard: 112–113
fascism: 7, 11, 38, 39, 49, 52, 63, 77, 79,
    81–82, 85, 88, 89, 90, 99, 103, 113,
    114, 117, 122, 242, 264, 273, 276,
    279, 285, 286, 288, 302, 308 n.7
Fedayeen-e Khalq (People's Fedayeen):
    120, 121

Federation of Workers' Councils and
    Unions (Iraq): 192
Filtzer, Don: 34, 63
Fisk, Robert: 169, 198–199, 205, 266,
    267, 280
Ford, Glen: 281
Foucault, Michel: 149
Free Syrian Army (FSA): 4, 5, 217,
    220, 223, 232, 234, 238–239, 244,
    246–248, 251, 252–253, 255, 256,
    257, 258
FSB (Federal Security Service of the
    Russian Federation): 66–69, 74

Gaddafi, Moammar: 247, 269,
    270–271
Galloway, George: 148
Gaza: 116, 270, 284
General Federation of Iraqi Women: 156
General Federation of Iraqi Workers: 194
General Federation of Trade Unions
    (Syria): 266
Geneva Conventions: 71, 232, 295
genocide: 8, 13, 35–36, 69–70, 89,
    100–109, 112, 113–117, 139, 151,
    161, 169, 184–185, 187, 275, 277,
    295–296, 298–299, 300, 307 n.3
Georgia: 4, 29, 32, 55–58, 67, 300
Ghouta (Damascus): 217–219, 245,
    248, 258, 267, 272
glasnost: 39, 64–65
globalisation: 41–42
Goldman, Emma: 54
Gorbachev, Mikhail: 9, 39–40, 45, 64–65
Green Movement (Iran): 141–143, 144,
    146
GRU (Russian Military Intelligence): 67
Guatemala: 26–27
Gutman, Roy: 100, 104, 244, 253, 261

Halabja: 161, 219
Hands Off Syria Coalition: 274
Hariri, Rafiq: 203–205, 206
Hariri, Saad: 205
Harvey, David: 41–42
Hashd al-Shaabi (Popular Mobilization
    Units): 187, 188, 189, 191, 192
Hassan, Budour: 276
Hekmat, Mansoor: 120–121, 127, 148,
    308 n.3
Herman, Edward S.: 115–116, 117
Hersh, Seymour: 267, 280
HESCO: 221–222
Hezbollah (Lebanese): 3, 5, 12,
    132–133, 149, 180, 203, 205–206,
    215, 217–218, 225–227, 229, 232,
    233, 243, 246, 248, 262, 276, 284,
    293, 299, 305 n.3
High Negotiations Commission
    (HNC): 262
Hilferding, Rudolf: 22, 24
Hitchens, Christopher: 98, 107, 168
Hitler: 8, 36–37, 39, 46, 52, 63, 72, 87,
    104, 116, 286, 288, 306 n.3
Hobson, J. A.: 21
Hoff, Brad: 4–5, 11, 13
Holocaust: 63, 77, 89, 104, 116
al-Hourani, Akram: 195–196, 197
Human Rights Association in Syria
    (HRAS): 201
Hungary: 35, 37, 64
Hussein, Saddam: 43, 107, 125, 132,
    151, 153–156, 157–168, 170, 171,
    172, 173, 174, 179, 200, 219, 268,
    282, 283

Idlib: 85, 217, 233, 234–235, 248, 258,
    263, 267
imperialism: 6, 10, 21–32, 35–42,
    45–51, 58, 60, 152, 196, 274, 275,

287, 288
British: 23
Iranian: 132, 138–139, 183, 187,
189, 191, 229, 273, 276
Russian: 8, 10, 13, 21, 28, 35–36,
37–39, 40, 47, 62, 71–72, 79,
83, 117, 238, 248, 255, 273, 276,
284, 302
US: 3, 11, 26–28, 37, 40, 44, 47, 125,
147, 149, 173, 175, 248, 264
Western: 1, 12, 27, 47, 139, 149, 284,
287
India: 25, 28, 42, 152, 265, 294, 306
n.4, 308 n.7, 309 n.3
inequality: 48, 49, 58, 210, 262, 287, 301
International Criminal Court (ICC):
205, 219, 261, 296–298, 299–300,
301
International Criminal Tribunal for
Former Yugoslavia: 108, 109, 115
internationalism: 15, 39–40, 57–58,
279, 287–291, 302
international law: 44, 111, 112, 217,
245–246, 254, 260, 291, 292–297,
300
International Monetary Fund (IMF):
41, 45, 97
Iran: 12, 26, 44, 119–150, 157, 263,
274, 277, 287
and Al Qaeda/ISIS: 214, 220,
229–231
democratic revolution: 119–122
Green Movement: 141–144
media: 14, 85, 148, 279
nuclear deal: 144
oppression of women: 130–131,
136–138
persecution of minorities: 129–130
political prisoners: 126–128,
134–135

torture, rape and mass executions:
126–129, 134–135, 148
exporting Iranian Islamism: 2, 3, 5,
132, 133, 157–160, 167–168,
171–172, 176, 180–182, 183,
186–192, 205–206, 215,
225–229, 231–232, 242, 248,
273, 275–276, 277, 293, 299
Iran-Iraq war: 157–160
Iran-Contra affair: 125
Iranian Communist Party: 308 n.2
Iraq: 2–4, 5, 6, 10, 11, 45, 85, 124,
151–194, 200, 202, 206–207, 230,
231, 264, 269, 275, 305 n.1, 308 n.4
effect of sanctions on: 164–167, 300
invasion of Kuwait: 163
political prisoners: 155
relations with Iran: 125, 132–133,
138, 139, 154, 157–160,
188–192
Shia Islamist militias: 175–178,
186–189, 217, 220, 226, 227,
242, 243, 246, 293, 305 n.3
torture, rape and mass executions in:
154, 155, 178–179, 187
US war (1991): 163–164
US/UK occupation (2002): 43, 44,
168–175, 293
WMD: 12, 43, 282
Iraqi Communist Party: 152–153
Iraqi Federation of Trade Unions
(IFTU): 174
ISIS/Daesh: 2–6, 11, 17, 51, 173, 179,
182, 183–189, 214–215, 219–225,
230–231, 232, 235, 248, 253,
257–258, 268, 281, 305 n.1
Islamic Revolutionary Guard Corps
(IRGC, Pasdaran): 123, 124, 126,
140, 143, 144, 146, 158, 171–172,
228, 230, 299

Quds Force: 132, 133, 172, 180, 187, 190, 191, 225–227, 229–230, 232, 243, 246, 262, 299

Islamic Supreme Council of Iraq: 171, 189

Israel: 42–43, 44, 116, 125, 132, 133, 149, 152, 159, 160, 199–200, 205–206, 226, 248, 270, 279, 283, 298, 300, 301

Izetbegović, Alia: 105

Jabhat Fatah al-Sham: 221, 238–239, 246, 248

James, C. L. R.: 59

Jazeera: 251, 253

Jewish Anti-Fascist Committee (USSR): 63

Johnson, Chalmers: 40–41, 43–44

Kadivar, Mohsen: 146

Kadyrov, Ramzan: 71, 73, 75

Karadjis, Michael: 4, 5, 255

Karadžić, Radovan: 100, 105, 283

Kazan Tatars: 59, 72

Khamenei, Ali: 128, 130, 132, 133, 135, 138, 140, 143, 144, 146, 159, 180, 186, 188, 189, 226, 228, 229, 277, 279, 283

Khatami, Muhammad: 138, 139–140, 144, 146, 147, 156

Khomeini, Ruholla: 119, 120, 121, 122–129, 131, 132–134, 143, 149, 157, 159, 160, 168, 192, 283, 308 n.5

Knott, David: 217

Kobani: 251–252, 253, 254, 257

Kosovo: 97, 98–99, 110–113, 114, 116, 117

Kosovo Liberation Army (KLA): 110–111, 112

Kovalev, Sergei: 66, 68, 69

Krupskaya, Nadezhda: 55–56

Kuomintang: 38

Kurds: 5, 51, 129–130, 147, 152, 155, 157, 159, 160–161, 167, 168, 170, 172, 173, 181, 184–186, 188, 231, 249–252, 254–257, 262, 308 n.3

Kurdish Democratic Party (KDP, Iran): 129

Kurdish Democratic Party (KDP, Iraq): 155, 160, 168, 185

Kurdish Regional Government (KRG): 184, 185

Kuwait: 159, 162–164, 165, 166, 168, 200

Lebanon: 132, 133, 138, 193, 195, 198, 199–200, 202–206, 207, 215, 225–226, 227, 229, 231, 262, 269, 277, 293, 294, 299

Lemkin, Raphael: 8, 35–36, 102, 295, 305 n.4

Lenin, V. I.: 9, 22–25, 28–32, 38–39, 41, 46, 53–59, 61–62, 83, 87, 117, 121, 127, 275, 286, 289, 306 n.6, 308 n.3

Le Pen, Marine: 52, 82

LGBT rights: 42, 44, 47, 50, 51, 80–81, 89–90, 177

Libya: 45, 159, 207, 214, 243, 247, 264, 269–272, 275, 298

Litvinenko, Alexander: 68–69

Local Coordination Committees (LCCs): 210, 215

Luxemburg, Rosa: 22, 23, 31, 32, 38, 285–286, 287–288, 305 n.2

Magnitsky, Sergei: 74

Makhlouf, Rami: 210, 261

Malaysia Airlines Flight MH17: 92–93, 282

al-Maliki, Nouri: 2, 3, 172–173, 180–184, 186–188, 190–192, 207
Mao: 38, 120
Maoist(s): 13, 304 n.5
Marković, Ante: 97
Marx: 22–23, 31, 38, 60, 121, 275, 305–306 n.2
Marxist(s): 13, 22, 31–32, 48, 52, 58–59, 60, 63–64, 120, 121, 127, 249, 274, 287, 288, 308 n.2
Mashkadov, Aslan: 66–67, 71
Mattick (Sr.), Paul: 34, 41
Melman, Seymour: 40–41
MI6: 26, 149, 270
Mikhoels, Solomon: 63
militarism: 41, 43, 47, 51
Milne, Seamus: 2, 3, 5, 11
Milošević, Slobodan: 95, 98, 99–100, 104, 110, 112, 113, 116, 283
Mladić, Ratko: 105–106, 109, 183
Moadamiya: 218, 260
Mohajedin-e Khalq (People's Mujahedin): 120, 121, 128
Montazeri, Hossein Ali: 128, 133, 141, 146
Mossadegh, Mohammad: 26, 27, 120, 121, 144, 149, 308 n.2
Mousavi, Mir Hossein: 132, 141–144
Mustafa, Seema: 4, 5, 11

Naame Shaam: 227–229, 232
Nasrallah, Hassan: 180, 203, 225–226
national liberation/independence: 25, 29–32, 56–59, 65, 66–67, 72, 87, 88, 99, 100, 110–111, 113, 151, 160, 189–194, 200, 202–204, 242, 249, 287, 288, 293, 301, 305 n.1
nationalism: 49, 50, 57–58, 78–79, 81, 87–88, 90, 92, 95–96, 97–105, 107, 108, 110, 113–117, 121, 122, 134, 151, 153, 179, 187, 195, 203, 252, 254, 289, 296, 308 n.3, 309 n.5
NATO (North Atlantic Treaty Organisation): 40, 83, 85, 92, 95, 104–106, 112–113, 115, 184, 214, 270–271
Navalny, Alexei: 76
Nazis: 36, 46, 49, 63, 71, 77–79, 81–82, 88, 89, 97, 98, 101, 112, 114, 117, 229, 238, 264, 269, 286, 295, 305 n.4, 306 n.3
Nemtsov, Boris: 75–76, 84, 92
neoconservatism: 9, 39, 42–43, 44, 46–47, 52, 71, 83, 125, 170, 308 n.4
neoliberalism: 41, 50, 91, 288, 289–290
Netanhayu, Benjamin: 43, 44, 279
Non-Aligned Movement (NAM): 64, 97, 157, 298
NotGeorgeSabra: 3, 5, 12
Novaya Gazeta: 73, 86, 235
al-Nusra Front: 2, 214, 220–221, 246, 248, 252, 255, 267

Obama, Barack: 2, 3, 4, 11, 44–45, 51, 116, 144, 184, 186, 191, 243, 245–249, 263, 268, 272, 275, 281, 299
Ordzhonikidze, Sergo: 55, 57
Organisation for the Prohibition of Chemical Weapons (OPCW): 245, 263, 267
Organization of Ukrainian Nationalists (OUN): 87–88
Organization of Women's Freedom in Iraq (OWFI): 176, 177
Ottoman: 28, 31, 97–98

Pahlavi, (Shah) Mohammad Reza: 119, 120, 121–122, 124, 127, 128, 129, 131, 136, 148, 157, 160, 307 n.1

Palestine: 44, 116, 125, 149, 199–200, 204, 212, 217–218, 232, 242, 276–277, 279, 283, 284, 288, 300

Palmyra: 224–225, 241–242

patriarchy: 30, 48, 49, 50, 79–81, 133, 138, 265

Patriotic Union of Kurdistan (PUK): 155, 160

Pentagon: 240, 244, 257

People's Democratic Party of Afghanistan (PDPA): 37–38

perestroika: 39, 64–65

Peshmerga (Kurdish): 160, 168, 184, 185, 188, 253

Petras, James: 52, 114

Physicians for Human Rights: 233, 260

Pilger, John: 6–7, 9–10, 93, 267, 280

Pillay, Navi: 219, 261

PKK (Kurdistan Workers' Party): 249

Poland: 28, 31, 37, 46, 49, 64, 87, 289

Politkovskaya, Anna: 73–74, 280, 290–291

Poroshenko, Petro: 75, 90

Postel, Danny: 141, 147

Potarskaya, Nina: 6–7

Press TV: 14, 148, 186, 279

protectionism: 24, 25, 288–289

Putin, Vladimir: 4, 7–10, 13, 45–47, 52, 66–71, 73–77, 79–86, 88, 92–93, 222, 232–238, 242, 251, 256, 258, 262, 263, 268, 275, 277, 279, 280, 281, 282, 283, 299–300, 306 n.6, 310 n.2

PYD (Kurdish Democratic Union Party)/YPG: 3, 249, 250, 251–258

racism: 9, 28, 39, 49, 50, 51, 69, 70, 77–79, 269, 271, 281, 287, 288, 289, 290, 310 n.5

Reagan, Ronald: 125, 206

Reich, Wilhelm: 49

Republica Srpska: 100, 108, 109

revolution: 3, 8, 15, 16, 21, 27, 28, 29, 30, 31, 33, 34, 38, 48, 51, 53, 54, 59–61, 62, 63, 64–65, 75, 91, 92, 95, 119, 122, 127, 128, 129, 131, 139, 143, 146, 147, 148, 150, 151, 152, 189, 191, 195–197, 209, 210–212, 214–216, 217, 243, 247, 252, 253, 255, 256, 258–259, 262, 265, 266, 269, 271, 272, 276–277, 279, 285–287, 288, 290, 301, 309 n.2, 310 n.3

Rojava: 251, 253, 255–256

Rosdolsky, Roman: 288

Rouhani, Hassan: 138, 144–145, 146, 229

Rugova, Ibrahim: 110, 111

Russia: 12, 14, 31–40, 45–47, 53–86, 98, 107, 108–109, 112, 113, 247, 249, 269, 270, 283, 295, 299–300, 301, 307 n.2, n.4, n.6

and Chechnya: 66–71, 73, 74–75

and Crimea/Ukraine: 6–10, 51, 52, 75–76, 81, 83, 87, 88, 92, 293, 299–300

democratic revolution: 64–65, 286

Eurasian supremacism: 77–79

imperialism: 13, 28, 32, 35–39, 40, 47, 51, 55, 58, 62, 83, 275–276, 284, 301–302, 306 n.4

propaganda: 12, 14, 63, 84–86, 92–93, 238, 240, 274, 280, 281–282

revolution: 28–30, 53–54, 59

state capitalism: 32–34, 45, 47, 63

in Syria: 215, 219, 222–225, 232–242, 245, 246, 248, 253–256, 258, 261–263, 273–275, 287, 291, 293, 305 n.3, 309–310 n.2

Russian Orthodox church: 79–81

Russian Social Democratic Workers' Party: 31
Russia Today (RT): 84
Ryzhkov, Vladimir: 9–10

al-Sadr, Muqtada: 177, 179, 180, 181, 189, 190, 191, 192–193
Sahwa (Awakening Councils): 179–180
Saleh, Hadi: 170, 174
Sarajevo: 102, 103, 104, 105, 106, 115
Sarkohi, Faraj: 136
Saudi Arabia: 5, 147, 156, 159, 163, 186, 189, 207, 225, 230, 231, 243, 275, 294, 309 n.2
SAVAK: 120, 122, 134
Serbia, Serb: 85, 95, 96, 97, 98–108, 109, 110–117, 242, 296, 307 n.3
Serge, Victor: 38, 54, 62
Shahak, Israel: 49
Shariatmadari, Mohammad Kazem: 120, 125–126, 133
Siegel, Jacob: 4
Sistani, Sayyid Ali: 177, 184, 186, 190, 193
Smith, Ashley: 247, 259, 269, 287
Soboul, Albert: 285
socialism: 15, 27, 29, 31, 32, 34, 38, 48, 54, 59–61, 63, 64, 83, 87, 92, 95, 117, 121, 123, 127, 131, 138, 151, 152, 155, 168, 196, 198, 229, 251, 264, 266, 270, 274, 275, 281, 284–287, 288, 289, 302, 306 n.5, 307 n.4
Socialist Workers Party (SWP): 12, 148
Soleimani, Qassem: 172, 180, 181, 188, 190–191, 226, 227, 228, 229, 232
solidarity: 6, 12, 13, 15, 58, 119, 138, 147, 148, 169, 194, 211, 251, 265, 276–277, 284, 285, 289, 290
Sontag, Susan: 104

sovereignty: 7, 13, 30, 39, 113, 182, 190–191, 204, 242, 266, 271, 289, 291–293, 295, 296, 299
Soviets: 53–54
Soviet Union (Union of Soviet Socialist Republics, USSR): 8, 13, 26, 29–30, 33–40, 46, 47, 56–62, 63, 64–66, 77–78, 84, 87–88, 121, 152, 159, 198, 237, 240, 249, 281, 288, 294, 295, 301, 306 n.3, n.4, n.5, 308 n.2
Sputnik: 84–85
Srebrenica: 105–106, 107, 108, 115
Sri Lanka: 14–15, 18, 51, 307 n.4, 309 n.3, n.4, n.6
Stalin, J. V.: 9, 15, 32–37, 38–39, 46, 47, 52, 54–58, 59, 61, 62, 63, 66, 71, 83, 87, 88, 154, 161, 274, 286, 288, 289, 306 n.3, n.5, n.6
Stalinist(s): 13, 35, 46, 47, 50, 52, 63, 65, 72, 83, 85, 88, 117, 119, 149, 198, 252, 269, 274, 275, 276, 284, 287, 289, 301–302, 306 n.3, n.5
Stein, Jill: 274–275
Stop the War Coalition (StWC): 12, 148, 185, 269, 272–273
Sultan-Galiev, Mirsaid: 59–61
Supreme Council for the Islamic Revolution in Iraq (SCIRI): 167–168, 171–172, 177, 189
Syria: 18, 85, 132, 133, 138, 173, 195–277, 305 n.1, n.3
democratic revolution: 3, 12, 18, 197, 209–212, 258–259, 276–277, 309 n.1
Free Syrian Army (FSA): 4, 5, 217, 232, 244, 246, 252, 255, 257–258
Greater Syria: 199–200
occupation of Lebanon: 200,

202–206
political prisoners: 201–202, 210, 248, 259, 263
refugees: 1, 237–238, 269
Syrian Arab Army: 241, 266
torture, rape and mass executions: 198–199, 201, 211–212
war: 1, 12, 213–219, 225–229, 232–237, 239–241, 248, 261–263, 309–310 n.2

Tammo, Mashaal: 251
The Syria Campaign: 1, 6, 260–261
Third World: 25–28, 38, 41–42, 51, 61, 294
Tito, Josip Broz: 37, 95–96, 97, 98, 99, 116, 307 n.2
totalitarianism: 37, 40, 63, 65, 72, 90, 134, 168, 198, 209, 262, 279, 285, 286, 287, 290, 302, 305 n.5, 309 n.5
Traboulsi, Fawwaz: 210
trade unions: 38, 48, 49, 54, 92, 120, 134, 148, 162, 170, 174, 194, 197, 266, 294
Trotsky: 22, 23, 31, 33, 35, 38, 54, 56, 61, 98, 286, 306 n.3
Trotskyist(s): 13, 33, 120, 306 n.5
Trump, Donald: 4, 10, 52, 82–83, 144, 263, 275, 279, 280, 281–282, 289, 310 n.2
Tudeh Party: 120, 121, 127, 308 n.2
Tudjman, Franjo: 99, 100, 104
Turkey: 5, 85, 129, 130, 159, 160, 207, 224, 225, 230, 231, 235, 238, 243, 249–250, 252, 253, 255, 256–258, 275, 293

Ukraine: 7–10, 28, 29, 31, 36, 51, 55, 72, 75–76, 81, 83, 84, 85, 86–93, 242, 280, 288, 293, 299–300

United Kingdom (UK): 23, 25, 168–169, 175–176, 179, 238, 241, 269, 293, 294, 295
United Nations (UN): 72, 83, 85, 103, 104–108, 130, 159, 163, 168, 169, 204–205, 219, 223, 233–234, 239, 240, 241, 260–261, 263, 269, 272, 299, 300–301
Charter: 292–293, 299, 300–301
General Assembly: 113, 295–297, 299
Human Rights Council (HRC): 14–15, 83, 219, 259, 261, 294
Mission in Kosovo: 112, 113
Office for the Coordination of Humanitarian Affairs (OCHA): 261
Protection Force: 105–106, 115
Security Council: 44, 103, 104, 113, 159–160, 163, 164–167, 203, 219, 241, 247, 260, 296, 298, 299–301
Universal Declaration of Human Rights: 293–294
United States (US): 2–5, 9, 24, 25, 44–45, 52, 78, 83, 106–107, 114, 124–125, 172, 179–181, 184–188, 194, 224, 241, 242, 272, 274–275, 289, 298–299
imperialism: 11, 13, 26–28, 37, 40–41, 42–44, 47, 147, 149, 159, 163–168, 169–171, 173–177, 179, 189–190, 206, 238, 243–249, 252–254, 257–258, 263, 282, 284
Unity of Communist Militants: 120
US Peace Council: 274

Varoufakis, Yanis: 290
velayat-e faqih: 123, 125, 139, 143, 146, 147
Veterans for Peace: 185

veto (in UN Security Council): 108, 219, 247, 298, 299, 301

Vietnam: 3, 27–28, 37, 168, 242, 267, 289

war crimes: 5, 13, 14, 44, 51, 70, 93, 108, 109, 217–219, 232, 241, 242, 249, 254, 260–261, 276, 295–298, 301

White Helmets: 235, 237, 268, 269

Wiesel, Elie: 104, 116

Wiesenthal, Simon: 104

women's rights: 42, 44, 47, 49, 50, 80–81, 127, 131, 134, 136, 137–138, 139, 145–146, 148, 156, 161, 170, 176–179, 191–192, 194, 196, 201, 203, 251, 262, 292, 294, 297, 308 n.3

Worker-Communist Party of Iran (WPI): 308 n.3

Workers' Democratic Trade Union Movement (WDTUM): 170, 174

workers' rights: 26, 27, 33–34, 48–49, 51, 54, 78, 92, 96, 127, 134, 141, 148, 153, 162, 174, 175, 192, 194, 201, 274, 288, 289

World Bank (International Bank for Reconstruction and Development): 41, 165

World Peace Council: 274

World Socialist Web Site (WSWS): 12, 264, 266

World Trade Organisation (WTO): 41

xenophobia: 50, 78, 288, 289

Yanukovych, Viktor: 7, 9, 83, 88, 90

Yassin-Kassab, Robin: 197, 198, 201, 202, 209, 210–211, 213–214, 215–216, 217–219, 251, 252–253, 263–264, 265, 269, 309 n.1

Yazbek, Samar: 216–217, 256, 268

Yazidi: 51, 151, 184–185, 193

Yeltsin, Boris: 39, 40, 45, 65, 66–67

Yemen: 133, 138, 191, 210, 214, 226, 275–276, 298, 307 n.2

Yugoslavia: 37, 95–97, 99–100, 103, 105, 108, 109, 112, 113–114, 116–117, 294, 296, 306 n.5, 309 n.2

Yusuf, Yusuf Salman (Comrade Fahd): 152

Zaitouneh, Razan: 201, 265, 290–291

Zeid Ra'ad al-Hussein: 83, 261, 281

Zetkin, Clara: 49

Zhirinovsky, Vladimir: 107, 117

Zinn, Howard: 283

About the Author

Rohini Hensman is a writer, independent scholar and activist working on workers' rights, feminism, minority rights, and globalisation. She has been published extensively on these issues, her most recent book being *Workers, Unions, and Global Capitalism: Lessons from India*. Originally from Sri Lanka, Hensman lives in India.